TO HECK WITH IT, I'M GOING HUNTING

7-25-16

Happy 'Birthday', Al, I love you, Jo!

To Heck With It, I'm Going Hunting

My First Eighteen Years As An International Big-Game Hunter

by

Arnold Alward

with

Bill Quimby

SAFARI PRESS INC.

Alward, Arnold

Second edition

Safari Press Inc.

2004, Long Beach, California

ISBN 1-57157-274-0

Library of Congress Catalog Card Number: 2002117782

10 9 8 7 6 5 4 3 2 1

Printed in Singapore

Readers wishing to receive the Safari Press catalog, featuring many fine books on big-game hunting, wingshooting, and sporting firearms, should write to Safari Press Inc., P.O. Box 3095, Long Beach, CA 90803, U.S.A. Tel: (714) 894-9080 or visit our Web site at www.safaripress.com.

This book is dedicated to my family—
my children and grandchildren, and those who will follow them,
but most of all to Janice, my understanding friend and lover.

TABLE OF CONTENTS

FOREWORD

The hunting instinct is an inherent characteristic of mankind and was, initially, necessary for the survival of the human race. This instinct has continued throughout history, and today it is manifested by the desire to hunt for sport. There are other factors that play into the desire for sport hunting, such as the ability to accept and respond to challenges and hardships, the curiosity needed to explore the world's environments and peoples, and the determination to collect species for posterity. All of these are indicative of Arnold Alward.

I initially met Arnold approximately twenty years ago at a Safari Club International convention. He was driven by the spirit of adventure and the desire to explore the world through sport hunting. Throughout the years, we have become very close friends. I also have had the opportunity to arrange many of his hunting expeditions, as well as the honor to hunt with him occasionally. Through my observations, I have concluded that Arnold is a very considerate and kind individual who can make the best of any adverse situation.

He has collected 320 different species of big-game animals from six continents, with 277 of them qualifying for the *SCI Record Book of Trophy Animals*. He is in the process of donating many of his trophies from his private museum at his home in New Brunswick to other museums, not only for scientific purposes but also so that generations to come will be able to enjoy them.

Arnold has achieved many of the most prestigious hunting awards, including the SCI International Hunting Award, all SCI Grand Slam awards, all SCI Inner Circles at the Diamond Level, the World Hunting Award Ring, and the Weatherby Big Game Trophy Award (1996). Not all of Arnold's achievements are in the field of big-game hunting, however. Among the many awards presented to Arnold has been Safari Club's 1993 Humanitarian Award and the Canadian Government Certificate of Merit Award. And while he was active in his businesses, he was recognized many times by his peers.

However, it is Arnold Alward's successes and contributions in the field of sport hunting that will long be remembered and appreciated by the sport hunters of the world.

Chuck Bazzy
Bloomfield, Michigan
September 2002

ACKNOWLEDGMENTS

There are many people in addition to my wife and family I would like to thank for helping me along the way. For starters, there were the dedicated employees of my former companies, who made all my achievements possible. Then there were my hunting partner and booking agent Chuck Bazzy; my taxidermist friend Kevin White, who personally drove my trophies from North Carolina to New Brunswick; Canadian hunting outfitter Fred Webb (formerly from New Brunswick), who told me about Safari Club International; Jerome and Halina Knap of Canada North Outfitting, who introduced me to the far north; Bob and Margaret Kern at the Hunting Consortium, who made my many trips to Asia memorable; Eduardo F. de Aroz at Cazatur in Spain, who helped so much in Europe; filmmaker Jack Hegarty, who shared cramped and leaky tents with me in Alaska and elsewhere; my plantation manager Brian West, with whom I am honored to work side by side; the late Dr. Jim Conklin, who introduced me to the SCI and Weatherby awards programs; the many members and staff of Safari Club International for innumerable things; George Roberts, who helped me keep a promise to a prince; Bill Harmer, who dropped me off and picked me up so many times at the Moncton airport and always wanted to hear about my adventures; Marcel Sodiro, with whom I hunted in Paraguay and Ecuador; and Bill Quimby, who took my notes and journals and turned them into this book.

It is a privilege to count all of you among my good friends.

There were many others, including the professional hunters, guides, hunting friends, and interpreters who took me to the tops of mountains and across jungles, forests, and deserts in search of game. If you are not mentioned here, it does not mean I have forgotten what you did. I thank you.

INTRODUCTION

I once read that a large percentage in the United States leave home and move to another part of the country at least once in a lifetime. Things are different in New Brunswick, our little corner of Canada. Many of us can trace our history in this region to the American Revolution. Our ancestors were among the seventy thousand Tories who remained loyal to King George III and fled the Thirteen Colonies into what was then called British North America.

My brother Ford, in his four-volume book *Benjamin and Oswald Alward, A Story of Two Loyalist Cousins and Their Descendants,* traced our family name back to the time of the Anglo-Saxons, in the 1060s. We Alwards have been farmers, blacksmiths, postmasters, medical doctors, grocers, merchants, mechanics, cheese makers, preachers and deacons, harness racers, mayors, fire chiefs, cobblers, baseball players, and, more recently, producers of agricultural lime and operators of transportation companies. Some of us fought for England in the 1770s and for Canada in its wars since then. A few Alwards died in those wars, but those who survived almost always went home to New Brunswick. We resisted change, and most of us moved only when forced to.

Thomas Alward, a beneficed English clergyman, was the first Alward to reach the New World. England's Act of Uniformity of 1662 literally put Thomas out of work, and he and his family had no choice but to leave England three years later. They immigrated to Woodbridge, a settlement in the colony of New Jersey, where Thomas's son Henry created a two-hundred-acre plantation in the wilderness.

Thomas Alward's descendants expanded the family's holdings, and when the fires of revolution roared across New Jersey a Benjamin Alward was among the founders of Woodbridge's loyalist committee. Supporting the British cause brought problems to the family, however. The Treason and Sedition Acts of 1795 and 1799 prohibited loyalists from selling land, voting, or working in certain trades and professions. Those who had served in King George's army were sent to prison. When Benjamin's lands were seized in 1777, the Alwards left New Jersey—the family's home for 115 years—and fled to New York to escape further persecution. The British government gave them free passage to the Saint John River Valley in Nova Scotia (New Brunswick was not created until 1784).

Our branch of Benjamin's family built a new life in the land. Others went to Ontario, and a few remained in the United States. My brother's research shows two of Henry's grandchildren, cousins Oswald Arnold and Benjamin Alward, were among the first settlers to reach the Saint John River. Oswald was not married when he arrived with the Spring Fleet on 12 May 1783. Benjamin, old and infirm, together with his adult children, arrived on the ship *Ann* on 24 July 1783.

When the cousins, Benjamin Jr. and Oswald, learned there was better land upriver, they—together with fifteen other families—moved to a place they named New Canaan. Although England gave them some support and free land, life was hard for these displaced loyalists. With axes they built log homes, and they covered their roofs with thatch or bark. They cleared maple, birch, elm, beech, and ash and created fields. They hunted moose, white-tailed deer, and black bear; made maple sugar and syrup; harvested butternuts; and grew wheat, corn, and barley.

Between them, the cousins raised twenty-three children. New Canaan was a strict, religious community that held regular prayer meetings and banned singing and dancing. Benjamin Jr. reportedly was a "stiff old Baptist," a deacon in the New Canaan church.

By the early 1800s, the Alwards and the Price and Keith families, assisted by local Indians, followed a hazardous portage called the Bridal Path to a place that would become known as Butternut Ridge (later renamed Havelock). Here they started all over again in what are now Kings and Westmorland counties.[1] This time they built their homes with lumber instead of logs.

Several incidents of note occurred in that region during the nineteenth century. The first began around 1825, when wolves moved into the area. As wolves will do, they soon began killing and eating the struggling farmers' livestock. *Butternut Ridge–Havelock, Our Proud Heritage, 1809–1989,* published by the Havelock Women's Institute, tells how the farmers responded:

> One night, the residence of James Keith was destroyed by fire. His sheep had to remain in the field all night and were nearly all destroyed by wolves. . . . The settlers had had enough of this wanton killing, so [they] decided to rid themselves of these troublesome animals. They armed themselves with guns, clubs, pots, pans, and anything that would produce a noise. They went through the woods in a long column in such a position that each man could distinguish the man on his left and the man on his right; thus, every animal was driven before them. This was known as the "Great Wolf Chase." It proved very effective. To this day, wolves are not found in the Havelock area.

Next came the flood of 1854, when a giant log smashed through the living room window of John Alward's homestead. No flood before or since has raised our area's rivers as high as they were that year.

In 1876 the Intercontinental Railway opened, linking New Brunswick and Nova Scotia with Montreal. Then the Canadian Pacific Railway line opened, connecting Montreal to Moncton by way of northern Maine. These lines finally linked rural New Brunswick to the outside world by land. We could now ship our lumber, crops, and minerals across North America. It should have been a time of plenty. Instead, Canada's growth declined. Industrialization was occurring in the central part of the country, not in the Maritime

1. The Prices and the Keiths, like the Alwards, were loyalists who had moved from New Jersey to New Brunswick after the American Revolution. My mother was a Keith. Her father (my grandfather) was born in 1868 near our current residence. It is said I got my love of hunting from him.

Provinces. The major agricultural areas were far to the west. Even worse for New Brunswick, the United States and Europe had imposed tariffs, limiting our exports. Our province's economy did not recover until the twentieth century, when we began shipping potatoes and launched a major pulp and paper industry.

The author was about eight years old when he posed with "Topsy." Learning to ride him served the author well on horseback hunts all over the world.

As I said earlier, we Alwards have always been loath to leave a place we like. Of my parents' four children, only one has left New Brunswick. All our children are within a few miles from us. We have spent nearly 220 years in this spot. I don't expect many of us will be moving anytime soon.

Though I became interested in hunting at an early age, I could never have predicted that I would travel to the very top and bottom of this planet, visit all seven continents, and hunt on six of them. By 1998, I had taken nearly three hundred types of big-game animals on six continents in sixteen years, and I had received the highest honors in international big-game hunting. I would make more hunting trips to the Northwest Territories, Quebec, California, Pakistan, Iran, Siberia's Kamchatka Peninsula in Asia, and the island of New Caledonia in the South Pacific—the adventures that fill this book.

Many events shaped my life and led to my wandering.

In 1938, the year I was born, my father, Roy Alward, then twenty-eight, risked everything he owned and went into debt to buy a limestone quarry, a tractor-driven crusher, and an old horse. He bought all this for $1,500. He knew nothing about the business. As a lifelong farmer, however, he knew that the soil in our region was chemically unbalanced. By adding lime, it could become fertile and arable, capable of producing two hay crops in a single season. Dad's Havelock Lime Works produced the agricultural lime New Brunswick's farmers needed, and the business eventually flourished.

Dad and my mother, Ella, went through rough times in their early days together. Mother sewed all of our family's clothes, making them out of any fabric she could find—including Dad's worn-out shirts and pants.

I was seven in 1945, when Dad decided to move the lime works to Havelock, a distance of seven miles. Our new home had been used for butchering hogs. Dad announced we were moving into it. In his book *Give Me Fifteen Minutes,* which commemorates his life with my mother, he recalled our first night in that slaughterhouse:

> That night, we slept on the studio couch, and the four children slept on the floor. There were no doors on the building, and some of the windows were out, but from then on it was to be home for us. The pot they used to scald the pigs with was still there, and there was manure on the walls of the linter, where the pigs were kept before they were slaughtered. This was like a side porch that you step down into. Well, we went to work cleaning the place up, with Gillette's lye and a broom. We had a kitchen and a living room, and we put up partitions in the linter, making two bedrooms for the children, and put gyprock on the kitchen and the living room.

Mother did the cooking on a wood stove. We had no running water, telephone, or electricity. Those things would come later. I did my homework by the oil lamp, the only source of light. Over the years, that converted slaughterhouse came to be a real home for us. Dad completely remodeled the original structure, adding a wing with a basement and a brick fireplace. No one seeing the place would ever have guessed its history. Today it serves as a laboratory for the lime works.

Ours was a loving family, and my two brothers Ford and Walter and my sister Elsie and I were happy growing up in Havelock. Ford was seven years older than I, Elsie was three years older, and Walter was three years younger. We had chores, of course. Dad kept horses and cattle even after buying the quarry, and it was our job to care for them. I will never forget having to mow our large lawn with a mower that I was too short to push. It seemed to take forever.

There was always someone who needed help with haying in the summer. In the fall there was wood to cut and pile, and in the winter we had to bring it into the house. Our water came from an outside pump, and when I was younger I needed to stand on something to reach the pump handle. At potato-digging time, Dad had me help our neighbor pick his potatoes in exchange for free milk. I picked the potatoes, carried them in a basket, and dumped them into wooden barrels. The rows seemed much longer than they actually were. I also snared rabbits and received twenty-five cents a pair. I remember the postmaster asked me to snowshoe two miles to his father's house after a heavy snow. The snow had drifted halfway up his doors. I spent seven hours shoveling him out, and for this I received a quarter!

We were expected to do other things, but we also had time for ourselves. We played baseball in the summer and hockey on an outside rink in the winter. (We spent more time keeping the ice clean than we did skating.) We missed few Sundays at church in Havelock, going to Sunday school in the morning and Sunday evening services every week.

Dad loved music. He would play the Jew's-harp, a harmonica (he called it a "mouth organ"), or a guitar in the evenings, and the entire family would sing along with him. At first we sang hymns, but as his guitar playing improved we added Hawaiian and Spanish music. Later, he taught himself to play the banjo, formed a small band, and played for village benefits. I was only about two at the time, but I remember watching in awe as he played a harmonica with his mouth, a guitar with his hands, and drums with his feet—all at the same time. His band grew to an orchestra with six young women and five men, all in matching uniforms made by Mother and two girls from the orchestra.

Everyone said I took after my grandfather, an avid outdoorsman and hunter. He died in 1966 at ninety-eight, when I was twenty-six. As do all boys, I started hunting small game, mostly rabbits and raccoons, with a .22 rimfire. During my teens, I moved up to white-tailed deer, hunting them as much as was legally possible near our home every fall. As I grew older, business and family left little time for hunting.

Something happened when I was in the first grade that would have a lasting effect on me. It was midwinter, and Mother had given me permission to go into the woods where the men were lumbering. When I reached the place, they were gone, and I became totally lost in the woods when I tried to follow them. I wandered for hours on horse trails until I came to a two-track road. I didn't know whether to go right or left to get home, but I made my choice and kept walking until I came upon my Uncle Jack on a sled pulled by a team of horses. It was after dark, and I can't tell you how relieved I was when I saw Jack's lantern in the woods.

Jack took me to his home and fed me before taking me to my distraught parents. All the men were in the woods looking for me. I cannot go near Keith Road without thinking about that long day and how I found my way to safety. Traumatic as it was, the experience gave me confidence in myself. Never again was I lost, no matter where in the world I went. My hunting partners have said I have an acute sense of direction. I don't know how I do it, but it began with spending that cold day wandering around without the slightest idea where I was.

Later, as Dad's business prospered and he had more time, Dad enjoyed dressing up in flashy cowboy clothes and putting on shows at county fairs and gatherings with a horse he named Scout the Wonder Horse. Dad had taught Scout twenty-one vaudeville tricks, including kneeling and stomping out numbers on command. Scout won the first horse show he ever entered and continued to bring home ribbons wherever Dad took him. I looked forward to those trips with Dad each fall. We only traveled fifty miles at most, but that was the farthest I would get from home during the year. I made many friends at the fairs and shows, though I would see those friends only once a year.

We children had a pony named Topsy, and I showed him at some of the fairs. According to Dad's book, I was "a real horseman" at a very young age. Learning to ride as a youngster served me well when, years later, I hunted on horseback in several countries.

In the early 1950s Dad bought eight purebred Hereford cows, and he kept buying cattle until he had a herd of 150. Because he thought thirteen was his lucky number, he entered them thirteen at a time at the local fairs and won so many ribbons that Mother used 222 of them to make a quilt. The quilt turned out so well that she made another using the ribbons Scout won.

My childhood ended abruptly in 1954, when I walked out of my eleventh-grade classroom, convinced I knew everything I would ever need to know. I started work at Dad's lime plant the next day and never returned to school. People who know little about rural New Brunswick in the 1950s are surprised to learn my parents gave me no argument. It was a different world then (only one boy finished high school that year), and I could be useful at the plant.

Eventually, I would work at just about every job at the lime works, but for the first few months I spent most of my time shoveling lime and loading hundred-pound bags of the stuff into boxcars. To earn more than Dad was paying, I moved to Toronto and got a job at Coutt's Hallmark Cards as a mail server for seventy-five cents an hour, working nine to ten hours a day, five and a half days a week. I went to Toronto with $600 in savings, but it quickly disappeared when I started buying food and paying my friends' rent at the rooming house after they were laid off. One day I woke up and decided I didn't like Toronto. I called my sister, borrowed $75, and flew back home to Moncton. It was the first time in my life I had ever been on an airplane.

I was nineteen then, and one of the people I wanted to see at home was Janice Spinney. I had met Janice a couple of years earlier when her parents, Louis and Hazel Spinney, moved to New Brunswick from Nova Scotia. Louis had moved his family into a house half a mile up the road from ours and had gone to work at the new cement plant in Havelock. Janice and I had gone out together a few times before I left for Toronto, and I had her on my mind when I returned from the big city. We soon decided we wanted to share our lives and were married in October 1957. Catherine Elaine (Cathy) was born in July 1958, followed by Debra Ann (Debby) in March 1962, Eric Arnold in December 1963, and Scott Andrew (Scotty) in September 1967.

After we were married, I got a job in Moncton, working on a survey crew for the railroad. They were building a "hump yard" in Moncton, where an engine could push

Janice and the author on their wedding day, October 1957.

a string of railcars to the top of a hump, allowing each car to roll down to the track they wanted it on. There were perhaps forty tracks. It eliminated a lot of shunting. Missing Havelock, I called Dad a couple of years later and asked if he could use another man, and Janice and I moved back within a week.

Havelock Lime Works was still producing agricultural lime, and we were also selling grit to poultry farms under the name of Eastern Shell Bone Products. It was about this time that Dad went to the Bank of Nova Scotia for a loan of $50,000 for operating capital. He never forgave that bank for turning him down. The Bank of Montreal quickly approved him for the same loan, and it received all of our business from that day on. It was a policy I continued when I ran the companies.

After returning from Moncton, I got serious about helping Dad expand the business and began taking on more responsibility. In 1964 we incorporated as the Havelock Lime Works Ltd., and I became a vice president. Three years later, we had a $100,000 annual payroll and were producing more tons of agricultural lime per hour than Dad had produced in his entire first year in business. The by-products from the agricultural end of the business were showing a profit, too. We now were selling poultry grit, fertilizer fillers, concrete aggregate, stone for chip sealing, calcium limestone for pulp and paper, and materials for roads and driveways.

We then began the process of forming another company, Havelock Processing Ltd., a million-dollar lime-processing plant that would enable us to produce both calcined and hydrate lime to sell to mines and pulp mills. During the process, my sister Elsie died of heart failure in 1970 at thirty-five, leaving a husband and two children. Elsie had had a problem with high cholesterol levels (it was called "hardening of the arteries" then), even before leaving school. When she worked in Toronto, the doctors experimented with various types of new drugs. Dad was leaving most of the daily operation of the companies to me by then, and I took on even more responsibility after Elsie died.

In 1971 I formed A&M Transport Ltd. Soon I had fifteen Kenworth trucks and twenty-four trailers and was delivering lime products across eastern Canada and across the U.S. border into Maine. Three years later, I built another $500,000 processing plant. We now had three plants and storage facilities operating twelve months a year. When Dad retired in 1974 and I became president and chief executive officer of the companies, my first step was to build a new crushing and screening plant that would increase our production from 1,600 tons per day to 2,500. Two years later, we built another lime plant and increased our total production by fifty tons per hour. By 1978, when I became a vice president of the Canadian Lime Institute, my transport company had doubled in size, and we were one of the largest businesses in New Brunswick.

To celebrate Mother and Dad's fiftieth wedding anniversary in 1978, Janice and I planned for a big family gathering at our home. I commissioned an author to work with Dad and publish his book, *Give Me Fifteen Minutes*. (The title referred to the time Dad went to the lime quarry to buy a load of lime for his farm and went away owning

Mom and Dad at their 50th wedding anniversary with our daughter Catherine and husband Bernie. Within three years we would lose my parents and daughter.

the business.) The book and the anniversary celebration were successful. Less than a month later, Dad suffered a heart attack and died suddenly.

Two years later, in 1979, our daughter Catherine, who was married to Bernie Demont, was six months pregnant when she was diagnosed with leukemia and given only a short time to live. While undergoing treatment at a hospital in Nova Scotia, she gave birth two months prematurely. Jeremy weighed less than two pounds at birth and was rushed to the children's hospital next door. For a while we thought we might lose him, but he was released three months later. Cathy, who had come home in remission on Christmas Eve 1979, underwent a bone marrow transplant in October 1980. She seemed to do well for a while, but right after Christmas her health started deteriorating rapidly. She died on 26 February 1981.

A few months later, Mother died, too.

The deaths of my loved ones changed me forever. I no longer had any interest in working. The excitement I had once felt in watching our businesses grow was gone. While in Kenya on a photographic safari with Janice in 1983, I decided to sell the companies and follow my lifelong love for hunting.

Life is too short, I told myself. I intended to live every day to the fullest.

AFRICA CHANGES MY LIFE, 1983–84

One year after we lost our daughter, Janice and I had to get away and do something different to help us forget the past year. We booked a twenty-one-day African photo safari in Kenya.

On 26 February 1983, along with our friends Gerry and Mark Pearson from Alberta, we flew to London and then on to Kenya. Our schedule called for three days in Nairobi before driving on to Mountain Lodge, where we would see our first African animals in the wild. Every morning and evening we would sit on the verandas and watch the antelope, warthog, zebra, and elephant come to drink. I was fascinated and thrilled. More than that, I was hooked on Africa. It was a pity, I told myself, that Kenya had banned hunting before I discovered this beautiful land and its wildlife.

From Mountain Lodge our tour took us to Samburu Lodge, another day's drive over extremely rough and dusty roads. We stopped briefly to visit and photograph a Masai *manyatta,* a hodgepodge of low brown huts of brush plastered with mud and cow manure. The people there were accustomed to having their photos taken. They wore their traditional dress—red blankets and spears for the men, and lots of brass jewelry for the women. I never learned whether they changed to western clothes after the tours left, but I doubt it.

While we were at Samburu, we left the camp very early each morning and drove around in Land Rovers, looking at and photographing game until around 9:30 A.M., when we returned to the lodge to eat and rest. Around 3:30 P.M. we went out again.

In addition to the Big Five (lion, buffalo, leopard, elephant, and rhino) and giraffe, impala, warthog, and wildebeest, we saw animals that I never knew existed until then. The various sable and roan antelopes, elands, duikers, dik-diks, hartebeests, and gazelles were new to me. I listened to everything our guides told us during the day, and after dinner I read everything I could find in my guidebook about the animals we were seeing. Right then and there I decided that all of this was too good not to be shared. Wouldn't it be great if someone assembled a collection of mounts of every African animal so that people who couldn't go to Africa could see them up close? From there, it wasn't a great leap to include every big-game animal in the world in this collection.

I had no idea how many types of game animals there were on the planet, but I was determined to find out. For some reason, though, I set my goal at two hundred species. Until then the only hunting I had done was for deer, bear, and moose near my home in New Brunswick, and I had made one trip for a caribou in Newfoundland in 1979. There was no reason why I couldn't be the hunter to put

Janice and the author stand on the equator near Mount Kenya Lodge during their trip to Kenya in 1983.

Janice at a Masai manyatta, *a house made entirely of sticks and cow dung. Kenya.*

this great collection together, I thought. I had no idea what realizing my goal would require, where it would take me, or where I might go for information.

From Samburu we flew down to the Amboseli Game Reserve. From the lodge and everywhere we drove, the sky was dominated by snowcapped Mount Kilimanjaro—Africa's highest mountain, the majestic peak that Ernest Hemingway had made a household name—across the border in Tanzania. It was the Africa of Isak Dinesen's *Out of Africa*—short grass plains with views that went on forever, green hills, blue mountain peaks rising above layers of white clouds, and animals, lots of animals. Zebra with wildebeest, and lion, leopard, and cheetah nearby waiting for something to make a mistake. Hartebeest, gazelle, and impala. Cape buffalo with heavy curved horns. Tall, spotted giraffe that ran with rocking gait. You name it, we saw it on my first safari.

Amboseli was (and still is) best known for its elephant, and the four of us saw these awesome beasts every day. Hearing an elephant trumpet and seeing one fan itself with its oversized ears were things this New Brunswick deer hunter would never forget. We drove up to one small family group of elephant and parked close enough to hear the strange rumbling sounds their stomachs make. When the matriarch mock-charged our Land Rover, I suddenly realized just how dangerous hunting an elephant might be.

From Amboseli we flew to the Governor's Camp in the Masai Mara Game Reserve and camped in tents on the banks of the Mara River. This large reserve was loaded with game, as were the other areas we visited. I most remember the hippo. There were dozens of them in the river's pools, and I never grew tired of watching them surface, just their eyes and nostrils showing. From the shore we'd snap photos when they opened their mouths and yawned, displaying their sharp ivory teeth. I was surprised to hear the tour guide say that the hippo is one of Africa's most dangerous animals until he told us that these three-ton giants kill dozens of humans every year. The danger comes, he said, when someone gets between the beast and the water. Hippo aren't very smart. Instead of running around you to reach safety, a hippo is just as likely to run right over you, cutting you in half with its terrible teeth as it passes. A hippo came very close to our tent one night.

After leaving the Masai Mara reserve, we flew on to the Mount Kenya Safari Club, the comfortable and scenic inn built by American actor William Holden and other investors. I was disappointed that there were no game drives there, but I enjoyed looking around this historic place. During Kenya's heyday of safari hunting, all the professional hunters (called "white hunters" in those days before political correctness) and their clients would stop at the lodge and swap stories about their safaris. It wasn't unusual, I was told, to meet such people as author Robert Ruark; African hunting legends Glen Cottar, Bill Woodley, John Lawrence, Syd Downey, and John Kingsley-Heath; and an assortment of movie stars and major and minor celebrities.

We returned to Nairobi and spent a couple of days shopping and visiting the local sights before flying to London, where we stayed at the St. James Club for three days and toured the city. We were back in Moncton on 12 March. The experience had changed my life. An elk hunt I'd already scheduled for that fall in Montana would launch my quest to assemble this great collection of the world's game animals. I had to start somewhere, and North America was as good a place as any.

Even before my Kenya photo safari, I had wanted to hunt an elk. Our moose in New Brunswick are big, and, even though their antlers can't compare with those from Alaska and the Yukon, they have respectable racks. Nonetheless, I wanted an elk. In my mind bull elk are the handsomest of North American deer. I wanted a trophy bull with at least six long tines on each of its long main beams. To hunt such a bull, my friend Dave Drury and I flew to Great Falls, Montana, in early November. We rented a car and drove to Helena and booked motel rooms for the night. I did all the driving because Dave had broken his ankle a few weeks before and was still in a cast. I was exhausted after a long day of traveling from Moncton. Even so, I had trouble getting to sleep. It was our first hunting trip outside Canada, and I was excited about what we might experience during the next few days.

We spent the next day driving to a small town called Toston, where we booked rooms at the Mustang Motel. The next morning we pulled into Crow Creek Outfitters' camp, a working cattle ranch that had leased its hunting rights to our outfitter. We would sleep, cook, and eat in one of the buildings the ranch used only during the summer, we were told. One glance told me we were in trouble. The shack was small and filthy, and it had a musty odor that smelled a lot like urine, very possibly rat urine. We would have to haul our water from an outside pump a long distance away. Our "bathroom" was a stinking outhouse behind the building. Our camp was nothing like what our booking agent had advertised.

Dave and I had booked a two-by-one hunt, which meant we shared a guide. After introducing ourselves, we climbed into the guide's four-wheel-drive pickup truck and started driving around the ranch on rutted logging roads, stopping every once in a while to look for elk with our binoculars. We saw no elk at all that afternoon and only a few cow elk and their calves the next day. The bulls were nowhere to be seen. Even the young spikes and ragged-horns were in hiding.

On the third day the guide and I made a short drive and pushed a three-point bull to Dave. He killed it with his second shot. On another drive that same day, I jumped a yearling bull with long spikes, but it offered me only a quick shot, and I missed. Those two young animals were the only two bull elk we saw on the ranch.

Our licenses allowed us to take two mule deer each, and Dave and I shot three

The author's boys began hunting at an early age. Scott poses with his first deer. New Brunswick.

Once the author and his associates decided to build a gun range, the work went fast. Here, they install the gate on the main road. New Brunswick.

bucks between us. We saw perhaps twenty or thirty bucks on the ranch, and we shot the only one that was large enough to mount. It really wasn't a trophy.

In my journal I ranked the hunting on that ranch as only fair and the quality of the animals poor. Our booking agent hadn't done us any favors. At the end of the week Dave and I drove back to Helena and got a motel. The first thing I did when I reached my room was to strip off my clothes and take a shower. Then Dave and I found a place to eat. The next morning we drove to Great Falls, only to learn that a snowstorm had closed the Denver airport and we couldn't get back to Canada through the mile-high city as we'd planned. We could fly to Las Vegas, where we might be able to catch a flight to Toronto, so that's what we did. We spent three days in Vegas, enjoying the sun and the casinos, before we flew home. Those three days helped make up for our disappointing elk hunt. If our booking agent had truthfully described the camp and the hunting conditions, we might have felt differently. Because of his glowing reports, though, we arrived in Montana with delusions of passing up a dozen or more trophy elk before we finally settled on bulls that would make the prestigious Boone and Crockett record book. We went away without seeing a single mature male elk.

Incidentally, I still see that agent's name mentioned in hunting magazines by the writers whose hunts he has arranged. I never used his services again, which was his loss. It would not be the only hunt that would disappoint me over the next eighteen years. I would eventually learn to accept the fact that not having things go as planned is a part of hunting. But this was my first hunt in another country, and Dave and I had expected a lot more than we got.

It was Fred Webb who first told me about Safari Club International and the conventions it holds each year in Nevada. I'd known Fred, a native of New Brunswick and owner of one of Canada's largest outfitting companies, for some time. Anyone who has met the man knows he uses "colorful" language when he gets to talking. His stories about the convention led me to join the club and attend its 1984 convention in Las Vegas. I was like a kid walking into a toy store for the first time, and it hardened my resolve to begin the quest to collect two hundred specimens of big-game animals. There were nearly a thousand booths on the exhibition hall's floors, including booths for outfitting companies from all over the world, custom gunmakers, taxidermists, hunting gear manufacturers, wildlife artists—you name it. I'd never seen anything like it. At its evening banquets the club sold hunts, paintings, and custom rifles to raise money for its programs. The Saturday grand finale banquets are where the major pieces go on the block, however, and on that Saturday night in February, I got involved in bidding on a beautiful double rifle.

It was from the SCI Big Five Masterpiece Series, five rifles custom built by some of the finest big-game hunting

Janice and the author at their first SCI convention. Las Vegas, 1984.

rifle manufacturers and decorated by well-known engravers. The 1984 rifle was a double-barreled .375 Holland & Holland built almost entirely by hand by F. W. Heym of Germany and heavily engraved and decorated with scenes of African Cape buffalo. It came in a handmade wooden case with cleaning accessories, a handmade Damascus-blade knife with a Cape buffalo horn handle, and an extra set of sidelocks. It was a beautiful, one-of-a-kind rifle, and I had to have it. My bid of $65,000

brought the audience to its feet, applauding, and it bought me a rifle.

According to *Safari* magazine, it was the most anyone had ever paid for a modern-made firearm. But how do you put a price on a one-of-a-kind masterpiece? My "record" didn't last long. A few years later, someone paid more than $100,000 for a rifle at another SCI auction.

I didn't take the buffalo rifle home with me right away because F. W. Heym was so proud of it, they asked me to allow them to display the rifle at international firearms shows in Nürnberg and around the world.

I spent a lot of time with the *SCI All-Time Record Book of Trophy Animals,* browsing the pages of its Africa edition, comparing the animals I had seen in Kenya with photos of the animals taken by SCI members. What interested me most were the descriptions of animals by Jack Schwabland, whom I would meet years later. It didn't take me long to realize that the world had many more varieties than the two hundred I had set as my goal and that it would be impossible to collect all the species and subspecies of Africa alone. I used the record book, as well as *Safari* magazine and the SCI World Hunting Awards programs, to plan my hunting. Since 1984, I have attended every SCI convention except the 1999 convention, when I was late returning from a hunt in Pakistan.

I was forty-six when I sold my three largest businesses to Dickinson Mines in 1984 and set out to devote my life to the outdoors. Much of my time on would be spent hunting animals, but I also got deeply involved in wildlife conservation programs and in the property I call White Pine Lodge. There I built a twenty-foot dam, which created a ten-acre lake. We have planted more than a million trees and have created areas for wildlife habitat. We have fifteen miles of well-maintained roads on the 3,500 acres.

Looking back at what I used to think was important, I can truthfully say I don't miss the pressures of running those businesses, not one little bit.

MY FIRST HUNTING SAFARI, 1985

After our photo safari in Kenya in 1983, I wanted my sons to share my fascination with the African continent and its wildlife. Later, they were both busy with their own families, so my first African safari, in 1985, was to be the only major hunt on which both of my boys were along.

Most hunters purposely avoid going through London to reach Africa because of the way British Customs and airlines officials treat gun owners. (I hadn't yet heard the horror stories about hunters who arrive at Gatwick Airport with their firearms and need to fly out from Heathrow—or vice versa—and can't get their guns transferred.) Fortunately for us, Chuck Bazzy of Safari Adventures, our booking agent, arranged for a company called Safari Services to keep our guns and ammunition under bond while we visited London. James Pedder owns and operates the company. He meets his clients at the airport, drives them into London, arranges day rooms or hotels and tours, and then makes certain they and their firearms make it onto their airplanes when they leave England.

Pedder got my sons, Eric (then 22) and Scott (then 17), and me through Customs without delay when we reached London. We were taking four rifles to Africa: a 7mm Remington Magnum, Eric's .30-06, a .338 Winchester Magnum, and a .375 side-by-side double rifle I'd bought the previous year in Las Vegas. Pedder locked the rifles and ammunition in a trailer behind his little van, then drove us into the city, where he had reserved hotel rooms for us. The next morning Eric, Scott, and I watched the changing of the guards at Buckingham Palace before Pedder drove us to Windsor Castle and the Castle Hotel. Two days later, he took us to Gatwick Airport and checked our rifles on through to Zambia. I was excited that we finally were on our way.

A brief stop in Cameroon was the only thing that broke up the long trip south from London, and we were on the ground there only long enough to take on more passengers. Our outfitter, Geoff Broom, and his son, Russ, were waiting for us when we landed in Lusaka, Zambia, in Central Africa. We had booked a three-by-one, twenty-one-day package, meaning the three of us would share one professional hunter—Russ—for three weeks.

Russ didn't waste any time getting the safari under way.

After stopping to pick up some supplies at a little store on the edge of the city, the four of us headed for the Kafue Flats in Russ's four-wheel-drive vehicle. It was interesting to drive through Lusaka. It must have been a grand and beautiful city when it was the capital of Northern Rhodesia, but it had seen better days. I saw no new buildings under construction,

Russ Broom, Scott, Eric, and Geoff Broom on their first safari with the author. Zambia.

The author is thrilled with his first greater kudu. Zambia.

and all the businesses and homes had iron bars on the windows. Most buildings and homes were surrounded by high walls topped with broken glass or barbed wire to discourage break-ins. Hundreds of people sat around or walked aimlessly. Even the government buildings downtown looked as if they hadn't been painted—or even cleaned up—in decades.

Although the flats are only about a hundred miles from Lusaka, the road was in such bad shape that it took us more than three hours to get there. The road had been paved many years earlier, but years of neglect had left it so full of deep potholes that everyone drove in the dirt along its edge. We could make only forty miles per hour or so in the best places. I was particularly interested in the large number of people we saw along the road waiting for a ride or just standing there, perhaps waiting for something to happen. Some held up small, dead fish, obviously hoping that someone would stop and buy them. A quarter-mile beyond where they stood, we could see their homes. Some were made entirely of poles and grass; others were constructed of concrete blocks topped with corrugated sheet metal. They were no larger than an average small bedroom in Canada or the United States, and entire families lived in them. Although a few had electrical lines running to them, I doubted they had heating or cooling. This was early in my international hunting career, and I wasn't accustomed to seeing such poverty. Over the next dozen years I would see such conditions (and worse) many times in Africa, South America, and Asia.

We were on the flats to hunt lechwe, a handsome antelope with long, swept-back horns and a body about the size of a mule deer. There are three subspecies: red, black, and Kafue Flats. We would hunt the Kafue Flats lechwe first. As its name suggests, it is found only on Zambia's Kafue Flats, a huge wetlands with absolutely no cover. We had no trouble finding lechwe. There were hundreds of them on the flats. The problem was trying to decide which male had the best horns and then getting close enough to shoot it. After a frustrating hour of slogging through shallow water and mud, Russ pointed out what he thought was the best ram in a herd that was watching us from about two hundred yards away. One of the trackers set up the shooting sticks (three thin poles tied with a piece of inner tube at the top to form a tripod). Shooting from the sticks, Eric made a beautiful shot and killed the first trophy of our safari. An hour later, just before dark, I shot a ram.

The next morning, after Scott shot his lechwe, we drove back to Lusaka and spent the night in the Pomlozi Hotel. Early the next morning we boarded the Brooms' private airplane and flew to the Luangwa Valley, unquestionably the best hunting area in that country, then or now. We landed on an airstrip Geoff had built near his camp along the river. As with most hunting camps in Zambia, his was constructed entirely with native materials. Everything in the camp, including the fences, doors, shutters, roofs, and walls, had been made with poles ingeniously lashed together with strips of bark and thatched with strawlike elephant grass.

After lunch Russ drove us to his camp about fifty miles and four hours away. My sons and I were amazed by the amount of game we saw along the way, especially the elephant. When we drove up on them on the road, they'd trumpet and whirl around, leaving clouds of dust as they ran away. Sadly, unmerciful poaching over the next ten years decimated the elephants in the Luangwa Valley and elsewhere in Zambia.

I was immediately struck by the difference between this countryside and Kenya's. It was June, the beginning of winter in the Southern Hemisphere, but the leaves had not yet fallen. The final colors of autumn weren't as gaudy as New Brunswick's. They were subtler, but splendid nonetheless. I saw none of the short grass plains I had seen in East Africa. The Luangwa Valley and other hunting areas of Central Africa are forested, with only the *dambo*s (clearings) offering long views. In addition to elephant we saw occasional groups of sable antelope, impala, warthog, and fawn-colored Lichtenstein hartebeest on the primitive road and in many of the *dambo*s we passed.

They did all the cooking at our new camp outside over open fires and on a small wood stove, then served the food under a semi-open thatched dining area. Our meat came from the animals we shot. (We didn't eat zebra, hippo, baboon, lion, or leopard, however.) According to Russ,

the cook previously had worked as a chef in a hotel in Lusaka.

After a light breakfast, our first day of hunting in the Luangwa Valley began at first light, as the four of us left camp in the Land Rover and forded the Luangwa River.[1] The river was infested with crocodiles, and we saw several of them near the vehicle nearly every time we crossed the water.

Two days before our lion hunt, I shot a hippopotamus, and Russ used his Land Rover to drag the oversized carcass to a place where we could move up to it from downwind without being seen. After we had left, the men removed the teeth with their axes and slit the belly to make it easier for the lions to feed. When we returned the next morning, big chunks of the hippo were missing, and there were tracks of lion and hyena all around the carcass. One of the men inspected it closely and proudly held up a long, coarse hair.

"That's from his mane," Russ said. "See how his tracks are so much bigger than the others. It's a good male."

The men got busy and built a screen of grass and brush in front of a termite mound about thirty yards from the hippo. According to Russ, the prevailing wind blew from the bait to our blind, and this should enable us to slip up on the lions while they were feeding. The men cleared a half-mile-long path, removing all leaves

---

1. Before we left this camp, Russ and I crept quietly to the edge of the riverbank, overlooking a sandbar where a big croc had been seen. It was still there. I found a rest and shot when the cross hairs of my scope were focused on a tiny spot on its head. Russ shook my hand when the crocodile stiffened and flapped its tail but didn't move from where I had shot it. If it isn't anchored with a brain shot, Russ said, a crocodile's first response is to run into the river, from which it often can't be recovered. This was an old croc, over thirteen feet long, and I was happy to take it for my collection.

The first leopard the author took on his first hunting safari. Zambia.

Eric with the Cape buffalo he took in the Luangwa Valley. Note its excellent spread. Zambia.

and twigs, and marked it with bits of toilet paper so we could follow it in poor light.

Even before we reached the bait that afternoon, Russ took one look at the trees around it and announced the lion weren't there. If they were, he said, the birds would be sitting in the trees instead of circling and landing on the carcass. Nonetheless, as we walked up to the bait with our rifles ready, we spooked jackals, vultures, eagles, and storks feeding on the meat. The hippo was covered with white bird droppings and feathers, but there were no fresh lion tracks around it. The pride probably wouldn't return until after dark, Russ said. Even so, we stayed in our blind, watching the carcass until it was too dark to see anything, before driving back to the camp. Russ was confident we'd find the lion at the bait at first light.

It was still dark the next morning when we drove to our path in the Land Rover. As soon as Russ turned off the lights and quietly opened the door, we heard the loud roar of a male lion on the bait. There was no mistaking it. It was the same raspy sound that famous lion makes at the start of every MGM movie. Russ grinned and loaded his .458 Winchester Magnum, resting its barrel on his shoulder, muzzle pointing forward. I loaded my .338 Winchester Magnum with 250-grain Nosler Partition handloads and put the sling over my shoulder. The tracker Russ had chosen carried only a crude ax. Its blade had been forged from a truck's leaf spring, then fitted into the knobbed end of a thirty-inch-long piece of hardwood root. Though he doubted we would need the tool, Russ said axes are more

maneuverable than rifles and just as effective against angry lion at close quarters.

"Ready?" he whispered.

I nodded and fell in behind him, and the lion roared again. If our luck held, we were going to be within thirty yards of that lion and its mates in just a few minutes. Russ was with me, so I wasn't afraid. But it was exciting.

We were lucky. The lion were still feeding when we moved up to our screen of grass in the dark. However, we could see only dim, gray shapes in the poor light when we peeked through the hole in our blind. I couldn't see the cross hairs in my scope at all. Russ put a finger to his lips. We would have to wait until the light improved. I was watching the largest moving shape in my scope when I saw a lioness effortlessly rip off a good-size hunk of hippo meat. She then walked over to the front of our blind, plopped down, and began eating—just three or four long steps from where we were standing. When I looked up to see what the male was doing, I saw it begin to move slowly away from the bait. Russ had said lion usually head for thick cover at the first hint of daylight if they've fed all night. By now, I could see the lion clearly in my scope. Russ nodded when I glanced at him. I put the cross hairs on the lion's shoulder, aiming for where I thought the center of the opposite shoulder would be, and fired. The lion jumped straight up and flopped around on the ground, roaring as it died. Russ slapped me on the back and we shook hands. I had taken my first African lion.

The author's Luangwa Valley lion had only the beginnings of a mane, but he was proud of it. It was the first of several lion he would take in Africa. Zambia.

Jack Hegarty (left) filmed the author's stalk on this moose for their video company. Newfoundland.

Although we believed the lion was dead, we circled it cautiously, both of us ready to shoot if it showed the slightest sign of life. Before we relaxed, Russ had me fire into its spine for insurance. Unloaded guns and dead lions can kill you, he said.

I was amazed at the size of the animal. I'd seen lions in circuses and zoos, but I never realized just how large they were until we began loading this big cat into the Land Rover. It weighed more than four hundred pounds and was nearly as large as a spike elk. It had a massive head, with very long teeth. As we were driving back to camp, I wondered what had happened to the lionesses, especially the one that had been feeding near our feet. It could just have easily bolted through our screen of grass—right into us—when I shot its mate.

In addition to taking hippo, lion, lechwe, and crocodile at this camp, we also took two leopard, buffalo, bushbuck, warthog, wildebeest, waterbuck, zebra, puku, impala, oribi, baboon, and greater kudu. We took the leopards at sundown, luring them to my rifle with impalas we hung in trees. We stalked the buffaloes and antelopes after we found their tracks along the area's two-track roads, or we drove up on the animals that had made the tracks.

We spent our last night on the Luangwa in Geoff's camp before flying on to the Bangweulu swamps to hunt sitatunga, a strange-looking, shaggy antelope with long, splayed hoofs that allow it to move around in muddy swamps.

Our camp at the edge of the swamp was similar to the others we'd seen—a compound with several thatched structures and a semi-open dining area. The huts, or "chalets," were comfortable, and their thatching gave them a distinctive sweet odor. According to Russ, they needed to be burned and rebuilt every few years to rid them of the mice, insects, and snakes that eventually found homes in their roofs and walls.

The Bangweulu swamps were loaded with game. There had been hundreds of lechwe on the Kafue Flats, but there were thousands of black lechwe in the Bangweulu. Again, we had trouble deciding which one to shoot and then getting close enough to shoot it. I finally took a beautiful ram with 28⅜-inch horns that would become the number one entry in the SCI record book at the time.

Other than the lechwe, our primary goal at Bangweulu was to collect a sitatunga. I sat in blinds for hours, walked along the fringes of reedbeds, and rode in *mokoro* (dugouts) mornings and evenings, but I never saw a shootable male. My sons and I did take lesser game such as tsessebe, common reedbuck, and another oribi.

We returned to Lusaka after twelve days of hunting and drove to the Kafue Plateau, where we took sable antelope and Lichtenstein hartebeest. In Zambia, hunters must purchase licenses for each animal before hunting, so I bought two licenses for everything Russ said we might encounter. I shot one of each, and my sons shared the other permits.

Russ suggested that I have our African trophies mounted by a company called Taxidermy International in Raleigh, North Carolina. Russ had gone to the university there and knew the owner, Dick Idol, an author of articles and books on hunting white-tailed deer. Taxidermist Kevin White was in the process of buying the company. When I returned from Zambia, I flew to North Carolina to meet Kevin and see his work. I later arranged for Russ to ship my trophies to him. Since then, Kevin has mounted nearly two hundred trophies for me, and our families have become good friends. After the first shipment, whenever he had forty or fifty mounts ready, he would hire a rental truck and fasten them to the floor and walls inside and drive up to New Brunswick with his wife. It eliminated crating and shipping problems, and we enjoyed their visits. I took Kevin on his first trip to Africa, and Janice and I spent a lot of time with the Whites at SCI conventions.

I don't know how a first hunting safari could have been any better than this one. We took twenty-one different types of animals—including three members of the Big Five—and most of them qualified for the SCI record book.

ALASKA, THE YUKON, AND BRITISH COLUMBIA, 1986

In the spring of 1985, two months before my sons and I went to Zambia, I hunted black bear with Fred Webb, a well-known Canadian hunting outfitter, at his camp in New Brunswick. When a downpour kept us from going out one day, Fred showed us a video he and Jack Hegarty, a friend from Maine, had filmed a year earlier at Fred's caribou camp at Ungava Bay. Fred said he and Jack would like to produce hunting videos commercially but lacked the capital. I talked with Fred later and said I might be interested in investing some money if the videos promoted the benefits of regulated hunting to nonhunters.

A month later, Fred and Jack showed up at my office with several videos Jack had made with fly-fishing expert Lee Wulff. They were of professional quality, and, according to Jack, he could lease the rights from Wulff to allow us to market them. Before our meeting was over, the three of us agreed to form a company called North American Outdoorsman. I was to be president of the company and would handle the financing. Jack would do the filming, and Fred would set up the trips. By early 1986, all the paperwork was behind us, and our new U.S. corporation was a reality.

We filmed our first video in Newfoundland in September 1985, before we had formalized the company. Fred contacted an outfitter named Gerry

Pumphrey, who guided Fred's clients when they hunted in that province. Jack went over a week early to collect some scenery and wildlife footage. I took a ferry across to Newfoundland and met Fred and Gerry, and we flew in Gerry's floatplane to his camp on a wilderness lake. It didn't take us long to recognize that Gerry ran a good camp. The log cabins were comfortable, the cook knew what he was doing, and there was plenty to eat.

While Jack was waiting for us to arrive, he had gone out with two hunters from Pennsylvania and had filmed one of them taking a black bear and a caribou. After we arrived, Jack filmed me hiking with two guides, climbing, and passing up several small bull moose. I knew enough about marketing to realize that a hunting video that didn't show someone taking an animal wouldn't sell. I also knew that my taking a small bull wouldn't be much better than shooting none at all. After a week of hunting, it looked as if we might have to abandon the project. Luckily, on the day before we were scheduled to go home, we found a nice bull, and I shot it while Jack filmed the action. Its antlers were 41 inches wide. It wasn't the biggest moose in eastern Canada, but it was a trophy bull by Newfoundland standards.

We spent the rest of the day quartering the bull and carrying the pieces

Rick Furniss's sturdy horses helped the author and his companions cover a lot of ground in sheep country. Yukon.

The author's first Dall sheep, number one in his quest for a Grand Slam of North American Wild Sheep. Yukon.

Rick Furniss's Dall sheep camp in the Ogilvie Mountains. Yukon.

Fishing legend Lee Wulff shows the author's salmon to their guides. The author holds the fishing rod. New Brunswick.

to a place where a helicopter could pick them up. We had worked hard for a week in cold weather, and Jack and I were exhausted by the time we were ready to leave Gerry's camp, but we had some good footage. We called the video *The Big Three in Newfoundland.*

For our next film project Jack and I chose an Alaskan brown bear hunt with outfitter Kelly Vrem. It began with Jack and I meeting in April 1986 at the airport in Anchorage and checking into the Golden Lion Hotel. The first thing we did after reaching our rooms was to call Kelly's office. The news wasn't good. We apparently had arrived too early. None of the hunters in Kelly's camp had taken a bear that season. The bear obviously were still in their dens, so Jack and I rented a car and spent a week sightseeing. We drove up to Mount McKinley and on to Fairbanks, then circled back to Anchorage. Jack filmed a lot of scenery for the video.

After returning from Fairbanks, we chartered a floatplane to fly us to Kelly's camp. Two or three hunters were there when we landed on Jude Lake in Unit 16, and none had taken a bear. After we unpacked and got settled in the log cabin assigned to us, Kelly explained how we would be hunting. While we stayed in camp, pilots in four Super Cubs would fly out in four directions and look for a suitable bear. When they found one, the plane would fly back to camp and get Jack, our guide Bob Adams, and me. It was (and still is) illegal for hunters to shoot game the same day they've been in the air, so the plan called for us to land near the

place the bear had been seen and spend the night in a small tent. The next morning we would follow the bear's tracks on snowshoes and try to catch up with it.

But the bears weren't cooperating. Jack and I spent the next four or five days waiting in camp for someone to find "our" bear. The few bear the pilots saw weren't anywhere near where we could get to them, and only one was large enough to be worth going after, Kelly said. Our time was running out, so a pilot flew us to another area, and we landed with skis on a snow-covered ridge. We stayed in tents and traveled around on snowmobiles, glassing the big valleys from the mountaintops, looking for bear tracks in the snow. We covered a lot of ground, but again we saw no shootable bear.

With only two or three days left, we moved to still another area and spent many boring hours watching an old moose kill. If the bear had left their dens, they weren't moving around, and they certainly weren't interested in rotten moose meat. Bob was worried about the weather. It had been getting warmer, and the snow would soon be too soft for a plane to land and take off on skis. That meant we would have to wait until the ground was dry enough to use wheels on the plane. How long that might be was anyone's guess.

On the day we were supposed to be picked up, Bob walked the ridge where we had landed and found his worries were justified. The snow was turning to mud. When Kelly flew over us, Bob waved him off. A couple of hours later, Kelly returned, circled, and dropped us more food. Back at his camp, Kelly followed the weather reports, and three or four days later he took advantage of a heavy frost and landed his Super Cub near us just after sunup. We loaded our gear and took off without any problems.

It had been an interesting and physically demanding hunt, but we had no footage of shooting a bear. Without that we had no video.

Our company eventually offered twenty-four video titles, including sixteen we leased from Wulff, three that Fred and Jack had completed earlier, and a couple of videos Jack leased from people he knew. The Tennessee company that handled our marketing set up a toll-free number to take orders, and they did the copying, storage, and shipping. The quality of our productions was topnotch, and we received two Teddy awards at the National Outdoor/Travel Film Festivals sponsored by the Michigan Outdoor Writers Association. (Our video *Courageous Lake Caribou* won the best hunting award in 1986–87, and our *Ungava Char* won the best fishing award in 1989.) We also filmed a total of four Alaskan brown bear hunts that we never marketed. Jack and I spent a lot of time together during those years. We traveled to Alaska four or five times, sharing many a night in little tents in bad weather. Fred later left the company, but Jack and I kept it going until 1990. We are still close friends.

The problem was our films were just too good. Everything was shot on expensive 16mm film, professionally edited and dubbed, and transferred to videotape. We even hired professional announcer Curt Gowdy to narrate the later tapes. Unfortunately, by the time our videos hit the market, we had to compete with dozens of cheaply made hunting videos, as well as videos produced by amateurs who viewed them as a way to make their own hunts tax-deductible. We couldn't recover our costs when retail video prices dropped, so Jack and I agreed to shut down the company.

Jack couldn't accompany me on my last two hunts in 1986, but he should have—they would have made great videos. I began them by flying to Whitehorse on 29 July and checking into the Chilikoot Inn. Waiting for me was a hunter I hadn't met before, Larry Stone from the States. Both of us had booked Dall sheep hunts in the Ogilvie Mountains with outfitter Rick Furniss and would be sharing a camp in Rick's concession in the northern Yukon. Larry and I got along well, and after dinner in the hotel that evening we bought tickets for the Whitehorse Fabulous Follies. After the show, even though we planned to get up at 4:45 A.M., we spent an hour or so in the hotel lounge, talking about hunting.

We had breakfast in the hotel with Rick before heading to the airstrip. Larry had flown to Whitehorse in his own plane, so he flew to camp alone. I flew in Rick's Super Cub to his sheep camp, where I was to share a tent with Larry.

The staff at Rick's camp included main guide Bill Rankin, a cook named

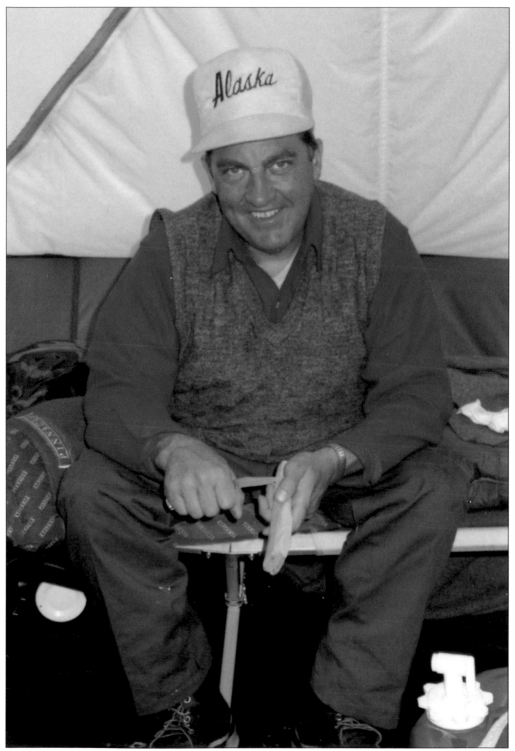

The author helps carve eating utensils, something the outfitter forgot to pack. Kelly's Camp, Alaska.

The brown bears, atop a high ridge, weren't moving that trip. Kelly's Camp, Alaska.

Bernadette, and my guide, Carl. We left camp on horseback each morning at first light and didn't get back until after dark. In early August that far north, sundown was at 10 P.M., which meant Bill and Carl got very little sleep. Rick hobbled the horses and turned them loose when they were at camp, allowing them to find their own food and water, which meant that every morning the guides had to get up early and find, catch, and saddle our horses. Bernadette made sandwiches of moose meat and fresh, homemade bread for us each night so we wouldn't have to return for lunch.

We rode each day up valleys and to the tops of mountains, glassing for sheep in all the likely places. Larry killed a caribou on the second day, and we didn't get back to camp until after midnight. We were seeing very few sheep, so we packed up the horses on the fourth day and moved to a spike camp on Castle Mountain, about four hours away. We had flipped a coin to see who would get the first shot of the hunt, and Larry had won. Now that he had taken his caribou, I would get the first shot at a Dall sheep.

Around 3 P.M. two days later, Bill and Carl spotted a good ram on a ridge across from us. The stalk took two hours of climbing through a boulder field, and we could get no closer than three hundred yards from the ram. After checking its horns again with the spotting scope, I found a rest for my rifle, found the ram in my scope, took a deep breath, squeezed the trigger as carefully as I could when the cross hairs were on its spine—and missed!

The ram didn't know where the shot had come from, and it ran downhill, toward me. My second shot, after the ram reached the bottom of the canyon and just before it went out of sight below us, also missed. I could hear the ram running in the loose rock straight down from us, so I leaned over the cliff, and when the ram came running into sight I killed it.

By now it was getting late, so while Bill and Carl went to retrieve the ram, Larry and I climbed to the top of the ridge and headed back on foot to the horses, two hours away. Bill and Carl caught up with us on the three-hour ride back to camp, but it was too dark to get a good look at my first wild sheep. I was pleased when we finally got to inspect it with the help of a lantern in the dining tent. Its horns were symmetrical, the longer one measuring 35¾ inches around the curve. The other horn was just an eighth of an inch shorter. It was a good head, and it easily made the *SCI All-Time Record Book of Trophy Animals.*

While Larry was hunting a ram the next day, Carl and I rode around the mountain and photographed the scenery. The day after that we left spike camp and rode back to sheep camp, where we spent the night. Larry flew home, and Bill, Carl, and I spent all the next day riding to Rick's main camp—three plywood cabins and a corral—on the banks of Hart Lake. According to Bill, we could catch lake trout if we had time.

I grew to appreciate Rick's horses after spending much time riding them. They were large, strong animals, almost large enough to be called draft horses, with huge feet that gave them stability while walking on the muskeg. A string of them, with their noses tied to their tails, had been brought in overland from the end of the road near the little town of Mayo in early July. Bill rode the lead mount; Carl brought up the rear. Camping out along the way, it took them three days to reach camp, and it would take them three days to make the return trip at the end of the season. There were wolves and grizzly bear in the area, but Bill said they rarely bothered the horses.

Carl and I stayed only that night at Hart Lake. The next morning we saddled our riding horses, loaded a pack animal with food and gear, and rode seven and a half hours to a big valley to look for a moose. We set up our little dome just in time that afternoon. The rain started a little before sundown and continued all through the night, and it rained off and on all the next day. We saw a few moose, but none of the bulls had antlers I wanted. I had taken eastern moose in New Brunswick and Newfoundland, and I wanted a moose with antlers not less than sixty inches wide. It was an achievable goal. Alaska-Yukon moose have the largest antlers of all the world's subspecies of moose, and the largest can have spreads approaching six feet.

Unfortunately, the weather didn't improve overnight. After breakfast the next morning, Carl and I packed up and rode eight hours back to the main camp— in steady rain every inch of the way. The following morning a small plane with floats landed on Hart Lake and flew me to Mayo, where I caught another plane to Whitehorse and had lunch with Rick. I'd had a good hunt and had taken a good ram. Rick said if I'd had more time, I would have taken a good moose, too.

After lunch I rented a car and drove to the little town of Atlin in British Columbia, where I had arranged to meet Jim and Charlene Matarozzo, owners of Diamond M Outfitters. After spending the night at their place, I chartered a floatplane to take me to their camp on Dry Lake, about two hours away by air. Waiting for me was Jim's camp manager and cook—a man I knew only as Elmer—and my Indian guide. I was there to hunt a mountain goat in the Cassiar Mountains.

I didn't get much sleep that night. Around midnight the wind came up, and it roared through our camp all night long, shaking my little tent. Just before daylight, Elmer announced that we might as well sleep late. It was blowing too hard to go out. We spent the rest of the day waiting for the storm to pass. We tried glassing from camp, but the Indian said we were wasting our time. There were no goats on this side of the big mountain above us, he said.

The wind died down that night, and we were able to ride out at seven o'clock the next morning. A two-hour ride got us to the top of the mountain, where we tied up our horses and glassed the country on the other side. Right away, the Indian spotted something at least a mile and a half away. With my binocular, all I could see was a white spot. If it hadn't moved,

I would have thought it was only a light-colored rock. The Indian walked back to our horses and returned with a spotting scope. After we set it up, I was able to inspect the first mountain goat I had ever seen. It was more cream-colored than white. I was amazed at the place it had chosen to spend the day. Only a goat could move around in a place like that. It was so far away I couldn't tell how long its horns were, or even if it had horns. My guide, however, said any goat found alone at this time of year probably was a billy. We would have to get closer and check the animal out, he said.

"First we eat," he said, as he took our lunches out of the saddlebags. "He's not going anywhere."

I kept returning to the spotting scope and looking at the goat while we ate. The animal was in a nearly inaccessible place.

As I expected, it wasn't easy to approach the goat. It took us at least four and a half hours to get around the basin without being seen and work our way to a place within two hundred yards above and across a little canyon from the goat. By then, we were close enough for my guide to get a good look at its horns. When he said they were about ten inches long, I sat down and found a rest. When I finally got the cross hairs under control, I aimed at the center of its shoulder and fired. The goat acted as if it hadn't been hit. It merely started moving uphill, almost in slow motion. My second shot put it down, and it rolled a few yards before coming to rest against a boulder. My first shot would have anchored any other animal, but that goat just kept going. "These are tough animals," my guide said.

If anything, my assessment of the terrain from afar had been on the conservative side. That goat had chosen an awful spot for its home. It was difficult and risky to reach where it had fallen. After skinning the animal, we packed its hide and meat on the horses. It was 10 P.M. before we reached camp, and we were exhausted. The billy's horns were 10⅛ inches long and later would rank very high in the *SCI All-Time Record Book of Trophy Animals*. The billy was in its summer coat, though, and its hair was thinner and not as long as it would have been if I had taken it earlier or later in the year.

My guide used a handheld radio to call the camp and ask for a plane to pick us up the next morning, but the rain and fog delayed its arrival until late afternoon.

When the four-seater, single-engine plane landed on the lake, Elmer and I said good-bye to the guide, loaded our gear, and flew out. The guide would stay with the horses until the next hunter arrived.

Back in Atlin, I stayed with the Matarozzos again. Another client, a man named Ed from upstate New York, was also staying there. Ed had taken a beautiful Stone ram, an animal high on the list of species I wanted to collect. The next morning was 18 August, a Monday. Charlene drove me to Whitehorse, where I caught the 6:30 P.M. flight to Vancouver, and I flew on to Toronto, where I spent the night before returning to Moncton.

I'd been gone three weeks and had hunted in one of the world's most spectacular regions. I shipped my ram and goat to Kevin White in North Carolina, and he mounted them life-size.

FOUR MONTHS OF HUNTING, 1987

You can forget everything you've heard about the comeback of the peregrine falcon and the American bald eagle in North America. The greatest conservation success story of the twentieth century was that of the southern white rhinoceros in South Africa. In the 1960s, when that country's nature departments began breeding white rhino on the Hluhluwe and Omfolozi game reserves in Zululand, the species was in danger of extinction. As the number of white rhino on those reserves increased, however, the wildlife managers took a bold step. Instead of restocking only the country's national parks, they auctioned some of their surplus white rhino to game ranchers and—more important—allowed the ranchers to sell trophy hunts. The money raised in the auctions helped sustain breeding programs. The hunters' trophy fees encouraged more ranchers to raise and stock more rhino.

When South Africa's white rhino restoration program began, black rhino were under no threat in East and Central Africa. In Kenya, the government had even paid professional hunters and game department staff to cull black rhino prior to opening new farming areas. What no one knew was that poaching teams (some of them sponsored by high-ranking Kenyan government officials) were gearing up to slaughter black rhino by the thousands.

Even before Kenya ended legal hunting in the late 1970s, poachers, fueled by the demand for rhino horn in the Middle East, were moving in. Within just a few years, black rhino numbers dropped drastically, and African governments everywhere ended legal black rhino hunting. Such "protection" did not slow the slaughter, however. There now was no reason for the local people to keep these dangerous and destructive animals around. Today, without legal hunting, the once-abundant black rhino is endangered. The white rhino has recovered and is thriving (and being hunted) on private game ranches all over South Africa.

When I booked my 1987 safari in South Africa, my primary goal was to take a white rhinoceros, a species that can be hunted nowhere else in the world.

James Pedder's smiling face greeted us when my son Scott and I landed in London on 11 February. (Unfortunately, Eric couldn't go with us on this trip.) It was just eighteen months since Scott and I had met Pedder, the owner of Safari Services, on our way to Zambia in 1985. As he had done then, Pedder got us through Customs with a minimum of delay, kept our rifles and ammunition under bond, and drove us to Windsor, where he had reserved a day room for us. After the long flight across the Atlantic, we were ready for a shower and a nap.

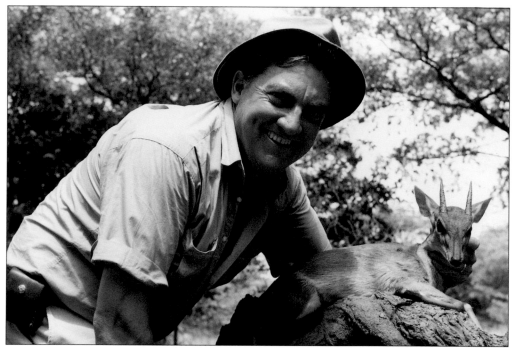

This little antelope is a trophy-class Livingstone suni. South Africa.

The vaal rhebok is a fine trophy. Long shots are the rule in its wide-open habitat. South Africa.

The author borrowed a .375 H&H Magnum from professional hunter Johnny Vivier to take his white rhino. South Africa, 1987.

That afternoon Jim drove us back to the airport for our 7 P.M. flight to Africa. Stopping in London even for just a few hours made a welcome break in the long trip halfway around the world.

From London, our South African Airways 747 flew to Nairobi, took on more fuel, and lifted off for Johannesburg. Getting through South African Customs was no problem at all. Scott and I merely pushed our luggage cart along a red line that led us to the police station, where they recorded the serial numbers and calibers of our rifles and issued us our permits. The entire process took less than ten minutes.

After leaving Customs, we stepped out into the crowded lobby and met our professional hunter and his wife, Johnny and Bev Vivier, and Johnny's tracker, a man named M'bella. M'bella loaded our luggage into his vehicle, and we climbed into Johnny's. Less than thirty minutes after landing, we were driving through heavy traffic on the left-hand side of the best highways in Africa. In Zambia, I had been struck by the litter and graffiti I had seen in Lusaka, as well as the idle people, the deteriorating infrastructure, and the pervasive poverty. South Africa's capital was nothing like Lusaka. Johannesburg was vibrant, modern, and prosperous.

Although this was in the days of apartheid, we saw none of the terrible abuses of human rights we had been reading about and seeing on television. Whenever we stopped for gas and food, Johnny and Bev treated all the people we met with true respect. They were more comfortable around the local people than I was. I was from a small town in New Brunswick, where we seldom saw anyone whose skin wasn't the same color as ours.

It was an eight-hour drive from the airport to the farm where our safari would begin. I planned to take as many of the country's unique game species as I could, especially the white rhino. I needed a rhino and an elephant to complete my collection of the Big Five of Africa. I had already decided to hunt an elephant somewhere else. Elephant can be hunted in South Africa, but the country was not known for producing big tusks.

At one time, when black rhino were hunted legally, they were the only rhino considered a member of the Big Five. The white rhino was too rare and wasn't considered dangerous enough. Instead of attacking humans without provocation, as black rhino frequently do, a white rhino's typical response upon finding a man in its domain is to run away. It also prefers open, grassy areas where it can be seen long before anyone approaches. The black rhino, on the other hand, lives in thick brush where it is nearly impossible for a hunter to see. Now that black rhino could not be legally hunted, Safari Club International was recognizing white rhino in its Big Five Award program. It was a logical decision. White rhino may be docile when unmolested, but they are considerably larger than black rhino and are therefore more difficult to kill. These three-ton beasts can be as dangerous as the black rhino or any other animal on this planet when wounded.

The author and his son Scott with a very good common nyala. South Africa.

A fine river-run salmon. Alaska.

The author and his son Scott with a Cape buffalo bull, taken in what then was called the Transvaal Province. South Africa, 1987.

The author had taken eastern Canada moose, but he found the size of the Alaska-Yukon variety truly awesome. Alaska.

Note the author's big smile about taking a good moose. Of course, he didn't have to carry it. Alaska.

After booking our twenty-eight-day safari with Mkuze Falls Safaris, I read everything I could find about rhino hunting. I knew where I would have to shoot to reach the brain, and where to shoot if it presented only a heart/lung shot. Any animal that weighs three tons deserves some respect. I didn't want to only wound mine.

In 1987 hunters were paying trophy fees well into the five figures in U.S. dollars for a white rhino. Game farmers kept a close eye on such expensive animals and weren't about to let them roam at will. They knew exactly how many were on their property, exactly where they fed and watered, and where they could be found during the day. They also knew before the hunt began exactly which animal their client would take.

We spent the night in a thatched rondavel at the farm where I would hunt my rhino. The next morning Scott and I left with Johnny, M'bella, and the farmer in a four-wheel-drive Toyota. Within a half-hour we found a small group of large gray shapes moving around in the thick brush near a water hole.

"See that one on the left, the one with the longest horn?" Johnny asked me, after consulting with the farmer in whispers. "You can just barely see its head."

"Yes."

"That's yours. We need to get closer, though."

The herd was about two hundred yards away and was paying absolutely no attention to us. I knew the only reason was that they couldn't smell us. Rhino have notoriously poor eyesight, but they have excellent noses. One whiff of our scent could send them stampeding deeper into the brush.

Fifteen minutes later we were within thirty yards of the rhino the farmer had selected. I was carrying a .375 H&H Magnum I had borrowed from Johnny. When the rhino turned broadside to me, I aimed about one-third up its chest, just behind the shoulder, and fired. That rhino and its companions bolted out of sight in less time than it takes to write about it. I looked at Johnny, and he looked at M'bella. The farmer had a grin on his face. He had seen my bullet kick dirt from the rhino's side, exactly where I needed to hit it.

"He won't go far," he said.

But a big rhino can take a lot of punishment. This one went around three hundred yards before it stopped near a big tree. When we caught up to it, I shot it again in about the same place, and it ran off again. When it had run less than one hundred yards, it went down in a cloud of dust. I now had four of the Big Five.

After taking some photographs and watching the farmer's men load the rhino into a big trailer, we returned to camp. My rhino "hunt" was over by 9:30 A.M.

We spent that afternoon driving around and looking for game. The farm had no shortage of zebra, blesbok, blue wildebeest, and impala, and we saw a few young kudu bulls, but Johnny said we would find larger ones at the next place we would be hunting. I passed them all up. I did shoot two small antelope—a Natal red duiker and a Livingstone suni.

The author and his guide Randy with a black bear. Its coat was much thicker than that of bears in New Brunswick. Alaska.

The author hunted four days before he found this 6x6 bull elk in a place called Bear Slide. British Columbia.

Johnny said I was lucky to take them both on the same day. They are harder to hunt than the larger antelope, and some hunters have spent days looking for them.

We left early the next morning and drove around six hundred miles to a place called Nottingham Road, where we hunted for three days without seeing an animal Johnny thought we should shoot. On Sunday we drove to Durban and stayed in a modern hotel overlooking the Indian Ocean and a beautiful beach. February is the middle of summer in the Southern Hemisphere, so Scott and I went for a swim. The temperature outside was 105 degrees Fahrenheit and muggy, but the water felt great.

The next day Johnny, Scott, and I caught an SAA flight south to Port Elizabeth, where a representative of Belvedere Safaris met us. Johnny would be only an observer on this leg of our safari. The professional hunter assigned to us for the next ten days was a man named Noel. Hunting with him, Scott and I collected southern greater kudu, Cape eland, Cape hartebeest, Cape grysbok, white and common blesbok, bontebok, fallow deer, giraffe, and southern impala. All were trophy animals, and all except the giraffe eventually would be listed in the SCI record book.

We then flew back to Durban and drove eight hours to Mkuze Falls, where Anton Marais, our outfitter, had a beautiful "camp" overlooking the falls. I've put "camp" in quotes because it was anything but what that word brings to mind. The lawns and hedges were immaculately groomed. Everything, including the rondavels, seemed new. There was even a swimming pool. I truly enjoyed sitting in the camp's *boma* above the river, watching colorful fish eagles swoop down and grab fish from the water.

During the five days we hunted at Mkuze Falls, I took a common nyala, another buffalo, and three or four smaller antelope. After that we drove to the eastern Transvaal, where we stayed at the Cheetah Inn and drove out to various nearby farms to collect the game animals of that region. By the time we returned to Johannesburg, Scott and I had taken thirty-eight animals, including a bat-eared fox and a black-backed jackal, and I had twenty-four more species for my collection. It had been a super safari.

Six months after returning from Africa, I met Jack Hegarty in Chicago, and we flew on to Alaska together. It was 18 August, and we planned to spend the next twenty-eight days making movies of hunting and fishing for North American Outdoorsman before returning to our homes on 13 October. The next morning we bought supplies and flew to King Salmon on the Alaska Peninsula. From there we chartered a small plane to take us to Tracy Vrem's camp, where we would fish for salmon and hunt barren-ground caribou. I'd hunted for a brown bear with Tracy's brother Kelly the previous year.

The camp consisted of four or five small tents for sleeping and a larger tent in which we cooked and ate. The tents had been set up along the edge of a river near a small airstrip where Tracy kept a

Super Cub and a four-passenger Cessna. Each morning Jack and I would climb into the Cessna, and Tracy would fly us upriver a few miles and land on a beach where we would go fishing. The river literally was full of humpback and pink salmon swimming upstream from the ocean to their spawning grounds, and we caught them on almost every cast. It gave us an eerie feeling to realize that every fish in the river was near the end of its life cycle. Dead salmon floating downstream reminded us that when these fish reached their spawning grounds, they would spawn and die.

Three days of catching all the fish we could catch was enough. Tracy flew Jack and me out to an area where we could hunt caribou with our guide, Bill Adams. We set up three small dome tents and climbed to the tops of mountains to glass. There were only a few caribou in the area, and I saw no bulls I wanted to shoot. Unlike the camp on the river, it warmed up in the middle of day, and swarms of big, black flies plagued us whenever the wind wasn't blowing. The heat and the flies had moved most of the caribou down the peninsula, Bill said. With our spotting scope, however, we could see small bands of caribou moving regularly along the base of Mount Peulick. It was too far to attempt to go there on foot, however.

After a week of hunting, with only two days left before we had to leave, Tracy arrived and flew us to the base of the mountain, where we again set up the tents and spent the night. The next morning we started climbing toward where we had

seen the caribou. To get there we had to cross four steep, slippery snowslides. We managed to get past the first three but had to turn back when we reached the fourth. It was just too dangerous.

The next morning we headed off in another direction. About an hour after leaving our tents, Bill pointed to a half-dozen light-colored spots that were moving about a mile away. Our binoculars showed they were all caribou bulls, and one of them had tall, heavy antlers. They were moving in a direction that would take them near us. I thought if we hurried we might be able to cut them off. A few minutes later, we were waiting for them to cross a rise about two hundred yards away. I passed up the first three bulls that trotted into sight. When the bull I wanted appeared, I kept the cross hairs slightly in front of the moving animal and squeezed the trigger. The bull went down on the spot and was trying to get up when I shot it again. Jack captured everything on film.

With our fishing and caribou hunt out of the way, Tracy flew Jack and me back to King Salmon, where Kelly Vrem's pilot was waiting to fly us to the Wood River Mountains in Wood-Tikchik State Park to hunt moose. We stayed at the main camp only long enough to drop off the gear we wouldn't need on the hunt, and then we flew to Dominion Creek. We landed on a sandbar and set up spike camp with domed tents. We spent a week there, hunting on foot and glassing for moose, but we saw no trophy bulls. As can happen in Alaska at that time of year, we were stuck in our tents for three of those days, trying to stay dry in downpours. On the eighth day the pilot returned and moved us to another area, where our camp had a comfortable wall tent. Even with a Coleman stove, it was very cold at night there.

We hunted by hiking and climbing low hills to glass the valleys and river bottoms. Walking wasn't easy, and even wearing hip boots there were places we couldn't reach because of the water. After four days of this, we were on a sidehill, looking across a series of beaver ponds, when we finally found a bull that warranted a closer look. It was across the river and so far off that all we saw at first were flashes of sunlight reflecting off the palms of its antlers. We were lucky, though. First we were able to find a place in the river shallow enough to allow us to wade. Then, being careful to stay downwind, we were able to get within one hundred and fifty yards of the bull. Compared to the moose I'd taken in New Brunswick, this one was a monster. It also was better than average for an Alaska-Yukon moose, I told myself, as I found a rest for my rifle and made certain Jack was ready with his camera. Then we waited until the moose was broadside, facing away from the water. When everything was just right, I held the cross hairs low on the animal, just behind the front leg, and fired. At the shot, it ran into the brush. Jack and our guide congratulated me, saying it had been a good hit.

We found the bull dead less than fifty yards from where I'd shot it. Jack filmed us shaking hands and measuring its antlers. He had the entire hunt on film and was smiling from ear to ear. Moose are supposed to be easy to hunt, but this one had taken twelve days of hard hunting on foot in bad weather, and our ordeal still wasn't over. We had to pack the moose to a place where we could put the meat, cape, and antlers on a plane and fly everything out.

We had scheduled two more hunts back-to-back in Alaska and British Columbia. After returning to the main camp, Jack and I packed our gear and flew to Bethel, where we caught a Mark Air flight to Anchorage. We had some time to kill before the next hunt began, so we spent the next two days driving a rental car down the Kenai Peninsula. On 19 September we left Anchorage to hunt elk, mule deer, and mountain goat with A-Bar-Z Outfitters in British Columbia.

After landing at an airport outside the town of Cranbrook, our guides, Fred and Bill Dubois, met us. We loaded our gear into their truck and drove to some corrals near Deer Lake, the trailhead for the five-hour horseback ride to their log cabin on Dutch Creek (in the mountains of) Kootenay National Park. We reached it just at sundown. Fred and Bill cooked our supper while Jack and I unpacked the things we would need for the next day's hunt. We were asleep within an hour after supper.

We hunted by riding the horses up the sides of the mountains to places where we could look across canyons into open meadows. Our guides took turns cooking and guiding. The warm weather was a welcome break for us but was not ideal for hunting. We did see game,

TO HECK WITH IT, I'M GOING HUNTING

however. There were small herds of elk in the valleys, and the bulls were in full rut, bugling and squealing at night and early and late in the day. There also were many goats on the steeper slopes. Mule deer were scarce, though. After passing up several smaller bulls, I shot a fine bull elk with six-by-six antlers on the fourth day. The next day we rode higher up the mountain and glassed a half-dozen goats before we selected a good billy. The stalk was moderately easy, and I was able to shoot it from around two hundred yards. As with my first goat, however, reaching the animal was not easy. It had died on a ledge overlooking a thirty-foot drop-off. If it had gone only a few more feet, it would have rolled a quarter-mile downhill.

We had seen very few mule deer, so Jack and I decided not to keep hunting for a buck. Instead, we returned to Cranbrook, stayed overnight in Windermere, and rented a car the next day. We spent the next couple of days at the Radium Springs Hotel and drove around Kootenay National Park. Jack was able to "shoot" elk and bighorn sheep at ridiculously close ranges.

By the time we left British Columbia, it was October, and although the autumn colors were beginning to fade, it was impossible not to be in awe of the spectacular scenery.

Jack and I then flew back to Anchorage, overnighted, and met Kelly Vrem again. After breakfast Kelly flew us to his tent camp in unit 16 near Mount Susitna, where he introduced us to our guide, Todd. We had relied on airplanes and snowmobiles on my first brown bear hunt with Kelly. This time we rode horses into the Mount Spurr area and glassed the mountains around us. It was colder now, and we would wake up every morning to find frost covering everything outside our tent.

We were glassing a likely looking hillside late in the afternoon of the second day when I caught a brief glimpse of something in a berry patch across from us in my binoculars. A moment later, a black bear walked into an opening. Todd said it was a big bear, probably an old boar. I was impressed with the way the sun glinted off its black coat. I enjoyed watching it. In New Brunswick, our cover is so thick we seldom see bear for more than a few minutes, and they seldom are more than one hundred yards away.

"Do you want to try to take him?" Todd asked.

I looked at Jack, then nodded at Todd.

"We need to stay high so we can see into the thickets," Todd said.

Getting within shooting range of that bear wasn't easy. Although black bear have poor eyesight, there is nothing wrong with their hearing or sense of smell. We had to stay out of sight, and we also had to move as quietly as we could and stay downwind. We made it, though. An hour after I first spotted the bear, we were standing over it. Its hair was thick, long, and glossy black. I helped Kelly skin it for a life-size mount, and Jack filmed us working. The trip had produced a lot of good hunting and fishing footage. We now needed only a good brown bear to make it complete.

It was not to be, however.

The morning after I shot the black bear, Todd, Jack, and I rode up the creek for four hours to another camp and spent the night. The next morning we immediately spotted a brown bear on a mountainside, but we were not able to get close enough to take it. It moved off every time we started a stalk, though I don't think it ever knew we were in the area.

The following day we found where a bear had been feeding on an old moose kill. That evening we went back before dark, tied up the horses, and crept to where we could see the kill. My heart raced when I saw a large dark shape moving around what remained of the moose. Then I saw another bear, a smaller one. It was a large sow with a two-year-old cub. Sows with cubs were protected, but I wouldn't have shot it anyway. We got back on our horses and headed back to camp. We were sopping wet by the time we reached it.

It rained continuously all night and for the next three days, forcing us to stay in camp. When the rain finally stopped, we woke up to a thick fog that restricted our vision to less than fifty yards. We tried riding higher on the mountain to get above it, but we couldn't. That afternoon the rain hit again and kept us in camp for another two days. When it finally cleared, it was the day we had arranged for Kelly to fly us out. I was beginning to think I was jinxed when it came to brown bear.

On the flight to Anchorage, Kelly said there were quite a few bear near Tracy Vrem's camp, where we had fished in August. There still were nine days left in the bear season, and with luck, I thought, I might get my bear after all. After we checked into a hotel in Anchorage, Jack and I phoned home and arranged to stay over another ten days. The next morning Kelly flew us to the fishing camp.

My luck didn't change. Although the weather cooperated and allowed us to hunt every day from that camp on the Alaska Peninsula, we saw no mature male bear. We found their tracks in the mud all along the rivers where they had been living and eating salmon. We even saw several small bear. The big old boars never showed themselves. We hunted until the last ray of light on 21 October, when the season closed, and I never fired a shot.

A cold wind was roaring across the runway when Kelly put his Cessna down in Anchorage the day he picked us up, giving us a hint of what it would be like when winter arrived in a few weeks. We had been gone for more than two months—the longest period I'd ever spent hunting and fishing. After three brown bear hunts, however, I still had no bear.

ONE YEAR, THIRTEEN HUNTS, 1988

For some reason, many hunters who have never hunted mountain lion or black bear with dogs believe that following a pack of trained hounds after game is not sporting. Others say it is too easy. Both of them are wrong. Another popular belief, among those who are not hunters, is that mountain lion are rare and threatened. That, too, is a misconception.

The reason few people see North America's mountain lion (cougar) is that these are nocturnal animals that rarely move around in daylight. They are so shy that many veteran houndsmen who spend their entire lives in the heart of prime mountain lion country will tell you they have never seen one of these cats when hunting without their dogs. It's not because there is a shortage of lion. There are more of them now than fifty years ago, when governments were doing everything possible to exterminate them. In fact, there probably are as many mountain lion in the western Rocky Mountains as there ever will be. That's because mountain lion are self-regulating when it comes to their territory. A big old tom will not tolerate another male lion on its home ground. When it finds a competitor intruding on an area it has staked out for itself, it will track down the newcomer and try to kill it. The victor in these battles not only wins the territory but gets to eat the loser, which it almost always does.

A tom mountain lion, like African lion, will kill and sometimes eat the cubs of any new female it comes across. I've been told toms do this because females that have lost their cubs soon become interested in breeding again.

Critics who have never hunted with dogs but criticize the practice also don't realize there is no guarantee the best pack of dogs will ever catch a lion or bear, even after the dogs have been started on a "hot" track. It takes only one young and inexperienced dog to start chasing a deer or an elk to pull away the rest of the pack. There's also the potential that even the best-trained hounds will lose the scent. Dogs can follow a days-old lion track amazingly well on the shady side of a hill. If the temperature is warm, and the track takes them around to the sunny side of that same mountain, they're just as likely to lose the trail, even if it's only a couple of hours old.

I hunted my only mountain lion in early January 1988 in Colorado. First I flew to Grand Junction and met my outfitter, Alan Baier. I spent the next hour driving forty miles to the little town of Collbran. When we reached Alan's Little Creek Ranch, I was introduced to houndsman Paul Janke, who would be my guide for the next ten days.

From the ranch we drove to Paul's home in Meeker, 130 miles away.

(Meeker was where Theodore Roosevelt killed a huge mountain lion that for many years was ranked number one in Boone and Crockett's *Records of North American Big Game*.) We spent the next three days driving the area's back roads in Paul's truck, looking for tracks in the snow that indicated a lion had crossed the road. When we found the tracks, Paul would unload two snowmobiles from his trailer and release his hounds, and we would start following the tracks and hounds in deep snow over mountaintops and through rugged canyons. There was nothing easy about it. In fact, we took those snowmobiles over places that were downright scary. Although we chased a lion every day, it wasn't until about 11 o'clock on the third morning that the dogs were able to catch up with a big tom and tree it.

If you've never heard a pack of hounds barking "treed," then you have missed one of the wildest sounds you'll ever hear in the wilderness. All the dogs are howling in frustration at not being able to get to the cat they know is above them. Some get so excited that they try to climb the tree themselves.

There is no hunt more exciting than following hounds. Once the cat is treed, however, the shooting is anticlimactic. When Paul and I climbed to where the dogs had treed my lion, the cat was about thirty feet up one of the tallest trees around. I got out my camera and took several pictures while Paul caught his dogs and tied them up—he didn't want me to drop a wounded lion on top of them.

When the dogs were safely out of the way, I killed the lion, a big male with a long, thick, golden coat. Paul rewarded his dogs by allowing them to maul the cat. I was worried that they might rip it apart, but they didn't damage the hide.

We loaded the lion on Paul's snowmobile and drove back to the truck, where he skinned it for a life-size mount. I'd enjoyed the experience, but it was the only time I ever hunted a mountain lion in North America. (A few years later I did take a South American puma.)

Paul then drove me back to Collbran and Alan Baier's ranch, where I spent two days looking for elk with Al and another man. We saw several bulls each day, but Al kept telling me we would see better ones. He obviously knew what he was talking about. On the afternoon of the second day, we drove up on a bull Al said I shouldn't pass up. It had six long tines on each antler, and its main beams were heavy and long. It was feeding in a meadow around six hundred yards below the two-track road we had been following, and it hadn't seen us. By keeping out of sight, we were able to cut the distance to under two hundred yards. It dropped at my shot.

When I had booked my lion and elk hunt with Al, I didn't know that his Little Creek Ranch was a game ranch stocked with a large variety of exotic animals from around the world, and I added seven species to my collection. Five years had passed since I had decided to assemble two hundred different species of game animals, and I now had taken more than fifty of them.

The only North American cougar the author ever hunted. He took it in early January, just before the SCI convention. Colorado.

Chamois were introduced to the southern Alps around the turn of the twentieth century. New Zealand.

After my hunt, Al and his wife Cheryl and I drove to Safari Club International's annual convention in Las Vegas. We checked into the MGM Grand Hotel and spent the next four days walking the convention's exhibit hall. I talked with the exhibitors and booking agents and bought several hunts at the club's fund-raising auctions before leaving for home on 24 January.

Five weeks after returning from Las Vegas, I was on the go again, flying to the South Pacific via Montreal, Vancouver, Los Angeles, and Honolulu, finally arriving in Naidi, Fiji, thirty-six hours later. I had left on 5 April, but I had gained a day because we had crossed the International Date Line. It was 6:30 A.M. on 7 April when I checked into the Sheraton Fiji Resort. I spent four days in Fiji, sightseeing, lounging on the beach, and thinking about my friend Bob Cusack, who had died the day I left home. Bob and I had known each other since we were twenty years old, and we had spent many happy days in a deer camp we'd built. I would have liked to attend Bob's services, but I couldn't cancel this trip. I was embarking on the most ambitious hunt I'd ever make: to take all fifteen types of game animals found in Australia and New Zealand in just two months.

Although it's not widely known, there were no big-game animals in Australia or New Zealand when Captain Cook sailed his First Fleet into the region. Cook and other early explorers began importing domestic swine, believing that they would provide food for future expeditions.

Much later, early British settlers imported Asian water buffalo from India to plow their fields and provide hides and meat. Some of their buffalo escaped into the rain forests of Australia's Cobourg Peninsula and multiplied, as did their domestic goats. By the late 1800s, hunters in Australia and New Zealand were purposely releasing game animals from all over the world so that they could hunt them. From Europe, they brought red deer, fallow deer, and Sika deer from an estate's privately owned herds, and chamois from the Alps. From Asia they brought tahr from the Himalayas, hog deer and barasingha (swamp deer) from India, Indian sambar from Sri Lanka and India, banteng from Java, and rusa deer from New Guinea, Java, and New Caledonia. From North America they brought elk, mule deer, white-tailed deer, and even moose.

Only the mule deer, barasingha, and, possibly, moose did not prosper. There are no wild mule deer or swamp deer in either Australia or New Zealand today, but random reports of moose sightings in New Zealand's Fiordland National Park persist.

I hired Australian outfitter John Steer to take me hunting for a hog deer. He met me in the lobby of the Melbourne Airport, and after a quick stop at his home in Rosedale we drove another three hours to his place near the town of Sale, where I stayed four days.

Hog deer were not as easy to hunt as I thought they would be. It's been said they were so named for their way of hiding in grass and brush until someone walks almost up to them and then suddenly jumping up and running away, low to the ground and with their heads down. Like wild boar, they do not leap or bound. We hunted by driving and glassing Victoria's lightly forested areas, where John thought we might find this little deer. In promising places, John and I left the vehicle and walked around, hoping to jump a hog deer. We saw a great many kangaroo but very few hog deer.

The first deer I saw was a female, and although it barked and didn't leap, it reminded me of our white-tailed deer as it ran off through the grass, waving its white tail. It was out of sight so quickly that I wouldn't have had time to get my rifle to my shoulder if it had been a buck. I was ready when a good buck got up the next day, however. As with all typical hog deer, it had only three points on each antler. Its longest main beam was 11⅜ inches, which ranked it among the top ten hog deer from Australia in the next issue of the SCI record book.

Leaving John, I caught a commuter flight back to Melbourne, stayed overnight at the Airport Travel Lodge, and flew across the Tasman Sea to New Zealand the next day. The four-hour flight arrived in Christchurch at 6 A.M., an early hour anywhere, but my outfitter for the next three weeks was waiting for me. I had met Terry Pierson at his New Zealand Wildlife Safaris booth at the SCI convention in January, and we spotted each other as soon as I cleared Customs.

I stayed in Christchurch for two days with Terry, his wife Gladys, and their three sons. Then, on 19 April, Terry and I drove about four hundred and fifty miles around the South Island to a place called Te Anau, where we checked into the Vacation Inn. From the inn we drove a short distance each morning to a heliport, climbed into a helicopter, and flew to various places in the southern Alps to hunt chamois, tahr, and elk. New Zealand was the only place I ever hunted where my guides used helicopters as if they were horses or Jeeps. According to Terry, dozens of helicopters had been brought to New Zealand and were used to capture breeding stocks of red deer for the country's growing deer farms. Capturing deer was a lucrative occupation while it lasted, but after the first generation of deer began breeding, the demand ended as quickly as it had begun. The pilots then turned to ferrying hunters and tourists around the mountains.

I had heard that a few hunters shoot their animals from the air, which was considered as unsporting as not bothering to get out of a pickup truck to shoot a pronghorn. Terry and I used our helicopter only to locate the game; then we would land and go off on foot. The first animal I took was a chamois, a little goatlike creature with stiff, coarse hair and small, hooked horns. It was by itself when we spotted it running across a deep canyon, so we landed on the opposite ridge, and Terry and I ran to where we thought it might come up. When it did, I killed it with my second shot. The next morning we found a small group of tahr— long-haired Asian goats that thrive in extremely steep terrain, much like our North American mountain goats—moving up a sharply sloped, boulder-strewn hillside. One of them was a trophy billy, Terry said.

This time the pilot flew past the tahr, then held the helicopter steady with one strut on an icy ledge while Terry and I jumped out. It lifted off and flew away while we waited for the group of tahr to reach us. When it did, my first shot dropped the animal Terry selected. It weighed nearly three hundred pounds, a much larger animal than I thought it would be. The blue-gray hair on its neck and belly was at least eight inches long. Its short, stubby horns curled back to sharp points and were more than a foot long. It later would rank among the top third of the entries in the SCI record book.

From the southern Alps we moved to Stewart Island, off the southern tip of the South Island, to hunt a white-tailed deer. There were so many deer that many areas were noticeably over-browsed. Like whitetails everywhere, these deer could become extremely wary when hunted. I had been around white-tailed deer all my life, though, and I shot a seven-pointer the first day. I knew that the antlers on the deer on this island typically are spindly with short tines, so I was prepared to shoot the first mature male we saw. It was a trophy by New Zealand standards, but I wouldn't have given that buck a second glance in New Brunswick.

Next we switched to hunting an elk, or, as the New Zealanders say, a wapiti. I found it interesting that they would use a name used by only one Indian tribe on the continent where the ancestors of these large deer were captured. It stems from

the fact that Europeans were using *elk* to describe the animal we call *moose* long before they encountered our elk. I've never understood why they didn't call them *red deer,* which are the same species as our elk. None other than U.S. President Theodore Roosevelt began the practice of calling them *wapiti,* but it was too late. North Americans weren't about to change.

At any rate, Terry and I spent several fruitless days flying through deep, snow-covered canyons and over mountains, trying to find a trophy bull. We saw several small herds of cows and young bulls in the thick brush, but we never saw one we thought was large enough to land and stalk. So, on 25 April, we drove back to Christchurch. The next morning we crossed the Cook Strait to the North Island on a ferry in 3½ hours, then drove to Masterton, where we spent the night. Two days after leaving the South Island, we were hunting red deer near Pongora on the North Island. Although most experts will say red deer and elk or wapiti are the same species, there are a few who disagree. There is no doubt that these two deer are very different. Elk have distinct dark manes and straw-colored bodies; red deer are the same reddish-gray color all over, and they have very short or no manes. The antlers of red deer can have a dozen or more points on each side, with the last three or four points forming *crowns* or *cups.* A mature bull elk rarely has more than six or seven points per side. The biggest difference is in their rutting calls. An elk bugles, grunts, and squeals. A red deer stag roars, sounding a lot like a

Himalayan tahr from Nepal were introduced to the Southern Alps more than a hundred years ago. New Zealand.

The author's South Pacific wapiti. Like many of the elk introduced to the region, this one had antler "crowns" like those on red deer. New Zealand.

Hereford bull. Despite these differences, red deer and elk readily interbreed and produce fertile offspring, which is why the majority of scientists say they belong to the same species. If they were not the same species, they say, their offspring would be like mules, unable to produce their own offspring.

New Zealand is the only place in the world where both deer have been introduced to the same habitats, and this has resulted in some interesting hybridization. Some elk have antlers that look like those of a red deer; some red deer have heavy manes and are slightly larger than other red deer. To make certain the larger hybrids do not dominate Safari Club International's South Pacific red deer category, the SCI record book also measures the skulls of red deer. If the skull is larger than a certain measurement, the animal is considered a wapiti.

This is confusing, but it really doesn't matter. Very few hunters other than New Zealanders hunt red deer in places where there are also elk. Instead, we outsiders are taken to hunting estates, where red deer are closely managed to produce the largest possible antlers. Elk are hunted either in the wild or on estates where they are separated from red deer to avoid contaminating the estate's gene pool.

At any rate, I shot a thirteen-point red stag on the second day, after passing up a half-dozen smaller stags. I also collected a wild turkey gobbler, a hedgehog, a weasel, and an Australian possum. This last animal looks nothing like its North American cousin. It has thick, luxurious hair all over, even on its tail. Opossums were introduced to New Zealand by farmers who wanted to raise them for fur.

Before leaving, I watched incredibly well-trained dogs herding flocks of sheep into corrals for sharing. The dogs responded to the sounds of a man's whistle to herd the sheep. I was also impressed by how fast the men worked to shear those sheep. Next, we drove to Lake Taupo, a large and beautiful lake in the center of the North Island, where I hunted Sika deer on a lumber company's plantation with a man named Don Craig. The deer here were not behind fences and were not easy to hunt. The rut was on, though, and Don knew where to look for them. Sika stags stake out small territories during the rut and defend them by stamping their feet and making deep whistling noises. I shot a good stag the second morning, a half-hour after sunup, but my bullet hit the stag too far back, and it ran off. There was a heavy blood trail at first, and we were able to follow it until early afternoon, when we lost the track. Don went back to his home and returned with a deer hound, and we picked up the trail again. By 4:30 P.M., even the dog had given up. We never found that animal. It bothered me that I had caused the stag to suffer. Terry and Don assured me that it wouldn't live through the night.

On 2 May Terry and I left for Rotorua and visited the bubbling mud springs. It was the first place that I saw the dark-skinned Polynesians called Maoris, the first humans to settle in New Zealand. That afternoon I added a wallaby to my collection.

From Rotorua we drove to the Wanganui River region, where we stayed with Paul and Maureen Bamber. The Bambers are a young and personable couple who have converted the historic ranch of Paul's family into a hunting estate. Their large home was built on a sharp ridge in the middle of the property. One side overlooks the steep canyons that run down into the Wanganui River Gorge. On the other side, volcanic peaks far in the distance make a spectacular backdrop on clear days. It was one of the most scenic sites I'd seen since the South Island's southern Alps. The Bamber estate is best known for the huge red deer antlers it produces, but it also has fallow deer, feral goats, Sika deer, and huge wild boar. Because of its steep terrain, we were able to do a lot of glassing.

I hunted there only one day, but I took a feral goat, a good fallow deer, and another very large red stag. We drove back to Christchurch that same day, arriving at midnight. The next day I boarded Mount Cook Airlines and flew back to Te Anau to try to find an elk again. After two days without seeing a good bull, I gave up and returned to Christchurch.

On 8 May I flew back to Melbourne and hunted deer with John Steer, taking both sambar and rusa deer, along with a blackbuck, in Victoria. Then John's partner, Peter Staple, and I flew to Sydney and caught an East West Air flight to Port Macquarie in New South Wales, where I took a chital (axis deer) the first day, then went swimming and sightseeing. It was there that I saw my first and only koalas

in the wild. We flew back to Sydney that night and stayed at the Airport Hilton.

On 13 May I flew from Sydney to Alice Springs and then on to Darwin in the Northern Territory to hunt banteng, water buffalo, and wild boar. As soon as I stepped out of the airport, the heat hit me. Although it was early winter in the Southern Hemisphere, the daytime temperature stayed around 96 degrees, and the humidity made it seem even hotter. The next day I chartered a small plane and took an hour flight to our banteng hunting camp, a group of tents near the beach on the Cobourg Peninsula. There are hundreds of miles of clean, sandy beaches and warm water, but my guides said swimming was out. The surf was infested with dangerous saltwater crocodiles, the most aggressive of all the world's crocodilians. We hunted hard for five days, but I never saw a mature bull banteng.

Next I flew to a place called Mountain Valley in the outback and was driven to the ranch house that would be our camp while I hunted water buffalo. According to my guide, there were at least twenty-five thousand free-ranging buffalo, along with hundreds of feral donkeys and wild horses, on a ranch of one and a half million acres. I shot a good bull the first morning, then we returned to the ranch. The next day we drove eight hours back to Darwin.

Taking a buffalo so quickly meant I had time to return to the Cobourg and try to find a banteng again. After five more days and a lot of walking in nearly 100-degree heat, I finally took a banteng. We then flew back to Darwin, where I

The author is trying to look like Crocodile Dundee. Australia, 1988.

shot a wild boar in a short hunt that same evening.

There was a message waiting for me at the hotel from Terry Pierson in New Zealand, so I called him. It had snowed in the wapiti country, improving my chances of finding a good bull, he said. I changed my flights and early the next morning flew back to Auckland and then on to Christchurch, arriving at 7:30 P.M. on 27 May. Terry met me at the airport, and the next morning we flew to Queenstown, where a helicopter took us across a lake and a mountain range to a ranch. We hunted from a truck and found a good bull right away. After I shot it, Terry and I skinned it, and we flew back to Christchurch the same day.

I said good-bye to Terry on 29 May and flew to Brisbane where I spent the next two days visiting the exhibits at Expo '88. I spent another three days sightseeing around Sydney, then flew to Papeete, Tahiti. I had left Sydney on 3 June and arrived in Tahiti on 2 June, losing the day I had gained when I first crossed the International Date Line.

I enjoyed the five days I spent in Tahiti. I sat on the beach, did some swimming in the surf, and relaxed. I spent 7 June, my fiftieth birthday, on flights to Los Angeles and Vancouver. I flew to Ottawa, Halifax, and Moncton the next day. It had been quite a trip. I had traveled more than thirty thousand miles in sixty-seven days, had used six currencies, and had gone through Customs and immigration posts with my rifle eighteen times. I'd enjoyed seeing the scenery and meeting people I will never forget. I'd taken all fifteen species introduced to the South Pacific, and all qualified for the *SCI All-Time Record Book of Trophy Animals.*

Terry Jacobs Taxidermy in Christchurch mounted my trophies, small animals, and birds, and shipped them by container to Halifax by sea. They arrived in Havelock a year later.

Less than two months after returning from the South Pacific, I left home on 29 July and flew to Whitehorse via Vancouver and Montreal to hunt Stone sheep with Jim Matarozzo's Diamond M Outfitters.

Jim's wife Charlene met me at the airport and drove me across the Yukon border into British Columbia to a small town called Atlin, around 120 miles away. It was 6 P.M. by the time we reached the Matarozzos' lodge. We still had another five hours of daylight, but I went straight to bed. (This far north, daylight was at 4 A.M.; dark came at 11 P.M.) It had been a long day.

The next morning Jim flew me in his Cessna 182 on floats to his camp at Desolation Lake, where I met John and Susan Jennings and their two sons, Jess (fourteen) and Jeramie (twelve). John was my guide, Susan the cook, and the two boys looked after the horses and did chores around camp. They assigned me a separate cabin; the Jennings family had rooms at each end of a cabin where Susan did the cooking. My hunt started on Monday, 1 August, so on Sunday we went for a ride and did some glassing. Although we spotted a few sheep, we didn't see a good ram that day. We left camp the next morning at 7:30 and rode about two hours to the foot of a mountain, where John said most of the better rams were. After tying up the horses, we climbed for a while, then spent the next hour or so with our binoculars and a spotting scope, looking for sheep. There were scattered patches of snow around and above us, and when the wind came up it was cold.

I had taken a Dall sheep in the Yukon in 1986, so I wanted a dark-colored Stone ram with good horns. North America's so-called "thinhorn" sheep—Dall and Stone—are closely related. The biggest difference between the two subspecies is their color. A true Dall sheep is totally white, with no dark hair anywhere. Stone sheep come in a variety of colors ranging from gray to brown to black. The problem is, no one has ever been able to draw a line where one subspecies ends and the other begins, and there is a lot of interbreeding in the Yukon and northern British Columbia. The offspring of this mating can be either white or colored. Both Boone and Crockett's *Records of North American Big Game* and the *SCI All-Time Record Book of Trophy Animals* list any American thinhorn sheep with dark hair in their Stone sheep categories. If dark hairs are found only on the tail, it's considered a Dall sheep.

It was a tall order to get a dark-colored Stone ram with good horns, and I passed up rams every day for four days. Those that had trophy-class horns were too light in color for me, and every dark ram we found had small horns. On Wednesday the fog rolled in, and we stayed in camp, hoping all day that it would clear enough so we could glass the mountains. It didn't. Fortunately, the wind came up that night and blew the fog away.

Finally, around 7:30 Friday evening— my last day to hunt—we found what I was looking for. John was using the spotting scope to check out a basin about a mile below us when he suddenly said, "I found one."

"Where?" I asked, moving over to the spotting scope. When I found the ram he'd seen, I turned back to John and saw that he was grinning. At that distance the ram's back and sides appeared almost black. Its head and neck were a lighter color, and its belly and muzzle were white. It truly was a handsome ram, and it had heavy and long cream-colored horns.

It took only a minute or two to decide the best route to reach the ram. John and I left the horses and took off on foot. We were able to keep out of sight in a gully for most of the stalk. When we crawled back over its edge an hour and forty-five minutes later, the big ram and two smaller ones were bedded near where we had seen them earlier. They were only about two hundred yards away and slightly below us. I had no trouble picking out the big ram. Its horns were huge compared to those on the other rams. I was shooting a 7mm Remington Magnum, and the shot was an easy one. When the big ram stood up and turned broadside, I centered the cross hairs on its shoulder and killed it.

"Good shot!" John said, slapping me on the back and gripping my hand. He was even more excited when we walked up to the ram. Every sheep hunter wants to take a ram with forty-inch horns, but not many do, especially today. The longest horn on my ram measured 40⅞ inches around the curve; the other horn was only slightly shorter. I could have hunted another month and not found a better one, John said.

By now it was 8:30 P.M. We had only two and a half hours before dark, and it would take much of that time to skin my ram for a life-size mount and bone out the meat. At 9:45 we finally were ready to leave. I carried the horns and cape; John carried the meat in his backpack. It took an hour and a half of climbing, walking, and stumbling to get to where we had left the horses; then we had a two-hour ride back to camp, most of it in the dark. It was 12:30 A.M. when we finally reached the corrals at the cabins. I had no trouble going to sleep that night.

The next morning, a Saturday, John used his radio to call Jim to fly in to get me. I was already packed when Jim put the Cessna down on the lake at noon and taxied up to the camp's pier. Ten minutes later we were flying back to his lodge. If we hurried, I thought, I could get to a hotel in Whitehorse that night and fly up to Rick Furniss's sheep camp in the northern Yukon the next morning. I hit the ground running, packed the gear I'd left at the lodge, showered, and had a quick lunch. Then Charlene drove me to the Westmark Hotel in Whitehorse, where I left my ram with Tim Cameron of Glacier Furs to be mounted life-size.

In the Westmark's coffee shop on Sunday, 7 August, there were seven other hunters who would be flying out together. After we introduced ourselves, we caught a taxi and went down to the docks on the Yukon River, where Rick had chartered two Cessnas to fly us to the village of Mayo, an Indian settlement on the river. From Mayo we flew to three different camps in an Otter with floats. At 1 P.M. three of us—a man named Mike and his fourteen-year-old daughter and I—were dropped off at a camp on Three Barrel Lake. The camp consisted of a large tent that was used for cooking and eating, two small wall tents for us, and two smaller tents for Bill Rankin and Sonny, our guides.

Bill and Sonny had been with me when I shot my Dall ram in 1986, and we spent a few minutes reliving that hunt. After Mike and I were settled in our tents, we met Cody, the wrangler who cared for the camp's twelve horses. Bill would be Mike's guide; Sonny would guide me.

We got a late start the next morning. After a big breakfast, Bill, Sonny, and Cody caught the horses and packed them with our tents and supplies. Around 11 A.M. the six of us left and rode four hours to where we would be hunting. When we reached the campsite, everyone helped set up the tents and get our spike camp in shape. This was to be our base for the next few days. Cody would stay at the camp while Mike and Bill hunted in one direction and Sonny and I in another.

The best area for big rams, according to Sonny, was another four hours away, which meant he and I rode eight hours round-trip each day. We climbed a lot of mountains and glassed a great many hillsides, but I didn't see a ram I wanted. The rams we found had black on their coats, which classified them as Stone sheep. I wanted a Dall sheep with larger horns than I'd taken on my first hunt there. We did see several good bull moose and a few caribou. We also spent two hours stalking a grizzly bear that was hunting a moose. When we got within fifty yards of it, however, we could see that it wasn't a big bear, and I decided not to shoot it. I almost had to kill it anyway. When the bear spotted us, it woofed, whirled around, and came running toward us. It didn't turn away until Sonny fired a shot into the ground below it when it was less than twenty yards away.

The day after the incident with the bear, Sonny and I left with a packhorse and a few supplies and traveled for three days, putting up our little tents wherever dusk (11 P.M.) found us. We did our cooking over open fires, and we covered a lot of ground. We didn't find any good rams, however.

On Sunday we rode back to the main camp, got more supplies, and rode nearly six hours to another area. We didn't see any sheep that afternoon or the next day. The day after that—my last day to hunt and my last chance to take a ram on this trip—Sonny and I found a small band of rams. One of the animals was worth a closer look, and we were able to get within 250 yards of it. I had wanted a better Dall sheep than my 1986 ram, and this was about the same size as that ram.

I set up the spotting scope and took a closer look at the ram's horns. Then I checked it once again for dark hair and found a place to rest my rifle. The ram staggered at my shot, then collapsed a few yards away. It wasn't as good a ram as I wanted, but I knew that when I shot it.

Sonny and I skinned the ram for a shoulder mount. Then we packed the cape, horns, and meat out to the horses and rode straight back to the main camp at Three Barrel Lake. The plane picked me up at 2 P.M. the next day and flew me to Whitehorse by way of Hart Lake and Mayo. I was home on 19 August, having taken half of a grand slam of North American wild sheep in less than three weeks. I would be home for only another

three weeks before setting off to collect number three in that slam.

I had booked four back-to-back hunts during thirty-two days beginning 8 September. They would take me from British Columbia to Utah, Colorado, and Texas. My first stop was Calgary, where a driver from Mitchell Cross Outfitting met me. We drove three hours to a town named Radium, where we spent the night before leaving to hunt Rocky Mountain bighorn sheep. Early the next morning we left on horses leading pack mules loaded with enough gear and supplies for about ten days in the Rockies. It took three and a half hours to reach camp, and, because of the steep terrain, we had to lead our horses and go on foot most of the way. Our camp consisted of three tents and an outside fire pit where we did our cooking. Grass for the animals was scarce, so the wrangler left us two mules and took the horses back off the mountain.

When the sheep season opened the next morning, 10 September, we walked out of camp, climbing one ridge after another, and glassed every promising basin. We picked up a few ewes and lambs, but the chances of our finding a good ram and being able to stalk it weren't good because we kept bumping into local hunters everywhere we went. After four days without seeing a mature ram, I decided to go on to Utah, where I'd drawn a Shiras moose permit, and continue my sheep hunt during the first week of October when things quieted down. After returning to Radium and Calgary, I flew to Grand

Junction, Colorado, where Alan Baier was waiting for me. Alan had set up my hunts for moose and pronghorn in Utah, mule deer in Colorado, and exotics in Texas.

Alan and I drove six hours the next day to Lone Pine, Utah, where we met Ken Aimone, the guide Alan had hired to pack us into the moose country. We spent the night in Ken's camp trailer, had a very early breakfast, loaded the horses and tack into Ken's trailer and truck in the dark, and drove two hours to a trailhead. By 6:30 A.M., we had unloaded and saddled up and were riding a trail that followed several streams past a long series of meadows and beaver ponds. We saw moose right away, but they were mostly cows with calves, along with a few small bulls. Three days later we still hadn't seen a good bull. I was getting discouraged. It takes a good dose of luck to draw a Shiras moose tag anywhere. The odds were best in Utah, but even there the chances for drawing a tag are so bad that some hunters apply every year for twenty years or more and never get to hunt a moose. Ken said the moose hadn't started rutting yet and suggested Alan and I spend a few days hunting pronghorn antelope and mule deer while he scouted for a bull for me.

Alan and I drove to a town called Vernal and checked into a motel. We ate our meals at local cafes and drove out onto the sagebrush flats to hunt. One thing about pronghorns: When you're where they are, it isn't hard to find them. We'd drive to high places to glass and would see scattered bands of antelope in every direction. Then we'd set up the spotting

scope and get a closer look at the horns on the larger bucks. By 10 o'clock on the second day, we had found a good buck with a herd of seven or eight does. Its head seemed black from nearly a mile away, and even at that distance we could see that its horns were tall and heavy. There was a two-track road that went near where the antelope were feeding, so we used it to cut the distance in half. Then we found a gully and followed it on foot, staying out of sight until we were about 275 yards from the buck. There was nothing to rest my rifle on, just sagebrush. So I sat down, put the cross hairs on my 7mm Remington Magnum just below the buck's back, and tried to hold them as steady as I could— and shot over it. The antelope didn't know where we were, and they started milling around. My second shot slammed the buck to the ground. It was a fine buck, with heavy, 13¼-inch horns and good prongs.

The next morning Alan and I drove back to Grand Junction and spent a few days hunting for mule deer. The third evening, there was a message to call Ken when we returned to our motel. It was what we had been waiting for. He had seen a big bull moose that day. We drove back to Lone Pine to meet Ken and rode to his spike camp. We spent most of the next two days looking for the bull he had seen, but we couldn't find it. Then, at 6 P.M. the second day, we spotted a good bull following a cow. The rut obviously was on now. We tied up our horses and checked the bull's antlers with our binoculars and saw it was a mature bull. Alan and Ken estimated that its antler spread was more than fifty inches. I decided to try to take the animal.

We had to wade and jump across a creek, then sneak through a small grove of trees to get within range. The bull was so much in love that it paid little attention to us. I found a good rest and shot it low and just behind the shoulder as it was quartering away. It ran only about thirty yards before it collapsed.

Compared to our moose in New Brunswick, this one had a smallish body. Its coat was a rusty, yellowish brown—not black—and it had a lighter "saddle." My guides' guess on the width of the antlers was right on. If its palms had been wider, my bull might have ranked among the top five or six in the SCI record book. I wasn't disappointed, though. Shiras moose have the smallest antlers of all the North American moose subspecies, and I had taken a good one. I could have hunted for years and not found a better bull.

It now was 6:30 P.M., and we had to work fast. The sun was on the horizon when we finished taking photos and gutting the animal, and we had a two-hour ride back to the truck in the dark and another hour's drive back to camp. We didn't reach our camp until 10:30 P.M.

We returned to the site at daylight and packed out the meat, cape, and antlers. It was 5 P.M. before we returned to Ken's camp trailer. As tired as we were, Alan and I loaded up our gear and drove on to Colorado without stopping. We reached Alan's ranch at 1 A.M. by driving straight through. We hunted for mule deer the next three days without seeing a shootable buck. While we were there, though, I collected a scimitar-horned oryx, an aoudad, and an addax on the ranch.

We drove back to Grand Junction and flew to San Antonio via Denver. We spent the next four days hunting exotics before flying back to Denver, renting a car, and driving to Colorado Springs again to try to find a good mule deer buck.

We saw only two coyote the first day of hunting with a guide named Paul Janke, and I shot both of them. Early the next morning Paul and I came over a knoll and immediately spotted a large group of deer feeding in a grove of pine trees. A closer look with our binoculars showed all fourteen were bucks, and they hadn't seen us. We spent the next twenty minutes deciding which had the best antlers, and we stalked it for an hour. After all the time I'd put into hunting for a mule deer, I can assure you that we were very careful not to be seen or heard. It took only one shot to drop the buck we had selected. I now needed only a bighorn ram to finish my hunt.

On 4 October I drove to Denver and turned in the rental car, flew to Calgary and rented another car, and then drove back to the Radium Springs Lodge. This time my guide was Lance McLean, and we would be hunting a place called Sheep Creek—a good omen if there ever was one.

About a foot of snow had fallen while I was in Utah and Texas, but most of it was gone when Lance and I, along with a man named Dean, who had been hired to help pack our gear in and my ram out, rode off into the Rockies again. There were patches of snow here and there, and there was frost every night, but it was warm and pleasant at midday.

I had a miserable first night at our camp. My stomach kept rumbling, and I felt weak. I kept waking up all night long, running out of the tent in my bare feet to go to the bathroom. Whatever I had caught wasn't pleasant. I kept drinking water, hoping to flush out the virus and avoid getting dehydrated, but it took that entire day before I started to feel better. That night the same bug hit Lance. Two days later Dean also had a bad case of diarrhea. We never did learn what had caused our problem.

We hunted by glassing from high ridges, checking the slopes and openings in the mountains across wide valleys, looking for far-off, light-colored rumps and amber horns. This time we had little competition. Most of the resident hunters had either gotten their rams or given up, and we now were seeing a few rams. British Columbia's game laws require a ram to be at least eight years old or have horns that make a full curve when viewed from the side. Only two of the rams we found during the first couple of days met those criteria, and I passed up both of them. One day, late in the afternoon, Lance spotted a ram at least a mile away with the spotting scope. It was too far to tell much about its horns, but they seemed heavy and out of proportion to its head and body.

"It's too late to try to get to him tonight," Lance said. "But we'll try to get a better look tomorrow."

"I just hope he doesn't move during the night," I said.

"He won't, unless something disturbs him," Lance said. "He should be pretty close to where he is now."

The next day we left our camp before daylight, dropped into a wide valley, and climbed up to where we had seen the ram the previous afternoon. Something must have spooked it during the night, though, because we never saw it again. At 4 P.M. we had climbed to the top of one of the highest peaks and were glassing the opposite slope when we spotted three rams about a mile away and a thousand feet below us.

"If we go after them, we won't be able to make it out tonight," Lance said. "We'll have to spend the night down there."

"Do you think we can get that big ram?" I asked.

"If we're lucky," he said. "If we're not, they'll move out of the country or move into the thicker brush where we can't find them again."

Lance and I started looking for things to mark where the sheep were. The brush was so thick that we wouldn't have seen them if we hadn't been so high on the mountain. Two hours later, after working our way into the basin, we were within a couple of hundred yards of where we had last seen the rams. When we didn't find them right away, I panicked. Had we spooked them? Then I caught a movement below me, and a ram stepped out of the brush, followed by two others.

From that distance it was easy to see that the horns on only one of the rams had a full curve. The other two were only three or four years old.

The author's Shiras moose is about as good as they come. Utah.

The hunting party had spent the night out, but the author was tickled pink about his bighorn ram. It was No. 3 in his Grand Slam. British Columbia.

This beautiful ram had everything the author wanted in a Stone sheep, including 40½-inch horns. British Columbia, 1988.

"That's not a bad ram," Lance said, while we were inspecting it with our binoculars. "Maybe you ought to think about taking him."

My first shot was a good one, and Lance and I were standing over the ram a few minutes later. Bighorns have larger bodies and horns with tighter curls than the Dall and Stone sheep I'd hunted, and I had misjudged it; I had thought its horns were smaller. The tape showed they were 34⅜ inches around the curve, and they held their mass out to their broomed tips. The ram later ranked about midway in the SCI record book.

While Lance skinned my ram for a life-size mount, I got busy collecting firewood. It was too late to think about trying to get back to camp that night. We would have to spend the night where we were, without a tent or sleeping bags. Fortunately, it didn't rain or snow, and we were able to stay moderately warm sleeping on the ground between two fires. I was glad to see the sun come up.

As soon as we could see, Lance and I had a conference. We could climb back over the mountain and return to our camp, or we could follow the creek down to a road and walk back to where we had left his truck. We chose the truck. After draping toilet paper on the trees at the site so Dean could find the meat, Lance put the ram's skin and horns in his backpack, and we started downhill. We had made the right choice. Going downhill was the fastest and easiest way out. It took us only about two hours to reach the truck.

While Lance and I drove the eighty miles to Cranbrook to have the British Columbia wildlife department check my ram's horns, Dean collected our camp and packed the meat off the mountain in a duffel bag on his back. That afternoon I drove back to Calgary, returned the rental car, and flew home.

It was 12 October when I returned to Moncton. I had been gone thirty-two days, had hunted nonstop, and had added sixteen species, including the exotics, to my collection. I had all the skins and horns shipped to Verrips Taxidermy Studio in Adkins, Texas. The mounts reached Havelock seven months later.

On opening day of our whitetail season in New Brunswick twelve days later, Alan called me at midnight. He had entered my name in a drawing for one of Colorado's best white-tailed deer hunting units, and I'd been issued a tag. The chances were good that I would take a very good buck, he said, because the area hadn't been open to hunting for fourteen years. There are thirty subspecies of white-tailed deer in North America, but for record-keeping purposes, Safari Club International has lumped them into six regional categories. Those in Colorado are classified as Texas whitetails, and I'd already taken a good buck in Texas. Nonetheless, I wanted to go. I had been away from home so much lately, and my anniversary was coming up in a couple of days, so I felt I needed to check with Janice before taking off again. Bless her, she understood. I flew to Denver the next day, where I met my guide, Bob. It was 25 October.

It took three and a half hours to drive from Denver to the town of Lemar, where I checked into the Cow Palace Inn. From there it was only a twenty-minute drive to the place Alan had leased for hunting. In addition to having deer on his farm, the owner raised pheasant and released them for hunters.

Bob and I were on the farm before daylight, hoping to catch a buck between one of the fields and the thick brush where the deer spent the day. As soon as it was light enough to see, we spotted several does and two bucks at the far end of a field, but they were gone before we could get within range. All I had brought on this trip was a carry-on bag, so I was using Bob's .300 Winchester Magnum. All the action had been at first light, but we spent a couple of hours after sunup looking for deer without seeing any. At 10 A.M. we went back to the motel, had an early lunch, and went to the shooting range and checked the scope on Bob's rifle. It shot where I aimed it. All we had to do was find a shootable buck.

I passed up several small bucks that afternoon and the next morning. At first light the third day, 28 October, we were at the edge of the field where we had seen the two bucks the first morning. We could see the dim shape of a deer moving away from us when we arrived, but it was still too dark to tell what sex it was. The light was better when a good buck walked out of the brush about fifty yards away, and I shot it. It was a gold medal ten-pointer with long tines. After photographing and

The author shot this gold-medal, ten-point white-tailed buck with a borrowed rifle. Colorado.

gutting the deer, we loaded it into Bob's truck and met the farmer, a man named Mitch. He said he had seen the buck several times in his fields but hadn't realized how big it was. He was so impressed with it that he called an artist friend, who drove to the farm and took a lot of measurements so he could do a bronze sculpture of it.

The morning after I took that buck, Bob and I drove seven and a half hours to Alan Baier's ranch, where Alan and I had dinner with Ed Weatherby, the son of the founder and now president of the Weatherby firearms company. I was on another airplane the next morning, flying from Grand Junction to Denver to San Francisco, and then to the town of Arcata. Alan had arranged for me to hunt a Columbia black-tailed deer with a guide named Charles Barnum. After checking into a motel in the nearby town of Eureka, I called Charles to let him know I had arrived, and he drove over to see me.

"I know you're ready to go hunting," he said across a restaurant table. "But there's no place you can buy a hunting license until Monday morning."

The Oregon border was just 150 miles away, and it was one of the states I hadn't visited. So I rented a car and drove north along the Pacific coastline on Sunday, returning to Arcata that evening, and checked into another motel after traveling more than four hundred miles that day. The next three or four mornings I would get up early and drive twenty-five miles to Charles's hunting area. The rut hadn't begun, and we didn't see many bucks. We spent a lot of time glassing the grassy meadows and openings, but the deer were spending most of the day in the thickets and steep, oak-choked canyons. After the third or fourth day, Charles spotted a small buck. I had planned to hold out for one with larger antlers, but my time was running out. We made a quick stalk, and I shot the deer from around 150 yards. It was pouring rain and almost dark when we reached where it fell. After gutting it, Charles and I hung the deer in a tree and drove back to his home. We retrieved the deer and photographed it the next morning.

I was back in Havelock on 6 November, three days after taking the buck. Waiting for me was the news that our video company had won the Michigan Outdoor Writers Association's Teddy Award for excellence in film production devoted to outdoor recreation, conservation, and travel.

I'd had a busy year, with thirteen major hunts (the most I ever made in a single year) in Colorado, New Zealand, Australia, British Columbia, the Yukon, Texas, and California, and I was happy to be home again.

A Desert Ram, A big tusker, And A Brown Bear, 1989

I spent the last two weeks of February 1989 in Texas, hunting exotics with Alan Baier. On the morning of 1 March Alan drove me to the San Antonio Airport. A few hours later I was leaving Tucson on an Aero Mexico flight to Hermosillo, the capital of the Mexican state of Sonora. We were to hunt desert bighorn sheep, which I needed to complete my grand slam of North American wild sheep, near Bahía de los Angeles. On the plane with me were Jack Newells and Ken Chew, who also would be hunting sheep. The three of us had booked our hunts with the Mexican government through a company called Sonora Outfitters.

After checking into our hotel, we met Norbert Bremer, a hunter who had taken a ram a few days earlier and was heading home the next day. At dinner that evening we pumped Norbert about what we could expect to find on our upcoming hunts.

I said good-bye to Jack, Ken, and Norbert the next morning and boarded a single-engine airplane with another hunter, a man named Bernard from Mexico City, who would be flying across the Gulf of California to Baja California Norte with me. Less than forty-five minutes after leaving Hermosillo, we were flying over deep blue water dotted with several arid, rugged islands. The largest, according to Bernard, was Isla Tiburon (Shark Island), one of Mexico's national parks. It had

once been the home of the Seri, the last Indian tribe to accept government rule in Mexico. Although Isla Tiburon is best known for a large race of mule deer found only there, desert sheep were transplanted from the mainland to the island in the early 1970s and were doing fine, he said. In summer the gulf just south of the island is one of the best places in the world to fish for nine-foot-long Pacific sailfish weighing up to 180 pounds, he said.

When our plane touched down at the small Mexican town of Bahía de los Angeles, a man called Luis Cordero met us. Luis didn't speak English, and I don't speak Spanish, but Bernard translated what he was saying. He would be going on to one camp while I went to another, Bernard said.

Luis and Bernard introduced me to three other men, who would be my guides. Only one of them could speak a few words in English. I said good-bye to Bernard and Luis and climbed into the men's old truck. After two hours of driving on a primitive road, we reached a place where the Mexican police checked my rifle and issued a permit allowing me to carry it in that state. Then we drove all the way back to Bahía de los Angeles and picked up supplies. We had another two-hour ride on a two-track dirt trail up a canyon to their main camp, consisting of three tents and an open *ramada* for shade. Under the

The author's Mexican sheep-hunting guides. Only one of them could speak a little English. Baja California, Mexico.

The desert bighorn ram that completed the author's Grand Slam of North American Wild Sheep. Baja California, Mexico.

crude roof was a little table and a stove made from an old oil drum. The wind was blowing hard, and two of the tents had blown down. Their stakes simply couldn't hold them in the loose, sandy soil.

For some reason we didn't spend the night there and instead drove back the way we had come for about an hour. Then my guides stopped and set up a small tent out of the wind for me. They slept on the ground in the open. I don't know how they did it. It was very cold. I was glad I had brought a heavy jacket.

We got up at first light and made coffee and tortillas filled with canned fish. Then we hiked up the mountain behind us, stopping frequently to glass. We went from mountain to mountain that morning without seeing a sheep. At 2 P.M. we were back to where we had spent the night, and the men began packing everything up. We then drove back to the main camp. They didn't bother to erect the two tents that had blown down, but they pitched the little tent for me. The wind was blowing hard, and it was getting colder by the minute. Even with wool pants and a heavy jacket, I couldn't get warm. The men sat around the campfire and talked for an hour or two after the sun went down, but I couldn't understand what they were saying, so I went to bed. The next morning we left early to hunt another mountain. We walked and glassed all day and again saw no sheep. It was dark when we finally got back to camp.

After the men woke me the next morning, they struck my tent and let me know that I should pack my gear. We then climbed into the truck and drove back to Bahía de los Angeles, where we had dinner and I checked into a motel. I didn't know it, but our next camp was another four hours away. It now was Sunday, 5 March, and I still hadn't seen a desert sheep. The four of us left very early in the morning and drove along a narrow, rough track for an hour before stopping to make coffee. I still couldn't understand what the men were saying, so I simply smiled whenever they tried to tell me something. We reached a valley around noon and stopped. Thankfully, the weather there was considerably warmer.

All four of us climbed a steep mountain and started down the other side, stopping at every likely place to check the country around us with binoculars. The vegetation was sparse, and it was all the same dull brown of the rocks. In the summer, I was told later, a few rainstorms bring out green leaves on the brush. In years of heavy rainfall, fields of wildflowers pop up everywhere in the spring. Now, though, I could have been on the moon. When we reached the valley floor, two of our men left us and started back over the mountain. The man who spoke a bit of English let me know that they would be bringing the truck around the mountain and that we would be spending the night where we were.

The next morning, after a breakfast of coffee, tortillas, and boiled beans, we loaded our backpacks with food, water, and our bedrolls and took off on foot again. We were going to hike over those rugged mountains until we found sheep.

I had seen no water except what we had carried during the past five days, and I had no idea what those sheep might find to drink. It was a long, hard climb up the mountain, but we finally reached the top at noon. My guides left me to watch a canyon while they went in different directions to glass the slopes below us. At 4 P.M. everybody was back, and we began hiking again. We found a place to camp just before dark, and while the guides were making camp and gathering wood, the one who spoke some English climbed with me to the top of a ridge. Almost immediately after we sat down with our binoculars, we spotted two rams below a steep cliff a long way off. My "interpreter" let me know that one of the rams was a good one. Unfortunately, there wasn't enough daylight left to try to take it that evening.

It was 6:30 when we got back to our little spike camp. To avoid spooking the sheep, we didn't build a fire, and the four of us went to bed without eating. I got very little sleep that night. I watched the stars most of the night and thought about the rams we had seen. We were up at 5:30 A.M. and climbed the mountain long before sunup. Even before the first glow of light hit the slope where we had seen the rams, we were using our binoculars, each hoping to be the first to see them again when there was enough light. We found a ram, but it was the smaller of the two we had seen the previous evening. The big ram was nowhere to be seen. It apparently had left during the night. I watched the little ram through my spotting scope and decided to pass it up.

I was feeling more confident after seeing my first desert sheep. We picked up our backpacks and walked away.

A couple of hours later, we located another ram on a slope across from us just 250 yards away. It was a mature ram with heavy horns, but its horns were not as good as those of the big ram we had seen the previous evening. The more I watched it, though, the bigger it seemed, and I decided to take it. The ram had no idea there was a human within a hundred miles when I found a place to rest my rifle, found the ram's shoulder in my scope, took a deep breath before gently squeezing the trigger—and shot over the ram's back. It was running over the ridge while I was frantically working the bolt, trying to feed another round into the chamber. When it appeared again, it stopped and looked back at us. This time I didn't miss. The ram stumbled and fell off a steep cliff and started rolling until it hit a thorn-covered mesquite tree.

It took us at least thirty minutes to climb up, around, and down to it. It was an old ram with broomed 32- and 33-inch horns that easily qualified for the *SCI All-Time Record Book of Trophy Animals*. More important, I had taken all four types of North America's wild sheep. After taking photographs, my guides skinned the sheep for a full mount and put the horns, skin, and meat on their shoulders. It was 10 A.M. when we reached the place where we had left our backpacks, and we were hungry. We hadn't eaten since noon the previous day. Cold tortillas, beans, and canned fish never tasted so good.

By 11 A.M. the temperature had reached 90 degrees, and it was getting hotter. We still had a three-hour hike to reach our vehicle, and our water was almost gone. Two of the men left us behind and took off at a brisk pace toward the truck. About two hours later, they returned carrying canteens. The water was hot, but it helped keep us going. I can't describe how I felt when we finally reached the truck with my ram. I was elated and exhausted. One of the roughest hunts I would ever experience was over. We were back in Bahía de los Angeles by dark, in time for my guides to call Hermosillo and arrange for a plane to fly me across the gulf the next day. We held a victory celebration in a restaurant later that evening. What a hunt it had been! I had taken my grand slam of four North American wild sheep in just seven months.

On 9 March David Miller and Bill Hurn were waiting for me when I cleared Customs in Tucson. David is a custom rifle maker, and I had arranged to meet him and pick up a .300 Winchester Magnum rifle he had built for me. I'd bought a Coues deer hunt in Mexico from Bill at the SCI Convention that January, and he'd come along with David to spend some time with me. Over breakfast I pumped Dave about the big elephant he had taken in Ethiopia the previous year. Although we hadn't discussed it before, I'd booked an Ethiopian elephant hunt with the same outfitter, and I wanted to know what to expect. Later, Dave and I toured Safari Club International's

headquarters and wildlife museum, and we went to dinner that evening. The next morning I was heading home for the first time in nearly a month.

On 20 March, less than two weeks after returning from Mexico, I was in Addis Ababa, the capital of Ethiopia. It had taken me more than forty hours to get there from Havelock, including an eight-hour layover to rest up in a day room in Frankfurt. My outfitter, Colonel Negussie Eshete of Rocky Valley Safaris, was waiting for me when I stepped off the airplane. I was pleased to see that he had arranged for an official to take my rifle and ammunition and accompany me through Customs. After registering my U.S. dollars and travelers' checks, I was issued several official-looking pieces of paper and was allowed to leave. In Ethiopia, the colonel said, the government controls all aspects of life and business, and trading in illegal currency is severely punished.

I spent the next two days at the Hilton Hotel, getting money changed into local currency and obtaining hunting licenses from the Ethiopian fish and wildlife agency. I don't know if it has changed since then, but in 1989 I was required to buy licenses for each species I intended to hunt.

Finally, on 25 March, Negussie's men picked up my gear and left Addis Ababa in two vehicles for Jima, a ten-hour drive. The colonel and I left the next morning in a small plane and met them at the Jima airport. We still had a five-hour drive over a practically nonexistent road to Negussie's main camp at a place called Bebeka. The camp was at the edge of a government-owned coffee plantation where elephant were threatening the crops. As many as thirty thousand laborers worked on the plantation during peak periods, Negussie said, adding that the workers were extremely poor and had to walk for miles to go to work. They carried for long distances all the wood they used for heating and cooking.

Our camp consisted of several thatched huts. Inside the one assigned to me was a single cot with insect netting. Even so, I sprayed everything with insecticide before going to bed. The food, served in a separate dining hut, was good.

A typical day at this camp began with breakfast at 5 A.M. By 6 o'clock, just before daylight, we would leave the camp and begin driving the forest trails, looking for elephant tracks. We didn't see a lot of game because the forest was too thick, but we did see and hear colobus monkeys in the trees everywhere we went. At noon we'd return to camp for lunch before heading out again that evening. At night I'd take a shower (they kept warm water in a barrel equipped with a tap and spray head), have dinner, and be in bed by 9:30. It rained for one or two hours nearly every day, and when it cleared it was warm and humid.

Elephant were coming out of the jungle and raiding the plantation at night, then returning to the thickets before sunup. We hunted them by driving around until we found fresh tracks, then following them on foot. We saw elephant nearly every day, but I kept passing them up. I had decided before going to Ethiopia that I would not take one with tusks smaller than seventy pounds per side. When Negussie showed me a seventy-pounder the first day, I decided to try to find a larger one. The forest was so thick that we had trouble seeing the elephant until we were almost at their feet, and this made for dangerous hunting. Twice females charged us. Fortunately, on both occasions they ran past us, missing us by only a few feet. According to Negussie, some of his clients have had to shoot in self-defense and had no choice but to go home with small elephant. We were allowed to shoot only one elephant, he said.

By the tenth day, I would have been glad to take a fifty-pounder. For two days we had been hunting with eight men in our party, including three Bushmen who had joined Negussie's trackers and skinners to help out in the tracking. Around 3:30 P.M. we were in an especially thick patch of forest when the trackers suddenly stopped. They apparently had seen or heard something. Negussie motioned for me to move closer to him as quietly as I could. My first sighting of the elephant was from less than twenty yards away. Through the leaves I caught a glimpse of a moving gray shape, then I saw a flash of white. The bull's tusks were heavy and long.

When I looked back, Negussie nodded to let me know this was a big elephant. I had brought a .458 Winchester Magnum, and when the bull turned slightly broadside I aimed at a spot behind its shoulder and slightly low to compensate for being so close. When my bullet smashed into its lungs, the elephant trumpeted and whirled before crashing off through the brush. We found it less than a hundred yards from where I'd shot it. Negussie and I approached it cautiously, ready to shoot again if it tried to get up, but it was dead. It was a huge animal, and its tusks were even better than I had hoped. The larger weighed 115 pounds; the other was 110 pounds. They would receive the number one SCI Major Award for Africa at the next SCI convention.

The men had to clear the brush from around the elephant so we could take photographs. We had just snapped the last picture when the skies suddenly opened up and started pouring rain. Within a few minutes, the Bushmen had built a crude shelter where they would spend the night and guard the bull. The rest of us were soaked by the time we reached the truck. It had been a long day.

The next morning Negussie sent eight skinners and helpers to the carcass to collect the parts I wanted—the tusks, an ear, and the four feet, which I intended to have made into stools. I went back to watch their progress around 10 A.M. and found that nearby villagers had learned of the kill and were waiting in the bush to retrieve the meat when we left. By the end of the next day, Negussie said, they would have packed away every edible scrap.

Later that afternoon we drove up on a small herd of East African defassa waterbuck, and I shot the male. We spent the next two or three days hunting for Nile buffalo but had no luck.

On 3 April we left Bebeka and drove five hours to a place called Gojeb, where Negussie had arranged for us to stay in one of the huts in the village. It was only around 1 P.M. when we arrived, and, soon after getting our gear put away, we drove out to look for a Nile buffalo, which Negussie said could be found nearby. We found a few tracks, but they weren't fresh enough to try to follow that late in the day.

The next morning we woke to a heavy rain, and we didn't start hunting until it stopped around 7 A.M. The dirt roads had turned to slippery mud, and our driver had trouble keeping the truck on the tracks. We found no buffalo sign at all, but I did take a good Abyssinian bohor reedbuck and a colobus monkey for my collection. The only game we saw during the next two days were several small groups of female waterbuck.

On 5 April we drove back to Jima. Negussie and I left for Addis Ababa in a small plane while the men drove the vehicles there. The next day, after the trucks caught up with us, we drove three hours to a place called Ziway, where we stayed in a small, rough-looking motel for three days. We drove out to hunt. I took a northern Grant gazelle and an Abyssinian greater kudu. I could see little difference between the kudus I'd shot in Zambia and South Africa and this one, except the Abyssinian kudu was a little smaller and paler.

On 9 April we drove to Asela at the foot of the Arusi Plateau, where Negussie had sent some of the men to set up a tent camp for us. I spent most of the first day hunting a Menelik bushbuck, which I shot late in the afternoon along a small stream. I also hunted hyena.

The next morning Negussie and I, along with seven men, started up a trail that led to the top of the mountain. Negussie had hired four horses, and he and I rode two of them; the other two horses carried our supplies. Along the trail we passed dozens of thatched houses where the local people lived. Some of the men were working their fields with homemade plows pulled by cows. When we finally reached the top, Negussie said we had reached an elevation of twelve thousand feet.

We were there to hunt a mountain nyala, a large antelope that bears a strong resemblance to a kudu but has smaller horns. The only place in Africa—or the world, for that matter—where it is found is in the high mountains of Ethiopia. Along with bongo and giant eland, it is one of the three most prized trophies on the continent. Negussie said one of the problems with hunting the mountain nyala is that the steep, brushy canyons where it lives often become choked with fog, making it impossible to see the nyala from any distance.

I was lucky. We had no fog, and I took a nice bull the second morning. Negussie and I had climbed to the head of a long canyon and were glassing the brush on the opposite slope when the bull stepped into an opening and began feeding. We had to move only a short distance to where I would have a 250-yard shot. I found a rest, waited until

I was breathing normally, and shot it. It horns were 28½ inches long.

The next morning we started down soon after first light. We'd only been on the trail for two hours when my horse fell as we were crossing a deep, narrow creek. It rolled on me, and I thought at first I had seriously hurt my hip and leg, but I was able to walk, which meant nothing was broken. I walked all the way off the mountain, trying to work the pain out of my muscles. That evening, when I undressed, I found the entire left side of my hip was black and blue. It took a week to clear up.

The next morning, while we were waiting for the men to load the trucks, one of them came up to Negussie and said something I couldn't understand. The colonel smiled and told me to get my rifle and follow him. We hadn't gone very far when he pointed to a small animal with a prominent dark stripe down its nose, watching us from a patch of brush about fifty yards away. "Shoot it," Negussie said, and I did. It was an East African bush duiker, a new subspecies for me. I had brought only a 7mm Remington Magnum with me to Ethiopia, and I had no choice but to use it to shoot the little animal. Fortunately, it didn't tear up the duiker's hide, and I was able to have it mounted life-size later. The men skinned it and salted the hide before we left for Addis Ababa in two vehicles.

We stopped in the city only briefly to buy more supplies before heading north. It was late afternoon when we reached a village with the unlikely name of Nazareth,

The author's newfound friends help him display his East African bush duiker. Ethiopia.

Fred Webb supervises the loading of the floatplane at the Yellowknife dock. Northwest Territories.

where we spent the night in a small motel. From there we drove to Awash, where we got rooms in another motel that would be our "base camp" for hunts in three different areas. We spent two days in the Danakil Desert, where I took a beisa oryx, a northern gerenuk, a Soemmerring gazelle, and an ostrich. In the mountains I took a Cordeaux dik-dik, a hamadryas baboon, and a lesser kudu. The temperature in both places was unbearably hot, especially at midday. We stopped several times to photograph caravans of camels along the way. Negussie had no idea where the nomads had come from, but they were going to Addis Ababa, where they would sell their cargoes.

The third area we hunted was reportedly a good place to find klipspringer, and it was. On 17 April we found a good male standing on the tips of its hoofs on top of a huge boulder, silhouetted against the blue sky, on the first low hill we stopped to glass. These little antelope weigh only about forty pounds, and I was worried that my 7mm magnum bullet would damage its coarse, blue-gray coat. It didn't.

The only other animal I wanted to take from this region was an Abyssinian bushbuck, which meant we had to travel to a small village and have someone in the Ethiopian game department issue me a permit. Permit in hand, and with two game department scouts accompanying us, we returned to where these bushbucks were supposed to be found. We spent a couple of days in the area but never found a bushbuck or its tracks. We left Nazareth on 19 April and drove back to Addis Ababa. I spent the next day getting cash from the local office of American Express (it took five hours), getting my flights changed, and making arrangements with a taxidermist in Addis Ababa to take care of my trophies, pay my ivory fee to the government, and crate and ship everything to my taxidermist in the States for mounting. I had taken seventeen animals on this safari, including the huge elephant that completed my Big Five of the dangerous big-game animals of Africa. Two days later, on 22 April, Janice met me at the airport in Moncton.

Nearly everyone who hunts anywhere in the Northwest Territories stays at the Explorer Hotel in Yellowknife before and after his hunt, so I really wasn't surprised when I saw a familiar face when I carried my bags into the lobby on 30 August. I had met Dr. Jim Conklin, a Pennsylvania plastic surgeon, at an SCI convention, and a friendlier guy would be hard to find. It was Jim who had encouraged me to become active in Safari Club International's awards programs. He also introduced me to the annual black-tie banquets of the Weatherby Foundation.

As I had done, Jim and his son Bill had booked caribou hunts with WebbQaivvik Ltd. on Lac de Gras, 180 miles north of Yellowknife. Jim introduced me to three other hunters he had met at the hotel, and two others were scheduled to arrive the next morning to accompany us to the same camp.

The next morning we were driven to Mike Freeland's office, where we made the final payment for our hunts, and to the fish and game agency's office, where each of us bought a license and tags to take two caribou, a wolverine, and a wolf. When we reached the floatplane's dock, we found the other hunters waiting for us. At 1:20 that afternoon we landed on Lac de Gras and taxied up to a little pier. Eight other hunters were lined up, ready to fly out after their hunts. All had taken caribou, and, although we didn't have much time to talk, they were enthusiastic about our prospects.

After Fred Webb greeted us, we moved our gear into the camp's eight-man "tent." It really wasn't a tent; a more accurate term would be a plywood and canvas cabin. Above its plywood walls and floor was an aluminum frame covered with a tarp. There were bunks with foam pads along the walls, with an oil stove in the middle. The dining tent, the guide's tent, a skinning tent, and a small office/radio room were similar except for their size. There also was a vented building for hanging meat. A more comfortable camp that far north would be hard to find, and every piece of it had been flown in on floatplanes.

Lac de Gras was about eighty miles long. Treeless sidehills, or eskers, covered with tundra and rock, sloped gently to the water. Any area that was about the same elevation as the lake was swampy and difficult to walk across. We hunted mostly from boats—with two hunters and one guide per boat—by moving slowly and glassing.

George Roberts of British Columbia and I were assigned a guide named John Franklin, an Inuit. Instead of taking the boat out the first day, the three of us walked quite a distance from the camp and glassed the country toward the end of the lake. There was no shortage of caribou. In fact, we saw several hundred of them, but there were no bulls George or I wanted to take on the first day of our hunt. It was warm enough that we didn't need jackets or coats except during the mornings and evenings. The days are long in the Northwest Territories in August, so it was a long time before sundown when we returned to camp for dinner at 5:30 P.M. We probably could have hunted another couple of hours, but we'd had a long day and were ready for dinner and a shower.

The shower was an ingenious thing. Water was pumped to a large barrel by a small, battery-powered pump, then heated with propane before being piped to the plywood shower building.

George and I were resting when four of the other hunters returned with the meat and racks of three caribou in their boats, so dinner in the dining tent that evening was a victory celebration of sorts. The food was good, as it always was at this camp, and there was plenty for everyone.

On day two George, our guide, and I left camp at first light and went up the lake by boat, spotting several bands of caribou along the way. Around 11 A.M. we found a bull with high antlers and lots of mass on top and above its nose, and George decided to take it. After a brief discussion on the best way to stalk the bull, we pulled the boat up on the bank, and all three of us went off on foot. Twenty minutes later, we were creeping over an esker when we found the herd looking up at us from around seventy-five yards away. The bull George wanted was standing off to one side, so he quickly sat down and killed it. It was the first central Canada barren-ground caribou I had seen up close, but I could see no difference between it and the caribou I'd taken in Newfoundland in 1973. After we photographed the animal, our guide skinned it and stripped the meat from the bones. He then wrapped the meat in the hide and made a package that he carried back to the boat on his back, using a tumpline attached to his head to help ease the load. It was obvious that he had done this many times, because the entire process took him less than thirty minutes. He had George carry the head. Inuit, he said, never bothered to save such things.

When we reached the boat, he stopped and built a little fire from dry driftwood and some of the larger pieces of dead tundra, then fried some of the fresh caribou meat and potatoes together for our lunch. It was delicious.

That afternoon we found a bull I liked across the lake, and by 3 o'clock I had it on the ground. It had good antlers, and I was pleased with it. We were back in camp at 5:30 and learned that two other caribou had been taken that day.

It was warmer on day three, with the temperature climbing past the seventy-degree mark by midday. Just before noon we saw a very large herd of caribou, perhaps five hundred of them, moving across a wide slope, but they were all calves, cows, and small bulls. After watching them for a while from the boat, we pulled ashore and used spinning rods with small spoons to catch grayling in the rapids that fed the lake. We could have caught dozens of them if we had wanted to, but we caught just enough for lunch. Our guide again built a small fire, and within a few minutes he had the fish baking in aluminum foil. We saw more caribou that afternoon, including a few good males, but George and I were more selective now that we both had bulls, and we passed them up. When we reached camp at 5:30, we measured some of the heads while waiting for the cook to prepare dinner. My bull's antlers scored 360 SCI points, which would rank the bull around the middle of the *SCI All-Time Record Book of Trophy Animals*. (I had it mounted by Hawkin's Taxidermy in Winnipeg.)

Our guides had some kind of disagreement with Fred Webb that evening, and two of them quit. I never did learn what had made the men so angry, but by morning Fred had things straightened out, and we were able to continue our hunt without any further problems.

On day four we took two boats with four hunters down the lake in a light rain. When a heavy fog rolled in, we pulled ashore and waited for it to lift—but it only got thicker. We were at least forty miles from camp, and we couldn't see more than fifty yards in any direction. When we started up the outboards and tried to run back to camp in the fog, both boats hit a reef of rocks, and their propellers were instantly ruined. The boats were equipped with 35-horsepower and 7-horsepower outboards, so we were able to use the small motors to get to shore, where our guides installed the spare parts they carried in the boats. We kept a closer lookout for reefs and debris on the water when we got moving again.

The fog started thinning at noon, and we were able to try hunting again. The other boat went to the far side of the lake; we moved along the shoreline on our side, checking out every inlet. Although we saw no large caribou bulls, our guide spotted a wolverine at the edge of the water, and we rushed to shore and ran up the bank, with all three of us—George, John, and I—shooting at the little animal. I am ashamed to say we fired a total of fifteen shots without hitting it. When it disappeared behind some rocks, we gave up and went back to the boat.

The next morning, our last day to hunt, we woke to find it raining, so we stayed in camp until 8:30, when it started to let up. We again went up the lake around thirty-five or forty miles, where we found a small herd of bulls. George shot the largest in the bunch, and after John packed it to the boat we crossed the lake and again ate fried caribou and potatoes for lunch. Soon after we got going again, we found another little herd of bulls, including one bull that was about the same size as the one I had taken earlier. We watched it through our binoculars for a few minutes, and I decided not to try to take it. We still had time to find a larger bull, I told myself.

A half-hour later, though, we hit a rock and broke the bottom off the base of the outboard and lost all of its oil. We had no choice but to head back to camp using the slower, smaller motor. If we had seen a good bull along the way, we would have stopped and tried to take it, but we didn't. My hunt was over. I wrote in my journal that evening that it had been a well-organized hunt and that I had seen good numbers of caribou in the area.

We were back in Yellowknife at 3:30 P.M. the next day, 6 September. George left that evening on a flight to British Columbia, and I met with Mike Freeland. I had booked two more hunts with his company—an Arctic caribou hunt in October and a polar bear hunt the next spring. I said good-bye to the other hunters the next morning and flew to Montreal. I checked into the Airport Hilton, where I had arranged to meet Jack Hegarty, the filmmaker and my partner in North American Outdoorsman. The Quebec-Labrador caribou hunt I had booked in northern Quebec with Ungava Bay Outfitters was scheduled to start on 8 September, and Jack was going with me to get some footage he needed to finish a video.

Jack and I caught a 7 A.M. flight and arrived in Fort-Chimo, Quebec, two and a half hours later on 7 September. Sammy Cantafio, my guide and operator of Ungava Bay Outfitters, was at the airport to meet us. The weather was deteriorating, and small planes were not flying, so Jack and I couldn't get to the camp that day as planned. Instead, we slept that night in

The author, his friend Jack Hegarty, and his guide Sammy Cantafio, operator of Ungava Bay Outfitters, take a break during the author's Quebec-Labrador caribou hunt. Quebec.

Outfitter Sammy Cantafio and the author with his Quebec-Labrador caribou. Quebec.

Sammy's office, along with Greg Steverson from Cabela's.

The weather report was favorable the next day, so the four of us—Sammy, Jack, Greg, and I—boarded an Inuit Air charter and, forty-five minutes later, landed on the water next to Sammy's camp. Just before we landed I looked out the window. The entire area seemed to be nothing but tundra and small lakes. Four hunters from Maine who were waiting on shore climbed into our plane within minutes after we left it. Their hunts over, they were heading back to Fort-Chimo.

There was still plenty of daylight left, but Canadian law did not allow us to hunt that day because we had been in the air. Instead, we left our rifles in camp and walked up on an esker and started to glass. The light drizzle that had made everything damp suddenly turned into a downpour and drove us back to camp. As with our camp in Northwest Territories, this one was also made of canvas and plywood.

It turned cold overnight, and we woke up to find a heavy frost covering everything. The rain had stopped, though, so Sammy was able to take us out in a boat to look for caribou. When we saw none, he decided that it wasn't worth trying to hunt in that area. As soon as we reached camp, he used the radio to call for a plane to pick us up and take us to another area that afternoon. I didn't have a lot of time. My son Eric was getting married on the sixteenth, which meant I would have to leave for home on the thirteenth.

Sammy's guides had been finding caribou for their clients around Lake Napthier, so, after leaving our gear in another plywood and canvas cabin, Jack, Sammy, and I took a boat down the lake and climbed to the top of a hill. There were small groups of caribou moving through the area, and Jack was able to film several of the herds. We returned to the same spot the next day, and by early afternoon he had photographed me shooting a very good bull.

We had lots of time and good weather for filming, and I had a tag allowing me to take a second caribou. I woke up the next morning with a sore throat and a cold, however. Although we returned to where we had been seeing caribou, I really didn't feel much like hunting. We saw several bulls that were about the same size as the one I already had taken, and I passed up all of them in the hope of finding a larger one. The following day Sammy called for another plane, and we moved to Lake Leopard so Jack could film a different area for our video. We saw a few cows and calves there but no good bulls. By now, I realized I was suffering from the flu and not a common cold. I felt very weak and was aching all over when I climbed into the floatplane at noon the next day, and the trip to Fort-Chimo and on to Moncton with an overnight stop in Montreal didn't help. Whenever one of the planes reached a certain altitude, my ears felt as if they were going to explode. It was an awful experience.

I had no time to rest. The day before the wedding I got a call from Canadian Customs. I needed to drive south to the U.S. border and clear a shipment of mounted animals that my taxidermist friend Kevin White had brought up from North Carolina. I was tied up at the border for six hours, and Kevin and I didn't get the truck unloaded until after midnight. I don't know how I did it, but the next day I made it through the wedding ceremony and the party afterward. Three days later I was scheduled to leave for British Columbia to hunt for a western Canada moose and a mountain caribou.

I was still feeling weak when I left Moncton on 19 September to fly to Montreal and then on to Toronto, Vancouver, Fort Saint John, and Watson Lake in the Yukon. A woman at the Air Canada counter gave me all the boarding passes I needed, and I boarded my plane. My ears didn't hurt as much this time, but I spent most of my time on the planes sleeping. After arriving in Vancouver, I boarded a plane heading to Whitehorse. Thinking that I would fly to Watson Lake from Whitehorse, I stayed on the plane when it stopped in Fort Saint John. At Whitehorse, however, I was told I was supposed to have disembarked at Fort Saint John and should have flown NWT Air from there to Watson Lake with a stop at Fort Nelson. They told me I should get back on the plane and fly back to Fort Saint John, then hop over to Watson Lake the next afternoon.

I rushed and got back on the plane as they were closing the door, then I suddenly decided I didn't want to wait a full day in Fort Saint John. The flight attendant checked with the pilot and opened the doors so I could get off.

As I was looking in the phone book for a bus company, a young fellow who had missed his plane to Vancouver told me I should be able to catch a truck to Watson Lake. I checked at a truck stop but found no trucks were going there that day. I eventually chartered a twin-engine plane to fly me to Watson Lake. My luggage had beaten me there, I learned, but the airport was closed for the night. There was nothing to do but call a cab and check into a motel.

The weather turned bad overnight, and we couldn't fly to the camp for two days. When the skies began to clear, Mark Sullivan, with whom I had booked the hunt, drove a hunter named Scott and me to the floatplane that would take us across the Yukon border into British Columbia to our camp on Tuya Lake near Cassiar. The closer we got to Cassiar, the more the weather improved, and the skies over the camp were clear.

The camp consisted of six or seven wall tents set on a bank near the lake. The largest tent served as a dining hall; the smallest was the shower room. Camp manager Mickey Overton introduced Scott and me to the other hunters—two men named Mark and Mike. Mickey assigned a man named Gene as my guide. There also was an Indian guide, whose name I never learned, and a cook named Eve. We stayed there only one night. After breakfast the next morning, we loaded our gear and supplies on packhorses and began the five-hour ride to the spike camp where I would hunt caribou. There were twenty-three horses in our string. We reached the campsite at 3 P.M., then pitched two wall tents and unloaded and hobbled the horses. Gene, Eve, and I would hunt mountain caribou from this camp; the others would ride six more hours to another camp to hunt moose the next day.

After breakfast, Gene and I said good-bye to the moose hunters and rode up to a high ridge, where we set up a spotting scope and started glassing. A few minutes later, we found a herd of about forty caribou across some beaver ponds a long way off. After studying them in the spotting scope, Gene announced that two of the bulls in the herd had impressive antlers. I took a look, too, but it was so far away that I could only see they had larger antlers than the others in the group. We had to get our horses across several streams and boggy areas to reach them, but we managed it. Unfortunately, we bumped into six caribou we hadn't seen, and they spooked the herd before we could get within range of the two bulls. We were able to follow the herd, though, and two hours later we were close enough to leave the horses and begin another stalk. A half-hour later, Gene and I were inspecting the two larger bulls with our binoculars from around two hundred yards away. I had seen enough caribou by then to know that these were only representative heads. Gene, however, said I should shoot one of them.

"There aren't a lot of caribou here," he said. "You may not see a better one."

I found a rest and shot what we figured was the larger of the two best bulls. When it staggered and started to run off, I shot it again, and it went down. It was one time I wished I hadn't listened to my guide. My assessment of its antlers had been correct. Nonetheless, it was my caribou, and I knew what I was doing when I shot it. We field dressed and removed the bull's head and cape, then loaded everything on one horse and headed back to camp. Gene and I took turns walking and riding the other horse.

Our spike camp was small but comfortable. They had brought plenty of food, and we had a portable stove that served for cooking and keeping the tent warm. We rolled our sleeping bags out on our saddle blankets for beds.

Our next camp was five hours away, so Eve and I started packing our gear and taking the tents down. Gene went off to catch our hobbled horses immediately after breakfast. An hour and a half later, we finally were heading up the trail. Our destination was a camp where other hunters had killed a moose a week earlier. According to Gene, there was a good chance a grizzly bear would be feeding on the boned-out carcass.

We hunted from that camp for two days and didn't see a moose or a bear. It was as if all the game had left the country. So we rode back to the main camp on the lake and spent the night there, then moved to another spike camp, where Gene said we would see plenty of moose. He knew what he was talking about. We were setting up our camp when a small bull walked up to the lake, less than one hundred yards from our tent. Its antlers were so small that I wasn't even tempted to shoot it. We spent the next two days riding to the tops of ridges and glassing the valleys and slopes. We saw moose up to three miles away every day, but there was nothing I wanted to take, and we moved to another area.

We had just gone to bed at the new camp when we heard a moose grunting very near our tent. When we peeked outside at first light, three cows and a fair bull were still feeding at the edge of the lake. I passed up that bull, and we found a better one an hour later. It, too, was feeding at the edge of the lake, and a short stalk brought us within 150 yards of it. I shot it with my 7mm Remington Magnum, and it went down. It was a beautiful bull with an antler spread of 59½ inches, an excellent western Canada moose.

It was still early in the day, so we were able to cut up the moose, remove its cape and antlers, and pack everything back to our spike camp on the horses. Instead of stopping there, we took down our tent and headed back to the main camp. It was 6 P.M. when we rode up to it, and Scott was standing outside waiting for us. He had been hunting with a bow and had turned down several caribou and moose, hoping to find better ones. He did kill a wolf with an arrow, however.

The lake was fogged in until noon the next morning, but as soon as it blew away a floatplane landed and took us to Watson Lake, where a local taxidermist took charge of my caribou and moose antlers and hides, later shipping them to Hawkin's

Taxidermy in Winnipeg. I flew home via Edmonton and Moncton, arriving there on 6 October. I didn't take the grizzly bear I wanted, and I would have liked a larger mountain caribou, but it had been a good hunt. I especially enjoyed packing into the British Columbia wilderness on horseback.

My next trip was scheduled to begin on 24 October, just over two weeks after I returned from British Columbia. It would take me to Victoria Island in the Northwest Territories for muskox and Arctic Islands caribou, to Alberta for a white-tailed deer, and to Alaska's Kodiak Island for brown bear and Sitka black-tailed deer—three back-to-back hunts in a total of thirty-three days. It's been said that bad starts can have good endings, and that's what happened here. Janice had driven me to Moncton to catch the 11:30 A.M. flight when I discovered I had left my carry-on bag containing my camera, shaving kit, and other things in Havelock. There wasn't time to return for it, so Jan agreed to ship it by courier to my outfitter in Alberta, where I would be hunting deer in a week or so.

I flew on to Edmonton, spent the night, and flew to Yellowknife, then on to Cambridge Bay on Victoria Island. On the flight to the island I met an Alberta taxidermist, and as we headed northwest across the Arctic Circle we passed the time talking about hunting. When we stepped off the plane at 4:30 P.M. on 25 October, the temperature was -10 degrees Fahrenheit with heavy wind. I wasn't dressed for such cold weather, and I envied the Inuit I saw at the airport, dressed in thick parkas and heavy clothes.

I had booked the trip through Jerome Knap of Canada North Outfitters, who worked with an Inuit cooperative association to put on the hunts. The taxidermist and I were met at the airport and were driven to a small motel operated by the co-op. For a little town the size of Cambridge Bay, the hotel was more than adequate. The rooms were clean and freshly painted. There was only one washroom to serve all the guests, however. The first thing we did was put on our insulated underwear, wool pants and shirts, and arctic coats and pants over that. Dressed properly, we were able to walk to the co-op's store to look around in relative comfort. That night the temperature dropped to -22 degrees Fahrenheit.

We met two other hunters—one from Mexico, the other from Spain—at the motel that evening. Both had taken muskox and caribou and were scheduled to fly home the next morning. I hadn't planned on taking a muskox. My primary purpose on this hunt was to collect an Arctic Islands caribou and complete a grand slam of North American caribou. Hearing the hunters talk about their muskox hunts changed my mind, and, when Bob and I went to the game department offices the next day, I bought a muskox tag also.

The co-op managers introduced me to my guide, an Inuit named Gary Angohiatok, and fitted me with a parka, pants, and mittens made from caribou hides. Gary had a sixteen-foot sled that he pulled behind his snowmobile with a twenty-foot towline. After loading the sled with our gear and an extra forty gallons of gasoline, I climbed onto the sled facing the rear so the wind would be at my back and got ready for a long, cold, and wild ride. Before we left town, we passed three or four local men driving snowmobiles, returning with caribou meat on their sleds.

At sundown four hours later, we reached our destination, a shack in the middle of nowhere, used primarily in the summer for fishing. There was no stove, and my little thermometer showed it was -5 degrees Fahrenheit inside when we arrived. Gary got busy and fired up a kerosene heater and a little Coleman stove he had brought with us, but they didn't help much. Four hours later, the temperature had climbed all the way to 32 degrees Fahrenheit. I climbed into my sleeping bag wearing insulated underwear, a wool shirt, and a stocking cap. It took a while, but the bag eventually warmed up, and I was able to fall asleep.

We had to melt ice to get water for our coffee when we woke at 7 o'clock the next morning. In October, daylight on Victoria Island is from 8 A.M. to 4:30 P.M. The sun never climbs very high in the sky and offers very little relief from the cold. All the lakes were frozen, and there were no trees. Surprisingly, the snow was only three to four inches deep. We saw quite a few caribou that first day, as well as several muskox—the first I had ever seen in the wild—but I passed up all of them when Gary said they were young animals.

The author's mountain caribou, taken with Cassiar Stone Outfitters. British Columbia.

Guide Barry Stewart and the author take a break from bear hunting on Kodiak Island. Alaska.

That evening Gary and I visited an Inuit man and his wife in a nearby hut. They were there to hunt for their winter supply of caribou meat. They invited us in for tea and some caribou ribs the wife had partially cooked. By 8:30 P.M. our hut had warmed up to slightly above freezing, but the floor was still cold when we climbed into our sleeping bags.

We drove the snowmobile around the area again the next morning but didn't see a caribou or muskox that Gary thought I should take. We spent the entire day out in the weather, and I was feeling ill when we returned to our shack and ate some soup before climbing into our bags. Around 10 P.M. I had a terrible urge to go to the bathroom, but I tried to control it. I didn't know how cold it was outside, but I didn't want to find out. By 11:30, I couldn't stand it a minute longer. I pulled on my boots and put on my parka and started out the door. I had gone only a few steps before I vomited. Then the diarrhea hit me. It was bitterly cold and windy, but I didn't want to go back inside until I had emptied my digestive system. I didn't think I could take the shock of going outside after getting warm again. My strategy apparently worked, because I felt fine the next morning.

A gentle snow was falling when we left that day, and we were able to drive up to a small band of caribou without disturbing them. Gary and I agreed that one of the bulls had better antlers than anything we had seen so far. I got off the snowmobile, made a short stalk, and dropped the bull with my first shot. All the caribou I'd taken

until then were pretty much alike. I doubt anyone could say for certain whether a head hanging on a wall was from a barren ground caribou, mountain caribou, woodland caribou, or Quebec-Labrador caribou. There would be no mistaking this caribou for anything but an Arctic Islands caribou, however. It was a smaller animal and much lighter in color than the other races, and its antlers were spindly and short. Even so, I had taken a trophy animal that years later would rank number eight in the *SCI All-Time Record Book*. Gary and I skinned it for a life-size mount; loaded the cape, antlers, and meat on the sled; and headed back to our shack.

We still had several miles to go when Gary stopped the snowmobile and pointed to a group of dark-colored objects at least a half-mile away. The falling snow had muffled our approach, and the little herd of muskox hadn't seen us. Gary and I left the snowmobile and used a low ridge to hide us while we moved closer. We were only about 150 yards away from the animals when we ended the stalk, and they still hadn't seen us. Judging muskox horns is not easy. You want a muskox with heavy bosses and long horns that swoop down and up, with no broken tips. A mere inch can mean the difference between a representative and a fantastic trophy. When Gary pointed to a bull standing off by itself and indicated that I should shoot it, I sat down and rested my elbows on my knees, centered the cross hairs of my scope on a spot just behind the bull's shoulder, and squeezed the trigger. I could hear the 7mm bullet slam into the bull, but, instead of dropping, it whirled around and started running off. Before I could work another round into the chamber, the muskox collapsed.

Our sled was loaded with meat when we returned to the shack in heavy snowfall at 4 P.M. The thought of spending another night in that cold hut was more than either of us could take, so we unloaded the sled and repacked it with the meat and all our gear. The load was so heavy that Gary had me ride on the snowmobile to give it traction as we headed back to Cambridge Bay, four hours away. About an hour and a half into the trip we stopped to check our load and discovered that my aluminum gun case had slipped from under the tie-down ropes and was missing. We unhooked the sled, and I stayed with the gear while Gary turned around and went back to find my rifle. It was snowing very hard by now, and the silence was eerie after he left. It was -10 degrees Fahrenheit, and I was alone in the arctic without any means of transportation other than my feet. All I could think was that if the snow and wind covered the snowmobile's tracks, Gary would never find me.

He still hadn't returned an hour later, and it was getting colder by the minute. Without the sled, I couldn't tell the sky from the ground. I had absolutely no idea which way was north, south, east, or west. I snuggled down in the snow alongside the sled to escape the wind, wondering what had happened to Gary. Had his machine broken down? Would he ever find me?

A half-hour later I was relieved to hear his snowmobile approaching. Gary said he'd had trouble following his tracks in the snowstorm and hadn't found my gun case. He would come back and look for it the next day, he said. At that point I was so happy he had found me that I didn't care if I ever saw that rifle again.

We reached Cambridge Bay around 10 P.M., six hours after sundown. It was Saturday night, and I can't remember any hot shower feeling better than the one I had that evening in the motel. It felt great to sleep in a bed in a warm room again.

There were seven other hunters in the motel, and when they and Gary left the next morning I was the only guest there. The motel manager left something for my lunch, locked everything up, and went out to visit someone. For the second day in a row, I felt lonely and abandoned until Gary returned with my rifle.

It was 30 October, and I had missed being home for another anniversary. I flew to Edmonton, where I left my caribou and muskox heads and capes with instructions to ship them to North Carolina. My next outfitter, Kirk Sharp of Wild Rose Whitetail Guiding Service, was supposed to meet me at the airport, but he wasn't there when I landed at 7:30 that evening. I waited an hour or so until Kirk paged me on the airport's loudspeakers. A freezing rainstorm had closed the roads, and he couldn't meet me until the next morning, he said. He gave me the name of a motel and said he would join me there for breakfast, which he did. While eating, Kirk surprised me by saying he had visited my lodge in Havelock with Dick Idol while I was hunting in New Zealand. I hadn't known that when I booked my hunt with him.

Kirk's place was near Innisfree, only ninety miles northeast of Edmonton, but it took us nearly two hours to drive there on the icy roads. Five other hunters and I would be staying in his home, Kirk said. One of the hunters had taken a good buck the previous day, the first day of the season.

I hunted all week with Mike Spat, my guide, but we saw only young bucks. The other hunters fared no better. Kirk said I could stay and hunt a couple of more days and see if my luck improved. I stayed, but I never saw any of the trophy bucks that make Alberta famous among deer hunters. On the last day, late in the afternoon, a small ten-pointer stepped into an opening about a hundred yards away, and I shot it. The carry-on bag I'd left in Havelock hadn't caught up to me, so I had to borrow Mike's camera to photograph it.

Mike drove me to Edmonton that night, 8 November. I flew to Seattle via Vancouver the next morning and met Jack Hegarty, who planned to film my Alaska hunt. We flew to Anchorage together and then on to Kodiak Island and checked into the Buskin Motel outside Kodiak that night. At breakfast the next morning, Jack said he had made arrangements to have Sam Fejes, our outfitter for the next leg of my trip, call us at 10 A.M. When we didn't hear anything by noon, we rented a car, intending to drive into town. When we returned to the motel for Jack's camera, there was a note from Sam. He was at the airport across the street from us. We had

almost missed him. Another hunter was due to arrive on the 3 P.M. flight, so we loaded our gear into Sam's Cessna and waited for a while. When the man arrived, Sam told him he would fly Jack and me to the south end of the island and return for him later that afternoon.

An hour later, Sam set the plane down outside a little settlement just off the beach. There were only a few houses and no roads. The only access to the settlement was by air or boat. We carried our gear down to a boat, and thirty minutes later we finally reached the bay that we would be hunting. After we got our gear ashore, Sam introduced us to Barry Stewart, our guide, and said he would return with the other hunter in the morning.

Our camp consisted of two small dome tents for the three of us. Our toilet was a trench in the brush, and there were only little propane stoves to heat our tents and provide a little light. The wind was blowing hard, rattling the canvas and adding to the feeling of remoteness on this lonely beach. After eating dinner we climbed into our sleeping bags to get warm. The wind didn't go away at sundown; it grew stronger during the night and kept blowing all the next morning. After breakfast we climbed through the thick brush above the beach and worked our way up to the plains on top of the mountain. We saw deer throughout the day, but no bears.

The weather was so bad that Sam could not return that day. The next day Jack, Barry, and I climbed to the plains again but turned around when it started to snow. By the time we reached our camp, the snow was six inches deep. It was the tail end of the storm, though, and we woke to a blue sky the next morning. We were getting ready to climb the mountain when Sam circled us in his plane and landed. He had brought a man with him to pack out our meat, along with some more supplies and the hunter we had met in Kodiak. After wishing us good luck, Sam and the hunter flew off to another area to hunt a bear.

Jack and I, along with the guide and packer, loaded the camp into our backpacks and began climbing over the ridges, heading to where the guide expected to see bear. Around 3 P.M., while we were hiking, someone spotted a bear on a far ridge. Leaving the packer to set up our two tents and make a camp in a hollow, out of the wind, Jack, Barry, and I went to get a closer look at the bear. When we got closer, however, we could see that it was only a small male, and we left it alone.

It was almost dark when we finally returned to our little tents. This hunt could not be called easy by any stretch of the imagination. That night the wind blew so hard that it ripped the tent our guide and packer were sharing in the hollow.

We hunted two more days, moving our camp each night so we could glass different mountain slopes each day. We were almost out of food and fuel for our little backpacker's stove, so we sent the packer back to the beach for more. The fog and rain meant Jack couldn't film, so

he spent most of the day in our tent while Barry and I hunted. Despite the windy, damp, and cold weather, we saw a lot of deer and a few bear each day. I passed them all up. At night I used our propane stove to try to dry my clothes.

It was warm and sunny when we found a bear a long way off in our binoculars the next day. After a quick look in the spotting scope, I decided to take it. It was the best bear we had seen, and our supplies were almost gone again. It took us two hours to reach the spot, and then we couldn't find the bear. Thinking it had left, we were ready to head back to the tents when we saw the bear coming toward us. When it reached the edge of a patch of ice sixty yards away, I was ready. My first shot broke both shoulders, and it went down roaring. My second shot killed it, but Barry had me shoot it again in the spine for insurance. Although I was looking for a much bigger bear, I was pleased with this one. It had broken my jinx. Brown bear are one of the world's largest land-dwelling carnivores, and mine must have weighed at least nine hundred pounds. I was especially impressed with the size of its head and feet. After photographing it, we skinned the bear for a life-size mount, packed the hide, and headed back to camp.

We had very little left to eat, but we didn't mind. I had taken my bear, and we would be returning to the beach the next morning. We had just finished a long, hard climb to reach the plateau the next morning when we reached a spot where the packer said he had seen a good buck on his trip to get supplies. Barry suggested that Jack and the packer continue on to the beach while we stayed behind to see if that buck would show itself. I had worked up a sweat hiking to the top of the mountain, and I got chilled when we sat down to wait for the deer. Two hours later, the sun was going down when I spotted the buck bedded on the flats. After setting up the spotting scope, we could see it had five points on each side of its antlers— exactly what I was looking for. Most Sitka blacktail develop only three or four tines per side, making a ten-pointer a fine trophy. It would not be an easy stalk, though. We were running out of light, and the buck had five does with five pairs of eyes guarding it.

We crawled to within three hundred yards of the buck before the does spotted us, and every deer in the little herd stood up and stared at us.

"Get down and don't move," Barry said. "Maybe they'll settle down."

And that's what they did. Sitka blacktail see very few humans, and after a while the deer forgot about us and bedded again, allowing us to get another hundred yards closer and kill the buck. It was nearly dark when we reached the animal and started field dressing, skinning, and boning out the meat. Barry and I kept watching for bear all the while. It was not unusual for bear to be attracted to the sound of gunfire during the deer season, he said. Rifle shots usually mean they will find something to eat, if only a gut pile. Even though we left the meat for the packer to bring in the next morning, Barry and I had

heavy loads. We finally staggered into camp three hours later. I was so exhausted that I thought I wouldn't be able to climb into my sleeping bag, but I felt like a new man after a hot meal. The packer said he was certain I had taken the big buck he had seen a few days earlier.

There was a third tent in camp that night. Sam had arrived that day to help us or fly us out if we were ready to go. He reported that the other hunter had taken a bear three days earlier and had left for home. I had two deer tags, and Jack wanted to film me shooting another buck. Before we left camp the next morning, however, someone from the village came to our camp and said a major storm with high wind was forecast for the next day. Sam asked us to stay in camp while he returned to the village and radioed the weather station to confirm it. At 1 o'clock that afternoon a boat pulled up to our camp. Sam had sent word that we were to pack up our camp and use the boat to get back to the village by 4 P.M. He wanted to fly us back to Kodiak before the storm hit.

We had three hours before we were to meet Sam, and the trip back to the village would take only a little more than an hour, so we moved slowly and glassed the country along the beach from the boat. A half-hour later we spotted a small herd of deer near the water. We went ashore and climbed the ridge above them. One of the deer was a buck, and I shot it while Jack filmed the action. It was not as big as my first buck, but it was an adult male with fair antlers. Working fast, we packed

Jack Hegarty and author with brown bear. Kodiac Island, Alaska.

Guide Barry Stewart, author, and packer on brown bear hunt. Alaska.

it to the boat and arrived at the village just as Sam was landing his plane. Sam was concerned about all the weight we packed into his little Cessna, but we lifted off and arrived safely in Kodiak after dark. It was snowing when we checked into the motel.

A foot of snow had fallen during the night, and the high winds had built high drifts along the roads. All flights off Kodiak were canceled that morning, but we were able to leave for Anchorage later that afternoon. Jack and I reached Seattle at 11 P.M. to learn that my rifle case wasn't with our luggage. I reported it missing, and Jack and I headed for a motel. We had been on the go since daylight, and a week of hard hunting had exhausted us. I caught a flight to Vancouver and on to Moncton; Jack flew back to Florida the next day. It had been a long month of hunting, but I had collected a few more species. I was home by midnight that night. My rifle caught up with me the next day.

Three days later, on 30 November, I was in Tucson shaking hands with Bill Hurn again. He had booked a hunt for Coues whitetail and desert mule deer for me with Roberto and Ramon Campillo of Sonora Trophy Hunting, who were brothers. We visited briefly before I boarded my flight to Hermosillo. Immediately after that hunt, I was booked for a southeastern whitetail hunt in West Virginia. I would return to Havelock on 22 December if everything went as planned.

Someone from the outfitter's company was waiting in Hermosillo to drive me to the hunting area, and four hours later we were parking in the yard of a ranch house called Rancho el Datil. It was 5 P.M., less than an hour before sundown.

The ranch consisted of forty thousand acres of rugged hills and wide, bush-covered valleys. The headquarters where I stayed was comfortable, and the meals (they were cooked outside and served inside) were good. My room had twin beds and a corner fireplace that I used for heat. My guide, who spoke English, said two other hunters would be joining me the next day. We would be hunting from four-wheel-drive vehicles, from horseback, or on foot, he said, depending upon the area we hunted that particular day. The terrain was typical of much of that part of northern Mexico—arroyos (sandy gulleys) with rocky ridges and low hills covered with a variety of cactus and dry-looking mesquite trees. Nearly everything had thorns. As far as I could tell, the only water in the area was in the *tanque*s, the shallow ponds made by the ranch owners to collect water for their cattle. We left the ranch each day at 7 A.M. and returned for lunch at noon, when it began to get hot. After a two-hour siesta, we'd return to the hills, hunt until dusk, and be back at the ranch house at 6 P.M.

I hunted on this ranch for seven days and saw only three small bucks. The two hunters who arrived after me took two deer—a good buck and a younger one. On 8 December my guide Ramon and I drove back to Hermosillo and then to a place called the Miller Ranch. It was 10 P.M. when we pulled off the highway and took a narrow, winding, rocky road up into the mountains. We reached the ranch an hour later, only to be told that four police officials from Mexico City were due to arrive and would be hunting there instead of us. The Campillo brothers had arranged for me to hunt on another ranch. Although I was given a bed, I didn't get much sleep. Ramon and the Miller Ranch foreman woke me up at 4 A.M., saying we needed to get started. The other ranch was across the mountain on an even worse road than the one we had driven the previous evening. We spent the next three hours in a bouncing truck, using four-wheel drive in low gear all the way.

Ramon said another guide and horses were supposed to be waiting for us, but the ranch house was deserted when we finally reached it. Ramon couldn't understand it. Three other hunters would be arriving that afternoon, and nothing was ready for them, he said.

We were in Coues deer country, though, so we took off on foot, climbing the rocky hills and glassing the canyons and ridges ahead of us. This ranch was at a higher elevation than Rancho el Datil, and the vegetation was different. The southern slopes of the canyons had open patches of grass, and the northern slopes were covered with small oak trees. Here and there were sotol and clumps of bear grass. Some of the hillsides were covered with ocotillo—long sticks covered with thorns. There was water there, too. Minuscule amounts would seep out of the ground and drip over the rocks before going underground again, and wherever there was water we found deer tracks and droppings.

Ramon and I had been gone for only a couple of hours when we caught a glimpse of something white moving rapidly under the oak trees across the canyon. Ramon was saying, "Shoot! Shoot!" except that it sounded more like "Chute! Chute!"

My third shot hit the running deer, and it rolled a few yards downhill, kicking. It was dead by the time we reached it. It was a buck, but it was far from a trophy. Ramon felt bad about misjudging its antlers. I don't remember whether we took photos of it, but we did field dress it and pack it out. We carried that little deer uphill, downhill, and across steep draws. By the time we reached the ranch house, I would have sworn that ninety-pound buck weighed at least four hundred pounds.

Ramon and I fixed ourselves some lunch and slept for three hours. When the other hunters arrived at 10 P.M., we drove back to Hermosillo. It took five hours, and the roads weren't any better than when we had last driven them. It was 3 A.M. when I finally reached a motel room and fell into bed. At 11 A.M. a man named Roberto drove me to the Campillo brothers' office, where I was offered the opportunity to take another Coues deer later at the Cerro Colorado Ranch, supposedly their best area for Coues deer.

That afternoon Roberto and I drove north and west toward the Arizona border to another ranch, where we hunted desert mule deer for the next two days. The country was mostly flat and was covered with paloverde and ironwood trees. The only places where we could see more than fifty or sixty yards in front of us were in the sandy arroyos. We hunted by driving the primitive dirt roads, looking for deer tracks crossing the roads. If they were fresh tracks made by a single, large deer, we would follow them on foot for an hour or so, hoping to catch a buck in its bed. There were big bucks with antler spreads of thirty inches or more in this area, Roberto said, but we didn't see one.

Late in the afternoon of the third day, we drove back to Hermosillo and continued on to the Cerro Colorado Ranch, arriving there at 11 P.M. to find everyone had gone to bed. Roberto and I found an empty room, and I fell asleep almost immediately. There were five other hunters at breakfast the next morning, including Tucson rifle maker David Miller and Steve Comus, who later became the director of Safari Club International's publications. I was encouraged to hear that all but one of them had taken good bucks during the previous few days.

Calin, the guide assigned to me on this ranch, spoke no English, but we somehow managed to communicate. We began seeing deer within twenty minutes after leaving the ranch house. They did not run in herds. Instead, we would see a doe with one or two fawns, or a single small buck. Almost always these deer would see us first and run away with their white tails wagging, just as all whitetail do. At 10 A.M. Calin and I found a buck feeding in a stand of ocotillos and were able to watch it in our binoculars long enough to see that its antlers were better than those on the other bucks we had seen.

To stalk it, Calin and I climbed the back side of the hill the deer was on and worked our way across to it as quietly as we could move over the rocky ground. When we were about seventy-five yards from where we had last seen the deer, it jumped up and threw up its tail, ready to run. I made the fastest shot of my life and killed it.

We had judged its antlers well. They were heavy, wide, and tall, with three long tines and an eye guard on each side. Rarely do these deer grow more points than this. Its short muzzle gave it a mouselike look, and its ears and antlers were much longer in proportion to the size of its body than those on the whitetail I'd hunted elsewhere. The rut was starting, and its neck was swollen. Its short coat was a light gray, and the inside of its legs and belly were pure white; there was not a hint of brown anywhere on it. It definitely was a pretty little deer.

After lunch Calin took me out to look for a javelina (collared peccary) before we left for Hermosillo, but we saw none. I called home from my motel room that evening and arranged to stay another five days to try to find a mule deer. The next morning I was driven back to the ranch I had hunted earlier, only to learn that none of the seven hunters in camp had taken a deer after four or five days of hunting there. My luck was no better than theirs, and I left Mexico without a mule deer. I'd had a good hunt in Sonora, though, and I'd taken a good Coues deer.

Instead of returning to New Brunswick, I flew to Morgantown, West

Virginia, to hunt a white-tailed deer with Pete Frazee of the B&C Game Ranch. I was shocked when I stepped outside the airport to find snow and a bitterly cold wind. After Mexico, it was like stepping into a frozen food locker. We hunted by walking the roads the next morning, but the snow was crusted and noisy, and all I saw were flashing white tails disappearing into the trees. This was a game ranch, and there were a lot of deer there, but it was far from easy hunting. Give any whitetail a hundred acres of woods, and you may never see it again. I stayed in a blind that afternoon while the people at the ranch tried to drive a buck to me, but I saw nothing I wanted to shoot. We hunted from a four-wheel-drive vehicle the next

morning and spotted a good ten-point buck in a field three to four hundred yards off. I managed to get close enough to shoot and photograph it before a minor blizzard struck. By the time we reached the lodge, the visibility was down to just a few yards.

I flew to North Carolina the next morning and spent the day with my friend Kevin White, going over how I wanted the animals I'd taken that year mounted and arranging to get my elephant tusks through Customs. On 21 December Janice met me in Saint John, where we stayed overnight and did some Christmas shopping.

That ended a full year of hunting for me in 1989.

SEVEN COUNTRIES IN 143 DAYS, 1990

In January 1990, in addition to attending Safari Club International's annual convention in Nevada, I unsuccessfully hunted white-tailed deer in Florida and spent five days in Texas hunting exotics with Alan Baier. As was happening with increasing regularity, my rifle (as well as a suitcase with the clothes I planned to wear at the convention) didn't reach San Antonio when I did. I was able to borrow a rifle and take the exotics I wanted, so it wasn't the worst thing that could have happened. My rifle case and my clothes showed up before I left for Reno.

As with previous conventions, I saw many people I knew, and at one of the evening banquets I received the SCI First Pinnacle of Achievement Award. For four days I wandered around the exhibition hall, talking with outfitters and booking agents. Before the convention ended, I had booked three separate African safaris, as well as hunts in Mongolia, British Columbia, and Mexico for later that year. These were in addition to the muskox and polar bear hunts I'd already planned for 1990.

Later in the year, Jack and I shut down our North American Outdoorsman video company. It was not something we decided to do overnight, nor was it a unilateral decision. We both had realized for some time that it would never be a profitable business, and we needed to get on with our lives. Looking back, the best thing about launching that company was that I got to know Jack. We're still very good friends.

It was 1 April when I landed in Cambridge Bay, Alaska, en route to hunt a barren-ground muskox, and not much had changed in the village since I'd left it five months earlier. There still wasn't much snow on the ground, and the temperature still was -10 degrees Fahrenheit. After buying my license at the game department's office, I joined seven other hunters and flew to Perry Island, arriving there late in the afternoon. The camp's manager, Bob Lloyd, greeted us, got us settled into our plywood cabins, and explained how the hunt would be conducted. All eight hunters would have individual guides, and we would hunt from the camp in snowmobiles towing *qamuliks* (sleds) with long tow ropes, exactly as I'd done in October. For safety reasons, two hunters and two guides on two snowmobiles would hunt together.

Perry Island's muskox country differed little from the area around Cambridge Bay—endless miles of snow and ice with scattered pressure ridges on which we would drive the snowmobiles, stopping to glass. It seemed to be much colder, however. My thermometer showed it ranged from -12 degrees Fahrenheit to -16 degrees Fahrenheit during the day. High wind

The author took this barren-ground muskox on Perry Island near Cambridge Bay. Northwest Territories.

Hunting polar bear in the high Arctic with a dog team made for many new experiences. Northwest Territories.

dropped the windchill factor even lower than that and caused us to lose two days of hunting because of whiteouts.

Around midday on the first day, the guides spotted three wolves. They immediately unhooked the sleds, leaving us behind, and went roaring after them on their machines. A half-hour and perhaps twenty shots later, they returned with two very dead wolves. Before skinning their animals, they pitched a tent so Bruce (a bow hunter on the second snowmobile) and I could have lunch out of the wind. We traveled around seventy-five miles that first day but never saw a muskox.

We did see a lone bull the next morning, and Bruce shot it with his bow. While the guides skinned it, I checked my thermometer. It was -18 degrees Fahrenheit.

The temperature continued to drop during the next two days, and the winds picked up. We saw only a few muskox. The fourth day the visibility was reduced to almost nothing, and we were back in camp by noon. It didn't clear up until 6 April, a Friday. By then, the seven other hunters had taken five muskox bulls. I still had seen nothing I wanted.

The winds returned with a vengeance on Saturday, blowing so hard I couldn't see the guide's hut just seventy-five feet from ours. On Sunday we were able to go out again. We had just driven over a ridge when my guide suddenly stopped our snowmobile. We had spooked a small herd of muskox, and he wanted to watch to see where they would go. When they seemed to calm down, we waited until

they had moved over a far-off ridge. Johnny, my guide, didn't want to drive too close and get them running again, so we drove as far as we dared, then followed them on foot. By 3 P.M., I had the largest bull in the herd down. Even before he and the other guide started to skin it, Johnny called our camp and told someone there to hold the airplane due to arrive that day. Now that I'd taken my muskox, I could fly out on it.

We photographed my bull, then unloaded our sled, and I got on it. It was a wild and bumpy ride—made even worse because Johnny drove faster than usual. We were back in camp in an hour, however. I was packed before the plane landed.

Johnny returned to the carcass to help the other guide skin my bull, and I flew on to Cambridge Bay with the other hunters. Only one of them had not taken a muskox. All eight of us checked into the co-op motel and had showers and hot meals before flying on to Yellowknife the next morning. It had been a much tougher hunt than I'd experienced in October.

It was Monday, 10 April, when I boarded a plane heading from Yellowknife in Northwest Territories to Resolute Bay on Cornwallis Island, one of the Parry Islands in the Arctic Ocean. A man from Bangkok who had been in our muskox camp was with us. His name was Sonny, and both of us had booked polar bear hunts immediately after our muskox hunts. After the five-hour flight, we checked into the dome-shaped Norwic Motel and met its nine other guests. Two were also bear hunters; the other seven were on a tour that would take them to the North Pole and back. This far north we had only about two hours of darkness. In just two weeks the sun wouldn't set at all.

The weather—with high wind and -15 degrees Fahrenheit (and falling) temperatures—was so bad that it cut visibility down to practically nothing, and we were forced to stay in the motel for three days. Although I would have liked to be hunting, the motel was warm and the meals were good. It was managed by the same company that had a contract to clear snow from the airstrip and the village roads. Although we were required to hunt from dogsleds, we were allowed to use a snowmobile to carry our gear, fuel, tent, and food, which meant I would be hunting with two Inuit. My guide, David, would handle the dog team while his helper, a man named Ekaksok, followed us on a snowmobile. Each of the three other hunters going after polar bear also would be hunting with two Inuit, a dog team, and a snowmobile.

It was Friday the thirteenth when we learned we were to meet our guides in a village of 125 Inuit approximately four miles from the motel at 3 o'clock that afternoon. At the village we were all outfitted with caribou parkas, pants, and gloves.

My hunt finally got under way around 5 P.M. Sonny and I climbed into separate sleds, and the dog teams, followed by two snowmobiles, took us out across the frozen sea. Traveling facing forward on a sled behind the dogs was considerably more comfortable than being towed backward on a long rope behind a snowmobile. Five hours after leaving the village, we stopped, and the guides set up two wall tents and began melting snow for water on a small Coleman stove. Our meals were prepacked in aluminum foil and were prepared by boiling. Until then I hadn't realized how cold I had been. It felt good to be out of the wind.

Before we went to bed that evening, our guides iced the runners on their sleds by rubbing them with a rag and hot water, a process they would repeat each day. They fed their dogs seal meat only every second or third day. They had nothing to eat between those feedings.

Camping with Inuit in subzero temperature was not entirely unpleasant. We stopped often during the day and boiled tea. At night I slept in two sleeping bags—a large and heavy one on the outside and a lighter, smaller one with a heavy flannel zippered lining inside that. Before I crawled into my bag, I pulled on a set of insulated underwear over my long johns and put on wool socks and a wool cap. I slept warm, and the heat from our little stove felt good when they lit it in the morning.

The wind whipped up a whiteout the next day, keeping us in our tents. When it cleared the following day, the plan was for Sonny and his guides to go in one direction while David and I went in another. Before we separated, however, we spotted a bear, and the Inuit turned their dogs loose. Within just a short distance, they had circled the bear and bayed it. It was a big male, and Sonny shot it.

We spent the night in our tents at that spot, and the guides skinned the bear. The next morning Sonny and his guides went back to the village, while my guides and I went to look for another bear. That night they set up the tents near a twenty-five-foot-tall ice ridge from which we could glass. We stayed there for two days and spotted three small bear, but I had decided I would take a big male or none at all. The third day we packed up and took off across the ice again. An hour or so later, our dogs hit a fresh bear track and went crazy. David couldn't control them; they dragged us over chumps of ice so bumpy that I had trouble hanging on. When we finally got near the bear, David let three dogs go to stop the sled (the ones still in harness couldn't pull it). At that moment we hit a ridge that was much rougher than the ones they had taken us over.

The three dogs quickly surrounded the bear and bayed it, but it was a young animal, and I didn't want to shoot. David and Ekaksok had a tough time calling the dogs off but finally were able to get them under control and allow the little bear to run off.

When the wind came up again and cut our visibility, we stopped and set up the tents again. Although we didn't speak each other's language, I could tell David was ill and hurting. Ekaksok, who knew a few words of English, said David had stomach cramps. The next day David took the snowmobile and returned to the village, saying we should stay where we were until he sent another guide out. The new man arrived at 7 P.M. that same day, and we packed up and traveled until 11 P.M. without seeing a bear track.

We continued on the next day, hoping to cut another track. It was still extremely cold, but the weather had cleared up considerably. Unfortunately, we had just enough fuel for our stoves for one more day, and our dogs hadn't eaten in three days. We had no choice but to turn around the following day and return to the village. We arrived at the motel at dusk (1 A.M.), and I got another room. Before I left my guides, we made plans to get more supplies and go out again the next afternoon. The next morning, however, I learned that my new guide's teenage daughter had been accused of shooting and killing her boyfriend while they were drinking. The village leaders didn't want my new guide to take the dog team out without David's permission. David, though, was on Baffin Island, where he had been airlifted for surgery. Unless Jerome Knap, my outfitter, could convince them otherwise, my hunt was over. After telephone calls back and forth, I was told I could continue hunting, but only after the village held a memorial service for the dead boyfriend. I would have to wait at least two more days in the motel, and there was a possibility the weather would keep me inside even longer than that. Instead, I opted to return home and come back later. I reached Havelock on 22 April, after stops in Yellowknife, Edmonton, Toronto, and Moncton.

It was 2 P.M. on 18 May when I checked into the Norwic Motel again. The weather had warmed up a few degrees, and we had twenty hours of daylight every day.

It was snowing and the wind was howling the next morning, so we didn't get out that day. At 6 P.M. on Sunday, 20 May, I got word to get ready to go. This time my guide would be Terry Monk. Ekaksok again would go along on a snowmobile. I was relieved to know that both spoke some English.

We finally got under way at 8:30 P.M. and traveled until midnight, when we set up the camp and ate something. At 2 A.M. the sun still hadn't set. According to Terry, supposedly one of the better Inuit guides, we would be hunting at "night" because the bears moved around more then, and traveling was easier on the dogs. With the sun hanging just above the horizon twenty-four hours a day, it really didn't matter to me. Like jet lag, it took a while for my body to get accustomed to hunting all night and sleeping during the day.

We didn't leave that first camp until 4 P.M., when we headed across the ice to Devon Island. We only saw a sow with two beautiful small cubs that night. The next day, 22 May, the wind blew so hard we didn't leave until 10 P.M. It was warmer now, and much harder for the dogs to travel. At 1 A.M. we spotted our first bear while glassing from the top of an ice pack. When we got closer, I decided to take it. As David had done, Terry released three dogs and the chase was on. When the dogs bayed the bear, I ran up to it and shot it in the heart. It ran only around thirty yards before dropping. It was a nine-foot bear, a trophy animal. After photographing it, I helped Terry and Ekaksok skin it for a life-size mount. We

were finished at 2:30 A.M., so we boiled some tea and prepared something to eat. My thermometer showed it was 15 degrees Fahrenheit.

Terry and Ekaksok each had a bear tag, the last two remaining tags in the village, and they were allowed to hunt with the snowmobile. They fed the dogs and tied them up, and we went hunting for their bear on the snowmobile and its sled, leaving the dogsled behind. Right away we spotted a bear track and followed it until we caught up with bear. It was 8 A.M. when Ekaksok shot it. While they were skinning it, I boiled some tea for all of us. At 10:30 A.M. we were on our way again when the Inuit spotted another bear on an ice pack. After unhooking the sled, Terry went after it on the snowmobile, leaving Ekaksok and me with the sled. Terry had been gone less than a half-hour when we heard him shooting. Thirty minutes later he returned smiling. The three of us had taken three bear in ten hours that day.

After skinning Terry's bear, we headed for the coast of Devon Island and visited the spot where explorer John Franklin's ship was crushed by ice when he was trapped there in 1845. All that was visible was a monument and a mast sticking out of the ice. We made camp there, fixed lunch, and slept for four hours before heading back to retrieve the sled and dog team. It had been a very long day, and we still had a long way to go to get back to Resolute Bay. It was 11 P.M. when we finally reached the motel.

I flew home the next day, after arranging for an export permit for my

The author's Arctic Islands caribou completed his Grand Slam of Caribou and ranked number eight in the SCI record book. Northwest Territories.

A very good Asian wapati. They closely resemble the elk of North America. Mongolia.

bear's hide and skull and tipping Terry and Ekaksok. I was back in Havelock on 26 May, only seventeen days before I would leave on a trip that would take me to the opposite end of the globe.

Namibia and South Africa are about as far south as you can get from Resolute, Northwest Territories, without landing in Antarctica, but that's where I was headed just over two weeks after my polar bear hunt. When I reached Namibia on 15 June, Jan Oelafse of Mount Etjo Safari Lodge met me at the Windhoek airport and flew me in his plane to his lodge, a comfortable, well-kept place with heated rooms and separate bathrooms with showers. Jan introduced me to Fred Bezuidenhout, my professional hunter. Fred and I spent a half-hour discussing the animals I hoped to take, and then I went off to my room for a quick nap.

Two hours later, Fred woke me. He, his tracker Buckie, and I had a two-and-one-half-hour drive in Fred's Volkswagen van to a motel about fifteen minutes from a place where a farmer had seen a cheetah the previous day. When we did not find the animal the next morning, Fred drove me to the Etosha Game Reserve, about an hour's drive from my motel, and we watched zebra, giraffe, elephant, springbok, and other game at the water holes. The Sand Pan was dry now, Fred said, but if I returned during the rainy season dozens of square miles would be covered with water, attracting thousands of pink flamingoes.

We didn't find the cheetah until the next evening, just before sundown. It was about a half-mile away when Fred spotted it with his binoculars. It was more interested in a herd of springbok than in us, and we were able to approach within rifle range without too much difficulty. Cheetah have a poor sense of smell, Fred said. We needed only to move quietly and stay out of sight. I killed it with my first shot. While we were snapping photos, I spent a lot of time inspecting the cat. Its spotted coat was beautiful, and I could see why it was so prized when cheetah coats were fashionable for women. Outside Namibia, before conservation steps were taken, the fur trade came very close to eliminating the species. In Namibia, though, there always have been plenty of cheetah, even though they are considered vermin and are fair game for every farmer.

We spent the next few days at the lodge, where I took a Damara dik-dik, a Kalahari springbok, an Angolan roan antelope, and a Cape eland. On 24 June Fred, Buckie, and I drove about 250 miles north to a German family's farm near the Angolan border to hunt a black-faced impala. These are identical to the impala in East and Southern Africa, except for a black blaze on their faces, and are not difficult to hunt. Because they are found only in Angola and this small corner of Namibia, Safari Club International has given them a separate category in its record book. The ram I shot on that farm was a good one. Its 24¾-inch horns still rank number three in the *SCI All-Time Record Book*. In the two remaining days of my stay in Namibia, I collected a genet and a caracal (African lynx).

The "five-star" restaurant at Luangwa Crocodile Safaris' main camp. Zambia.

The facial markings tell the story: This is no ordinary impala. It's the rare black-faced variety. Namibia.

I had heard rumors of riots and unrest in Zambia while I was in Namibia, and when a telex I sent to my outfitter there went unanswered I called him. Zambia was having some problems, he said, but there was no reason I should change my plans. There had been rioting and some deaths in Lusaka, but things had cooled down, he said.

I arrived in Lusaka in the evening of 29 June and didn't know what to think when only one other passenger disembarked. Worse, there was no one to meet me, and I wasn't sure what to do with my rifle. Monat, a representative of Luangwa Crocodile Safaris, arrived at the last minute. I wasn't sure what she was saying at first but eventually realized she was having trouble saying "Alward." She was late because of a curfew, and she had had to get a special permit to travel to and from the airport.

On the drive to the hotel I saw firsthand that some of the rumors I had heard in Namibia were true. A curfew was in effect from 6 P.M. to 6 A.M., and I didn't see a single person in the streets. Downtown Lusaka was deserted, too. I saw cars that had been turned over and burned. When Monat dropped me off at the Continental International Hotel, I went to my room and called for room service. I didn't leave my room that night.

Monat was supposed to meet me in the hotel lobby at 6:30 the next morning to take me to the airplane I had chartered to fly us to the hunting camp, but she was late again. There were dozens of soldiers in the hotel lobby and on the street. The government had been overthrown during the night, she said, and she wasn't sure if it was safe to drive to the airport where my charter was waiting. I told her it was up to her; I was in no hurry to go anywhere, especially if there might be a revolution under way. We waited until she said we should go.

People were lining the streets and cheering as we drove past them. There were armed men in uniform everywhere. The TV station was surrounded by tanks and soldiers, and the street was barricaded. Monat said the station had been seized during the night. The people in the street apparently believed they had a new government and were clapping their hands and chanting. After fifteen minutes, we drove into a ditch, around the blockade, and past the tanks. At the airstrip no one knew who was in control, and the guy who ran the charter service said he hadn't been able to find a pilot who would go up during the unrest. No one knew who had control of the air space, he said. I sat down with a book and told the man I was content to wait.

Four hours later, someone said it was safe to leave. The people trying to seize control had broken into the TV station and had broadcast that the old government was out. There had been no coup, however, and the opposition leader was sent to jail. He later "accidentally" died in his cell.

We felt better when Lusaka was far behind us. Our destination was a camp in the Luangwa Valley near the place Scott, Eric, and I had hunted with Russ Broom on my first trip to Zambia. High on my list of the trophies I wanted to take from this area was another lion, so the first thing I did was shoot a hippo for bait. Unlike the time the boys had been with me, the lions didn't find this one. We watched the carcass for several days, and only hyenas, jackals, and birds fed on it.

Next we flew to the Bangweulu swamp, where I concentrated on collecting a Zambezi sitatunga. We spent the mornings and evenings in blinds the outfitter had built in the trees overlooking promising places. During the middle of the day we hunted from boats that they poled through bogs. We saw several sitatunga, but it wasn't until the third afternoon that we found a big male in a spot where I could shoot it. After returning to Lusaka and finding things had quieted down, we flew to a concession bordering Kafue National Park to hunt a Crawshay defassa waterbuck and a Livingstone eland, two species I hadn't taken during my previous trip to Zambia.

I was told that the park's game scouts had killed a dozen poachers and had seized twenty pairs of small elephant tusks the week before we arrived. We saw several antelope that had been snared and left to die. After taking a waterbuck the second morning, I was ready to get out of Zambia. I could hunt an eland elsewhere.

On 15 July I caught a flight to Johannesburg and checked into the Airport Holiday Inn. The next morning I flew on to a South African town named Vuylaid and was driven to Mkuze Falls, an hour and a half away. I had booked a ten-day safari with Mkuze Falls Safaris, the same company Scott and I had hunted with in 1987. Instead of Johnny Vivier, my professional hunter this time was a young man named Mark. I also had a much smaller list of species I wanted to collect.

We began by hunting bushpig, trying—without success—to intercept a herd that was damaging a farmer's crops at night. After two days we drove five hours to Durban on the Indian Ocean and spent the night in a hotel, before driving on to an area where Mark thought I could take a blue duiker, the smallest member of the duiker family. Its horns are very short (those on the world record are only slightly over two inches). Mark set up a drive with thirty men and dogs and placed me where he thought I might get a shot. The strategy worked, and I shot two blue duiker that day before we drove back to Mkuze Falls.

The next morning Anton Marais—my outfitter—and I drove twelve hours to the Transvaal to hunt a bushpig, a Limpopo bushbuck, and a Sharpe grysbok. Our first stop was the farm of Philip Nel, a former Zambian, who had just purchased the place. We spent two days and nights on Nel's farm and found lots of evidence of at least two herds living in the area, but we never saw a single bushpig. On the third day Anton and I drove to Messina, where we spent the night. The next day we traveled on to the Limpopo River, the border between South Africa and Botswana, and checked into another motel. Our first evening's hunt produced nothing. The next day we moved

The author's Altai argali, his first Asian sheep.   Mongolia.

to a lodge on the river, and I was able to take two Limpopo bushbuck and the grysbok I wanted. The bushpig continued to elude me, though.

Anton had hired another professional hunter, a man who was dating the daughter of the farmer who owned the land we planned to hunt, to help me find a bushpig. When the guide didn't show up, Anton called his home in Botswana and learned the man had been killed when his vehicle collided with a truck. I was beginning to wonder what would happen next. My polar bear guide's daughter had murdered her boyfriend, and now a professional hunter had been killed before I could meet him. Anton had the unpleasant task of calling the farmer and telling him that his daughter's boyfriend was dead. He drove me to Johannesburg the next day, and I began the long trip halfway around the globe to Havelock. I had been gone for forty-four days, and it was good to get home.

Igor Panin, a representative of the hunting company with which I had booked my first Asian hunt, met me when I landed in Moscow, helped me through Customs, and arranged for the police to hold my rifle until I was ready to leave for Mongolia. It was 22 August, 5:30 P.M., seven hours ahead of New Brunswick time. It was my first trip to the Soviet Union, and I was interested in seeing everything we passed on the drive to the National Hotel across from Red Square. Before Igor left me, he and I agreed to meet for breakfast at 9:30 A.M. After the long trip from Havelock, I had no trouble falling asleep.

Ordering breakfast was difficult, to say the least. Igor was late in arriving, and the waiters in the coffee shop couldn't understand me, nor could I understand them. Although their Russian probably wasn't the best, a couple from France who spoke some English saw my plight and helped me order something. I had eaten and was ready to go when Igor finally arrived and took me on a tour of Red Square, the Kremlin, and several very old cathedrals. He spoke North American English without an accent and was very knowledgeable about everything we saw. After lunch he drove me back to the airport and helped get my rifle on the 6:30 flight to Mongolia. It was my first experience with a Soviet airport. This one was packed with people, all of them pushing and shoving, trying to jockey a position at the front of the lines. I hadn't seen anything like it before, but I would later encounter similar conditions in Ulan Bator and Beijing. I had first-class tickets, so I had few problems after checking my bags at the Aeroflot counter. Seat numbers apparently weren't assigned in coach, though, and there was a mad scramble when everyone was allowed to board.

Five hours after leaving Moscow, our plane landed in the middle of the night near the Mongolian border. I never learned why, but we had to wait there an hour and a half before we took off again. It was 8 A.M., five hours ahead of Moscow time and twelve hours ahead of New Brunswick time, when we reached Mongolia's capital. From the air the green, rolling hills around the city reminded me of New Zealand.

"Welcome to Ulan Bator," I heard someone say when I left the airplane. The man said his name was Ganbat, the interpreter assigned to me for the duration of my stay in his country.

The old Hotel Ulan Bator, a twenty-minute drive from the airport, must have been a grand place in its heyday. The marble columns and staircases were right out of the 1920s. My suite had two rooms with a separate bathroom. However, the furniture in the sitting room might have been made in Russia fifty or sixty years earlier and had seen better days. The carpeting was threadbare, and the elevators were very slow. One minute I would have hot water in the shower; the next minute it would be cold. The toilet paper was only a little more than two inches wide, and it reminded me of the rolls of crepe paper we use as decoration at birthdays and weddings. Breakfast, lunch, and dinner were served in a large, hollow-sounding ballroom with a neon-covered Wurlitzer jukebox. It was an interesting place, especially when I thought about all the famous hunters who had stayed there over the years.

Juulchin, the national tourism agency, had its office on the mezzanine, so I stopped by the next morning to pay the balance due before my hunt began. I would hunt for thirty days from three camps for five different animals—Altai

argali, Gobi argali, Asian ibex, maral stag (wapiti), and Siberian roe deer. The price was $37,500, including airfare, trophy fees, meals, and accommodations. That was a lot of money then (and now), but it was a bargain when you consider what it costs to hunt these same species today.

We had to wait until Monday to leave Ulan Bator, so Ganbat took me to the Buddhist monastery. Monks in red robes sat and chanted, while a line of faithfuls walked around the walls of the monastery lighting candles, stopping every once in a while to kiss a photograph or some item that had been left in the thick candle wax. Outside, pigeons walked among the feet of people lined up to get inside. Whenever something frightened them, they would rise up at once, beating their wings frantically like a swarm of gnats.

Next we went to the national museum, where old hunting equipment and the best heads of all the native big-game species taken in Mongolia were on display. Although the taxidermy was terrible, I was especially interested in seeing the mounts of the animals I would be hunting on this trip. If I shot a Mongolian record, Ganbat said, I would be required to trade it for one of these heads. Hunters were not allowed to take world records from the country.

Outside, Ulan Bator was a bustling city of about 500,000 people. The streets were clogged with buses packed so full of people I wondered how they could possibly get another soul inside. There were a few cars, too. According to Ganbat, the Mercedes and Russian-built luxury

The author took this very good central barren-ground caribou at Lac de Gras. Northwest Territories.

The 49-inch horns on the author's Gobi argali ram ranked in the top twenty of the SCI record book. It dropped at his shot. Mongolia.

vehicles belonged to military officers and high-ranking officials of Mongolia's Communist Party. Very few ordinary citizens owned their own cars, he said.

We left the hotel the next morning at 4 o'clock to drive to the airport for our 6:30 A.M. flight. Ganbat had checked a pile of gear and a large amount of food with my baggage, and we and forty-eight other people boarded a Mongolian Airlines twin-engine airplane. Four hours later, we were on a dirt runway outside a little town called Vegi. According to Ganbat, someone was supposed to meet us when we landed, but no one was there. He scurried around and finally found someone to drive us to an inn in the town. While I rested in the lobby, he spent the next two or three hours looking for our driver. When he finally found the man, we loaded our gear and food into his small Russian Army Jeep and drove out of town, heading for our camp. Including Ganbat, the driver, and me, there were six people packed into that little vehicle. The other three were two men from the Mongolian wildlife department and the driver's girlfriend, who was hitching a ride to her village near our camp. We had gone only a few miles, after clearing a police roadblock at the edge of the city, when one of the Jeep's tires blew out. We had to unload everyone and everything to reach the tools needed to replace it with the spare.

There were no roads as such. Instead, there were dozens of tracks heading across valleys and passes. It was as if no one wanted to drive where anyone else had gone. Five hours later, at 5 P.M., we finally reached the village where the girlfriend's mother lived. Deluen was like no other place I'd seen. There were only a few small frame buildings. All the other structures were yurts (the Mongols pronounced it *gers*), the dome-shaped felt and canvas structures I would come to see all across Asia.

The girlfriend's mother welcomed us and started preparing tea when we arrived. It was the first yurt I had ever entered. A cast-iron stove that burned wood, coal, or yak dung was in the exact center, surrounded by beds along the walls. Above the stove, the canvas roof could be opened to let light in and smoke out. Everything made of wood—the door, the bedframes, and all of the yurt's long, thin rafters—were brightly painted in matching designs. There were no chairs or tables; we all sat on the floor. According to Ganbat, the diet of the average rural Mongolian consisted of cheese and other food made from milk—from cows, yaks, goats, camels, or horses—and mutton.

We stopped at quite a few homes during my four-week stay in Mongolia, and each was the same. Our hosts would always insist that we drink the tea they made on top of their stoves by boiling water in big dishes and adding coarse tea leaves and goat's milk. It smelled like a cheese factory to me, and I had a hard time drinking it from the bowls (about the size of a cereal bowl). My hosts and guides could drink a half-dozen bowls of the stuff per sitting, jabbering all the while in Mongolian as I waited to get moving again.

After leaving the girlfriend with her mother, we drove to another group of yurts, where we stopped and visited a man who was retiring from the wildlife department. The men in our Jeep had brought him a colorful badge and some money for the occasion. Our hosts served us tea, sugar cubes, and hard bread. Before we left, they brought out something they called "homemade beer." Made from mare's milk, it was mostly white, but there were streaks of blood in it. It smelled so awful I didn't try tasting it.

Before we left, our host played a homemade instrument (which looked a lot like a guitar except that it had only two strings) while his granddaughter sang. I couldn't understand a word anyone (except my interpreter) said. Before we could leave, everyone had to taste the man's homemade vodka. After an hour and a half of this, we finally were headed for camp, another hour's drive away. We reached it at 9 P.M., just as it was getting dark, and I was shown the yurt I would share with an American hunter who had arrived there before me. The man seemed familiar, and when he said we had met in Darwin, during my hunting in Australia in 1988, I remembered him. I've since forgotten his name, however.

The camp was at an elevation of five thousand feet at the foot of the Altai Mountains in the western corner of the country. According to Ganbat, we would ride horses up to the eleven-thousand-foot level to hunt an Altai argali—a 450-pound animal with the largest, heaviest horns of all the world's wild sheep—and a Siberian ibex, a two-hundred-pound wild goat with scimitar-shaped, knobbed horns.

Our mornings began at 6 o'clock, when a woman built a fire in our stove to warm our yurt before we got up. A few minutes later, she would bring our breakfast and place it on a small table near the stove. About a half-hour later, our hunting party—Ganbat, a guide named Enkee, a wrangler, and I—would climb aboard four little Mongolian horses and ride up into the treeless, rock-covered mountains. Until the sun was well up, it was so cold I was glad I had brought a warm coat. The little ponies were amazing. Although they were not much bigger than the Shetlands children ride at carnivals, these horses carried us over very steep and rough terrain. They never stopped and seldom stumbled, even when stepping over boulders.

We hunted from the horses for two days and saw sheep both days, but we saw no mature rams. The third day we left camp in one of the Jeeps and drove until dark to another area. That night we parked in front of a farmer's yurt, went inside and had tea, and slept on his floor. The Jeep was able to take us partway up the mountain the next day, and then we walked over the mountain and met the Jeep on the other side hours later. It was hard work, and we repeated the process the next day without seeing a good ram.

The third day we drove to the Chinese border and stayed with another Mongol family for a few days, using the man's horses to ride the ridges and glass the valleys. I saw my first good Altai argali ram there. It was a long way off, and there was absolutely no cover that would hide us during the stalk, but we tried to go after it anyway. An hour later, we were above it and about three hundred yards away. I knew where my 7mm

Remington Magnum was shooting at that distance, and I took careful aim, but I missed. We never saw that ram again.

I didn't miss the next afternoon around 5 o'clock, when Enkee and I carefully crept over a rocky ridge and found ourselves within two hundred yards of a small band of ibex. Ibex horns are deceiving. To me they all look as if they're way too large for the animals that are wearing them. Enkee, however, was able to use his hands to indicate which one I should shoot, and I killed it with my first shot. It was a fine trophy. Its 39½-inch horns are still ranked in the bottom third of the *SCI All-Time Record Book of Trophy Animals*. After skinning it, we rode for nearly four hours, mostly in the dark. I was sore all over and tired when I finally got to sleep that night. We tried hunting this area for an argali the next day, then returned to our first camp.

Another yurt had been erected in our absence for Prince Abdorreza Pahlavi of Iran, who had brought his own cook with his own food and two men from Poland. Only the Prince could speak English. He was there to inspect a game preserve that was being funded by his conservation foundation in Paris.

I hunted on horseback from this camp for two more days, and on the morning of the third day—the day before I was scheduled to travel to the Gobi Desert—we spotted a good ram on a hillside at least a mile and a half away. There was very little cover, and to stalk it upwind Enkee and I had to make a wide detour to get above and around it. It was

5 P.M.—eight hours after we had first seen the ram—before we crawled into shooting range. This time I didn't miss. After packing the ram back to the camp, Ganbat and I loaded our gear and left for Vegi at midnight, arriving there at daybreak. By 9 A.M. we were on a flight back to Ulan Bator. It had been a long and hard hunt, but I'd taken a good ram and an excellent ibex.

Ganbat and I spent that day at the hotel, salting the capes and buying more supplies. We left Ulan Bator the next day on a train. It took ten hours to reach SeinShand in the eastern Gobi Desert. Ganbat had gotten us a compartment with pull-down beds, so I was able to sleep during much of the ten-hour ride. We spent my first night in the Gobi at a hotel—if it can be called that—in SeinShand. Although there was no place to buy anything to eat, my interpreter had brought some food with him (something I recommend for anyone who hunts in Mongolia).

We left at 1 P.M. the next day by Jeep to go to the East Gobi Camp, a seven-hour drive over very rough roads. It was dark when we reached it. From this camp I would hunt Gobi argali (a wild sheep that is slightly smaller than the Altai argali and that has shorter, heavily corrugated horns), white-tailed gazelle (also known as the Hillier goitered gazelle), and Mongolian black-tailed gazelle.

The Gobi where we hunted was not covered with sand, so it was not what most people consider a desert. A few widely scattered low bushes and short grass covered the wide, flat valleys and hillsides.

We hunted it from a vehicle and on foot, driving or climbing to the top of low hills to glass. We found a small herd of black-tailed gazelle right away the first morning, and I was able to take a good male with 12½-inch horns without too much trouble. We spent the rest of the day searching for sheep but saw only ewes and young rams. Late in the afternoon of the second day, we drove about thirty miles to another area to hunt a white-tailed gazelle. We found scattered herds of a hundred or more of the little animals almost as soon as we reached the area. I shot two the first hour; then we went back to hunting sheep.

Just before dark, we were heading back to our camp when we drove up on five rams, all of them trophies. When they stopped and looked back from about two hundred yards away, Ganbat and the local hunting guide pointed to a ram standing by itself, and I shot it. Its 49-inch horns, the largest taken in the Gobi Desert that year, still rank number sixteen in the *SCI All-Time Record Book of Trophy Animals.*

We left camp at noon the next day for the seven-hour drive to catch the 11 P.M. train to Ulan Bator, arriving the next day at 11 A.M. I still had some time left, so Ganbat went to see about arranging a forest hunt for me. I salted my capes on the hotel's roof and put my tags on them; returned to my room; unpacked, showered, and shaved; and was ready to take a nap when Ganbat returned at 4 P.M.

"You can hunt," he said. "But we have to leave in the next half-hour and drive to the camp tonight."

I couldn't have been happier. I'd heard about Mongolia's maral stags (Asian wapiti) and Siberian roe deer, and I was ready to hunt them.

Neither Ganbat nor the driver had been to that camp before, and it wasn't long before we were lost. It had rained for two days there, and everything had turned to slippery mud. When we stopped at a lonely yurt at 9 P.M., the driver told Ganbat we still had twenty-five miles to go. At the speed we were averaging, that would take at least an hour.

We stopped and woke people up six more times before our Jeep eventually got stuck in the mud at 1 A.M. Ganbat and the driver jacked up the Jeep and gathered stones and piled them under the wheels. Three hours later, we were on our way again—but for only about a half-hour. Then we were stuck again.

"It's too late to try to get it out tonight," Ganbat said, after saying something to the driver. "We'll have to sleep in the Jeep and dig it out tomorrow."

The Jeep was too crowded and I was too cold to sleep. I was wide awake when the sun came up at 7:30. A heavy frost covered everything when the driver climbed a hill and spotted some yurts a mile away and walked over to them. It was our camp. He was back in less than an hour with another Jeep to pull us out. It felt great to get something to eat and get warm again.

Late that afternoon we crossed a wide valley and drove to the edge of a series of long, shallow canyons covered with trees in full fall foliage. As soon as the driver turned off the Jeep's engine, we began

The author's western Canada moose hunt has a happy ending. British Columbia.

The "crown" on this bull's left antler is found on many Roosevelt elk. British Columbia.

hearing bugling in the canyon above us. Scientists say North America's elk originated in this part of Asia and moved to our continent on a bridge of land across what is now the Bering Sea. The squeals and grunts those stags were making sounded identical to the sounds I've heard rutting elk make in Colorado in the fall. Ganbat, a local guide, and I started walking toward the bull, hoping to see it before it saw us. It spotted us, though, and the next thing we saw were elk running through the trees. I picked out a bull with tall antlers and sent a bullet at it. It was running flat out through the trees, and I shot behind the animal.

It was snowing when we reached our camp. The next morning the ground was covered with three or four inches. I would have thought fresh snow would make tracking easier, but we hunted two more days before I found a stag I liked and shot it. It had six long points on each side of its antlers, a good trophy. I could see very little difference between it and a North American elk, except that its rump was slightly redder and its coat was a bit darker.

We returned to the same group of shallow canyons and ridges the next morning and started glassing the openings in the larch trees above us. We saw quite a few elk, but we also found the roe deer we were looking for. As we started up the canyon toward it, we spooked another buck, and it ran some way and stopped and barked at us. Ganbat urged me to shoot it, and I did. The Siberian roe deer is not the same species found across Europe. At about 120 pounds, it is much larger. It also

has larger antlers. The main beams on my buck were 12½ inches long, which would qualify it for the *SCI All-Time Record Book of Trophy Animals* years later.

We were back in Ulan Bator on 17 September. Two days later I was in Moscow and Frankfurt. After spending the night in Montreal, I flew to Moncton and drove home. I had taken all the major big-game species in Mongolia except moose, bear, and wild boar in a month of hunting. It had been a great experience in an interesting country.

Only six nonresident Roosevelt elk hunting tags were issued on Vancouver Island in 1990, and I had one of them when I flew to Campbell River to meet Wayne Weibe of Pacific Rim Outfitters. It was 29 September, less than two weeks after I'd returned from Mongolia. Wayne was waiting for me at the airport with another hunter, a man named Gary Primm. Gary, a Nevada casino owner, had just arrived on his own jet from Las Vegas with his pilot and hunting agent, Peter Bollo. He and I would both be hunting grizzly bears on the British Columbia mainland; then I would try to fill my elk tag on the island. I also had obtained permits for Columbia black-tailed deer and black bear, in case I got a chance to take one of them.

Wayne took us to the Dolphin Inn Resort Cabins, where he had rented a cabin that would sleep six men. The next day we flew over to the mainland in a floatplane and stayed at a lumber camp on Knight Inlet, where about twenty people harvested timber. All their food, supplies, and equipment had to be brought in on barges, Wayne said. There were no roads to the place, but logging roads had been bulldozed across the area so that the timber could be hauled to the wharf. My elk season started on Saturday, so I planned to hunt bear until Friday noon and return to the island. If I hadn't taken a grizzly bear by Friday, I could return after the elk hunt. Wayne had arranged for us to stay in the camp and eat in its dining room. My bear guide was a man named Terry Shendruk.

Terry and I saw females and young male bear every day but no large, old boars. We usually left camp at 6 A.M. and returned at 10 A.M., and we had lunch and rested before going out again at 3 P.M. to hunt until dark. Salmon were running in the creek, and we did a lot of sitting and waiting for a bear to come out of the thick brush to feed. Although we hadn't seen the larger males, the place was loaded with bear. They had beaten paths on both sides of the creek and had left half-eaten fish every few yards. One day a grizzly bear walked up to the end of a bridge just thirty feet away from where I was sitting. It stood there for a couple of minutes and turned around and walked away. Terry warned me to avoid getting myself in a position where I suddenly walked up on a bear and spooked it. It could be dangerous, he said.

Neither Gary nor I had taken a bear by Friday afternoon, so I boarded a floatplane and flew back to the island.

All six of the nonresident elk tag holders were hunting with Wayne Weibe.

We each had a guide, and mine was a man named Robbie.

Two other hunters and I hunted out of the cabin, each going in a different direction with our guides. Robbie and I spent most of our time near the Salmon River, riding in his truck on old logging roads and glassing the cutover areas on the mountain slopes. We saw lots of elk on opening day but very few after that. The local hunters were out in force and pushed most of them back into the woods. Two of the nonresidents shot their elk on opening day, but none of the rest of us saw a good bull that day. By Wednesday, everyone in our group except me had taken an elk, but several of their bulls were not even representative heads. We were driving approximately 250 miles a day, returning to the cabin around 8:30 P.M. I was getting tired.

Because of my bad luck, the guides said I had to be from Newfoundland and started calling me "Newfie." Hoping to change that luck, I shot the first four-point black-tailed buck we saw the next day. By now, the two grizzly bear hunters had returned from Knight's Inlet. Neither had taken a bear.

As their clients were heading home with their bulls, two of the other guides rode along to help me find an elk. We found a good bull on 6 October, but I missed two shots at it as it moved through the brush. It was the first mature bull I had seen in a week of hunting. The next day was a Sunday, and I was scheduled to fly back to the lumber camp and resume my bear hunt. Around 9 A.M., however, Robbie spotted a group of elk on a hillside.

This buck's 33-inch rack makes it a very good desert mule deer in anyone's book. Mexico.

There was a large bull with about a dozen cows. My first shot knocked the bull down. It kicked a few times but never got up. The drizzle that had been coming down all morning suddenly turned into a downpour, so we returned to the truck and called Wayne on the radio while we waited for the rain to let up. By the time Wayne and the other guides reached us, Robby and I had taken photos and had caped out the bull and quartered it, and we were getting ready to load everything in the truck. It was the best elk taken on the island that year, a beautiful bull with seven points on one side and six on the other. After the teasing I'd received, I called it my "Newfie elk."

By 2 P.M. we had returned to the cabin, and I was in the air again, heading back to Knight's Inlet. I hunted morning and evening for four days without seeing a mature bear, and my time was running out. It could have snowed any day, and the lumber camp was shutting down the next day for the winter. That evening, as we went out, I told my guide that I would take any bear over seven feet. As we neared the creek, we saw ripples and knew a bear was in the water around the corner. We moved in as carefully and as quietly as we could until we were close enough to see the bear. It was less than forty yards away. It was the best bear I had seen during the entire week, and I shot it. Its hide squared seven and a half feet. Although it was not as large as I had hoped to take at the start of the hunt, I was happy with it. Its hide was in good shape, and it had long, luxurious hair. It was dark by the time we skinned it and packed the hide and skull back to the truck.

I had taken that bear just in time. The lumber camp shut off its furnace and drained the water to the cabins the next morning. Our plane arrived at 9 A.M. and flew us back to Campbell River. I was back in Havelock on 20 October. Since 17 May, I had been in New Brunswick only fifty days. My next hunt wouldn't start until a month and a half later.

I was back in Mexico en route to Rancho el Datil exactly one year after unsuccessfully hunting there in 1989. I was again looking for a good mule deer buck. With me were Roberto Campillo, one of the brothers who operate Sonora Trophy Hunters, and a hunter from Mexico City. After an hour and a half of bouncing over a rocky road, we pulled up to the ranch house at 8 P.M. to find it deserted and the house locked up. Roberto was checking to see if the tack room was open when the owner arrived. He had driven there from Tucson that day.

We had breakfast at 5 A.M. each day, and were out hunting by 6:30 A.M. On the days we didn't ride out on horseback, someone would drive us someplace and arrange to pick us up later at another spot. We always took a lunch with us, although on a couple of days we returned to the house at noon. It would be cold when we left. By 9 A.M. it would start warming up, and by 11 it would be too hot for walking. As the deer were doing, we would find a shady place and take a nap until about 2 P.M., then hunt till dark at 5:30.

I don't think I ever got used to the cactus and having everything I touched stick to me. We saw deer every day for the next two days, but they were mostly does and yearlings. The few mature bucks we saw always managed to spot us before we saw them. Then, on the third day, a guide named Beto Diaz and I rode out from the ranch house on horseback and found the tracks of a very large deer in an arroyo.

Beto spoke absolutely no English, but he was a world-class tracker. According to Roberto, he had learned the skill from his father, who had guided Jack O'Connor (the longtime gun editor for *Outdoor Life* magazine) years earlier. We tied up the horses, and he and I followed the tracks for the next forty-five minutes through groves of paloverde and patches of prickly pear. Suddenly he stopped and silently pointed. Sleeping in the shade of an ironwood tree a hundred yards away was a mule deer buck. It hadn't seen us. A quick look at that deer with my binoculars was all it took for me to decide to take it. This was the type of desert deer that had brought me to Sonora. Moving as slowly and as quietly as I could, I found a place to rest my rifle and shot the buck in its bed. Its antlers were 33 inches wide, a good buck in anyone's book. I stayed with it while Beto retrieved the horses and the camera I had left in my saddlebags. After photographing the deer, he rode back to the ranch, leading my horse. An hour or so later, he returned in a truck with Roberto and drove me back to the ranch. Beto and I hiked up into the higher hills that evening to look for a Coues deer but saw only does.

Soon after the Mexican hunter in our camp shot his buck the next morning, we had lunch and left for Hermosillo. After stopping in the city to buy more food and supplies, we left at 7 P.M. to drive to Rancho la Cienega. It was three hours off the main highway on narrow, winding, rough mountain roads. Everyone at the ranch had gone to bed by the time we finally reached it, but we all found a place to sleep. I don't know what the elevation was, but it was cold at night in the mountains.

I had taken a javelina and a good Coues deer the previous year, but I was looking for better trophies. Two other hunters were already in camp—a young man from Michigan and Jack Newells, a seventy-four-year-old from California. Jack and I had met the previous year in Hermosillo when we were both on our way to Baja California to hunt desert sheep.

I hunted from a truck that morning with Alex Rubio, my guide, but saw only does. Late that afternoon the Mexican hunter and I both shot javelina from a small herd our guides had found with their binoculars. Javelina are not pigs, but, like domestic swine and wild boar, they are nearsighted and very easy to stalk if you approach from downwind. When spooked, though, these little creatures can be very tough to hit. When the herd is broken up, there are "pigs" running everywhere. I suppose my javelina weighed about fifty pounds or less on the hoof, which is typical for these animals. Unlike wild boar, the

javelina with the longest tusks are the youngest animals. Older ones break their tusks and wear them down when rooting. The oldest sometimes have only smooth knobs where their tusks once were.

Alex and I went out on foot the next day, 6 December, and saw several bucks in the first hour. None interested me until we came upon two bucks pushing each other around on a sidehill across a little canyon.

"Grande," Alex said, as we watched them in our binoculars. I had seen enough Coues deer bucks to know one of the deer was a trophy-class buck. *Grande* was one of the few Spanish words I understood.

After watching the deer for a few minutes, Alex and I talked with our hands and agreed that I should shoot the largest buck, which I did. I was a little disappointed when we reached it, because it was not as large as the one I'd taken the previous year. It was a good buck, though.

After photographing it, Alex carried the buck to the roadside. We then walked back to the ranch, where Alex sent someone in a truck to pick up my deer. The Mexican hunter went out that evening and the next morning but didn't take his deer. We left at 2 P.M. on 7 December and drove back to Hermosillo.

That ended my hunting for 1990. I had hunted in Texas, British Columbia, the Northwest Territories, and the Mexican state of Sonora in North America; Namibia, South Africa, and Zambia in Africa; and Mongolia in Asia—seven countries on three continents in 143 days—and had added forty more specimens to my collection.

FIVE COUNTRIES ON THREE CONTINENTS, 1991

In 1991 I began the year by hunting wolf and lynx from a two-seat Super Cub in Alaska. The U.S. government and the State of Alaska both prohibit hunting big game the same day a hunter has been up in an airplane, but wolf and lynx are exceptions. Landing and shooting is permitted, provided the hunter has same-day airborne permits and does not shoot from the airplane. I spent ten days in Alaska that February, but the weather kept us grounded for six of those days. I never saw a wolf or a lynx on that trip.

As happened after the attack on New York City's World Trade Center in 2001, many people wouldn't fly during the Gulf War. It made traveling interesting, to say the least, when the airlines started cutting their flights. I had booked a twenty-eight-day safari in Cameroon and was supposed to go direct from Montreal to Paris on 25 February. When that flight was suddenly canceled, it created a chain reaction that kept the people at the airline counters scrambling to get me where I was going and back. In addition, a layover in London caused me to arrive at Charles de Gaulle Airport at 10 A.M., two hours later than I had planned. It didn't matter, though. I now had a flight out of Orly Airport, on the other side of the city, leaving at 7 P.M. for Rome and on to Douala on Cameroon Airlines. I do not speak French, but I managed to get through the airport, catch

a shuttle to a day room to shower and rest up, and take a taxi to Orly on time.

Rome, however, was shrouded in fog, and we circled for forty-five minutes before turning around and flying back to France. We spent two hours on the ground in Marseilles before resuming our flight, finally landing in Douala four hours late. AfricSafari, my outfitter, had someone waiting for me. She helped me clear Customs, gave me my licenses, collected my final payment for the safari, and drove me to an air charter service nearby. By noon, I had embarked on a three-hour flight to the small village of Kika.

My professional hunter, Rene Ruchaud, and his camp manager, Max, greeted me when I stepped out of the plane in the middle of hot, humid Equatorial Africa. If anywhere on that continent can be called a jungle, what we saw during the forty-five-minute drive to Rene's camp in southern Cameroon certainly qualified. The forest was thick and dark, and vines hung from nearly every tall tree. The Tarzan movies could have been filmed anywhere in that rain forest.

My "room" was a tent with a cot covered by mosquito netting. There were insects of every size, shape, and color in this camp, and I'd smear insect repellent all over myself and fall asleep listening to their various noises.

On a typical day for the next two weeks, we left camp at 6 A.M. and drove on old logging roads to the place we would hunt that day. When we reached a trailhead, we'd go off on foot. When the trackers found the tracks of a solitary bongo, we'd follow them for hours until we either lost the track or spooked the animal. The bush was so thick we sometimes got within twenty or thirty yards of a bongo before it went crashing away through the brush. We could hear it but couldn't see it. It was frustrating. We usually returned to camp by 1 P.M.— when the temperature hit 90 degrees Fahrenheit—and had lunch and a nap before going out again at 3:30 P.M.

The old trails were overgrown and difficult to follow. There were gorillas, too. I don't think I ever got used to suddenly coming upon them in that brush. We saw them every day, and old silverback males mock-charged us twice. There were quite a few forest and pygmy elephants, too. I thought the first pygmy elephant I saw was only about half-grown, but Rene claimed they do not get any larger. It was only about six feet tall at the shoulder, and its tusks were pink.

For eight days we walked ten to fifteen miles a day in nearly unbearable heat. We had been following still another bongo track for about an hour when our Pygmy trackers suddenly stopped. Rene slowly pointed to a spot in the wall of brush ahead of us. It took me a second or two, but I finally was able to see it—a bongo was staring at us, motionless, not more than twenty yards away. The brush was so thick I couldn't see its horns or much of its body, but Rene urged me to shoot

it. I slowly brought my .300 Winchester Magnum to my shoulder, put the cross hairs on what I figured was the shoulder, and fired. The animal was instantly out of sight. I wanted to rush forward, but Rene stopped me.

"Wait a minute," he said in his heavy French accent. "Bongos are dangerous when they're wounded. They can kill you with those long horns."

After we had waited a few minutes to allow the animal to die or grow weaker, the trackers picked up the blood trail. Two hundred yards later, we found the bongo dead. I had seen life-size mounts of bongos at the SCI conventions, but I didn't realize how large these animals are until I walked up to mine. This powerful antelope must have weighed five hundred pounds. Its coat was a bright chestnut red, with light-colored stripes on its sides. I had not seen its horns when I shot, so I was relieved to see it was a mature male that qualified for the SCI record book.

The word that there was an animal down quickly spread through the jungle's insect world. A cloud of big flies and bees swarmed on the bongo as we started photographing it, so it was hard to sit still for the photos. Before starting to skin the bongo, the Pygmies built a smoky fire on each side of it. I wore a mosquito net over my head and waved a branch over the animal as they worked. It was as if every insect in Africa were feeding on that carcass.

The next day we left early and drove forty-five or fifty miles to the Sangha River, the border between western Cameroon and the Congo, where Max had hired some people to take us out on the river in their dugouts to hunt forest sitatunga. The local people didn't show up as agreed. After waiting about an hour for them, we gave up and drove back to camp. We returned the next day to find three men with a small, narrow canoe that had been hacked and burned from an old log. Rene took one look at it and told the men to come back the next day with a larger, safer one. We drove back to camp and returned to the river in the morning. We never saw the men again, and I didn't get to hunt the forest sitatunga I wanted from this area.

Several types of duiker—a family of miniature antelope with short horns—are hunted only in Cameroon or in this small region of West Africa. I shot five species in the two areas we hunted during the safari—Ogilby,[1] Peters, red-flanked, western bush, and blue. We took two of them by calling them to us. Typically, we'd find a place to stay out of sight and would wait until the forest quieted down. Then one of the Pygmies would start making sounds with his throat or call by suddenly exhaling air from his nose or patting the ground. When the calling worked, a duiker would arrive, apparently looking for what it thought was a female, and I'd shoot it with Rene's shotgun.

On 13 March Rene and I left the southern forest and returned to Douala. The next day we flew five hundred miles north to Garoua. This region was a narrow strip of land sandwiched between Chad and Nigeria and was as different from the southern forest as night and day. Garoua was a savanna with scattered trees and openings and many small villages with thatched homes along the roads. It was good to be able to see more than a few yards again. Although we were farther from the equator, it was hotter and drier near Garoua. It was 80 degrees Fahrenheit and very humid when we checked into a motel at 7 P.M.

The safari company's owner, a Frenchman named Maurice, and Igor, the camp manager, met us with a vehicle and took us to a place where I bought more licenses. It was a four-hour drive to our next camp, and only the first hour was on a paved road. The rest of the way was rough and dusty. Around 2:30 P.M. we finally reached the camp—an old cement-block building with open doors and windows, near a village called Ndok. Thankfully, there were fewer bugs in the savanna.

It was approaching 100 degrees Fahrenheit when we went for a drive at 4 o'clock that afternoon. We saw a few animals, but I didn't take anything that day. What I really wanted from this area were a giant eland and a dwarf forest buffalo.

My opportunity came just after daylight on the third morning, when we found where a herd had crossed the road during the night. Rene and I, along with two trackers, left the vehicle and followed the tracks on foot. Four hours later, we found the animals feeding in a thicket, unaware that we were downwind. When Rene pointed to a bull, I shot it with the

1. My Ogilby duiker was a very good one. Its 3¾-inch horns are ranked number four in the *SCI All-Time Record Book of Trophy Animals.*

This buffalo from the Garoua area is smaller than southern Africa's Cape buffalo, and its horns are a different shape. Cameroon, 1991.

.300. It was a very good bull. (Ten years later, it still ranks number four in the *SCI All-Time Record Book*.) It took the trackers an hour to skin it and hang the meat in trees where the local villagers could retrieve it. We finally got back to the truck at 2 P.M., eight long hours after we first found the tracks. After lunch and a nap, we went out again.

We had been gone for only a short while when I suddenly felt a severe pain in my side. Rene stopped the truck several times, and I tried to walk it away, but nothing helped. The pain got worse. I hurt so much I couldn't stand or lie down for more than a few minutes at a time. I had them drive me back to camp. By now it was dark and so hot in that concrete building that I went outside and rolled in the cooler dirt. I could hardly stand the pain, and I had absolutely no idea what was wrong. There was nothing I could do. I thought I had come to my end. I had no more painkillers left. I was at the point where I was thinking about my past.

Rene was the only person in our camp who spoke some English, but his accent was so thick I sometimes had trouble understanding him. Around 9 P.M. Rene said the closest hospital was back at Garoua, four hours away, and they wouldn't treat me until morning. I didn't think I could make the trip anyway. The pain was so bad I was afraid I would pass out. Later, one of our men told Rene there was a doctor in a village two hours away, so I limped over to the truck, and we headed off for help. I'm sure you could still find my fingerprints on the handle

over the door I clung to as we drove to that village. I felt every bump.

It was midnight when we reached the village, but we had no idea where to find the doctor until the trackers found a man to show us the way. By now I was lying in the back of the vehicle, barely able to walk or talk. In French, the doctor told Rene he had no medicine and couldn't help me. I was thinking that I might be passing a kidney stone.

Next, Rene drove me to a church where a priest and a nun saw me. Then we went back to camp. The pain gradually subsided, and I eventually was able to get some sleep. I was sore the next morning, but the severe pain was gone. I still don't know for sure what it was, but my self-diagnosis probably was correct. A doctor I spoke with later said I could have aggravated the condition by being dehydrated and drinking a lot of water while tracking my buffalo.

Whatever it was, I recovered enough to hunt morning and evening until 26 March, and I took most of the animals I wanted from this area. It was one of the toughest safaris I ever made, because of the heat, insects, living conditions, food, and language problems. We did most our hunting on foot in heat that kept us covered with sweat. I took eleven species of game on this safari, including Central African giant eland, western hartebeest, western kob, Nigerian bohor reedbuck, western roan antelope, sing-sing waterbuck, and civet, in addition to those I've already mentioned. Because we weren't able to hunt on the river,

AfricSafari's owner invited me to return the next year at no charge. I left Garoua on 27 March for the long trip back home and never returned.

It was during this period—after returning from Cameroon and before leaving for Tanzania—that I decided that hunters and shooters in Havelock needed their own shooting range. The new Canadian firearms law was strict. Anyone who wanted to sight in a rifle or test a new handload outside of the hunting season had to obtain a permit from a government agency ten miles away. In addition, the permit had to specify where the firearm would be fired and the exact times the shooter would take it out of his home and return with it. It was inconvenient, to say the least, especially when the officials began requiring us to get our permits the day before we would be using them. We had no choice but to comply, and we'd get our permits and fill them out by saying we would be shooting at an old gravel pit or some isolated place.

One of my employees, who also did some shooting, said if we formed a club and had a registered shooting range, the club could issue the permits to its own members. To be registered, a club needed ten members and its own shooting range. It didn't take me long to sign up more than the minimum number of members. I then leased twelve acres to the club for twenty years for one dollar a year and used my company's equipment to scrape out the shooting lanes and build up berms. The other members and I cut cedar logs on my property and built a clubhouse. The Havelock Sportsmen's Club was born.

I served as the club's president for the first two years, and I may have used the range more than any other member then, shooting and testing loads. Although we built traps and laid out trap and skeet ranges, few shooters use them now. Most of the members are riflemen.

As the years went by, I used the range less and less. Nowadays, I go there only to check my rifle's zero before a hunt. I became a life member seven years ago.

I may hold some sort of record for having my rifle case temporarily lost by airlines, and it happened again on my safari to Tanzania in 1991. When my plane landed at Kilimanjaro International Airport on 26 July, my rifle wasn't with my baggage. The last time I had seen it was in London, where someone in the security office assured me it would be put on my Air Tanzania flight. I should have been used to this by then, but I wasn't.

Waiting for me at the airport were Tanzania Hunting Safaris' representatives Pete Lawrence and Michael Angelides. They helped me file a missing article report and said they would pick up my rifle when it arrived the next day at noon. They drove me to the Mount Mara Hotel, and I got a room for the night. When I saw them the next afternoon, they said I would have to use their rifles. Mine hadn't arrived on the noon flight, and they said I would be leaving for my camp on a charter flight in less than an hour.

A mature bongo, one of Africa's three most coveted spiral-horned antelope. Cameroon, 1991.

My professional hunter was Nicky Blunt, one of the better-known professionals during the heyday of East African safari hunting and "one of the most highly regarded professional hunters of his generation," according to Anthony Dyer's book *Men for All Seasons*.

Nicky was waiting for me when the little plane touched down around 1:30 P.M. near what he called "the Koga Camp" in the northwestern part of the country. It was a tent camp with a thatched dining area. My first order of business was to sight in the 7mm Remington Magnum I was borrowing. That done, we returned to camp and had dinner.

Around 10 o'clock the next morning, Nicky and I, along with three of his men, left on a twelve-hour drive to the area where I would be hunting an East African (also called Speke) sitatunga, a shaggy, swamp-dwelling antelope with lyre-shaped spiral horns. Most of the long trip was on dirt roads, and when we finally pulled off the main track I was sure we were near our destination. According to Nicky, though, we had another three or four hours to go. There were no signposts; we simply followed a series of two-track trails that ran in the direction Nicky wanted to go. It was 10 P.M. when we finally pulled up to a hut at the edge of a cluster of thatched mud dwellings and found our local guide. We pitched our tent near their huts and unpacked only what we would need for the night.

I woke the next morning to find every boy and girl in the village watching the men load our gear again. Nicky warned me that if I gave one kid something, the rest of them would swarm all over us, and we might never get away. Lake Sagale, where Nicky was taking me, was four hours away. When we finally reached it, I found it was about a mile across and approximately three miles long. It was only one to three feet deep, and large patches of reeds and grass grew out of it. By now, I had hunted in Africa enough to know this was prime sitatunga country. The reeds provided cover, and the water and mud kept the animals safe from most predators.

It was 4 P.M. by the time we drove around the lake and set up the tent. Nicky and I found a high spot and sat there with our binoculars until dark without seeing anything other than egrets, cranes, and a large assortment of water birds. If there were sitatunga on that side of the lake, we didn't see them.

The next morning we moved the camp to the other side and spent the entire day glassing from various spots overlooking the lake. Our last "glassing station" was in a tree that allowed us to see over a sea of reeds and check out the scattered openings around us. Just before dark, Nicky tapped my shoulder and pointed. In the middle of the lake, a long way off, two sitatunga were moving across a clearing. We were too far away to try to shoot one of them, and it was too late in the day to try to get closer. I could only watch as they stopped to feed.

Until now, we had spent most of our time on the edges of the lake. The next morning, though, we started wading toward

The author could see little difference between the sing-sing waterbuck and other African waterbucks. Cameroon.

Nicky Blunt and the author with his East African (or Speke) sitatunga. Tanzania.

where we had seen the sitatunga the previous evening. The water ranged from knee-deep to crotch-level, and whenever we stepped into a particularly muddy spot we would sink another foot deeper.

"Welcome to sitatunga hunting," Nicky said.

I didn't bother to reply. I was too busy trying not to slip and fall in the mud. I also was keeping an eye out for crocodiles. Virtually every large body of water in this part of Africa has crocodiles. Fortunately for us, they didn't bother us.

About an hour after we entered the water, one of the men stopped and nodded toward an animal standing in the reeds two hundred yards ahead of us. We could see only parts of it; we couldn't tell if it was a good male. While we were trying to get a better look, the sitatunga bolted and disappeared in an instant.

We spent the rest of the day on a small mound in the middle of the lake, and we saw only two females at dusk. Then we sloshed for the next two and a half hours in the dark to get back to camp. Two days later, after failing to see a good male sitatunga within rifle range, we moved the camp over a ridge to another lake with the same name. Nicky was able to hire two local men to pole us around in their canoe. On my seventh day of hunting, around 1 P.M., we came upon a sitatunga in its bed. I was ready when it suddenly jumped up, and my bullet struck behind its shoulder as it was quartering away. When it dropped, it sent up a spray of water. The men were excited as we poled over to retrieve it. I was relieved that the ordeal was over. I'd

had enough hunting in that muddy marsh to last a lifetime. I had taken a good sitatunga, though. Its 24⅞-inch horns recently ranked number fourteen in the *SCI All-Time Record Book of Trophy Animals.*

Next, we returned to the Koga Camp. Although we saw very few game animals in the four days we hunted there, I managed to take a topi and a roan antelope. The stalks were nothing unusual. We found the animals while we were driving around; we got out and walked a short distance, and I shot them.

Next we moved to Lake Rukwa, where I would hunt a bohor reedbuck. It took us five hours over rough roads to reach the hunting company's Runga camp, about midway in the trip. When we arrived that evening, there was a party of seven people from the United States already at the camp. The company's owners—George Angelides and Gerard Miller—were guiding them. The people I met there that evening said the area was loaded with game. It certainly didn't sound like the place I had been hunting.

Nicky and I and three or four men left in the morning and had a three-hour drive to the lake. We had to cut our own trail the last two miles to reach a large, flat area on the edge of the lake, but it was our best campsite so far on that safari. The lake's water and reeds had attracted a great number of birds, as well as bohor reedbuck, small groups of zebra and impala, and other game. We stayed there only one night, and I shot two animals: an eastern bohor reedbuck with 10-inch horns and an East African impala.

Gunwriter Jack O'Connor called the East African greater kudu the "gray ghost of Africa." Tanzania.

The local fishermen behind the boats of the author and his party are loading their catch in a dugout to take to a nearby market. Tanzania.

Compared to the impalas I had taken in southern Africa, the horns on this one seemed too large for the animal. It ranked about midway in the SCI record book.

Early the next morning we packed up and returned to Runga camp, where we spent the night. We left for Koga the next day. We devoted the next few days to hunting for eland, greater kudu, and waterbuck—we even put out a lion bait— but I didn't fire a shot at Koga. I had a list of twenty-four animals that I wanted to take in Tanzania, and I hoped to get at least twenty of them before the safari was over. So far, two weeks into this safari, I had taken only five.

I was a little disappointed in Nicky as a guide. He just couldn't seem to arrange a day without some sort of problem, and his people weren't very efficient. I also was tired of driving around Koga without seeing the game we wanted. When Nicky said Masailand had the animals I wanted, I suggested we go there. We flew back to Arusha the next morning and then drove to Masailand. I took a Thomson gazelle on the way.

Masailand also was a disappointment. There were Masai camps and cattle everywhere. All I shot during three days of hunting there was a hartebeest. On 14 August we spent five hours driving to Arusha, where my missing rifle finally caught up with me. I stayed at the Dik Dik Motel and hunted on Mount Meru with guides from the government wildlife college. They charged $500 a day, and each hunter was allowed two animals per day. I took a suni, a Harvey red duiker, and a

bushbuck. I enjoyed hunting on Mount Meru, and I enjoyed the people we met there. It seemed we were always on the move on the trip.

I wasn't happy that I wasn't allowed to hunt from the Runga camp, the only good area in my outfitter's concession. The owners were guiding and catering to a group of people who had booked a hunt after me, and they took them to the Runga camp. Nicky had planned for us to hunt there, but he now had to find other places for us to hunt.

I was scheduled to leave Arusha at 10:30 P.M. on 28 August, and Michael was supposed to take me to the airport. When he didn't show up, Nicky called, and I learned Michael was waiting for someone to show up with an export permit for my rifle. It had been one minor crisis after another throughout the safari. After Nicky drove me to the airport, I checked in at the airline counter, but I couldn't clear Customs until my rifle export permit from the police arrived. Michael didn't have my permit when he showed up at the airport. He hadn't been able to find the man who supposedly had it. When Nicky and Michael finally got things squared away, I boarded my plane just as the door was closing.

I landed in Moncton on 29 August, one day before my rifle case got there. I had taken seventeen of the twenty-four species I had hoped to take in Tanzania on that trip, and several of them were gold-medal animals, so I have to say it was a successful safari. If I had been allowed to hunt from the Runga camp, and if we hadn't wasted all those days driving back and forth to the other camps, however, it would have been much better.

Imagine landing one afternoon at the airport in Moscow, rifle in hand, and finding no one there to meet you. You've been told you need a special permit for your rifle, but you don't know where to go to get it. Your next flight is from an airport an hour and a half away, and you don't have any way to get there. To make matters worse, there aren't many people around who speak English, and you don't know a single word of Russian. That's exactly what happened to me in September 1991.

I had booked a hunt for snow sheep, Siberian moose, Eurasian brown bear, and reindeer through Safari Outfitters of Cody, Wyoming, and it was getting off on the wrong foot. I finally got through Customs with my rifle and found an official who kindly paged the person who was supposed to meet me. When no one showed up, I got a cab and somehow found a way to let the driver know I wanted him to drive me to the other airport. Once there, however, I learned that the 8:30 P.M. flight to Magadan had been delayed until 3:30 A.M.

I couldn't check my bags or my rifle on my flight at that rundown airport, so I sat on them to make certain no one stole them. Around 8 P.M. a woman who could speak a little English walked up to me and said I could take another flight that was leaving in thirty minutes. When I went to check my bags, I was hit with an excess baggage fee. Trying to argue would have been a waste of time. No one would have understood a word I said.

At the departure gate I met three people from Germany who also were hunters flying to Magadan. One of them could speak a little English. The Germans also spoke no Russian, so the four of us were clueless about what people around us were saying, but it was great to have someone with whom I could communicate during the eight-hour, nonstop flight across eight time zones.

I felt better when we landed in Magadan at 1 P.M. the next day and found the outfitter's representative and an interpreter waiting for me. A half-hour later, they helped me check into a hotel. I was asleep exactly one minute after hitting the bed. I felt better that evening, when the two men took me to dinner. Bad starts very often have good endings, I told myself.

My problems weren't over, however. The next morning I was supposed to take a one-hour commercial flight to Seimchan and hook up with a helicopter that would fly me to my hunting camp. At the airport we were told our plane had mechanical problems and was grounded. There was nothing we could do, my interpreter said, except hire a car and drive to Seimchan.

I enjoyed the seven-hour drive through interesting, mountainous country, past dozens of small gold-mining camps along the rivers. It was 3 P.M. when we reached the city. It was cold, about 32 degrees Fahrenheit, and there was some snow on the ground, but I was dressed for it.

At dinner that evening, after I had taken a room at a place they called a hotel, my interpreter introduced me to Khalil, the hunting company's local manager, and Valera Skirda, my guide. Khalil spoke enough English that we were able to communicate, but Valera spoke only Russian. He proved to be a good guide nonetheless.

We wanted to fly to the camp the next morning, but the helicopters weren't flying on Sundays, so we had to wait until Monday, when we didn't get under way until 2 P.M. An hour later, the large, military-type transport chopper dropped us off at the campsite. It started to snow while the men were setting up our two tents, and it continued off and on all through that first night. We woke the next morning to find three inches of snow covering everything.

We climbed a mountain above our tent to look for snow sheep that first day. As soon as we reached the top, thick fog rolled in, making it impossible to glass. We waited a couple of hours for it to burn off, and when it didn't we headed down to the camp. We hunted that mountain for a week, and every day it snowed and the wind blew. We did see a few ewes and lambs, but no mature rams. On the eighth day my guides were able to reach the airport on their radio and arrange to have a helicopter fly us out that day. During the flight we spotted some rams on a mountain slope below us. We had the pilot drop Valera and me off; then

we hiked to where we had last seen the sheep. We were lucky. The little herd had not gone far, and I was able to shoot the largest ram from about two hundred yards with my 7mm Remington Magnum. When we walked up to the ram, I was struck by how much it resembled the Stone sheep of British Columbia. Its horns were 30½ inches long around tight curls, and it weighed about two hundred pounds. It later would be listed as number fifty in the *SCI All-Time Record Book of Trophy Animals* in the Siberian snow sheep category.

I spent the rest of the hunt "camping" in the hotel in Seimchan and flying out each day to look for game. We did not hunt from the helicopter. Instead, it dropped us off each morning in promising places and picked us up and flew us back to town each evening. I was able to take the three other species I wanted—a Siberian moose, a brown bear, and, on the last hour of the last day, a reindeer.

The skins of my trophies weren't dry enough for me to take them to Magadan and Moscow the next day, and I had to leave without them. Khalil promised to have them shipped to Canada later, which he did. He flew back to Moscow with me, along with my interpreter and another representative of the hunting company, a man named Vladimir. We spent the night at the Intourist Hotel in Moscow. Khalil drove me to the airport early the next morning so I could catch the 7 A.M. flight to Bulgaria. I had come to know and like Khalil during this two-week hunt. I'd had dinner at his home in Seimchan three or

A very cold camp in the heart of snow-sheep country. Siberia.

The author's Siberian snow sheep reminded him of the Stone sheep of Canada. Its horns were 30½ inches long. Siberia.

four times, and I'd met his family. One of his two children spoke some English, and we all got along very well. I was genuinely sorry to have to say good-bye to him.

After a disastrous start, Khalil and Valera had saved my hunt. I had taken every animal I wanted because of their efforts. As my plane lifted off, I promised myself that I would return to Russia someday.

A man named Nasco, a director of hunting for the Bulgaria Service, and a woman named Milka met me when I landed in Sofia. They took me directly from the plane to a hunters' lounge while they cleared my bags through Bulgarian Customs and got my gun permit. When we stepped out of the airport, a van with a driver and interpreter—and all of my gear—were waiting for us on the curb. After my experience in Moscow two weeks earlier, I was impressed.

It was a beautiful day, and I enjoyed the six-hour drive through the rural countryside. We stopped only for lunch along the road through several large farming areas. Interestingly, the farmers were still using small wagons and donkeys to work their fields and deliver their crops.

When we reached the hunting estate around 5 P.M., George (the estate's hunting director) and Eugeni (my guide) were waiting for us. Neither could speak English, but Milka had come along as my interpreter. At dusk they drove me around to see the estate, and we saw several young red stags and hinds. The real hunt wouldn't start until the next day. I would be hunting European red deer, wisent (European bison), and roe deer before driving south to hunt brown bear and Balkan chamois.

There was no shortage of game, but the gamekeeper who accompanied us let me know with nods of his head and motions with his hands that I should wait for better trophies. On the second day we were watching a roebuck a couple of hundred yards away with our binoculars when the gamekeeper nodded his head and pointed to my rifle. It was an easy shot, and the little deer dropped in its tracks. Its antlers had three points per side and were "pearled," meaning covered with bumps—a sign of an older animal. It was better than just a representative head, and I was happy to have it. It was the best of the two dozen roebuck we saw during the first two days. We were seeing a large number of red deer, too, but the gamekeeper kept saying I should wait.

We hunted for my wisent the third day. The largest game animals in Europe, these closely resemble North American bison but have longer legs, straighter horns, and bushier tails. The wisent, like the North American bison, was teetering on the brink of extinction a hundred years ago. Wisent have recovered, however, and they now can be hunted in Bulgaria, Poland, Russia, and Austria. Unfortunately, as with hunting American bison today, hunting the wisent is not very challenging. My guides drove me to where they knew a herd was staying, and we walked slowly and quietly through a stand of trees until we reached its far edge. In the meadow in front of us were fifteen to twenty shaggy brown

Europe's wisent, or bison, greatly resemble their North American cousins. Bulgaria.

The gamekeeper needed only a quick glance at this stag's antlers to let the author know this was the red deer he wanted. Bulgaria.

animals. The gamekeeper pointed out the bull I was to shoot, and I killed it. It was a good representative trophy.

To complete my hunt on this estate I wanted to take red deer and fallow deer. We had spent a lot of time every day looking for a good red stag, but we didn't find one until the last morning of my hunt. Again, taking it was nothing like hunting an American elk, to which red deer are closely related. The rut was on and the stags were roaring, making them easy to locate. The gamekeeper didn't hesitate when we came upon this particular stag. One look at its antlers was all he needed. I should shoot that one, he indicated, and I did.

That same afternoon they drove me to an area where fallow deer gathered during the rut. It was a sight to behold. The stags were running around grunting, trying to hold their territory against intruders. I shot perhaps the fifth or sixth good stag we found.

Next on my itinerary were bear and chamois hunts from a comfortable lodge in the mountains near Izvoz, about eight hours away. I hunted chamois in the mornings. In the evenings I sat in a high seat (an elevated blind) over bait that had been set out for bear. The chamois country was very steep, and the animals were scarce. Although we saw several from far off, I never was able to get close enough to take one. Two days before I was scheduled to leave, I shot a representative bear just after sundown. I had passed up this same bear several times, but when we realized it was the largest in the area, I shot it.

On 19 October we drove back to Sofia, where I caught the 1 P.M. flight to Frankfurt. It had been an interesting hunt, with excellent accommodations. It was my first experience with the European trophy fee system. In Bulgaria, and elsewhere in Europe, the hunter pays a fee for each animal he takes, based upon its trophy quality. Taking a gold-medal red stag, roe deer, or fallow deer, for example, can be very pricey.

The next morning I flew from Frankfurt to Madrid, where I learned that the passengers were let out at one terminal while their baggage went to another. For some reason it took longer than usual to clear Customs, and then I had to get to the other terminal, where my guide, a man named Rodrigo Fajardo, was waiting for me at the baggage drop. Next I had to take my rifle to the airport's police station and get a firearms permit. All of this took nearly two hours, but finally Rodrigo and I were on our way.

Three hours later, we pulled into a village at the foot of the Sierra de Gredos, where I would hunt a Gredos ibex, one of the four types of Spanish ibex recognized by Safari Club International. We didn't stay in town long. Rodrigo found a telephone and called the Gredos Mountain Reserve's office, and a half-hour later two gamekeepers arrived and took us to a small but comfortable lodge in the mountains.

The next morning Rodrigo, three guides, and I began our hunt. We had only two horses: I rode one; the other was a packhorse. The four other men walked.

The trail we followed was steep and long, but after four hours we were near the top and had found in our binoculars a small group of ibex across a canyon. One of the males was a good one, and, although this was my first day of hunting, I decided to take it. It was a long way across the canyon to where the animals were feeding—maybe three hundred yards— but my 7mm Remington Magnum was sighted in to shoot to point of aim at 250 yards. I found a rock I could rest my rifle on, used my jacket to cushion it, put the cross hairs on the billy's spine, and squeezed the trigger. The ibex simply collapsed. It was dead before we heard the smack of my bullet hitting it.

Scientists say Spanish ibex are goats and not true ibex. I must admit that the 30½-inch horns on mine looked nothing like the horns of Asian ibex. They flared out in a *V* shape, then turned sharply in at the tips. After photographing and caping the billy, the men brought the horses over, and we packed it down the mountain.

It was still early after we had dinner in the village, so I packed up my gear, and we drove to Las Arripas, the hunting lodge Eduardo Araoz owns in the Toledo Mountains. (Weatherby Award-winner Ricardo Medem had built it when he still owned Cazatur, the hunting company I was using. Araoz was now one of the owners of Cazatur.) There were two couples from Texas and California hunting Spanish red deer on the estate when I arrived. I spent only two nights at Las Arripas, taking a mouflon and a wild boar. There were plenty of red stags

on the estate, but when we couldn't find a good one Rodrigo and I drove around the mountain to another estate. There were fewer stags there, but they were larger than those we had been seeing. I was surprised to see how spooky they were. If one of them spotted a small part of us from three or four hundred yards away, it would throw up its head, stare at us, and run away. The terrain consisted of small valleys surrounded by gentle hills, but those hills were covered with high brush. The stags were out of sight in an instant in that stuff.

The stag I shot was standing in one of the many firebreaks that had been cut on one of the hillsides when we first saw it. The wind was drifting from the deer to me, so I was able to use the brush to cover my approach. When I was about two hundred yards away, I found a rest, put the cross hairs on its shoulder, and squeezed the trigger. The stag bolted at the shot, but it ran only about thirty yards before falling. Its antlers had eight points on one side and seven on the other, with main beams nearly three feet long. It was smaller than the red deer found elsewhere in Europe, weighing only about two hundred pounds. But this was a Spanish red deer, one of the smallest races, and my stag was a good one that would qualify for the *SCI All-Time Record Book of Trophy Animals.*

Rodrigo drove me back to Madrid the next day, where I met Eduardo Araoz. Rodrigo drove us to the airport, and Eduardo and I caught the 9 P.M. flight to Barcelona. Rodrigo planned to drive there and hook up with us later. Eduardo

The author and his guides with his Gredos ibex. Spain, 1991.

The author shot two Spanish ibex on his first trip to Spain. This is the Beceite variety. Spain.

and I landed in Barcelona at 2:30 A.M., then rented a car and drove two more hours to a village called Tortosa, where we checked into an ancient castle that was being used as a hotel. We had traveled all night. The only sleep I got was on the airplane, and I was very tired. Nonetheless, daylight found Eduardo, a gamekeeper, and me climbing the nearby Beceite Mountains to hunt another race of Spanish ibex. We saw only females and young billies after glassing for most of the day. Then, just as we were getting ready to come off the mountain, someone spotted two big males near a far-off peak. It was too late to try to go after them, but we made a mental note of where they were so we could try to find them the next day.

Rodrigo was waiting for us at the hotel when we got there. He had driven all night and most of the day and was as tired as we were. After eating something, we all went to our rooms and crashed.

We were back on the mountain the next morning, just as the fog moved in and it began to rain. We stayed in the vehicle until the storm passed at 2 P.M., except that I got out to pick a few olives and almonds. They were the first I'd ever picked from trees. When things started drying out, we started climbing on foot, looking for a place to glass from.

An hour later, we spotted several female ibex on a rocky hillside. After watching them for four or five minutes in our binoculars, I picked up a movement near them. I had to concentrate on the spot, but I eventually was able to make

out the horns of a big billy in its bed. I'd seen only its head move, but that was enough. We'd found the ibex I wanted.

As we started moving around the steep canyon, trying to cut the distance to the ibex, the rain came back again. We stopped behind a boulder about 150 yards below the ibex. Although all of the ibex were bedded within a few yards of where we had seen them an hour earlier, they were above us, and all I could see of the billy was its head and horns. I set my rifle on a rock and got ready to wait for the ibex to stand up. Meanwhile, we were getting soaked, and it didn't look as if the rain were going to stop anytime soon.

When the rain turned into a downpour, Eduardo whistled, and all the ibex jumped up. I was ready, and when the billy turned broadside I shot it—too far back! My second shot killed it as it was going over the ridge. It was still raining hard when we reached the animal and started skinning it. Scientists say the Beceite and Gredos ibex are the same subspecies, but there were visible differences between this ibex and the one I'd taken earlier. Its 31-inch horns were thicker and of a different shape, and its coat was a different color.

We were exhausted, wet, and cold when we reached our vehicle at 5 P.M. By now, the rain was coming down so hard it was difficult to see the road more than thirty or forty yards ahead of us. The track had turned to mud, and water was running everywhere. I cannot describe how it felt to finally reach our hotel after spending the day out in that storm.

The first thing I did was to call Janice. This was 26 October, our thirty-fourth wedding anniversary. Then we showered and shaved, changed clothes, and went to a seafood restaurant to celebrate my second Spanish ibex. As tired as we were, we partied until midnight.

Eduardo flew back to Madrid the next morning, and Rodrigo and I drove to the Pyrenees to hunt a chamois. Four hours later, after driving on mountain roads and through tunnels, we reached a ski resort in an alpine valley surrounded by high mountains. We were only a few miles from the French border. The place was so quaint and picturesque it reminded me of Switzerland. We hunted there for two days, spending both days glassing and climbing without seeing a male chamois. It was raining when we called it quits at 6 P.M. on the second day. My tickets called for me to fly home the next day, so, instead of spending the night at our hotel, we began the long drive back to Madrid, arriving there at 3:30 A.M. on 30 October.

A world meeting on terrorism in the Middle East was taking place in the city, and my hotel was not only crowded but heavily guarded. When I arrived with my rifle case in the middle of the night, it was like setting off an alarm. The police inspected my firearms permit closely and went through my luggage before they would let me check in.

I slept until 10 A.M. before meeting Eduardo in the lobby and settling up my account. Two days later, after spending the night in Frankfurt, I was back home. I had been gone six weeks. I'd had good hunts in Russia and Bulgaria, but I was a bit disappointed in Spain, and not just because of the weather. Every animal I took there was larger than the SCI record book minimums, but the overall quality of the game wasn't as good as I had hoped. There were still four species in Spain and a Balkan chamois in Bulgaria that I hadn't taken.

SOUTH AMERICA MAKES IT SIX, 1992

The year 1992 got off to a good start for me, with a Canada lynx in February and an Alaskan wolf in March. I had hunted these two animals for several years, and both had eluded me. I shot the lynx south of Fort Saint John in British Columbia the first day I hunted with Barry Tompkins' Big 9 Outfitters, and we spent what was left of the two-week hunt unsuccessfully trying to take a wolf. (We saw two wolf but weren't able to get close enough to either of them.) The lynx completed my SCI Grand Slam of the Cats of the World. A month later, with Dan Troutman's Alaska Sport and Recreation, I shot a black male wolf and a red fox on the Ivishak River in the northern Brooks Range.

We used snowmobiles for both hunts, but we found the wolf by following its tracks in the snow on foot. Hunting British Columbia and Alaska in February and March was not easy. The wolf hunt was especially tough because our snowmobiles kept getting stuck in the spring snow, but it completed my SCI Diamond Level of the Trophy Animals of North America. Taking that wolf meant I had collected forty different species and subspecies of the larger game animals in North America.

Over the past seven years I had hunted on five continents—North America, Africa, Asia, Europe, and Australia. South America was about to become the sixth

when I landed in Buenos Aires on 20 April after stops in Halifax, Toronto, and São Paulo, Brazil. Jorge (George) Gonzales, whom I had met at the SCI convention that January in Reno, helped me obtain my rifle permit and get through Customs. It was a good thing he was there, because very few people at the airport spoke anything but Spanish.

George had a car and driver waiting for us outside, and an hour later we were at another airport, where we were met by Maximo Ricardi, the agent who had arranged my hunts in Argentina. After a quick meal, George and Maximo saw me board the 5:30 P.M. flight to Barscilla on the Argentine border with Chile.

Two hours later, an interpreter named Gustavo Ayciriex met me at Barscilla and drove me to Parque Diana, a large hunting estate and five-star resort about two hours away. I was the last hunter of the season, and I had the place to myself. After two full days and one night of nonstop traveling, I was exhausted and went straight to my chalet without eating when we arrived at 10:30 P.M.

The next morning I met Beat Affolter, my guide. Beat spoke a little English, but Gustavo stayed with me all the time I was at Parque Diana. I had booked only a mouflon and a fallow deer hunt, but when I was quoted a special price for a red deer and an alpine ibex, I expanded my hunt to include those two extra species. It rained all the first day and off and on for the rest of my stay. The weather was colder than I expected, and one night we got two inches of snow. The game was hard to find, but after four days I had taken the four species I wanted from Parque Diana, and all were fine trophies.

The last evening there I was invited to dinner with Francisco Moya, the estate's owner. I left at noon the next day from St. Martin de los Andes on 24 April and flew back to Buenos Aires. George again met me there, and he stayed with me until I boarded the 7:30 P.M. flight to Bahía Blanca. German Rossi, the son of Pablo Rossi, owner of Hucal Safaris, was waiting for me there. German would be my interpreter while I hunted axis deer, wild boar, and puma with his father's company.

German and I left my hotel early the next morning and drove to an estate a few hours away, where I collected an axis deer. There really wasn't much hunting involved. We drove around and saw several bucks, and I shot one. We were back at my hotel that evening.

The next morning we drove three and a half hours to a town called Rio Colorado, where Pablo Russi was waiting to guide me for my boar and puma. Pablo ran Hucal Safaris, and he and his son German were among the friendliest and most likable of all the great people I have met on my travels.

We stayed in a rented cabin, and Pablo cooked some of the best meals I have ever eaten. We hunted wild boar from a baited stand, which the boars visited late in the evening. As I recall, we spent a couple of nights in that stand before a really good boar showed up and I shot it.

We hunted the puma with a pack of hounds, driving around until we found a fresh track and then releasing the dogs and going off on foot through the brush. It was tough work keeping up with the pack. After several false starts, we hit a very hot track and spent the next three hours following the dogs before we heard them barking. The rest of that hunt was anticlimactic. The dogs had run a puma up a tree, and I shot it.

I spent five days with German before he and Pablo drove me to an airport to catch my flight to Buenos Aires. They knew I didn't speak Spanish and wanted to make certain I would have no problems, so they stayed with me till I boarded the plane. As my plane was moving down the runway to take off, the pilot suddenly cut the power. The captain announced something I couldn't understand and taxied back to the ramp, where people outside started climbing onto the plane's wings. Thirty minutes later, the captain made another announcement, and we started down the runway, only to turn around again at the last possible minute. There was another announcement when the plane came to a stop, and all the passengers started leaving their seats. I followed them back inside the terminal. I tried to ask someone at the airport's police station what was wrong, but no one there spoke English.

I took a good look at the passengers who had been on my plane, so I could

Author and guide with a Canada lynx taken north of Fort St. John. British Columbia.

Pablo Rossi and the author with his South American puma. Argentina.

The author with a red deer taken while hunting in South America. Argentina.

follow them if they boarded another flight. I spent the next hour reading a book, looking up frequently to make certain the people I was watching hadn't left. While I was reading, a man sat down next to me and asked me something in Spanish.

"Oh, English," he said in a thick accent when I said I didn't understand him. Our plane had a mechanical problem, he said.

We finally got into the air four hours after we were scheduled to leave and flew to Buenos Aires without any problems. I was worried that we would be so late that no one would be at the airport to meet me. I was relieved to see George's smiling face as I left the plane.

On 30 April George and his driver, Guillermo Massum, drove me three hours to Rancho Corona, where I would hunt feral goat and blackbuck. My room was in a lovely old hacienda that had been built in a scenic setting. There were interesting and unusual things throughout the house. In one room, for example, the floor had been made from the knee bones of cattle inlaid in mortar.

We were served a lunch of barbecue beef. Then George and I drove out to where blackbuck had been seen. These little antelope seldom stray far from the territory they stake out, so it didn't take long to find the buck I wanted. Then we headed for Gualeguay in the province of Entre Ríos. It was 10 P.M. when I checked into the hotel. The next morning we drove another three hours to La Paz, where I would hunt Asian water buffalo and gray-brown brocket deer. A few miles past the village, we pulled off the highway and

drove up to a four-wheel-drive vehicle. Inside was a driver and the owner of the ranch where we would be hunting.

After three days of steady rain, the dirt roads had turned to slippery mud, so we left our car and transferred our gear into the Land Rover. There was water everywhere. While driving to the ranch house, we spotted several buffalo and tried to approach them on foot. We spooked them, though, while wading toward them. After leaving my gear at the ranch house, we went out again and set up a small drive. My hosts stationed me at a spot they thought the buffalo might run past, but I had to stand in knee-deep water to have a clear view in the direction from which they might come.

I was standing there, waiting for the drive to start, when I felt something slithering up my leg. A small water snake had crawled into my pants. I was terrified. I knew that harmless water snakes outnumber the venomous types just about everywhere in the world, but I dare anyone to ignore a snake in his pants. Trying not to panic, I loosened my belt and slowly lowered my trousers. When I found the snake, I flicked it off my leg, and it swam away from me. I was relieved to be rid of it. I never learned whether or not it was a poisonous variety.

A few minutes later, I spotted three or four buffalo heading my way. They weren't badly spooked, but I could tell they were trying to escape something behind them. In the distance I could hear the guides moving toward me. When the buffalo were about seventy-five yards away, I shot the largest bull with my .300 Winchester Magnum. The bull ran a few yards, splashing water three or four feet in the air, and collapsed at the edge of a little island.

I shot a gray-brown brocket deer the next morning. At daylight we were driving on one of the many muddy roads on the ranch, slipping and sliding all over the place. Just as it was getting light enough to see, my driver suddenly stopped the Land Rover and started saying, "Shoot! Shoot!" A small deer was standing just off the road. I jumped out of the vehicle with a shotgun loaded with buckshot. There wasn't enough time to see if the little deer had antlers. I was relying on my guide when I pointed the gun at it and fired. The deer went down kicking. When I walked up to it, I was relieved to see that it was wearing a pair of slim, four-inch spikes on its head, the sign of a mature buck.

Although brockets are not the smallest of the world's deer (that honor goes to the twenty-pound southern pudu of the Andes), this was the smallest adult deer I had taken until then. It weighed only about thirty pounds and probably stood no more than two feet high at the shoulder. Its coat was a dull, gray-brown color. Taking it left only peccary on the list of species I wanted to collect in South America on this trip.

To hunt peccary, Guillermo and I drove twelve hours through the province of Santa Fe and on to a village in the province of Santiago del Estero. After a night in a hotel, Guillermo and I met a man who took us outside town a few miles. There we hunted collared peccary, the little

piglike animal they call javelina in Arizona, New Mexico, and Texas. Like the peccary in those states, Argentina's peccary form herds, have poor eyesight, and seldom leave their small territories.

Our guide took us to a brushy area along a small river. After walking a mile or so, checking the open areas to the front and sides of us, we bumped into a herd of ten to fifteen animals, confused and running this way and that. I shot the largest I could see. It later would rank very high in the South American category of the *SCI All-Time Record Book of Trophy Animals*.

The peccary ended my first South American hunt. I had taken twelve different species in three weeks. Next came a six-hundred-mile drive back to Buenos Aires and a brief stay there before heading home. Argentina was cooler and flatter than I had expected, but I'd enjoyed the experience and had met some interesting people. I'd had absolutely no problems. I still see George and German at the SCI convention each year, and they always give me an *embracio*, the hug reserved for special friends of Spanish-speaking people.

I was flying south of the equator again, less than three months after returning from South America. This time my destination was western Tanzania, where I hoped to take some of the East African species I hadn't taken on other safaris. After having so many problems with airlines losing my gun cases, I made it a point to check my baggage when I reached Nairobi. I had a six-hour wait.

As I had feared, my rifle was missing. Someone at the airline's counter told me it probably was going on to Tanzania on the same plane I'd just left. He said he would call Dar es Salaam and have them ship my rifle back if it was on that plane. It would be returning at 10:30 that night, just one hour before I was due to fly out.

The airline gave me a meal, and I read until I was able to get my boarding pass at 9:30 P.M. At 10:30 the airline attendant found me. My rifle wasn't on the plane from Dar es Salaam, he said, which meant it must not have made it out of Frankfurt, where I'd spent the night. Just before it was time for me to board my plane, however, the same man returned and said my rifle had been found, but I would need to have it cleared by the Kenyan police. It was close, but I got the permit, the police put my gun on the plane, and I was in Kigali, Rwanda, an hour later. I don't know what I would have done if they hadn't found it at the last minute. Very few outfitters keep in their camps spare rifles suitable for the animals I would be hunting.

Peter Byabato, with whom I had booked this safari, met me in Kigali. He helped me clear Customs, and we loaded my gear into his Toyota Land Cruiser. Peter would be staying in Kigali while I traveled on to the camp with my driver Ali, the guide Saidi, and two other men. Only Ali and Saidi spoke English. The camp was four hours away, near Burigi, just across the border into Tanzania. I'd flown into Kigali because it was the closest airport to the hunting area serviced by commercial airlines at the time.

This was two years before Rwanda's tribal rivalries exploded and Rwandan soldiers and Hutu thugs began slaughtering minority Tutsi tribal members by the hundreds of thousands. Even in 1992, this small, poor, and vastly overpopulated country wasn't a safe place to be. I felt better when we finally reached the border, got through Rwandan Customs, drove across the bridge, and entered Tanzania.

For some reason the Tanzanian officials were in no hurry to stamp my papers and let us go on. The Customs officer stared at me and fingered my passport, then stared at me some more. I had obtained a Tanzanian firearms permit before leaving Canada, but he wanted to check the serial numbers on the permit against those on my rifle, then check everything again. He even counted my cartridges, twice. He moved in slow motion when checking the passports of the other men in my party, and seemed to take forever when inspecting our vehicle and its papers. It was dark when we finally were permitted to go on. An hour and a half later we drove into camp. Although I hadn't eaten since Nairobi, I wasted no time in finding my tent and getting into bed.

There was a lot of game in the Burigi area—I saw fourteen different species the first morning—but I had taken all of them on previous safaris. I did take a very good East African defassa waterbuck with 33¾-inch horns (it still ranks number four in the SCI record book) during the two days we hunted there.

At 4:15 A.M. on the third day, 3 August, we left that camp and drove fourteen hours to our next camp. The road was rough and covered with deep potholes all the way. We stopped only in a couple of villages to buy tea or Coke.

Rainer Jocch, one of the hunting company's directors, greeted me when we arrived at the camp at 6:30 P.M. After I stowed my duffel in my tent, I joined him for dinner. Peter had not yet been able to get the permits I needed to hunt Roberts gazelle and Nyasa wildebeest in my next camp in Tanzania, he said. He expected to get them in a day or two, however. According to Rainer, our camp was only about a mile upriver from where I'd camped a year earlier.

My primary goal this time was to collect an East African greater kudu, which I hadn't taken in 1991. While hunting for that kudu, Rainer and I drove up on a big lion. I'd taken other lion, but this one was a big one with an exceptionally thick golden mane, and I decided to try to take it. We drove past the lion and parked the Toyota out of sight, then carefully worked our way back to the cat. When we were about fifty yards away from where it was standing under a tree, I shot it. As many lion do when fatally hit, this one leaped into the air roaring, then collapsed kicking where it had been standing.

Quite often in Africa, after taking a lion or leopard, the guides and staff celebrate and do a special dance to honor the taking of the cat. So, before returning to camp, they stopped and decorated our vehicle with tree branches and sang as we drove into camp to tell everyone we had taken a lion. That evening, while we were

sitting around the campfire, they started dancing and chanting. They then picked up my chair with me in it and paraded around as they danced.

A day or so later, my guide and I were in the back of the vehicle when the black driver suddenly stepped on the gas and started driving like a madman. He and the government game scout had seen some buffalo poachers. A minute or so later we spotted a man running away and began chasing him with the truck. Our wild ride didn't stop until the man had led us to a flat, muddy area where the truck couldn't go, and the game scout jumped out with his rifle and ran after the man.

While we waited for the game scout to return, we spotted a Cape buffalo near our truck. Only its head and half of its body stuck out of the mud, but we could clearly see a spear stuck in its side.

"The bloody poachers wound them and chase them into the mud, where the buffalo get mired down and are easier to kill," my guide said in disgust.

I couldn't leave the buffalo to die of starvation in that mudhole, so I shot it.

I took my East African greater kudu on the sixth day, after following its tracks for an hour or so. As kudu sometimes do, this one was standing motionless in the brush, apparently convinced we wouldn't see it if it didn't move. Although it wasn't a gold-medal animal, it was a fine trophy. The SCI record book recognizes five greater kudu categories, but I'll be darned if I can tell the difference among them. This one may have been slightly smaller,

Professional hunter Peter Byabato and the author with a heavy-maned lion. Tanzania.

The entire staff staged a victory celebration when the author brought in his lion. Tanzania.

but it looked exactly like the ones I'd taken in Zambia and South Africa.

Now that I'd taken the kudu, the next species I wanted were the Roberts gazelle and Nyasa wildebeest, and for these we would have to return to Arusha. We left at 3 P.M. on 10 August and checked into the Mount Meru Hotel in Arusha at 6 o'clock the next morning, after eighteen hours of nearly nonstop driving over very bad roads. The roads improved only during the last two hours.

That afternoon Saidi left to check about the permits I still needed and didn't return until 11 o'clock the next morning— without them. I still had one week left in the safari, and the gazelle and wildebeest were the only two species I wanted to hunt. I was ready to end the hunt that day if I couldn't get the permits I needed. At $800 a day for seven days, the hunting company stood to lose a considerable amount of money. Saidi relayed my message to Rainer, and both came to my hotel room. After a brief discussion, they said they could get the permits for both animals if I paid an extra $1,500 and our hotel bills. Sure enough, Saidi arrived with the permits the next morning, and we drove on to the Serengeti, where I shot an impala and a Roberts gazelle, a small antelope with unique horns that rise straight up before flaring out to the sides.

We then returned to Arusha, and I chartered a plane to take Rainer and me to the famous Selous Game Reserve in the southeastern corner of the country, where he had arranged for me to hunt a Nyasa wildebeest. These smallest of all wildebeest were plentiful in the open savannas there, and collecting a good male took only a couple of hours. I still had a day left to hunt when we returned to Arusha, so we moved on to Mount Meru to look for a bushpig. Unfortunately, I did not break the jinx that had plagued me every time I hunted this animal, and I left Tanzania without seeing one.

My problems with airlines weren't over, either. I was supposed to fly from Arusha to Nairobi on 17 August, but, when I called to confirm my flight, I was told all flights to Nairobi had been canceled a week earlier because of a lack of passengers. I could drive to Nairobi in about four hours and catch my scheduled Air Zimbabwe flight to Harare, but I wouldn't be able to cross into Kenya with my rifle. I had two choices: I could leave my rifle behind, or I could charter a plane to take me to the Nairobi airport—for $1,050. I decided I wanted to keep my rifle.

Two familiar faces were smiling at me when I cleared Customs in Harare and stepped into the airport's lobby. One was Russ Broom, with whom my sons and I had hunted in Zambia in 1985 on our first safari. Standing next to Russ was my friend and taxidermist Kevin White from North Carolina. Kevin had arrived earlier in the day to join me for a week on my safari as an observer. Then we would go to Victoria Falls to do some whitewater rafting.

I was after a Livingstone eland, and I also hoped to break my bushpig jinx. We spent the first three days in the north at a place called Camp Kabuba without seeing

Tracker "Jairos" followed the author's bushpig to its bed and helped the author break his jinx on this animal. Zimbabwe.

The author and his taxidermist friend Kevin White are on a whitewater raft on the Zambezi River below Victoria Falls. Zimbabwe.

The author's best-ever Cape buffalo. Tanzania, 1992.

a good eland, then flew to another area in the south.

It hadn't rained in twenty months in this area, Russ said, when I remarked how dry it was around our new camp. It made seeing animals much easier—there was no grass to hide them—but it also made it harder to approach them. Many of the water holes had dried up, and we found a great many carcasses and a few antelope that were so emaciated they surely could not have survived more than a few more days. Every edible plant they could reach had either died or had been eaten. A third or more of an area's game population might die of starvation in droughts like this one, Russ said. Warthog usually were the hardest hit.

Eland, the tallest of all the antelope, apparently are not bothered by drought. Only giraffes can reach the leaves on the small trees on which they feed.

It didn't take me long to realize that eland cover a lot of distance when traveling between their feeding and bedding areas. We spent two days on foot, tracking them for many miles both days. We were almost ready to turn around and head back to the vehicle at noon on the second day when we suddenly came upon the herd of thirty or forty eland that we had been tracking since sunup. They were bedded in a spot where we would not have seen them in a wet year. Like oryx, both sexes of eland have horns, and, also like oryx, those on the females sometimes are longer but thinner. I wanted a big male, which meant we not only had to check out their horns but had to look for the patch of hair on the forehead, which only male eland have.

Eland are exceptionally wary animals, and before we could locate the best bull in the herd, they all suddenly jumped to their feet and began milling around.

I already had my rifle up, and when I found the best bull I quickly centered the cross hairs of my 7mm Remington Magnum on a spot on its shoulder. The eland flinched at the shot, then started to run off as if it hadn't been hit. Just as it was going out of sight, I shot it again. Eland weigh more than half a ton and can be hard to kill. Although I had broken its shoulder, we had to track it for another mile before I could get close enough to put it down.

I spent the rest of the safari hunting for bushpig. I'd lost count of how many days I had hunted for this animal on all my safaris, and I had only caught glimpses of bushpig when we least expected them and were hunting something else. Bushpig are nocturnal animals, and I guess I could have hunted them at night with spotlights on some farmer's field, but I never did. As it turned out, I didn't have to. Almost unbelievably, our tracker was able to follow a pair of bushpig for three and a half hours to their bedding area. The first pig we saw was a female asleep under a tree. I carefully took another step and spotted the male. It was only twenty yards away when I shot it. I had broken my jinx!

This was Kevin's first trip to Africa, and he had not planned to hunt. However, a hunter has a hard time being only an observer on a safari. Before the week was over, he had borrowed my rifle and shot an impala and a greater kudu. We flew back to Harare on 25 August, spent the night, and flew to Victoria Falls the next morning.

After checking into our rooms at the grand old Victoria Falls Hotel, Kevin and I walked about a quarter of a mile to the falls. It was the first time I had ever seen Africa's greatest natural wonder. Even though the drought had lowered the Zambezi River, the falls were spectacular. That evening we took a cruise on the river above the falls. The next morning we ran the eighteen rapids below the falls in a seven-person inflatable boat, which promptly flipped and dumped everyone into the frothing water on the very first rapid. We made it through the seventeen others without a problem. Visiting Victoria Falls was a great way to end Kevin's first trip to Africa. I don't know why I waited so long to go there.

Five weeks after returning from Africa, I was shaking the hand of Peter Swales of Sports in Scotland in a Scottish town called Inverness. I had booked back-to-back hunts in Scotland, England, and Spain through Cazatur, the company with which I had hunted in Spain in 1991. First on my agenda was a Scottish red deer. Thirty minutes later, I was in my room at the Lovat Arms Hotel in a village named Beauly. After a shower and a nap, I went downstairs at 6:30 P.M. for a steak. That evening Stewart Richardson, who had arranged this leg of my tour, stopped by, and we talked about my upcoming hunt. In the dining room were two Americans,

Frank and Audrey Murtland from Michigan. Both were SCI members, and I had seen them at the club's conventions, although we hadn't been introduced. We had an enjoyable visit, and I learned that Audrey had taken a good red deer that day with a handgun.

In Scotland guides are called "stalkers," and the stalker who would be guiding me was a man named Mike Purcell. Mike picked me up at the hotel the next morning at 9 o'clock in his half-ton truck. We reached his place in the highlands too late for a morning hunt, so we fed his pheasants—several thousand of them—and his ducks. We went out at noon and climbed the heather-covered hills.

I had done my research and knew the deer I would be hunting were only about the size of the little Spanish red deer I'd taken the previous year. I also knew that some outfitters were importing larger European red deer. I wanted only a pure Scottish red deer, even though I knew these had small, spindly antlers that could not compare with those on the red deer from Bulgaria, for example.

Mike and I climbed the hills and saw only a few females and small stags that afternoon. It was interesting to see him pull out his long telescope, lie on the ground, and use parts of his body to steady the instrument.

"We Scots like to do things the traditional way," Mike said, when I asked why he didn't use a binocular or spotting scope on a stand.

After checking the hills near his home, Mike drove me to an area where he said a good stag had been seen regularly just before dark. We hunted there until last light, then returned to my hotel after seeing only a few more females and small stags.

We saw only young stags again the next morning, so Peter suggested we try hunting a feral goat that afternoon and come back that evening to look for his big stag. These goats, according to the *SCI All-Time Record Book of Trophy Animals,* have been running free in Scotland for a thousand years or more and are thought to have originated when bezoar ibex from the Middle East were released there. Stir the genes of feral domestic goats into the pool with the bezoar goats over many generations, and you have a unique breed. The same herds can have billies with horns like ibex as well as horns that look like any domestic goat's, and strange combinations of both types.

It didn't take long for us to find a herd and stalk it within two hundred yards. I wanted to shoot the largest billy from there. It was an easy shot for my 7mm Remington Magnum, I told Mike in whispers. But he wanted me to get closer, so we crawled for thirty or forty more yards and stopped when the goats started looking in our direction. I was ready to shoot, but Mike shook his head. After a minute or two, the goats started feeding again, and we crawled some more. This time I didn't look to Mike for permission to shoot, and the billy dropped in its tracks. Mike's reluctance to allow me to shoot at any distance over a hundred yards was typical of Scottish stalkers, I learned later. Other hunters have told

me their stalkers also wanted them to get very close before shooting.

After photographing my goat and taking it back to Mike's place, we returned to the spot where we hoped to find the big stag. When it appeared at dusk, only about fifteen minutes before it would be too dark to shoot, we made a short stalk, and I shot it from about 150 yards. I was happy to see it was a true Scottish deer and not something imported from the Continent.

Next on my agenda in this three-country European hunt was England, where I would be hunting non-indigenous deer. It was 11 October when I arrived in London. James Pedder helped me get my rifle through Customs and introduced me to my driver. Three hours later, we reached Devon, where I asked the driver to take me to Brickleigh Castle. The first Alwards to reach North America had come from this area. I couldn't go inside the castle, but I did take some photographs for family history that my brother Ford and I eventually would publish. As I walked around the little chapel on the castle grounds, it was interesting to think that my ancestors had worshiped there more than four hundred years earlier.

About an hour after leaving Brickleigh, we stopped in front of an old home made of hand-cut stone, where John Willet, my guide in that area, lived with his wife. I had taken a hog deer in Australia in 1988, but I wanted a buck with larger antlers. England's hog deer were imported from India and Pakistan, as are the hog deer now found in Australia. The hunt took all of three hours, and I collected a fine buck with John's help. My driver then took me to Welling by Somerset that evening, where I stayed at Greenham Hall.

The next morning we drove another three and a half hours to the Woburn Estate northwest of London, where I met Kenneth Whitehead at the Bedford Arms Hotel. Whitehead—one of the few true authorities on the deer of the world—was eighty-four then, but in very good health.

The estate had a palatial castle with beautiful, well-kept grounds where several varieties of deer wandered at will. According to Whitehead, the original Duke of Bedford began importing live deer from all over the world to England in the early 1900s. Some of them, such as the Reeve's muntjac and water deer from China, escaped, multiplied, and spread far from Woburn. Others have always been kept in large enclosures. I hunted with Whitehead for two days and took a muntjac, a water deer, a Sika deer, a Soay sheep, and a Père David deer. What we did might best be described as "collecting." In 1992, however, this was the only place in the world where some of those species could be taken.

Jack Hegarty had arrived in Madrid a few hours before I did on 14 October, and he was waiting for me at the airport when I cleared Customs outside Spain's capital. I was glad to see him. Jack and I had become good friends while we were trying to get our video company going, and he would be traveling with me as an observer during the two weeks I hunted in Spain. (Jack's wife had died in an accident the year before, and I had invited him to join me in Spain to help forget the tragedy.) With Jack was my guide Giuseppe from Cazatur.

We began my hunt by driving to the Pyrenees, on Spain's northeastern border with France, and getting rooms in a town called Benasque. A gamekeeper joined us after breakfast the next morning and drove us to a hunting area nearby, where we picked up a local wildlife officer. (All hunters in this area were required to be accompanied by someone from the government.) After a long drive to the top of the steep, rocky mountains, we left the vehicle and went off on foot. We spotted chamois right away, but they were so far off it was hard to judge their small, hooked horns. We spent the next forty-five minutes or so trying to get a closer look but eventually decided there were no good bucks in the group. An hour after lunch, we found another small group of chamois feeding near a patch of snow. They hadn't seen us, and the wind was right, so we were able to climb higher than they were and stay out of sight as we came around the mountain. It wasn't long before we ran out of cover, though.

The gamekeeper and I sat down and, with our binoculars, spent a few minutes trying to decide which buck I should shoot. There was no way we could get closer without spooking the entire herd. It would be a long, uphill shot at a small animal, but I thought I could make it. I found a good rest for my rifle, put the cross hairs on the buck's spine, and tried to get off the best shot I could. I hit the buck, but it began running uphill anyway. When it stopped to look down at us, I shot it again. This time the chamois dropped, then started sliding down the slope and over a small cliff. When it hit a boulder, it flew high in the air, crashed into the rocks, and continued sliding. It didn't come to a stop until it was about fifty yards from us.

My first thought was that it must have broken its horns in that spectacular fall, but they were intact. After taking photos, my guides skinned the buck for a full mount and carried it down to our vehicle. It was dark when we reached my hotel, and all I wanted to do was eat something and go right to bed. Unfortunately, it is almost impossible to find a restaurant that will serve dinner before 8 or 9 P.M. in that part of Spain. While Jack and I waited to go eat, the gamekeeper measured the horns of my chamois under both the C.I.C. (the major European hunting organization) and the Safari Club International measuring systems. My chamois ranked close to the middle of the SCI record book, and would have qualified for a C.I.C. silver medal if I had entered it.

We slept late the next morning. I wasn't scheduled to hunt a Cantabrian chamois in the western part of the country until 19 October, three days later. When we were unable to get an earlier starting date, we joined Giuseppe in driving a couple of hours into the mountains to visit one of his friends. We could have stayed in the hotel, but we wanted to see the countryside. The next day we left for a small mountain town called Ruesga and checked into a hotel. Jack had not felt well

all day and went straight to bed. Our room was so cold he slept with his clothes on.

Meanwhile, Giuseppe and I had dinner with one of Giuseppe's former clients. Afterward, before we went upstairs, he had the hotel make a special tea for Jack from local herbs. He said Jack would feel better in the morning after drinking it. The remedy apparently worked, because Jack felt fine the next morning and was able to accompany Giuseppe and me to a place in the mountains where the local hunting club was staging a *monteria* (wild boar drive).

For a Spanish hunter, *monterias* are important social events. The hunters dress from head to toe in loden green hunting togs with matching hats and gloves. Meat is barbecued and cocktails are served after the hunt. Someone usually plays a guitar. Sometimes professional dancers are hired to perform for the guests. The hunting event that most reminds me of its colorful ceremonies would be an English fox hunt. In a *monteria,* however, the hunters are stationed along openings and fire breaks, and dogs and their handlers move through the brush toward them, trying to push the boars to the guns.

Each shooter is assigned a limited shooting zone and can shoot every boar that passes through it. The shooting isn't easy, because the fire lanes usually are less than twenty to thirty feet wide, and the boars literally race across them. The hunter's only warning comes when he hears a boar crashing through the brush toward him. He will have less than a second or two to find the running animal

The author and his party stop for a rest while hunting in northern Spain. Note the village far below them, as seen through a hole in the rock. Spain.

The author's southeastern Spanish ibex. Spain.

in his sights, shoot, and hope that he has led the animal enough.

Although Jack and I were only observers, we enjoyed watching the *monteria* and the post-hunt festivities. I was surprised to find that many of the Spaniards spoke very good English; then I learned some of them had attended college in the United States.

Afterward, we drove another three hours to our hunting area and spent the night at the gamekeeper's home. There were no hotels nearby. We were up at daylight and hiked a long way, following a brook up a narrow gorge. It was a beautiful place, and we kept climbing higher. After we gained some elevation, we climbed to a ridge and spotted some chamois almost as soon as we started glassing. Unfortunately, we spooked them before I could get into rifle range. It was hard to tell at that distance, but at least one of them might have been a good buck.

We glassed until just before sundown without seeing another chamois and returned to the gamekeeper's home after dark. All my life I've heard about "sunny Spain," but so far I've never seen anyone write about how cold it can get at night in a rural home. An hour or so before I had to get up in the morning, I put on more clothes and crawled back into bed. I couldn't go back to sleep and was awake when the gamekeeper got up. We were climbing another canyon at first light. As soon as we gained some elevation, we sat down with our binoculars and started glassing the opposite slope as the sun was lighting it up. We found several bucks right

away, but they were at least eight hundred yards away. Crossing that deep canyon took about an hour, but the bucks were gone when we got to the place we expected to see them again.

While we were sitting there, glassing another canyon, Giuseppe and the gamekeeper were talking in Spanish. Suddenly Giuseppe grew angry. When I asked him what was wrong, he said the gamekeeper had told him the reason we were seeing so few animals was that the manager of the reserve was selling illegal hunts. Soon after that the sky grew dark, and it started to rain—a drizzle at first, then a real downpour. We soon were soaked and cold, and Giuseppe's temper mounted.

When we returned to the house, the manager was there, and Giuseppe and he were soon arguing loudly. Suddenly Giuseppe said we were leaving. I can't describe how I felt, but I certainly wasn't happy about cutting my hunt short. Instead of driving all the way back to Madrid, we stopped in a small town and checked into a hotel just after 10 P.M. Our rooms had no heat, and we were so cold we got very little sleep for the second night in a row.

Disappointed was not the word for how I felt by the time we reached Madrid at noon the next day, and I asked to be reimbursed for that part of my hunt. I felt better when Giuseppe told me they would try to get me another permit and take me to another chamois area after I'd hunted the two ibex I wanted.

That afternoon I rented a car, and Rodrigo Fajardo (my guide in 1991), Jack, and I drove south from Madrid to a town called Bailén, where we spent the night in a heated hotel. On this leg of the trip I would be hunting Ronda and southeastern Spanish ibex, which scientists say are the same subspecies of Spanish goat as the Beceite ibex. The SCI record book separates what it calls the "Mediterranean race" into three categories for record-keeping purposes. There is a good reason for this. There are distinct differences among the three animals, especially in the shape of their horns.

We left Bailén at 4:30 the next morning and drove three and a half hours to the Ronda Mountains, where we met the reserve's gamekeeper, who would be my guide. After getting rooms in a local hotel, we changed into hunting clothes and left the hotel on foot to look for ibex. We found ibex tracks and droppings, and even saw a few female ibex and young billies that afternoon, but we saw no mature males. I was exhausted, and my legs were hurting when we got back to the hotel after dark.

We climbed the mountain again the next morning, but instead of starting out from the hotel, we drove to where we could hunt another major system of ridges and canyons. By noon, I was getting discouraged. My hunting permit allowed me to hunt in the reserve for only two days, and it would expire in only a few hours. Around 3 P.M., however, Rodrigo looked behind us and caught a quick glimpse of a male ibex crossing a ridge, heading toward us. Something or someone had spooked it, and it wasn't aware we were there. Only Rodrigo had

seen it, but it was a very good male, he assured us. While the ibex was crossing the canyon, we all quickly got ready. I found a steady rest for my rifle and sat down. When the ibex finally came into sight, it was climbing a peak to the right of us. I found it in my scope and squeezed the trigger when everything felt right. It was closer to three hundred yards than 250, and I didn't hear my bullet strike the animal before it was out of sight. I was certain I'd hit it, though.

We spent a good fifteen minutes or more trying to find that ibex, but all we found were tracks where I'd last seen it. There was no blood. I was ready to give up when the gamekeeper said something in Spanish. My ibex had died in a ravine about fifty yards from where we expected to find it. It was a good one. Nearly ten years later, its 25⅝-inch horns would rank number seven in the *SCI All-Time Record Book of Trophy Animals.*

Rodrigo and the gamekeeper decided that we should get off the mountain by going downhill in the opposite direction from where we had left the car. It took us two hours to reach a narrow mountain trail. Rodrigo and the gamekeeper left us there with my ibex, and he walked two or three miles to get the car. Jack and I were wondering whether we should build a fire to stay warm when we heard the vehicle coming to pick us up. It was long after dark when we reached the hotel. I was exhausted, and the muscles in my legs felt as if someone had been pulling on them. I had a permit that allowed me to hunt a southeastern Spanish ibex for the next two days, but I was too tired and sore. I told Rodrigo to take a day off. There was no way I could get up and go hunting the next morning.

Instead, Jack and I spent the day touring the Rock of Gibraltar, which was only about ninety minutes from our hotel. We took a ferry across to Africa and back and did some shopping. At 7:30 P.M. Rodrigo drove us to Granada. The next morning at 6 o'clock we drove into the mountains and met the local gamekeeper. An hour later, the gamekeeper parked his Land Rover near the mountain's summit, and we went off on foot. It didn't take long for the gamekeeper to find the ibex. There were half a dozen of them on a rocky slope six hundred yards away, but we couldn't get closer without them seeing us. The best plan was to wait to see what the ibex would do. We waited for two hours, and the ibex hadn't moved more than one hundred yards in all that time. Most of them were bedded when we ate lunch. I kept sneaking a peek at them with my binoculars and finally decided we had to do something. Those ibex might stay there until the next day if nothing bothered them.

Leaving Jack and the gamekeeper's son, the gamekeeper and I tried to close the distance to the ibex by working our way around a rocky ledge. Just as we had feared, the animals spotted us and ran until they were out of sight. We were lucky, though. While we were trying to find them again, we found another herd that hadn't been disturbed. Again, this new herd spotted us before we could get within range.

We had spent the last four hours unsuccessfully stalking two different herds of ibex. We had very little daylight left, and I was certain we would be wasting our time if we stayed until dark. I was making plans to return a few months later and try again when we heard rocks rolling in the canyon below us. Rodrigo spotted them first: a male with a female, climbing toward a ridge. Again, it was too far to risk a shot. When they moved into a gully and were briefly out of sight, Rodrigo and I hurried to get closer. When the ibex reappeared across the canyon, I got ready for one of the longest shots of my life. I held the cross hairs of my 7mm Remington Magnum's scope slightly over the billy's back and shot. The animal bucked, but then it started running as if it had never been hit. I was working the bolt on my rifle when the sound of my bullet striking the billy reached us. My second shot killed it.

The sun was going down when we reached the animal, and our cameras were in the packs we had left with Jack and the gamekeeper's son. It was dark when we started off the mountain with the head and cape, 9 P.M. when we finally reached the truck, and 11 P.M. when we got back to the hotel. It had been a long, hard day.

The next day was 26 October, our thirty-fifth wedding anniversary, and I called Janice. I'd missed a lot of family celebrations since starting this quest to collect the world's major game species, but she always supported me.

We were back in Madrid at 1 o'clock that afternoon. It was Monday, and Jack and I weren't due to leave for our homes until 7:30 Wednesday morning, when Eduardo said he had obtained another Cantabrian chamois permit. It would take some luck and a lot of driving, but maybe I could take one before leaving Spain. This time I would be accompanied by Jose Cavestamy, my new guide.

Jose, Jack, and I left Madrid at 5 o'clock that afternoon and didn't stop until we reached a very small town in the mountains where I would be hunting. At 7 A.M., the four of us—the local gamekeeper, Jose, Jack, and I—were hiking up a mountain trail. Compared to where I had hunted chamois earlier, this was much easier going.

By 9 A.M., I was stalking a lone chamois we had spotted from a half-mile away. We were almost to the spot from which we figured I could shoot when the buck spotted us and ran off. It didn't go far before stopping, though. My first shot put it down. My companions were impressed! I was happy to have that chamois. It not only completed the list of animals I had gone to Europe to hunt but was a good trophy. At about fifty pounds, the Cantabrian chamois is the smallest of all chamois, and its horns are comparatively short and slim. Its 7⅛-inch horns, however, would later rank number twenty-one in its category in the *SCI All-Time Record Book of Trophy Animals.*

It was raining when we came off the mountain with the little buck, but we decided we could make our flights in the morning if we left for Madrid right away. We got fewer than five hours' sleep that night, but Jack and I were home the next day.

It had been a hectic three weeks. I have no idea how many miles I traveled across Europe in those three weeks, or how many miles I walked. It had been a great hunt. But I was glad it was over.

FOUR CONTINENTS, TEN COUNTRIES, 1993

At its 1993 convention in Nevada, Safari Club International honored me with its Humanitarian Award. For several years I had been donating the cost of the airfare to send underprivileged young people to Africa to hunt. The popular program was the brainchild of SCI past president Vern Edewaard of Michigan. A month earlier I had obtained the first nonresident woods bison tag the Northwest Territories' Department of Renewable Resources had ever issued. I asked Brian West to go along. Brian works at my lodge and has always been a good companion on a trip.

The wind was blowing, and so much snow was falling when Brian and I left Havelock on 6 March that we thought the airport at Moncton might cancel our flight. We were able to leave for Edmonton, though, and spent the night there before flying on to Yellowknife. Jerome and Halina Knap's Canada North Outfitting had arranged my hunt. Bill Tait, who represents the company in Yellowknife, met us at the airport, and with him was Bob Lloyd, a taxidermist from Red Deer, Alberta, who would go with us on the hunt.

Bob had a half-ton pickup truck, and he drove Brian and me to Fort Providence, where we checked into the Snowshoe Inn. That evening my two Indian guides met us at the motel, and we discussed my hunt. They had taken supplies to our camp that morning and had left behind our cook Johnny and wildlife officer Tom Chown to get things ready for us.

We stopped by the game department's office to get my special license and tag the next morning. By 11 o'clock, we were on the road in two vehicles. Ten miles north of Fort Providence we parked the trucks and went off on three snowmobiles. Brian and I each rode behind a guide, and Bob drove a Skidoo towing a sled. It was very cold—minus 4 degrees Fahrenheit or so—but we were all wearing insulated snowmobile suits, so it wasn't too bad. The only problem was that it was hard to move around in that bulky clothing.

It was a two-hour drive through brush and woods and across open areas and frozen lakes to our camp—two small but comfortable insulated buildings made of plywood. Just as we reached it, snow started falling. It felt good to get inside and warm up again. It was still snowing an hour later, but we went out and drove around on the snowmobiles, looking for bison. It soon was snowing so hard we couldn't see, so we returned to camp, had supper, and talked about the animal I was hunting.

Only about 1,500 woods bison were known to exist in 1922, when Canadian wildlife authorities created a park in northern Alberta and Northwest Territories to protect them. To stock the park, they captured more than six thousand plains bison in central Alberta and released them in the park with resident woods bison. Over the next six years the transplanted plains bison not only contributed the wrong genes to the herds but introduced tuberculosis and brucellosis. When the authorities finally realized in the mid-1930s what they had done, the park's herd had increased to twelve thousand animals, and the pure woods bison no longer existed—or so everyone thought. In 1957, however, authorities found a few woods bison, separated from the hybrid herds by ninety miles of muskeg. They checked these animals and found them to be free of the plains bison's genes and diseases. Six years later, in 1963, they released eighteen of these rare bison into the newly created Mackenzie Bison Sanctuary on the northwest side of Great Slave Lake.

By 1992, those eighteen animals had increased to more than two thousand. Canadian wildlife authorities have carefully watched this purebred herd, stationing people along the river to keep the herds from mixing when the river freezes over. Hunting helps keep the two herds from crossing. It also raises the money needed to manage and protect them.

Brian and I began the hunt in the morning on sleds behind our guides' snowmobiles, with Bob on the Skidoo, towing an empty sled. An hour later, we spotted our first herd of more than a hundred animals. It was a sight to see, but there were no old bulls, and we left them alone. It was very cold when we crossed a wide, frozen lake an hour later

and drove to another area our guides said the bulls were using. At noon we stopped, built a fire, and ate lunch before leaving on the machines again. The few bulls we saw didn't stand around and stare at us, as I've seen other bison do. These were wary and wild animals, and they avoided openings. They would run into the willow thickets as soon as they saw or heard us.

After catching a glimpse of a very large bull in a herd of ten to fifteen other bulls, my guide Edward and I spent an hour following them on foot but never caught up to them. Once they were spooked, these bison ran for long distances! Next we found another big bull with three smaller ones, but they ran off before we could approach them. At 5:30 P.M. we left the area and had a very cold two-hour ride back to camp.

Tom, the wildlife officer, thought we should keep hunting where we had seen the bulls, so we left at 6:30 the next morning to try it again. All we saw before noon were glimpses of dark-colored shapes running through the willows. Woods bison were hard to approach, and it also was nearly impossible to get a good look at their horns. For a record-book animal, the size of the animal isn't important. It's the horns that count, and bison horns need to be thick and long. Those on many older bulls are worn or broken off.

Edward and I followed one herd's fresh tracks on foot for two hours, but we spooked the herd before we ever saw the animals. Around 5 P.M., as we were crossing the lake again, Edward spotted six bison in the willows, and we immediately altered our course to get downwind of them. We parked the machines and walked back to where we had seen them. I had taken off my snowmobile gear and was wearing white coveralls for the stalk. (It was fine as long as I kept moving. I immediately felt the cold whenever I stopped.) We got quite close to the little herd, but we could only see one animal at a time and couldn't tell which was largest. We knew all six were bulls, but we never could get a good look at their horns. When they began moving away from us, we went on our knees in the snow, moving from bush to bush after them. My coveralls did little to keep my legs from getting wet and cold.

It was close to sundown when we caught up with the herd and found an old bull moving across a small opening. The only horn I could see was thick, heavy, and long. I put the cross hairs on the bull's shoulder and shot, and it surprised me by collapsing in its tracks. My assessment of the horn I'd seen was correct: It was heavy and long. The other horn, however, was worn down and three or four inches shorter. My first reaction was disappointment, but that quickly left. I had taken a rare animal in fair chase, an animal found in very few collections. While Edward called the others on the radio to tell them I'd taken my bull, I took a closer look at it. Jack Schwabland, author of the text in the *SCI All-Time Record Book of Trophy Animals,* wrote that the woods bison is darker, larger, and warier than the plains variety, and this hunt had certainly proved him correct.

Brian, Bob, Tom, and the other guide drove up on their snowmobiles a few minutes later. After Tom took a blood sample and inspected the carcass, we took photos, and the three men started skinning the animal, using the lights of their snowmobiles. While the guides and Bob were working, Brian and I made a fire and tried to stay warm. It was 10 P.M. before we had loaded the meat, hide, and head on Bob's sled, and another two hours before we were back in camp. It had been a long day, and everyone was cold and close to exhaustion, but Bob and Edward brought the bison's cape into the cabin and worked until 2:30 A.M. to prepare it for salting and drying. Just before I went to bed, I had to step outside and was struck by the beauty of the northern lights. I had seen the phenomenon many times before, but I have never ceased to be awed by it.

We slept late the next morning, then packed our gear and boxed up some of the bison's meat and its cape and horns. In Fort Providence I paid the trophy fee and received an export permit. Bob took the horns and cape back to Edmonton to mount for me, and Bill Tait showed Brian and me around Yellowknife. It had been a tough hunt, but I had enjoyed it. Even though they were not used to trophy hunting, our guides knew what they were doing and were pleasant to be with. Every time I see the mount of that bison's head it brings back memories of a great hunt. The year after my hunt, authorities closed the woods bison hunt in Northwest Territories for a few years.

Two weeks after returning from Fort Providence, I left home on an airline ticket

The author's wood bison was one of the first in recent times taken by a trophy hunter. Northwest Territories.

The author and his guide, "Hawkeye," with the author and his Himalayan tahr. Nepal.

valid for around the world with two side trips. In Bangkok I spent three days with a fellow I called Sonny instead of trying to pronounce his Thai name. I'd met him while hunting polar bear two years earlier. We then hooked up with Chuck and Karen Bazzy and Carl Ross from the United States. Sonny showed me around Bangkok, and Chuck and Karen and I took a tour on Bangkok's busy, crowded river. There were people living on boats and in houses on stilts in the water. Many of them were selling things from their boats. It was very hot—at least 85 degrees Fahrenheit—and humid. The sights, smells, and sounds were all foreign to us, and very interesting.

From Bangkok, Chuck, Karen, Carl, and I flew three hours on Thailand Airlines to Nepal, where the daughter of T. J. Thapa, the owner of Nepal Wildlife Adventures, met us in Katmandu. I had corresponded with her while she completed the paperwork for our rifles and ammunition, and it was good to meet her in person. She took us to Nepal's wildlife office, where authorities issued our hunting permits for blue sheep, Himalayan tahr, and Indian muntjac and then brought us to our hotel.

Blue sheep really isn't a sheep, but it isn't a goat, either. (Scientists call it a "pseudosheep.") It is also called bharal. Safari Club recognizes three categories: Chinese bharal, dwarf bharal, and Himalayan bharal, which I would be hunting on this trip. Blue sheep in Nepal are found up to 21,500 feet, higher than any other game animal in the world.

That afternoon we hired a taxi for a quick tour of the city of half a million people. It was like stepping back in time. The streets were jammed with carts and bicycles and lined with stalls. Just about anything you could imagine finding in Asia was on sale, including hashish, but there was nothing that interested me. Men ran alongside the taxi, hawking goods. Holy men, sacred cows, beggars, and dirty young kids roamed the streets. We saw crumbling shanties, crowded bazaars, and elaborate pagoda-style architecture. Then there was the traffic, the noise, and the smell of sewage and exhaust fumes. It was impossible to escape this atmosphere.

I am glad we took the time to see Katmandu, but I can only describe it as a poor, dirty, backward, Third-World place. What I did not realize was how extremely volatile its politics were. Just three years earlier, angry street demonstrations and labor strikes had forced King Birenda[1] to proclaim a new constitution that vastly reduced his own powers in what had been the world's last absolute monarchy. A year later, in 1991, a new government was formed. While I was there in 1993, that government was on its last legs and ultimately collapsed the next year. Today, I'm told, Maoist communists are trying to take control.

---

1. King Birenda, with Queen Aishwarya, Prince Nirajan, and four others, were shot to death in 1999 by Crown Prince Dipendra, who then shot and killed himself. News reports say the prince killed everyone in his immediate family over the queen's alleged objection to a bride he had chosen.

On 6 April we flew seventy-five minutes in a helicopter to a small village, where two hunters from Alaska who had finished their hunts were waiting to fly back to Katmandu in the chopper. Both had taken blue sheep. Although we had only a few minutes to talk, Chuck, Carl, and I pumped them for information about what we could expect on our hunts.

The village of Dharapken was at 9,500 feet, and we purposely spent the day at a lodge there to acclimate ourselves to the elevation before moving higher. The next day Carl, Chuck, and I went off in three directions on foot with our guides. There were no roads of any kind within two days' walk, but we found people living and trying to subsist everywhere in the valleys and mountains. This was my introduction to the Himalayas, the roof of the world.

Our party consisted of thirteen men, led by the main guide, a man I called Hawkeye. The party included an assistant guide, who carried my rifle and pack, and ten Sherpas, who carried all our gear in large baskets on their backs, using tumplines on their foreheads to help steady their loads. The weight of each man's basket must have been considerable, because they were carrying four tents, our sleeping bags, cooking gear, and all our food, including two live chickens that they carried for two weeks. The chickens provided fresh eggs every day.

Our first camp was at about 11,500 feet at a place called Phagune Khola. It was in a basin surrounded by mountains that rose at least five thousand feet above us. While the men were setting up camp, Hawkeye and I sat down with our binoculars and began looking for sheep. We saw nothing that day or the next, but on the third afternoon—from our third camp—we found a large herd of sheep about two miles up the valley from us. It was too late in the day to try to stalk them, so we made plans to go after them in the morning.

We left before daybreak and climbed to a fifteen-thousand-foot, snow-covered pass. We crossed into the basin where we had seen the sheep the night before. The sheep were still there, but it was impossible to get close to them because there was nothing to hide our stalk. I didn't have a range finder, so I could only guess how far away they were, but I decided to try a long shot anyway. There were no boulders or logs to use as a rest, so I set my rifle on a pack and sat down. There were thirty to forty sheep, and it took a minute or two to decide which was the best ram. When I found it, I waited until my breathing was normal, then held the cross hairs a bit above the ram's back and squeezed the trigger. I wasn't surprised when I missed. The mud my bullet kicked up told me the ram was farther away than I thought it was. When the ram stopped to look back at us, I held higher and missed again. Two shots later, I killed it in its tracks. Hawkeye and the two men who had come with us cheered. It had been a very long shot. The ram's horns, like those of a tur, were only average at 22⅜ inches (they later would rank number forty-seven in the SCI record book).

I was glad my blue sheep hunt was over. Hunting at that altitude is hard work. Even though we went up in stages, human lungs do not function well at anything over thirteen thousand to fourteen thousand feet. I had headaches daily and was short of breath all the time I was there.

After we photographed my ram, Hawkeye signaled the men we had left behind, and they came up to us and packed the animal back to our camp. It was 4:30 P.M. before we ate our first meal that day. While I was eating, the men took down the tents. The wind was growing stronger, and they wanted to get at least one thousand feet lower that evening.

We made our next camp just before dark, and while I slept the men stayed up and smoked the sheep meat over the campfire. We packed up again the next morning and hiked for six hours down a long valley and over a couple of ridges before making our next camp at a place called Kang. This new area was steeper and rockier. High on the cliffs above us we would find Himalayan tahr, Hawkeye said. I had taken a tahr in New Zealand, so I knew what type of terrain the animals would seek—the roughest and steepest they could find.

We moved our camp to the top of the mountain the next morning and spent the next few nights there. One night the wind was so strong I thought it would blow my tent away, and when I went outside to answer the call of nature I had trouble standing straight. Being so high made hunting easier, however, because it allowed us to walk the tops of the ridges and glass across and into the canyons. We spotted several tahr a long way off but were unable to get close enough to shoot before they got onto the cliffs. The place was hard to get around in, and it was dangerous. Finally, after six days, we spotted a good male tahr across a rugged canyon. There was no way to get any closer—it was three hundred yards or more—so I found a good rest and held the cross hairs on the spine. The tahr was running when the sound of my bullet hitting the animal came back across the canyon. The ram ran a few yards and fell, then rolled down the canyon. It was out of sight before I could work another round into my 7mm Remington Magnum.

Hawkeye and I had to slide down our side of the mountain perhaps a thousand feet through brush and snow to reach the tahr. It had fallen off a cliff into a narrow creek and had gone over a twenty-five-foot waterfall before stopping in a small pool of water. It was a beautiful place to take pictures, but it was a terrible place to reach. My tahr's 12⅞-inch horns would later rank number twenty in the *SCI All-Time Record Book of Trophy Animals*, but I didn't care. I'd taken both of the animals for which I'd gone to Nepal, and I was relieved that my hunt was over. I had been so tired when I got out of my sleeping bag that morning that I had considered calling off the hunt.

Carl got to the lodge before us, and he also had taken his blue sheep and tahr. I still wanted to try to take an Indian muntjac, a small deer with little horns that grow from tall, hair-covered pedicels. There weren't many muntjac, but Hawkeye said we might find them along the river near the lodge, and we did. Just before dark that evening, a little buck stepped out of the brush and into an opening we were watching, and I shot it. It was an old male with a representative head, and I was glad to have taken it so quickly.

Carl and I waited two more days for Chuck and Karen to return to the lodge. Chuck had taken his sheep and tahr and spent another day looking for a muntjac without seeing one. On 22 April we flew back to Katmandu in the same helicopter that had taken us to the village. The next day I arranged to take an early tour by plane over Mount Everest, and later I flew back to Bangkok. Chuck, Karen, and Carl had an early flight back to the States, but I was able to spend some more time with Sonny. The next day I left on an eleven-hour, nonstop flight to Johannesburg.

I was in good shape for a man of fifty-five, but this had been a physically grueling hunt in the Himalayas. I was looking forward to being in Africa again, where the hunting usually is less demanding.

It was 2:00 A.M. when I arrived in Johannesburg from Katmandu, after spending all night in an airplane. I only had four hours before I needed to catch another flight to Kimberley, where I planned to collect an aoudad (Barbary sheep), but I needed to take a shower and rest up, if only for an hour or two. I was asleep within minutes after checking into my room. When the front desk called to wake me, I had been sleeping so soundly that it took a second or two for me to realize where I was. After a quick shower, I called a taxi and caught the 6 A.M. flight to Kimberley to meet Brent Hill. Hill was a professional hunter for Mkuze Falls

Safaris, a company with which I had hunted during previous trips to South Africa. We had a two-hour drive to the game ranch where we would hunt.

Free-ranging, truly wild aoudad are found only in North Africa, but they have been introduced to game ranches all over the world, including South Africa. I'd taken an aoudad in Texas several years earlier, but I wanted one with better horns for my collection. We saw several males in a small herd that evening, but I decided to see if we could find a larger one. I have no idea what time Brett went to his bed in the room we shared. I fell asleep with my clothes on as soon as I reached mine.

I shot a big male aoudad from a herd of about thirty animals the next morning, then spent the rest of the day resting. The next morning I flew back to Johannesburg and checked into the Airport Holiday Inn again. The day after that, 28 April, I was on an airplane heading to Nairobi, where I had arranged for someone to keep my rifle overnight. I spent that night in the Nairobi Hilton downtown and caught the 8:30 A.M. Ethiopian Airways flight to Addis Ababa.

I had spent a month hunting with Col. Negussie Eshete and his Rocky Valley Safaris company in 1989, and I immediately spotted him when I stepped off the plane. We spent the rest of the day talking about that earlier safari and buying my licenses at the game department. At noon the next day, Negussie and I, along with a government game scout named Nicole, were flying to Gambela, where Negussie had sent the vehicles a few days earlier. Nicole would travel with us throughout the safari.

The heat hit us like a slap in the face when we stepped off the airplane at Gambela, a city of 180,000 people and the capital of the Ethiopian state of the same name. After lunch, we left town and started driving south, following the tracks of other vehicles. There were no roads as such. Negussie simply drove in the general direction of our destination. Four hours after leaving Gambela, we finally arrived at the Gilo River, where we set up camp in the dark. Negussie thought it was fortunate that we had been stuck "only" once on the way there.

We had planned to cross the river and hunt along the Sudan border some thirty-five miles away, but the river was running too high and too fast to cross it. Negussie briefly considered having the men build a raft that would take his truck over, but he quickly abandoned that idea. It would be a long walk back to Gambela if something happened and our second vehicle broke down. We could only hunt on our side of the river, which we did for a week. The only animals I took were an Abyssinian bohor reedbuck (a medium-size antelope with forward-pointing horns), a tiang (an antelope related to South Africa's bontebok and blesbok), and a serval (a twenty-pound, catlike predator). I had hoped to take six species, but we never could get away from all the people who were living along the river. Negussie said the reason the game was so scarce was that many of those people had rifles and were poaching game and selling the meat. We

traveled long distances, and even tried making a spike camp under the trees and spending the night out, but the game in that area simply had been shot out.

On 7 May we gave up and drove back to Gambela. From there we hunted two days along the Baro River, where I shot a Nile bushbuck. On 19 May Negussie sent the vehicles ahead, and we flew back to Addis Ababa. Soon after that we traveled to Mount Kaka, where I hunted for four days at twelve thousand feet for a mountain nyala. I had taken a good bull with Negussie in 1989, so I wasn't too disappointed when rain and fog forced us off the mountain. In fact, I was happy to get to lower ground where it was warmer.

Trophy hunting requires a lot of traveling from place to place to reach different habitats, and all too frequently the best-laid plans can go wrong. An airline cancels a flight. The people who were supposed to meet me never show up. Rain turns the roads into bottomless mud. This time our problem was with one of Negussie's trucks. We had planned to spend the next day hunting, but we spent it in Awash instead. When we learned it would take several days to get the truck parts we needed, Negussie and I, along with three of his men, piled into the Land Rover and went hunting. With five people and all our gear, we were crowded and uncomfortable.

I was looking forward to sleeping in a real bed, but the only "hotel" in the small town where we spent the night was best described as a horse stall with a dirty, lumpy mattress. Safari Club International's founder, C. J. McElroy, in *McElroy Hunts Africa,* told of choosing to sleep on the floor in an Ethiopian hotel because his bed was infested with bedbugs. I guess I should have been thankful I had none in my bed.

The farther north toward the Red Sea we drove, the more arid the terrain became. When we finally stopped and built a camp under a small tree, it was in a place called Serdo. I'd seen all types of habitat in Ethiopia on this trip, from twelve-thousand-foot mountains to marshes and rivers, and now we were in this lonely desert spot. The place had no shortage of wildlife, though. We started seeing antelope right away, and I shot a very good gazelle with 10⅝-inch horns. It ranks number four in the Isabelline gazelle category of the *SCI All-Time Record Book of Trophy Animals.*

After returning to Awash, we drove to Harar Province, near Ethiopia's border with Somalia, and hunted for two days until I shot a Harar dik-dik with 2⅜-inch horns. I was happy to have it. As it often happens with dik-diks, I couldn't see its little horns when I shot it. It was a good trophy, though, and still ranks number eight in the SCI record book. We spent nearly all the next day driving toward Ethiopia's border with Somalia, where I collected a Phillips dik-dik. When we returned to Awash, Negussie sent the vehicles on to Addis Ababa, and he and I caught a commuter flight.

It took four hours to get out of the airport in Addis because of the strict security. Although we were arriving, not departing, we had to go through the x-ray machines four times. Negussie talked with one of the officers, who reported that an airplane had been hijacked somewhere, and the officials were on high alert, taking no chances.

One of the animals I really wanted on this trip was a giant forest hog, the largest wild swine on earth and the toughest of all to hunt. The largest boars can reach six hundred pounds and stand more than three feet tall at the shoulder. Before leaving home, I had arranged with Negussie to hunt one, but he hadn't been able to get the necessary permit before I reached Addis Ababa. Only one man could issue it, and he was out of town, so the first thing we did after I arrived was to find him. Although he issued the paperwork, it wouldn't be valid until it was stamped by a wildlife officer in the district where I would be hunting. The officer wasn't in his village when we got there, so we spent the night in his village and tracked him down in the morning. Permit in hand, I was authorized to take a giant forest hog, if we could find one. There was one catch. Another wildlife officer would have to accompany us, and he lived in another village.

The guy was out in the bush when we reached his village and wasn't expected to return until later that day. While we waited, I looked around. Cows roamed among the thatched homes, and there were dogs and chickens running around everywhere. I suppose the younger villagers had seen very few (if any) white men, because the town's little kids followed me everywhere

The author made friends for life when he bought sugar cane for the local kids. Ethiopia.

Whenever the vehicle became stuck, which was often, everyone was enlisted to help, including any locals who happened to be nearby. Ethiopia.

I went. After an hour or two, I sent one of our trackers to a little market to buy some sugar cane for them. When he returned, we chopped it up into eight- to ten-inch pieces and passed it out to the kids. Grinning from ear to ear, they started sucking on it immediately.

It was about nine miles to where we wanted to hunt, but the road was a muddy mess after all the rain. Some of the ruts were two feet deep and filled with water. When we tried to drive up a little hill, the Land Rover slid off the road and sank to its doors. Even with everyone in the crew helping, we couldn't get it out.

Negussie hired some men who had come walking along to help us get our second Land Rover over the hill. Some pulled on a long rope tied to the vehicle's front bumper while the others pushed. The spinning wheels of the Land Rover threw mud at the men in the rear, and they were soon covered with it. Once the vehicle was moving on its own power and started going over the hill, they followed alongside, pushing and pulling when we needed it.

When we were less than two miles from our destination, the Land Rover's axle broke, and we had to leave it. We walked the rest of the way in the dark, taking only my carry-on bag. We reached the place where three or four families lived in round huts with thatched roofs. We had planned to set up our tents there, but they were back at the truck.

Negussie was able to talk a family into renting us their hut and moving into another family's. We all slept on the floor.

When I woke the next morning, I was surprised to see that someone had been using the hut's wall as a chalkboard. All the letters of the English alphabet had been carefully written on it, along with some *X*'s and *O*'s. Negussie had built an open fire inside the hut to warm it up when two small, totally naked kids came in and stared at us with round eyes. I shared an orange, the only food I had with me, with them. We were friends forever after that.

It was raining outside, and the ground around the huts was a slippery goo. Negussie sent one of the men to get help pulling our truck out and instructed him to have it ready for us, then to return to Addis Ababa to buy another axle for the Land Rover.

We spent the next three days in that area, hunting on foot in rain and mud. Finally we bumped into a small group of forest hogs. I shot the largest I could see as it was running into a thicket. That finished my hunt. Negussie rented three horses, and he and I, along with the wildlife officer, rode them back to the truck while the others walked. When we reached the village, all the kids I'd given sugar cane ran out, shouting, "The white man is coming" in their language.

Our truck was ready, and the man had returned from Addis Ababa with a new axle for the Land Rover. Negussie sent some men to install it while we returned to Addis Ababa in the truck. We got stuck only once on the trip back.

I had taken only half the species I wanted on this safari, so Negussie offered me a special price if I'd return in February for the rest. The Gilo River would be lower, he said, and we should be able to cross it and hunt along Sudan's border where the animals I wanted were found. I never returned to Ethiopia, though. I'd already booked all the hunts I could make in 1994, and Ethiopia's political situation was not improving.

When I landed in Moncton on 30 May, after sixty days of continuous traveling and hunting, wouldn't you know it? My rifle case wasn't with my luggage! It didn't show up until seven days later. I will always remember this Ethiopian safari, especially the hunt for that giant forest hog.

I was in the Customs line in Buenos Aires twenty days after returning from Ethiopia. Someone from Adventure Safaris was supposed to help me get a firearms permit, but I never saw him. When I carried my rifle over to the airport's police station, there was only one man who spoke a little English. I needed a special form from the Argentine embassy in Canada, he said. The more I talked with him over the next hour, the more his story changed. I finally said I would leave my rifle at the police station and try to straighten things out from my hotel. It was then he said he would issue me a permit for $400. I knew that was far too much for a bribe, and he eventually settled for $250. As it turned out, I didn't need a rifle permit for Argentina right away. When my guide Jose Sorido met me at my hotel the next morning, he said a major snowstorm had closed all the roads in the northwest, where I wanted to hunt a Northern huemul.

Instead, Jose and I made plans to leave for Paraguay the next day. To pass the time until then, I went to one of the city's many leather shops to be fitted for a leather jacket and vest. They were delivered to my hotel by 8 o'clock that evening. I don't know how it is now, but for a city with a population of sixteen million the streets seemed very safe. I felt easy walking anywhere I wanted.

By noon the next day, I was in Asunción, the capital of Paraguay, with Jose Sorido. It was winter south of the equator, but it was a pleasant 60 degrees Fahrenheit in the city. In the summer, Jose said, the average temperature is about 100 degrees Fahrenheit, but it can hit 120 degrees Fahrenheit or more.

I was supposed to fly in a small plane from Asunción to the ranch where we would be hunting, but all the planes were grounded because of heavy cloud cover. Jose was going there in his truck, so instead of waiting another day I decided to go with him. I was glad to see the countryside. The terrain was flat, and we passed very few villages along the way. According to Jose, there were six million people in that country, but nearly five million of them lived in Asunción. That meant there were only about a million people scattered across a country the size of California. Most of the rural folk worked on Paraguay's many large ranches, he said, and never traveled far from where they were born. The men became gauchos (cowboys); the women raised children.

The country's per capita income was less than $2,000, less than one-seventh of neighboring Argentina's.

Three hours after leaving Asunción, we drove past a place called Pozo Colorado, left the main road, and traveled another two hours across three ranches before reaching a ranch house where Jose's son, Marcello Sorido, was waiting for us. He had driven to the ranch earlier that day. It was 2 P.M. As the only passenger on the trip across the ranches with Jose, I had opened and closed eighteen gates. Marcello wasn't so lucky. He had no passengers. He had to open the same gates, drive through, and walk back and close them before he could drive on.

After lunch, our gear was loaded onto an oxcart with two six-foot-tall wooden wheels pulled by a team of six oxen. It was the only way to get our equipment to our campsite on another ranch, Jose said. Jose, Marcello, and I rode horses, while the driver and another man rode in that cart for two and a half hours through mud, water, and groves of small palm trees. Finally we came to two huts constructed of palm thatching. Nearby was the airstrip I would have used if I had come by plane. Instead of housing me in one of the thatched structures, my guides erected a small tent for me. This suited me just fine, because I suspected thatched buildings in Paraguay were like those in Africa: They eventually became homes for every type of snake and bug in the area.

My enthusiasm for that tent dropped considerably when I returned to it after lunch one day to get something and found a snake crawling around on its canvas floor. Jose and another man killed it and said it was not a poisonous kind. I could only take their word for it. I knew nothing about South America's snakes.

We hunted from that camp on horseback with hounds for eight days, trying to find a jaguar, but all I saw were tracks. Our guide was a local Indian who spoke only his own language. I was told the man had killed dozens of jaguar and knew the area better than anyone. However, the cats stayed in the thick brush where the dogs couldn't follow them during the day, and moved out of it only at night to do their hunting. I did collect a white-lipped peccary and a brown brocket deer there, however.

On 2 July we abandoned the jaguar hunt and returned to the ranch on the oxcart. We reached Pozo Colorado just as it was getting dark. After getting something to eat, we drove another two hours on a muddy road to a city called Concepción in the center of Paraguay, arriving there at midnight. About fifty thousand people lived in Concepción, Marcello said. Its streets, parks, and buildings reminded me of places I'd seen in Mexico. Our hotel was comfortable, clean, and modern, a major change from the camp we'd left that morning.

Jose had hit a stump on our trip to the ranch in his half-ton truck, and we had to keep adding oil every fifty miles or so. When he took it to a garage the next morning, the mechanic told him the base of the oil filter was cracked and it would take a day or two to get a part shipped over from Brazil, some 120 miles away.

We left Jose's vehicle and drove in Marcelo's van for four and a half hours to another ranch, traveling across six ranches with forty-two gates. It was a pleasant change from the other ranch. This one had adobe walls, running water, and a generator that powered the electric lights in the house. For the next four days we would leave the house at daylight on horseback or in a truck. I took a South American puma right away. I spent the rest of my time there looking for a red brocket deer but did not see a buck.[2]

Our next stop was another ranch a long way from the main road. By now, the daily rains had turned everything to deep mud, and we could hunt only from horseback or from a gravel trailer pulled by a tractor. The elevation must have been higher than at the first ranch, because it was a lot colder in the mornings and evenings. After a couple of days of riding around without seeing any sign of a red brocket deer, my guides decided we needed to move to another ranch. Before we left, however, I picked a bag of oranges and grapefruit from the trees in front of the ranch house to take with us. They were delicious.

We arrived at the new area late the next day, after spending another night in Concepción. The next morning we were riding through a jungle on horseback, following a trail on the edge of a river, when my guides suddenly stopped and motioned for me to get off my horse and bring my rifle. At first I didn't see what Jose had seen. In the wallow of a clearing about seventy-five yards away was the dark shape of a large animal.

"It's a tapir. A big one," Jose said. "Shoot it!"

I quickly moved to a small tree, used a branch to steady my rifle, and shot the animal. When it did not go down, Jose and I ran after it. A hundred yards past where we had last seen it, we came upon the tapir again. This time my shot put it down. I wanted to rush to it, but Jose grabbed my arm and stopped me.

"They use their teeth when they're wounded," he said. "They can kill you if you get too close."

My tapir was a very large animal, at least 350 pounds, and six feet long. Its dark-brown hair was very short, and its feet and nose were unique. It had fourteen hoofs—three on each front foot and four on each hind foot (Jose said they helped keep the heavy animal from sinking into the mud)—and a long, flexible snout. That snout can be used as a snorkel when the animal is in the water, Jose said.

When my guides skinned it, I was surprised to see that its skin was nearly a half-inch thick. I had not planned to collect a tapir, but I was glad to have taken this one.

A couple of days later, I shot my red brocket deer, and we packed up and

2. It was in this area that I saw my first and only anteater in the wild. I was making a stalk through some thick brush when I had to slide over a blowdown. I looked down and saw the animal sleeping on the ground directly below me. I didn't disturb it.

headed back to Concepción. It had been raining heavily every day for at least a week, but this time the sky opened up and delivered a deluge. Water was rushing over the roads, and the flats around us had turned into lakes. Whenever we crossed a bridge, the creeks and brooks were at flood stage.

I was back in Havelock on 19 July, six weeks after I'd left. I'd visited a very interesting part of the world and had met some fine people. I didn't get to hunt a northern huemul or a giant peccary, and I had hoped to take a better red brocket deer. Despite that (and all the rain and mud), I had enjoyed the experience, and I'd added four more species to my collection.

The airport in Moscow hadn't changed much since I had last seen it in 1991. Unlike my trip to hunt moose, brown bear, and reindeer in Siberia that year, I was relieved to find that Trans Soviet Outfitters had sent an interpreter to meet me. Nickolay (or "Nick" as he asked me to call him) Khokhlov took me through Customs, helped clear my rifle, and drove me to a hotel. The next morning, 5 September, I was on my way to Kazakhstan to hunt one of the world's strangest-looking animals, a one-hundred-pound antelope called the Mongolian saiga. What makes it unique is its swollen nose, like a proboscis, with downward-pointing nostrils and translucent, lavender-colored, lyre-shaped horns. Scientists say it has changed little since the Pleistocene Epoch.

Nick and I flew on to Akmola in Kazakhstan the next afternoon. From there we were driven another 150 miles to the hunting area. The country was as flat as a Canadian prairie. It actually reminded me a lot of Canada's prairie country. The farmers were growing wheat and working their fields with combines, just as they do back home. And, as in Canada, we saw literally thousands of geese flying over and feeding in the fields. We finally reached our camp near a place called Tselinogad at 12:30 A.M., after seven and a half hours of driving. It felt good to get out of the vehicle and stretch out in a bed. The prefab building the government had brought in for its saiga hunters was comfortable and warm.

We hunted from the vehicle the next morning, stopping often to glass. By noon, my guide, a man named Leonid Lebedinski, found a good male saiga with horns that were considerably longer than those on the other males we'd seen that morning. I shot it as it ran past our truck. I was proud of the shot because these antelope can reach speeds approaching fifty miles per hour. Its horns were every bit as good as we thought they would be. Today, they still rank number seven in the SCI record book.

We stayed in that camp another two days and shot ducks on the lake in front of our camp before returning to Moscow, where Nick and I were immediately taken to another airport two hours away. Before leaving camp, we were told the country's president was due to arrive that day to hunt ducks. We left for the

The author's saiga antelope, one of the world's strangest-looking large mammals. Kazakhstan.

The author's East Caucasian tur. Compared to the mid-Caucasus, the terrain here was much gentler. North Ossetia.

Caucasus Mountains at 10:30 P.M. to hunt a little-known wild goat called the tur (the Russian word for goat). The *SCI Record Book of Trophy Animals* recognizes three types of tur, and I intended to take two of them on this hunt.

The game department's officials in Validacaurcus greeted us warmly when we landed in the Republic of North Ossetia, gave us a fine meal, and sent a man to drive us to the hunting area three hours away over a mountainous road. The mountains were rugged, with deep ravines and nearly vertical cliffs. In some places the slopes were so steep that dozens of tunnels had been punched through them for the road. It was almost dark when we reached the small, one-man tent that would be our "base camp." I'm not sure what the elevation was, but it was cold at night in those mountains.

The next morning, 11 September, I packed a small bag with the things I thought I would need for two or three days, and we left with five horses and eight men. We rode as high up the mountain as we could take the horses and made another camp. The next day we left on foot and hiked until about 1 P.M. We were hunting the eastern (or, as SCI calls it, East Caucasian) tur, a brown goat with very dark legs, a three-inch beard, and massive, smooth horns that curve behind its neck, with tips turning inward and upward. We were in prime eastern tur habitat, on the eastern slope of the Caucasus Mountains east of Mount Dykh-Tau. My guide was a grizzled Russian named Bazour.

We were staying high, glassing the steep, rocky slopes below us, when Bazour found a herd of tur on another mountain. After some discussion with the guide in Russian, Nick said we would go in one direction while the men went in another to get the tur moving. Bazour, Nick, and I moved about five hundred yards and found a place to wait. After thirty minutes, we had seen or heard nothing. I was telling myself the drive had failed when two brown animals came racing over the knoll behind us. Nick was saying they both were good males as I brought my rifle up. "Shoot the second one," he said.

I found the animal in my scope, pulled the barrel ahead of it, and shot. The tur staggered but didn't stop. It had slowed down somewhat when my second shot killed it. It was an old male with 31⅞-inch horns that would later rank number forty-eight in the SCI record book.

While the men skinned my tur, Nick and I started hiking back to our camp. It was already 5 P.M., and we had to hurry to get there before dark. The men arrived an hour or so later with my tur. I was so tired I ate only a piece of bread before crawling into my sleeping bag. Nick and I left before the others in the morning, heading down to where we had left our vehicle. I cleaned up in one of the streams and did my laundry while we waited for the men to catch up.

To hunt the mid-Caucasian tur, we traveled about 120 miles to the republic of Kabardino-Balkaria. According to Nick, Kabardino and North Ossetia were not good friends (he never explained why), so he arranged for a policeman to accompany us to the border. We had no problems, though. We parked our vehicle on the North Ossetia side, walked across the border, and got into a truck that was waiting for us in Kabardino. From there we were driven to a hotel in Nalchik, a city of some four hundred thousand people. After a week without a proper bath and very little food, a shower never felt better, nor has a meal ever tasted better.

The head of the area's hunting organization, a man about seventy years old, somehow learned I was at the hotel and came to visit me. With Nick interpreting, I learned I would be the first foreigner to hunt in this area during his lifetime. I could tell the man was proud of his region and of his life there. He had guided all the former leaders of the Soviet Union, he said.

We left Nalchik in a Jeep an hour before sunup and drove two hours to a mountain village, where we picked up my guide, a man named Herun. An hour later, after a very rough ride on a bad mountain road, we reached our camp, where Herun's two sons were waiting for us. According to Nick, the place was called Balkaria, and it was here that Herun expected to find my mid-Caucasian tur.

Herun woke us at 3:30 A.M. on 15 September, and we left camp on horseback. By daybreak we had ridden two hours and at least five miles up a steep mountain trail to where Herun wanted to start our hunt. Just as the sun was starting to light up the sky in the east, we tied up the horses, moved to the edge of a bluff, and started glassing. We found several

herds right away, but there were no old males. At 10 A.M. we rode back down the trail, reached a junction, and rode to another high mountain. We saw tur every time we stopped to glass, so there must have been a lot of them in the area. Unfortunately, there was no way to get close enough to any of those herds.

Late in the afternoon we found a lone male feeding on a far-off mountain. The spotting scope showed it was worth trying to take. We decided we might be able to get to it, shoot it, and get back before dark, but we had no time to waste.

As we were moving off our ridge, Herun spotted another tur about 250 yards across the canyon from us. He and Nick whispered a few words, then Nick turned to me and said I should shoot it.

It was not a difficult shot, but the tur didn't drop. Instead, it took a few steps, staggered, and fell over a cliff and rolled out of sight. The shot spooked at least twenty more animals that we hadn't seen, and they ran out from under the cliff, ran to the ridge, and stopped before going out of sight. I doubt they ever realized what had frightened them.

It was hard work climbing down to the animal and climbing back out of the canyon after posing for photos, but I managed to do it. I had taken a very good mid-Caucasian tur with 33⅛-inch horns that later would rank number one in the SCI record book.

As we had done with my first tur, Nick and I left the men to skin the animal while we went ahead. We were still a long way from camp, and it was getting dark, when we started following the wrong creek. We were stumbling around in the dark when we saw the light from a flashlight and heard the men yelling on the ridge above us. We had been walking in the wrong direction! If they hadn't found us, we would have spent a long, cold night on that mountain.

We spent the next night in Nalchik and flew back to Moscow on 17 September. There I was offered a hunt for a Marco Polo argali for $22,000—a discount of $5,000 from their usual price—after my Turkmenistan hunt. I had wanted to hunt this sheep for some time, and this was an opportunity to avoid making another trip to do it, so I arranged to have the money transferred to Alexander. We agreed that they would not let me shoot a ram with horns shorter than fifty-four inches. If I didn't take a ram that size or larger, I would get a $10,000 refund.

The next day Nick and I flew to Ashgabat in Turkmenistan, a three-hour flight. The city was much warmer (about 90 degrees Fahrenheit) and, with five hundred thousand people, much larger than I had expected. After lunch, we took a paved road for five hours across flat, arid plains, then turned off on a dusty dirt road and followed it for another two hours into the mountains. It was 2:30 A.M. when we reached the Badkhyz Reserve, where I would hunt a Trans-Caspian urial and a Persian goitered gazelle with a guide named Juma. The terrain was mostly flat and uninteresting, but there also were some low hills and a few deep canyons.

At daylight a driver drove Juma and me about a half-hour to a place where two horses were waiting for us. We saw a few urial, and one of them could have been a good ram, but I couldn't understand a word my guide was saying, so I didn't shoot. Nick rode with us the next day, and he was able to interpret when Juma found a small group of rams.

We watched a ram in our binoculars, and Nick said, "He says you should shoot the big one in that herd."

To reach the animal the three of us had to climb around the peak the sheep were on, then move down on them. It was easier said than done, but our plan worked, and I was able to shoot the ram from about 150 yards. It was a good ram with 35⅜-inch horns.

I was glad to be leaving the area. We had been hunting in a volatile corner of the country, along the border with Iran and only three miles from Afghanistan. Each country was patrolling its borders, and the military stopped us at least a dozen times.

We hunted the Persian goitered gazelle from our vehicle, and we saw several good males the first morning. Every one we saw was running, however. Nick didn't offer to guess the reason, but I was certain that poachers were regularly harassing these herds. The animals definitely knew a truck meant danger, and they knew enough to get as far from one as they could. Eventually we realized that to get a shot I would have to go on foot. Juma, Nick, and I left the truck on the edge of a canyon and worked our way down a canyon about a mile and a half to where Juma knew there was a spring. Someone had built a blind there. We waited in it for several hours without seeing a thing.

About halfway back to our camp, Juma parked the truck, and the three of us tried walking across a wide valley. We saw several herds containing up to fifty gazelle, including a very good male, but the animals would not allow us to get within five hundred yards of them. We also saw a herd of feral donkeys, which Nick called "zebras," and several wild boars.

On the way back to the truck that afternoon, Nick, Juma, and I stopped to rest after a long climb, and we spotted a herd of five male gazelle. Two of them were very good, Juma said, as we backed off the hill and worked our way around the little mountain on which we had seen them. Somehow they had seen or heard us, because they were running away when we came over the top. I shot quickly at what I thought was the largest gazelle, but I missed it before the herd went out of sight. When it reappeared, I was ready. Sitting down, with my elbows locked into my knees, I placed the cross hairs on the best gazelle's shoulder and killed it with my first shot as it was running uphill. It was a beautiful little animal, and I was happy to have it for my collection. As do all the types of goitered gazelle, mine had a conspicuous lump on its throat.

That evening in camp Nick hit me up for tips for the people in camp and at the Moscow office, and he wanted $300 to $400 for himself! I decided to pay the local people myself. As I went to bed, I told Nick he could wait until the end of the hunt for his tip, and I didn't think anyone in Moscow had earned one.

It was windy and dusty on the long drive back to Ashgabat. We spent the night there in the home of one of Juma's friends. The next day a government official issued the export permits I needed to take my trophies with me.

When we returned to Moscow on 24 September, we learned that one of Nick's close friends had died. It was not the only news. History was being written when we were in Moscow, and I wasn't comfortable about it. Three days before we arrived, President Boris Yeltsin had suspended the Russian Parliament and called for an election. To protest Yeltsin's move, leftists had barricaded themselves inside the old Supreme Soviet White House, and they were still there. Sporadic fighting was under way in the center of the city.[3]

Nick and I didn't wait to see what might develop next. At 11 P.M. we left for Tajikistan to hunt a Marco Polo argali, the world's largest wild sheep. On our plane to Dushanbe were two Spaniards who had booked a twelve-day argali hunt. (I planned to hunt only a week.) Before we landed, the captain came on the intercom and said something in Russian. According to Nick, the fighting was spreading across the country, and military officials had imposed a curfew from sundown to 6 A.M. The Spaniards and I were certain we were in the wrong place at the wrong time.

---

3. Ten days after we left Moscow, troops loyal to Yeltsin recaptured the White House in a bloody battle, and the old Parliament was dissolved. A new constitution was adopted in December 1993.

Nick, however, was not too concerned. We would have no trouble in the mountains where we were going, he said.

Because of the curfew, we couldn't leave the airport when we landed at 4:30 A.M., so we were taken to the V.I.P. lounge to wait with armed security guards. I stretched out on a coach and slept until Nick woke me at 7 A.M. A car was waiting to take us to a helicopter, he said. We had no problems at all on the drive to the heliport, and I saw nothing along the streets that gave any indication of the unrest that was under way. Nick and I, with the Spaniards and their interpreter, climbed into the helicopter and left for the mountains.

We dropped the Spaniards off at a comfortable-looking camp in a scenic spot, then flew over a ridge and landed. I would be camping at 12,500 feet, less than two miles from the Spaniards' camp. It was not a good campsite, and we were given very little equipment for high-altitude, cold-weather camping. (The daytime temperature would reach only about 35 degrees Fahrenheit.) We had no lantern, so my guides cut a window in my little tent to let in the moonlight. We ran out of gasoline for our little pump-up stove after four days. There were no chairs or anything in which to warm our water for washing. I was expected to sleep on the ground with only a thin mattress, and I had to pile all my spare clothing on top of my sleeping bag to stay warm. We didn't have adequate food, either. Our tent's homemade stove was fueled by dried yak dung and some roots the men had found. When it snowed—when we most needed the stove—the stove filled the tent with smoke. The only way we got relief from the smoke was to add so much fuel that the stove became white-hot. The smoke cleared up somewhat then, but it became uncomfortably hot in that little tent.

I wouldn't have minded all this if it had been a good hunt, but it was a disaster. The reserve may have been a good place to hunt in years past, but the only sheep tracks we found were in a small valley a long way from our camp. The Spaniards had hunted there for two or three days and had seen nothing.

When I agreed to stay a couple of extra days, I was moved to a tent where the Spaniards had hunted. The camp manager, who spoke some English, said Nick and my guide couldn't go there because there was no room for them. I made it very clear to him that he should tell my new guide not to let me shoot a ram under fifty-four inches, which he did.

The elevation was about 13,500 feet, and we were hunting up to 15,000 feet, where it was hard to breathe. After walking at least five miles the next morning, we finally found two different bands of sheep. The first herd saw us from a long way off and was running when we first saw it. The next bunch of rams was feeding at the base of some low hills across a valley, at least a mile or so away. To reach them we had to cross the valley and come up on them from behind. Finally, after a two-hour stalk in thin air, we had closed the distance to about three hundred yards. These were the first Marco Polo argali rams I had ever seen on the hoof, but I couldn't find a good ram in

The author shot this Trans-Caspian urial in the Badkyz hunting reserve. Except for the deep canyons, much of the terrain was flat and uninteresting. Turkmenistan.

Note how steep the terrain is where the author found his blue sheep. Nepal.

the bunch. The guide knew I didn't want to shoot any ram with horns shorter than 54 inches. I was certain the herd's best ram was smaller than that, but he wanted me to shoot it. When I wrote "135" (for 135 centimeters) on a piece of paper and showed it to the man, he nodded his head as if he understood and kept indicating that I should shoot the ram that was standing apart from its companions.

Against my better judgment, I killed that animal. When I saw my ram up close, I didn't need a tape measure to know it was not what I wanted. It was only a four-year-old with 49¾-inch horns, and no one would ever accuse it of being a trophy. When I left the guide and returned alone to the tent, the camp manager agreed the ram was too small and said he would help me find a better one. He never did. He did offer me a free hunt, but I suspected he didn't have the authority for that. I was so disappointed that I left the tent and walked—by myself—about three hours back to where Nick was, crossing a small river along the way. Nick was upset, too, and used the radio to try to get the helicopter to come get me, but the people in town kept giving us excuses for the delay. I finally realized they were waiting until the Spaniards were ready to go out.

I wanted to try hunting for an ibex, but my guide made only a halfhearted attempt at it. While returning to camp one day, we came across a small pack of wolves, and I shot one of them. By the time the Spanish hunters were ready to leave, bad weather had moved in. There was so much snow and fog that the helicopter was grounded for the next three days. When we were down to our last bit of food—a few packages of soup and hot chocolate that I'd packed in my duffel bag for emergencies—I shot a small ibex for meat.

We woke up on 9 October to find the storm had passed. Around noon we could hear the distinctive sound of the helicopter coming to get us. It may be a cliche, but that sound was music to my ears. I was never happier than when we finally left that miserable place and landed in Dushanbe. There would be no planes flying to Moscow for two days because of a fuel shortage, so we were put up in a flat, and the Spaniard's guide cooked for us. There was no hot water, but it was better than the tent we'd just left.

We heard shots in the distance each night, telling us that the fighting hadn't stopped. But Nick, the two Spaniards, and I had no problems when we walked to a market and back. There were very few vehicles on the streets. Those streets, incidentally, were wide and clean and lined with trees. It was hard to realize that the country was in such turmoil.

Back in Moscow, I complained about the hunt and the hunting conditions. I'd purchased my Marco Polo sheep hunt with the understanding that I would receive a refund of $10,000 if I didn't take a trophy ram. When I asked Alexander for my refund, he first responded by saying I had taken my ram. However, when I told him the camp manager had said I could come back at no charge, he agreed I could. He also agreed that a refund was due me.

I left Moscow on 12 October and was back in Havelock two days later, having been gone five weeks. I never saw that $10,000 refund, nor was I ever invited back for the makeup hunt I had been promised. The last I heard, the outfitter's U.S. office was saying everything would be straightened out. That's hunting in Russia, I guess.

Ray Young—a hunter from Moundsville, West Virginia—and I had both booked chamois, brown bear, and ibex hunts in Turkey with Orhan Konokci of Safari Tours in 1993, and we met for the first time in the airport outside Istanbul on 27 October. Ray had arrived an hour earlier, and he and the outfitter's driver were waiting for me after I cleared Customs.

On the drive to our downtown hotel, I looked at the sights. Istanbul was—and is—a historic, cosmopolitan city. It is a major seaport and Turkey's industrial and financial center, but it also is a resort, attracting thousands of tourists every year. We drove past ancient Byzantine castles, marble palaces, Ottoman villas, mosques with grand domes and minarets, kiosks, bazaars, and well-kept parks with flowers and magnificent old trees, as well as modern hotels and office buildings. Boats were coming and going on the Bosporus, the strait that separates Asia from Europe, while traffic flowed over its bridge, one of the longest in the world.

The guidebooks stated the population was six million; according to our driver, it was twelve million. The city was much larger than I expected, and it fascinated me. Ray wasn't as interested in seeing the sights as I was. He had hunted in Turkey in March. A heavy spring snow had closed all the mountain roads after he had hunted only two days, and he had spent a few days in the city. Ray and I walked to a crowded bazaar in a large, enclosed shopping area, where he bought some items for his pawnshop. I didn't buy anything, but I enjoyed shopping and watching the people. Virtually every race in the world could be seen there.

We flew to Erzuram the next morning, where a driver named Mustafa met us. We were on the western side of Turkey, near the Republic of Georgia. Fighting was going on to the north of us on the Black Sea coast, but Mustafa said we shouldn't worry, because we would be at least sixty miles from the contested areas.

To reach the hunting area, we drove north for two hours on paved roads before turning off on a winding, narrow dirt road that climbed up into the mountains. Whenever two vehicles met on that road, one of them had to back up to a wide spot to let the other pass. I don't know how many miles we drove—it was very slow going—but it took us two more hours to reach the house where we would be staying in the mountains. It was 5:30 P.M. when we started unloading our gear. The house was in a scenic spot, on a sidehill above a river, and each of us had his own room with a small wood stove.

Orhan Konokci was already there, as were three hunters from the United States. According to Orhan, we would hunt Anatolian chamois and Mideastern brown bear in the hills above the house. We would move to the Toros Mountains for the bezoar ibex, he said.

One of the Americans had already hunted in the mountains without taking a chamois. The two others went up when we arrived but returned, saying there was no snow to drive the animals down from the rough country they inhabited. Despite their dire predictions, my guide and I, along with an assistant and a mule, climbed to the peaks on the third day, following an old trail that went past a settlement with no other means of access. Our camp was an old stone and log house on top of the mountain. Its owners kept their cattle in corrals beneath the structure, which they used only in the summer. There were no beds, so we slept on the floor, and one of us would get up every so often and feed more wood into the small stove.

It was a long climb to where my guide expected to find the chamois, but we found fresh chamois tracks as soon as we reached a level with an inch of snow on the ground. We tried to follow them but eventually lost them. While glassing that afternoon, we saw a small group of chamois on another mountain, across a wide valley, but a heavy fog rolled in before we could go after them, and we returned to camp.

We tried hunting another spot the next day and spent most of the day moving down a long ridge, glassing as we went. At 3:30 P.M. the guide suggested that we come off the mountain and go to his house instead of climbing back to our camp. It was dark by 5 P.M., but by then we had reached a steep, winding

path that eventually led to a road. I was completely played out when I reached his house at 8:30. We had been going downhill on very steep slopes all day. My legs were cramped, and my toes were hurting. Although the guide and I couldn't communicate well, his wife knew what was wrong and got me a pan of cold water and salt in which to soak my feet.

After serving me tea, bread, honey, cheese, and grapes, the guide arranged for a vehicle to take us back to the main lodge. I didn't think it could be very far, but it took two hours to drive there. It was after midnight when I finally got to bed.

Two days later, I climbed the mountain again with another guide. Although it had been raining every day, the chamois cooperated, and I was able to take a good buck the second day. After photographing it, the guide and I returned to the lodge and found Frank and Audrey Murtland from Michigan there. I had met the Murtlands in Scotland in 1992. Their friend Kevin Downer, a taxidermist and booking agent from England, was with them.

I hunted for a brown bear for five days but didn't get one. Perhaps I should have said five nights, because we drove around after dark with a powerful light, hoping to catch a big bear moving about. Although I don't like jacklighting, it was legal there. It also was the only way they hunted bear, my guides said. We did see two small bears, which I passed up.

To hunt ibex we needed to move to the Toros Mountains in Antalya, a resort city of about five hundred thousand on the

The author's sleeping quarters high in the chamois hunting area. Turkey.

Scientists say the bezoar ibex the author shot in Turkey's Toros Mountains really isn't an ibex. It's a wild goat. Turkey.

Mediterranean coast. It was a three-day trip by car. I rode with Frank, Audrey, Kevin, and Orhan as far as Trahzon, then flew to Antalya the next day. My interpreter, a man named Baha, and his father drove me to the hotel. It was the off-season, and the hotel had very few guests. The temperature would drop to a chilly 40 degrees Fahrenheit or below that at night.

The hotel would be my "camp" for the next few days, Baha said. We'd leave an hour before daylight every morning and drive into the nearby mountains. A government gamekeeper would be my guide, and we would have two spotters to help us glass. Baha would go along with us and interpret for me.

We stayed on the mountain only an hour or two the first day because the wind was blowing so hard. The ibex were holed up in the canyons to avoid the wind, and we wouldn't be able to see them, the gamekeeper told Baha. I was optimistic about this hunt, having seen several females and a couple of young males on the way out. I also was relieved to see that the mountains were not as high or as steep as some of the other places I had hunted ibex.

Frank, Audrey, and Kevin reached the hotel that evening, and we had dinner together. The four of us planned to leave the hotel at 6 A.M. each day and drive to a game department office, where we would pick up our guides and spotters before going off on our separate ways to hunt. The wind had gone away by the second day, but it was raining off and on when my guide and I started up a trail in the same

area we had hunted earlier. We had gone no more than a quarter-mile when the drizzle turned to a downpour. My guides and I ran back to the vehicle, and I called off the hunt that day. I had all the early symptoms of the flu. I took some medicine at 10 A.M. and stayed in bed all day. I even skipped dinner that evening. I felt better the next morning and met Frank and Audrey in the dining room for breakfast. They had hunted in the rain and had seen several good ibex, but the animals were in places where they couldn't reach them. We all had only two more days to hunt, but none of us took an ibex that day.

On 16 November, our last day to hunt, Baha took me to a different area, where we climbed and glassed until noon. I was ready to give up when Baha suddenly said the spotters had found an ibex.

"Where?" I asked.

"On that far ridge."

It took me a minute or two to find it. "It's not very big, is it?" I asked.

"No, but where there's one male there usually are others," Baha said.

Forty-five minutes later, we had located five other males on that mountain, and all five were shootable. To reach them we had to slide down to the bottom of the canyon, then climb up to their level and work our way around the mountain. If we were lucky, we would come up on them in shooting range.

Luck was with us, and we were able to get within two hundred yards of all five ibex without alerting them to our presence. The problem now was deciding which one I should shoot. Baha had

To get our supplies to the jaguar hunting area across a river, we used this ox team and cart with high wheels. Paraguay.

stayed up on the ridge while the guides and I made the stalk. The head guide was motioning for me to shoot, but I didn't understand a word he was saying. I could tell he was getting frustrated. He finally got through to me by rubbing his head on a tree, which was what one of the ibex was doing. When a good shot presented itself, I had the animal in my cross hairs and squeezed off a shot. The ibex was out of sight in an instant; then we heard the bullet strike the animal. I had hit it, but where had it gone? The next thing I saw was the herd heading for the ridge. The guide was holding up three fingers and nodding his head. I shot the third animal in the line, and it dropped.

My first ibex had died where I had shot it. Now I had two. I would need to go to the bank to cash some traveler's checks.

The trophy fee for shooting a second ibex was $2,000.

Both were trophy animals, but my first ibex was the better one. Its horns were 31⅜ inches long and easily qualified for the SCI record book. Both were handsome animals, with gray coats and dark heads that were almost black, shoulder stripes, beards, and white underparts. Their horns were scimitar-shaped and had sharp keels and a few knobs. It is difficult to understand why scientists classify them as "goats" instead of "ibex." That sharp keel on their horns makes the difference, they say. The men field dressed my ibex and carried them off the mountain, then skinned them at the game department's headquarters.

I took Audrey, Frank, Kevin, and Orhan to dinner that evening. They'd had no luck on this trip and were going home the next day without having fired a shot. I accompanied them as far as Istanbul the next morning, and we all caught different planes. I was in Moncton exactly twenty-four hours later. It was a Thursday, and I had scheduled a whitetail hunt in Alberta starting three days later.

It was 2 P.M. on 21 November when my guide, Gerry Smith, drove me to the Inn at the Lake Motel in Sylvan Lake, Alberta. After flying to Edmonton that morning, I had driven south with Gerry to a town called Red Deer and then west for another fifteen minutes to the motel, which would be my camp for the next week. My friend and taxidermist, Bob Lloyd from Sylvan Lake, had arranged the hunt. In addition to a license for white-tailed deer, I also had tags to take mule deer and coyote.

Gerry had permission to hunt on a large block of private land, so we spent most of our time driving along its roads. The bucks were moving now, he said. It was the last week of the hunting season, and the rut was in full swing. Bob accompanied us the first morning, and we did see a small, eight-point buck and a coyote. I passed up the buck and missed the coyote. Bob stayed in town after lunch, and Gerry and I went out again. We saw only three does the rest of that day.

Four days later, we had seen perhaps a dozen antlered deer. I passed up a small ten-pointer and missed a quick shot at a better ten-pointer. The weather was perfect for hunting, with temperatures of about -6 degrees Fahrenheit at dawn and above freezing during the day, and there were about six inches of snow on the ground. Despite what Gerry had said, the big bucks just weren't showing themselves. We even tried rattling antlers to get a buck to come in, but none did. We saw three moose one day and a few mule deer does, but no bucks.

One of Gerry's friends had told him about a place we should check, so we went there late Friday afternoon and saw three does and two small bucks just at dark. At daybreak we were back at the same place, parked next to an oil-well pump, when three does followed by an eight-point buck came out of the brush and stopped about forty yards from the truck. It wasn't Alberta's best buck, but it was a respectable deer, Gerry said. When it turned its head and started trotting away down a road, its antlers seemed wide and tall. This was the last day I could hunt there, and it was a good buck. I stepped out of the truck and shot it.

We hunted for mule deer that afternoon but saw only females. That evening Bob and his wife, Nancy, and I drove to Red Deer for dinner. I was home the next night.

I'd had an interesting year, hunting in ten countries on four continents. I'd taken thirty-four specimens in 1993, and all were trophy animals—except for that Marco Polo ram in Tajikistan.

CHINA, NORTHWEST TERRITORIES, AND PAKISTAN, 1994

I was waiting outside the airline's gate when Chuck and Karen Bazzy arrived in Tokyo from Michigan on 22 April. I'd flown nonstop for thirteen hours from Toronto and had arrived six hours before them. The three of us then boarded another plane and flew four and a half hours to Beijing, where Wang Wei of the China Wildlife Association greeted us. We would spend the next four days sightseeing, before beginning our hunts for blue sheep and Tibetan gazelle. Our first order of business, though, was to leave our rifles with the airport police and catch up on sleep. I had been traveling for twenty-four hours straight since leaving Toronto.

Beijing was bustling with activity, its streets jammed with bicycles of every description—some carrying unbelievable loads. Modern hotels and office buildings stood next to tall, Russian-style apartment buildings that reeked of cabbage. As do other tourists in that huge city, we visited the Ming Tombs, the Forbidden City, the Heavenly Temple, Tiananmen Square, the Summer Palace, and the National Zoo. We even had a Beijing duck dinner at the restaurant where that delicacy supposedly originated. There were crowds of people everywhere. Although the temperature was only about 80 degrees Fahrenheit, it was uncomfortably hot and humid.

This hunt had been scheduled a month earlier, but Chuck had called me in Toronto while I was en route to China. Wang Wei had been unable to get me the permit I'd need to hunt a Gansu argali, the main animal I wanted on this trip, and he wanted me to wait. Returning thirty days later meant I would be able to hunt the argali, but I decided to go as planned and hunt the other species on my list.

After leaving Beijing, Chuck, Karen, and I flew to Xining, a city of one million at about 7,900 feet elevation, and spent the night. On 27 April, along with our interpreter, Hunguei Yang, we spent the next thirteen hours in a Toyota Land Cruiser, passing a hundred or more small, two-wheel tractors towing trailers loaded with people and their supplies. According to Hunguei Yang, the people were heading for the mountains to pan for gold during the summer. The road was paved for the first nine hours, as we climbed higher into the mountains and past patches of spring snow.

We stopped in Dulan for lunch at noon—and what an experience that was. For a week I had been looking forward to eating great Chinese food, but I would not find it on this trip. The food we call "Chinese" is nothing like what the Chinese people eat. Our Chinese food is vastly better, in my opinion. That opinion would not change throughout my first trip to China. One item we were served was a plate of more than two dozen chicken feet, which Hunguei Yang greatly appreciated, but we didn't try it. The "real stuff" was too exotic for me.

At 3 P.M. we left the pavement and continued on a dirt road for a while. We then drove up a dry riverbed for many miles. Around 6 P.M. Hunguei Yang announced that we had reached our hunting area, but neither he nor the driver knew exactly where our camp was. The driver stopped at a lonely yurt and asked for directions, and an hour later we found it.

Gou Li Camp was in a broad valley at thirteen thousand feet. Chuck and Karen were assigned one yurt, and I had another. There also were yurts for the staff and a separate yurt for cooking. Compared to what we had been eating, the food was good, and the staff even offered us American-style meals. In addition to Hunguei Yang, the staff consisted of cook Shi Ying Hong, waiter Saim Ji, housekeeper Jama, a camp doctor named Gli Xao Yan, two guides for each of us, and several other people Hunguei Yang said were "helpers." All were courteous and eager to please, but only our interpreter spoke any English.

Chuck, Karen, and I were tired and dusty after the long trip, and, because I hadn't yet adjusted to the elevation, I had a severe headache. After dinner, I went straight to my yurt and went to bed. I had just awakened at 6:30 A.M., feeling better, when a girl came in and dumped half a bucket of coal into the stove and built a fire. I don't know how cold it was outside, but a pail of water inside the yurt had a quarter-inch of ice on top. I waited until

the stove warmed up the place before I got up.

After breakfast, Chuck and I sighted in our rifles and left camp. Chuck and Karen and their two guides went in one direction, and my two guides—Yang Yong Hang Lt and Jincai—and I went in another. There were only three horses in camp, so Chuck, Karen, and I rode; the others walked. The terrain was hilly but arid, with little vegetation. The valleys were warm, but whenever we climbed a sidehill or a ridge, a cold wind would cut right through our clothes.

My guides and I saw several bands of gazelle before we stopped for lunch (bread, cookies, and mineral water), but we saw no sheep. That afternoon we found a herd of gazelle with a good male with 12-inch horns in the lead, and an hour later I was able to take it with a very long shot. It was not an easy stalk. There was little cover, and the terrain was mostly flat. Every time we would get within four hundred yards of it, the herd would spot us and drift off. Each time this happened, however, the herd would move just a little bit less.

My guides and I returned to camp before sundown to learn that Chuck had taken his blue sheep and a gazelle and had gotten back by 3 P.M. He was tired and sore and was not feeling well, and Karen had flu symptoms.

Breakfast the next morning was some kind of fruit juice, coffee, and toast. At 8 A.M. my two guides and I rode out on the three horses. Although they weren't much larger than Shetland ponies, our

My hunting friends Chuck and Karen Bazzy with our tour guide enroute to hunt Chinese bharal. China.

The author's Chinese blue sheep was smaller and of a different color than the bharal he shot in Nepal. China.

mounts were strong and had great endurance. They were only partially broken, however, and would try to bite or kick us the minute we let our guard down.

We hit pay dirt the second day, after spending all the previous day without seeing a sheep. There were so many animals that it was tough to decide which was the best male in the flock. It was impossible to count them, but I can truthfully say there were two or three hundred, maybe more. Several were trophy-class rams. With that many eyes, it didn't take those sheep very long to spot us. Each time we tried to move closer they would move away, staying just out of rifle range. Suddenly the entire flock froze and looked down the mountain. About three-quarters of a mile below, two wolves were moving around. A few minutes later, we could see six wolves. The wolves never tried to rush into the flock. Instead, they slowly pushed it over the ridge. We tried to follow them and got close enough to shoot at least twice, but an opportunity to take a good male never presented itself.

I was having trouble breathing when we stopped to have lunch and let the flock settle down. We were at fourteen thousand feet, and my lungs didn't function well at that altitude, especially after following the sheep on foot for several hours.

The flock was bedded when we caught up to it again. The wolves were nowhere in sight. By staying out of sight, we were able to get within three hundred yards of the flock and set up a spotting scope. We glassed that big flock for nearly an hour, trying to decide which ram I should shoot.

Whenever we picked one, another would stand up and block the shot. Then we'd see an even better ram. I already had my rifle resting on a boulder when what we thought was the herd's best ram stood up and walked a few steps away from the other sheep. My first shot put it down.

The tips of both horns were broomed, but they were heavy and thick all the way out. It was an old animal, a fine trophy, with 24⅞-inch horns that had 11⅛-inch bases. (It still ranks number five in the SCI record book.) Its body was noticeably smaller than that of the Himalayan blue sheep I'd taken in Nepal. It was light brown overall instead of grayish-brown, and its darker areas were brownish instead of black. We took lots of photos and were back in camp by 6 P.M.

Chuck and Karen still were not feeling well. Both said they ached and had colds, and they were looking forward to returning to Xining the next day. I invited my two guides to my yurt and tipped them; then we celebrated with the rest of the staff at dinner. It was quite a party. Although I couldn't understand them, I really enjoyed myself. There were some Tibetan helpers in camp, in addition to the Chinese, and we each sang songs in our own language. I didn't get to bed until 10 P.M.

It took us three and a half hours the next day to reach the paved road. We again stopped in Dulan at noon for lunch and drove another six and a half hours to Xining, where we spent the next two days. We were tired, but we felt better after hot baths and dinner. Hunguei Yang and our driver took us on a tour of Xining's sights the next morning. I was still on my quest to find some really good Chinese food, and a restaurant in one of the tourist places seemed to be my best chance. But the food wasn't as good as back home. They brought the cold things first, then lots of rice, soup, and a half-dozen different dishes. There was nothing sweet.

That afternoon Chuck and I measured our sheep and gazelle horns. I spent the rest of the day reading a book and writing in my journal, and skipped dinner.

Hunguei Yang and the driver took us downtown the next morning. We toured a crowded market where vegetables, fish, meat, and all types of things were for sale. That evening we had dinner with the general manager of the Department of Agriculture and Wildlife and his assistant. We were back in Beijing the next day. Wang Wei met us at the airport and drove us to see the Great Wall before taking us to our hotel. The next day, 4 May, we flew on to Tokyo, only to learn that our United Airlines flight had been canceled because of mechanical problems. People who had paid fares for that flight were standing around, not knowing what to do. I knew that Canadian Airlines had recently added a 6:45 P.M. flight to Vancouver and was able to change my ticket. Chuck and Karen flew Air China to Tokyo and made connections to the United States from there. I landed in Vancouver at 3:30 that same day, an hour and fifteen minutes *earlier* than I had left. I was back in Havelock the next day, after spending the night in Toronto.

I'd had a good hunt. There certainly was no shortage of blue sheep or Tibetan gazelle. Our camp was comfortable (and unique), its people were courteous and hard-working, and our guides knew what they were doing. Our tours of Beijing and Xining had been interesting. Although I didn't get to hunt a Gansu argali, I'd thoroughly enjoyed my first hunt in China.

I met Gerald Warnock, a well-known, international big-game hunter, for the first time over breakfast in the Leduc Motel in Edmonton on 9 May 1994. Both of us had booked hunts with Canada North Outfitting for barren-ground grizzly bears out of Cambridge Bay in Northwest Territories.

Canada North's representative, Bill Tait, was waiting for us when we landed in Yellowknife. Gerald and I had met Bill on previous trips, so we had no trouble recognizing him in the little airport. After paying our bills, Gerald and I got back on the same plane and flew on to Cambridge Bay. It was noon when we landed, and the temperature was down to 0 degrees Fahrenheit. There wasn't a cloud in the sky, and the sun was shining brightly. At the Arctic Hotel, the desk clerk jokingly said the town was experiencing a heat wave—it had been -5 degrees Fahrenheit the same time the previous day, he said.

After meeting our guides—Philip, Jack, and a helper named Henry—at the hotel restaurant, Gerald and I did some shopping. We left town the next morning with three snowmobiles, one each for Philip, Jack, and Henry. Gerald and I would ride in a *qamulik*, a sixteen-foot-long sled towed by a rope twenty feet behind one of the snowmobiles. Henry's snowmobile pulled our supplies on another sled. Sixty miles and an uncomfortable four hours later, we stopped for tea and a snack on the mainland across the Queen Maud Gulf from Victoria Island. The temperature was approaching -10 degrees Fahrenheit. According to our guides, sundown would be at 11 P.M.; sunup around 2 A.M.

We had seen a couple of herds of muskox and quite a few Peary caribou on the trip. The caribou, according to our guides, would move across to Victoria Island before the ice went out at the end of June.

We arrived at our campsite around 4:30 P.M. Our guides put up three tents, one for them, one for Gerald and me, and one for cooking and eating. Dinner—in frozen packages that they thawed and cooked in boiling water—was served at 8 P.M. They had frozen a variety of food, and it all tasted good.

We were too tired to sit up and talk, so we went to bed right after dinner. We'd heated our tent with a Coleman stove but had to turn it off before going to sleep. Keeping it on all night in that closed tent would have put us at risk of asphyxiation. As soon as the stove went off, though, the temperature plummeted. I don't know how cold it was, but it could have hit well below zero in the tent that night. I had a good sleeping bag and slept warm, however. The next thing I knew, Henry was lighting our stove again. It was 7 A.M.

Gerald and I stayed in our sleeping bags until it had warmed up a bit. The men had hot porridge and tea waiting for us.

The temperature outside was hovering around -10 degrees Fahrenheit when we left Henry with the tents to go hunting. Gerald and I were in the boxes on the sleds behind our guides' snowmobiles again. We would be traveling together for safety, so Gerald and I flipped a coin to see who would shoot if we found a good bear the first day. After that, we would alternate days. I won the toss.

We saw a few caribou, wolf, and wolverine tracks. At 11 A.M. we came across the tracks of a large grizzly in the snow. The tracks were frozen, which meant they could have been made during the night or three or four days earlier. We followed them anyway, hoping we might catch up to that bear. The bear seemed to prefer the rocky ridges where our snowmobiles couldn't go, and whenever we came to one of those places, we had to drive around it and try to pick up its tracks on the opposite side. When we went down steep grades, we'd unhook the sleds and push them down. Gerald and I had a rough ride. Around noon we found the bear's den, along with some sign indicating the bear had left it. It hadn't stopped once in two days and had covered an unbelievable distance. Eventually, though, we closed the distance and spotted the bear about a half-mile ahead of us. Bear do not have good eyesight, but there is nothing wrong with their hearing. As soon as the bear heard our machines, it whirled around and started running flat out.

The author rode in the box on this sled on his hunt for a barren-ground grizzly bear. Northwest Territories.

The barren-ground grizzly the author took near Cambridge Bay had a luxurious coat of hair. Northwest Territories.

The next few minutes of that chase were exciting. Being towed twenty feet behind a snowmobile going that fast is a lot like water-skiing, except the passengers in a sled have absolutely no control. When Jack made a sudden turn, my sled swung out and overturned, dumping me onto the snow. I wasn't hurt. Jack unhooked the sled, and I jumped on behind him as we roared to the bear. When we were about 150 yards away, I jumped off the machine and shot the bear. It was a big old male, covered with a very thick layer of fat. Our guides said they always hunted before it warmed up because the boars left their dens earlier than the females.

As soon as we'd taken photos, the guides erected a tent and set up a stove, and we had supper. After skinning the bear, we left at 10 P.M., just as the sun was going behind a mountain. It was 1 A.M. when we finally reached our camp, after a rough, cold ride. Although the sun was below the horizon, it never got dark. The sky was as red as any sunrise back home. During the "day," the sun never gets very high, and it doesn't give off enough heat to melt the snow.

It was as cold as ever when we packed up our camp the next morning and moved to the spot where Gerald would hunt his bear. We both had licenses to take seals, so we kept a sharp lookout as we traveled. We left at 2 P.M. and had a four-hour, fifteen-minute drive down Runklin Inlet to Bay Chimo, arriving at 6:15 P.M.

The wind was blowing strong, making it seem even colder than when we first drove into Bay Chimo. Only about fifty people live there, and when the days get longer most of them leave to go hunting or to visit Cambridge Bay. They return to collect eggs when the birds come back to nest. Once a year a barge arrives to service the fifteen homes on each side of the bay.

Our guides had homes in Bay Chimo, and Gerald and I stayed in one of them. It was cold enough to freeze meat inside when they opened it up, but it warmed up when they got the stove going. The house was made of plywood and was insulated. The beds had foam mattresses. I don't know about Gerald, but I felt like a new man after washing up, shaving, and eating dinner.

I was up at 7 o'clock the next morning after waking up several times during the night, sweating. My sleeping bag was designed for colder temperatures than inside an insulated, heated cabin, and it was uncomfortably warm. The wind had died down during the night, and the sun was shining brightly when we got under way again at 9:30 A.M. It was still very cold, however. Two hours later, we had seen no tracks. Suddenly we saw two bears ahead of us. When we caught up to them a mile later, the guide was convinced that one was a very big sow and the other was its cub, so we left them alone.

A short while later, we found another set of tracks and followed them for five miles until we came to an area literally covered with bear tracks of all sizes. Soon after that we found a dead muskox. The bears had ripped it apart, leaving tracks everywhere. We tried following the tracks from the carcass, but there were too many tracks, and the bears were going in every direction. We eventually gave up without finding a bear.

Around 6:30 P.M. we headed back to Bay Chimo. We'd had a nice clear day, and it had warmed up a bit since we'd left that morning. Without wind, though, the fumes from the machines were bad for us on the sleds. About a half-hour after we'd turned around, we drove up on a fresh set of bear tracks. About a mile later we found the bear. Gerald wanted to take it with his muzzleloader, but when he couldn't get the flint to spark he picked up his centerfire rifle and killed the bear—another big old boar.

Back in Bay Chimo we ate dinner and were in our beds by 2 A.M. We woke to find it had snowed during the night, and a high wind was blowing snow horizontally. I was glad we'd taken our bears and didn't have to go out again. Gerald and I rested while the guides fleshed and salted the hides of our bears. Henry learned that a plane would be landing outside the village the next day to take supplies to a bird-watching site, where biologists studied migrating waterfowl. Henry arranged for both of us to fly back to Cambridge Bay on it, but I decided to go back with my guide on his snowmobile. The weather forecast called for it to clear up and get warmer, and I wanted to take a seal and see the geese returning to their nesting grounds. After we put Gerald on the plane, the guides and I drove the snowmobiles to the nesting grounds and found the seals

sunning themselves on the edges of the ice. After watching literally thousands of geese landing, flying around, and on the water, I picked out a seal and shot it.

An elderly Eskimo man, who was traveling to Cambridge Bay to visit his family, came along about then. When we gave him my seal, his face beamed. He hadn't seen his family since the previous summer, he said, and he was happy to be able to take meat to them.

The first thing I did after checking into a motel in Cambridge Bay that evening was to take a hot bath. The woman at the airline ticket counter the next afternoon asked me where I was from. She had heard my name, she said. It turned out that she was from Hillgrove, just eight miles from my home. I was back in Havelock two days later, after staying overnight in Edmonton.

Hunting in the far north in the spring is tough and not without danger, but our guides knew what they were doing and were able to produce two very good bears for us.

Rohil Nana was a legend among hunters who hunted in Pakistan. Rohil was an executive for a tobacco company when SCI founder C. J. McElroy walked into a travel agency in downtown Karachi in the early 1970s and asked if the operator knew anyone who could take him hunting. (The fact that the travel agent spoke English was just one of the fortunate events that would change Rohil's life.) The agent introduced McElroy to Rohil because he knew that Rohil enjoyed hunting. Before that meeting, there had been no hunting outfitters in that game-rich country, and few trophy hunters had ever hunted there. Rohil went on to form his own hunting company and would guide virtually every foreigner who hunted in Pakistan for many years after that.

I'd been talking with Jim Conklin about hunting in Pakistan, and Jim introduced me to Rohil at the 1994 SCI convention.

It was 11:30 P.M. on 14 November 1994 when I landed in Karachi, after flying there via Halifax, Amsterdam, and Dubai in the United Arab Emirates in less than twenty-four hours. Someone from the hunting company met me at the airport and drove me a short distance to a hotel. I had booked a two-week hunt with Rohil Nana, Pakistan's only professional hunting outfitter.

Rohil had been young and physically fit when he began outfitting nearly thirty years earlier, but his health had seriously deteriorated by the time I met him in Islamabad. He'd undergone two recent heart bypass operations and was scheduled for even more surgery after I left Pakistan. (I saw him take a large number of pills when I was with him, and he frequently took oxygen during the day.) Rohil's health problems had left him thin and gaunt. He spoke a British-sounding English with a Pakistani accent.

Rohil said he had flown from Karachi to Islamabad the previous day to make certain that things were ready for my hunt. We would have lunch at the home of one of his friends in Islamabad, and then we would drive four and a half hours to Kalabagh in the state of Punjab, where I would hunt a chinkara gazelle and a Punjab urial in the Salt Range. According to Rohil, I would be the first trophy hunter to hunt there since a disease carried by camels had halved its herd of eight hundred urial three years earlier.

Kalabagh was crowded with trucks and animals of every description when we arrived there at 7 P.M. We had traveled over arid, featureless land that resembled much of southern Africa's terrain. The roads were so narrow that we sometimes had to move onto the dirt shoulder to avoid getting sideswiped by brightly decorated trucks. Every so often we would drive past men and women in traditional Muslim dress, leading or riding two-humped camels, and it would suddenly remind me that we were in Asia.

We did not stay long in the noisy city but went directly to the palace of Prince Azam. After I was introduced to the prince, a big man in his late thirties, I was taken to a large guesthouse overlooking the Indus River. Guards in uniform, as well as the household staff, met us when we arrived. The house was about four thousand square feet in size and had large rooms with high ceilings, marble floors, and chandeliers. Outside, there were marbled terraces. When I was invited to sign the guest book, I was surprised to see that Queen Elizabeth, Prince Philip, John and Jacqueline Kennedy, Prince Abdorreza Pahlavi of Iran, C. J. McElroy, and many other people whose names I recognized had stayed there.

The next morning the prince took us to a fort in the Salt Range above the river. To get there we had to cross the river on the railroad bridge. (A man was stationed there to stop traffic when a train was due.) We drove noisily across the planks laid loosely between the rails. We traveled with two vehicles ahead of us and one behind us, and each vehicle carried four armed guards wearing uniforms. The prince drove our vehicle. When we reached the fort, the guards jumped out and took positions before we left our vehicle.

The fort had a large staff. Their primary task was to protect the prince's property, but they also did a little subsistence farming and some housework and cooking when there were guests in the lodge.

Rohil was unable to go out the next day—he had to stay near his oxygen supply—so I left the lodge early with three of the guards (one spoke some English and was my hunting guide), and Rohil and the prince slept in. In the books of sheep hunters Rashid Jamsheed, Elgin Gates, and C. J. McElroy, the hunters talk of having seen herds of sixty or more Punjab urial when they hunted in this area two decades earlier.[1] The two herds we saw that day each had perhaps one-third that number, and they were extremely wary. I'd done my research before leaving home and had a pretty good idea what a trophy ram should

look like. When we found a male with horns that seemed to almost touch the animal's neck, I knew I was looking at a good ram. My guide agreed. We left the vehicle and made a long stalk across the wide, grassy plain that brought us to within two hundred yards of the herd. We waited a few minutes until the ram I wanted stepped away from the others, then I shot it. The animal dropped on the spot, and my guide—as guides everywhere do— grinned and slapped me on my back.

This ram was much redder than the Trans-Caspian urial I'd taken a year earlier in Turkmenistan. It had a long, black mane on its throat, a white bib, and a two-color saddle on its back. Its horns were 23½ inches long and would later rank number fifteen in the *SCI All-Time Record Book of Trophy Animals*. I was glad to add it to my collection. This small wild sheep is found only in the Salt and Kala ranges between the Indus and Jhelum rivers in Pakistan.

The three guards and I hunted the flats the next two days for a chinkara gazelle (also called Indian gazelle). We saw a few of these graceful, sixty-pound antelopes, but I was not able to collect a good male. There weren't many of them, and they were hard to see because of the high grass. It was obvious that they had been hunted before, because all of them were running

---

1. At dinner one evening Prince Azam said he wished he knew more about protecting his last herd of Punjab urial. I told him North American biologists were capturing wild sheep with nets and tranquilizing darts and using radio collars and other methods to learn more about them. They also were collecting eggs from the ovaries of Armenian sheep in Texas and implanting embryos. When I returned to New Brunswick, I called George Roberts, my hunting friend in British Columbia. George had helped transplant wild sheep, and he wrote a report that described various methods of capturing them. He also got in touch with Texas A&M University and obtained research papers on freezing eggs and implanting sheep embryos. Unfortunately, soon after we sent the report to Rohil, he wrote me to say the prince had died suddenly of diabetes. I never heard what happened to the report after that.

This Sind ibex was the largest the author could find in five days of hard hunting. Pakistan.

Outfitter Rohil Nana and the author with his Punjab urial. Pakistan.

The author rode a camel to hunt Blanford urial and enjoyed another different experience. Pakistan.

away from us and wouldn't stop until they had put a wide valley between us. My guides said it would be dangerous to follow them. There were "outlaws" in the mountains across the valley, they said.

I had heard shooting from heavy guns the first day we hunted on the flats, but no one with me spoke English, and I didn't know what was happening. Rohil later said the outlaws were shooting warning shots to tell us to leave the area. No one had hunted in that area for a few years, and they didn't know we were hunting. If they had known, they wouldn't have bothered us.

On 19 November Rohil and I were back in Islamabad in time to have lunch at his mother's home and catch the 3:30 P.M. flight to Karachi.

When Pakistan gained its independence from India in 1947, Karachi's population

was only 250,000. Today it has more than eleven million people and is suffering from growing pains. I found it dirty and crowded. Whole regions of the city were shanties and shacks slapped together from any kind of scrap the occupants could scavenge. The hotels and business districts were islands surrounded by poverty. We couldn't find a room because the World Wildlife Fund was holding a big meeting in Karachi, with Prince Philip as its featured speaker, and every room in every halfway decent hotel was booked. Rohil finally got me into the prestigious old Sindh Club, a private club with a ten-year waiting list of people who wanted to join. He and his family had been members for years, Rohil said.

The next day Rohil and I, along with a driver, drove four hours to Dureji in Baluchistan Province to hunt Blanford urial, Sind ibex, and Kennion (or Jabir) gazelle. According to Rohil, a tribal chief ruled the region, and the government had no control over it. Women were conspicuous by their absence in Dureji, as they were nearly everywhere I went in Pakistan. The few women I saw along the streets and in the shops were dressed entirely in black, and black veils covered their faces. Most of the men had beards and wore caps and long vests. Dureji was a collection of pole shacks with grass roofs. Rohil said few people had beds with mattresses. Most of them slept on mats on the floor.

Rohil and I stayed in a small house in the mountains above Dureji. For the next few days I got up early and ate something before joining the two men Rohil had hired to guide me. Most of the time we simply left the house on foot and began climbing the mountains that surrounded us. Twice, though, we rode camels when Rohil wanted to go with us. It was the first time I had ever hunted from a camel. I can't say I enjoyed the experience.

The mountains were not as steep and rugged as some of the other places I had hunted urial, but we did do a lot of climbing. I shot my Blanford urial first, a fine animal with 28-inch horns. Its body was twenty to thirty pounds larger than my Punjab urial's, and it was more grayish-brown than red. We saw a dozen or more males before I selected the one I took. These urial did not seem to be as wary as others I'd hunted.

Next, I made a good shot on a Kennion gazelle, which we found on the flats as we were driving to the place where I'd hunt a Sind ibex. Scientists say this animal, along with its cousin the bezoar ibex, is the ancestor of the domestic goat, and they classify it as a goat and not an ibex because the leading edges of its horns are sharp instead of flat. I don't know any hunter who would call it a "Sind goat," however. It looks like an ibex, walks like an ibex, and lives in the roughest country it can find, just like an ibex. It was tough hunting, and when we found a good male, more often than not it would be on a nearly vertical ledge that was impossible to get to. After five days of hunting, I shot an average-size billy. It was not as large as I'd hoped to take, but I was thankful that I was able to add it to my collection and end my hunt in Pakistan.

We drove back to Karachi the next morning, and I showered and ate lunch at noon. I was scheduled to fly home that afternoon, but I hadn't confirmed my flight the required seventy-two hours in advance. Rohil managed to get me a seat, however, and got me through Customs quickly, only to learn that my flight would be delayed for five hours. I was in Havelock the next day.

In my journal I wrote, "I am looking forward to hunting other species in Pakistan at a later date." Four years later, in 1999, I did exactly that.

PLAINS AND MOUNTAIN GAME, 1995

If you were to ask international hunters which animals that the Sudan is best known for, chances are most would tell you Africa's largest country is one of the few places, except for game ranches in Texas and South Africa, where one can hunt the Nubian ibex. Very few might say that eight of the SCI record book's twenty-four categories of African gazelle can be hunted there. In 1995 I booked a safari in Sudan with Angelo Dacey Safaris to take five of those gazelle—Eritrean, Heuglin, red-fronted, Sahara dorcas, and Isabelline—plus an ibex and a Salt dik-dik.

Port Sudan, a city of more than three hundred thousand on the Red Sea, is the Republic of Sudan's major seaport and rail and pipeline terminus. The center of trade, it has an international airport and an oil refinery. The Nile Valley outside the city produces a world-famous strain of cotton. Despite all this, Port Sudan and the rest of that country are rife with poverty, illiteracy, and lawlessness. Civil wars fed by Muslim fundamentalists in the north have flared up sporadically in the south since the 1950s. State departments of other governments regularly issue travel warnings, and foreigners need special permits to travel from one area to another. Most of the country's cities have imposed curfews.

It wouldn't have taken much research to realize that the Sudan was not the place for a non-Muslim North American to be on 2 March 1995, the morning I landed in Port Sudan's international airport.

I wasn't being reckless. I knew hunters who had recently hunted in the Sudan safely. They had experienced few problems and claimed they never felt threatened while in the country. Because they had hunted with an outfitter who knew how to operate amid Sudan's corruption and chaos, they were able to get in and hunt the animals they wanted and get out. As I went through Customs in Khartoum, I was hoping my safari would go as smoothly as theirs.

I'd traveled to the Sudan through Boston, Amsterdam, Cairo, and Khartoum, where Angelo Dacey had arranged for a man named Nichola to help me get the permits I needed to hunt and travel in his country.[1] After clearing Customs, he took me to a home, where I paid the balance of my safari fees, and saw me board the 10 A.M., one-hour flight to Port Sudan.

Angelo Dacey, my guide for the next three weeks, drove me into the city, where he picked up some supplies and had my licenses stamped. The Sudanese, I quickly learned, thrived on paperwork and red tape.

---

1. Nichola owned the rights to bottle Coca-Cola in Khartoum. He had bought, or was in the process of buying, Angelo Dacey Safaris from Angelo when I was there.

I had a license to possess a firearm and ammunition, a license to hunt, and a license to travel inside the country. Angelo and I didn't tarry in Port Sudan after leaving the government offices, and we were on the road out of town by noon. We had a hot, humid four-hour drive to the Red Sea Hills, where I would hunt a Nubian ibex about 150 miles south of the Egyptian border. The road was paved for the first hour and a half; then we turned off onto a two-track trail and traveled the rest of the way over rocks and sand. Our camp, at three thousand feet elevation, consisted of four tents set at the base of a rocky hill. Everything around us was nearly barren.

Angelo said we would find ibex in the mountains above us and Salt dik-dik and Eritrean gazelle on the flats nearby. As I've experienced in deserts elsewhere, there was a big drop in temperature as soon as the sun went down. I'd brought a light jacket and was warm enough at night. Our camp was comfortable and well stocked, thanks to Angelo's professionalism.

Scattered along the foothills around us were a few small bands of desert people, living in lean-tos or out in the open, wherever they could find some shade and a little water for their goats and camels. There was very little for their animals to eat, but they somehow subsisted. All the men were dressed in white robes, but I never saw a woman. I suspect they were like the few women I saw in the towns, who covered themselves from head to toe whenever they went outside.

I spent the next five days getting up at 5:30 in the morning and driving to whatever mountain Angelo had arranged to hunt that day. He had hired up to forty of the local people to serve as beaters. When the people worked their way over the ridges and toward us, the ibex, we hoped, would run past the spot where we were sitting. The hunt wasn't as easy as it sounds. The rocks on those mountains would crumble when I tried to grab a rock or use it as a foothold. It was so steep that I'd take one step up and slide back two in some places. It was far from easy just getting to the place where we would wait for an ibex to run past.

We saw a few ibex each day on these drives but none that I wanted until the morning of the fifth day. The older male ibex always seemed to know where we were and would turn and run down another canyon just before they came into range. On the fifth morning, though, the drive was almost over when a good billy bolted out of a steep canyon and came running toward me. I was ready with my rifle resting on my jacket when it came into range. I led it by several feet and fired, and the ibex rolled and slid a few yards down the hill. I was glad to have taken it. I didn't want to climb those rugged mountains another day. Now we could concentrate on the dik-dik and Eritrean gazelle on the flats.

Hunting the flats was much easier because we could drive, glass, and stalk. There was nothing unusual about collecting these two species. For the dik-dik, I merely stepped out of the truck and shot it. These little antelope weigh less than six pounds and have short horns. They seldom stand and allow

The author's outfitter Angelo Dacey hired these local people to drive a Nubian ibex to him. Sudan.

Outfitter Angelo Dacey and the author with an Eritrean gazelle. Sudan.

enough time for a hunter to inspect them with binoculars. I shot almost the same instant Angelo said it was a male. I was glad to have it.

The gazelle were a different story. We were seeing herds of them, but, like all gazelle, they were tough to approach on that flat, wide-open terrain. We chased them around for two days before I finally collected a respectable head. It was just in time, because we planned to move to another camp the next day, 9 March.

Angelo had arranged for Nichola to drive up from Khartoum—a distance of some seven hundred miles—to meet us in a village called Hadalia. I never knew how far he and I drove to get there, but it took us about eight hours. We arrived in Hadalia at 4 P.M. and found Nichola hadn't arrived yet. We waited in town for him until dark, then drove about a mile out of town and made camp alongside the road. Angelo didn't bother to set up a tent. The night was warm, and we slept under the stars. Except for the dust, it was quite pleasant. Nichola found our camp at about 11:30 that night.

We spent the next morning hunting a Heuglin gazelle in that area but didn't see a shootable male, and we left for a camp Nichola called the "bird camp," another eight hours south. Along the way we stopped to eat at a marketplace in a small village where goat and sheep meat was hanging in open stalls. Each of us picked a cut we wanted, and it was grilled on a piece of iron over an open fire outside. At 11:30 P.M. we pulled up to four or five dingy tents near a grove of some of the

few trees we'd seen in that area. I was not comfortable in this unorganized camp. The people there would not look directly at me and were inhospitable. I felt better when Angelo said we would spend only two nights there.

We spent the next two days hunting Heuglin gazelle on the plains about an hour from the camp. We didn't see many, but it may have been because the grass was so high. I finally took one just before noon on the second day.

That afternoon we crossed the Blue Nile and drove for two hours through a fertile farming area that was as flat as our Canadian prairie provinces, then crossed the White Nile and drove on to a town called Kosti. Before we could continue, we had to stop and get our paperwork stamped at the game department. That done, we left the main road and drove about an hour to a small village, where a local guide was waiting for us. From there we drove another five hours to a spot on the border between northern and southern Sudan. Until then, my stay in that country had been relatively safe.

Terrorists controlled southern Sudan, Angelo said, and we would have to avoid the areas where they were known to be. But first we had to get across the border. Few people were crossing it from the north in those days, and the man at the checkpoint didn't want to let us continue. Angelo talked with him for a while before he allowed us to cross, which he did, with the proviso that we would get permission from someone in another village. To see that we did, he sent a policeman to go with us. Two hours later, we located the official—a very friendly man—and had our paperwork stamped again. It was midnight before we reached the place where the local guide wanted to hunt. Instead of erecting tents, we merely set up some cots and slept in the open.

The next morning I woke to find myself in savanna woodlands, with a great deal of high grass. Some of the area had been burned, however, leaving large patches of bare, soot-covered ground. The gazelle were attracted to the new grass that was popping up in the open areas, and we drove up on our first herd less than half an hour after leaving camp. The burning that had made it easier for us to find the gazelle made it difficult to approach them. It took us thirty or forty minutes to get within range of the little herd. The gazelle saw us before I could find a rest for my rifle and started running. Leading the best male by at least six feet, I took an offhand shot at it when it lagged a bit behind the others in the herd—and shot behind it. Angelo consoled me by saying we'd find another herd, but we couldn't get close enough to the only herd we saw that afternoon.

Finally, very late in the afternoon of the next day, we found a good male, and I was able to take it. It was a good thing, because we didn't have enough water to stay there much longer.

We left the next morning for Khartoum, leaving our guide at his home. Around noon we stopped at another village and bought Cokes and fruit for lunch. We reached Nichola's place around 9 P.M. My room had an air-conditioning unit, but the city's power kept going on and off all night long.

A dorcas gazelle was next on the list of animals I wanted to take in the Sudan. It was a long way over bad roads to the area where we would hunt it, Angelo said, so we would be accompanied by another truck, just in case ours broke down. Because of the heat, we didn't leave until 4 P.M. and traveled much of the way in the dark. There was no road, only tracks, and there were fewer tracks the farther we went. At 9 P.M. our little caravan stopped for the night. We were only about an hour from where we would hunt, Angelo said. We slept under the stars again that night.

We left before daylight the next morning, leaving the second vehicle with a man, and drove over to the flats the gazelle were using. We started seeing them right away, but there was absolutely no cover to hide our approach. Whenever we drove up on a herd, the gazelle would spot our vehicle from a half-mile away and run off. Around noon, though, one of those herds allowed us to get within 350 yards, and I took the best male with a very long shot.

The wind was blowing off the Sahara, and it was dusty and very hot, perhaps 95–100 degrees Fahrenheit. After skinning my gazelle, we drove back to Khartoum. There was one more day remaining in my hunt, but it wasn't enough time to hunt an Isabelline gazelle. I'd taken one in Ethiopia on another safari, so I wasn't concerned. I spent the next day looking around Khartoum, a city of more than four million, where the White and Blue Nile Rivers meet.

Angelo Dacey and the author with a Heuglin gazelle. Sudan.

The author took his Greenland muskox during a break in the weather. After this photo, rain and fog moved in. Greenland.

I left for home at 1 A.M. on 22 March, with stops in Frankfurt and Boston, before landing in Moncton at 10 P.M. that same day. I'd had a good hunt and had taken some very good trophies in the Sudan. According to Angelo, I was the first hunter to take four different types of gazelle on the same safari in recent times.

Later, the SCI record book would rank my Heuglin gazelle's 11⅝-inch horns number one in that category. My red-fronted gazelle would rank number three, and the Sahara dorcas gazelle and Eritrean gazelle both would rank number fourteen.

It pleased me when Angelo said he had enjoyed hunting with me. We both enjoyed camping in the open and moving on the next day. We'd become good friends.

Exactly four months to the day after returning from the Sudan, I was stepping off an airplane in London en route to Denmark, where I would stop over before heading on to Greenland to hunt a muskox. First, however, I would spend four days hunting a European roe deer with British outfitter Kevin Downer.[2] I had taken a roe deer in Bulgaria in 1991, but I hoped to take a better one on this trip. My chances were good, because I would be hunting during the last week of July—the peak of the roe deer's rutting season in England.

After meeting me at Heathrow Airport, Kevin and I drove forty-five minutes to a village called Reading and had breakfast with Allan Hayward in his restaurant before driving to Allan's home in nearby Thatchin. For the next few days we would call our "camp" the comfortable guest area Allan had built on one end of his home. We hunted the areas he had leased from the local landowners.

At first light the next morning we were sitting in a high seat (an elevated blind) on the Chievley hunting estate, but all we saw that day was a small male roebuck and a female with her fawn. Kevin and I stayed in the blind until it got dark, around 9:30 P.M.

We were up at 4 o'clock and spent the morning on the same hunting estate. Instead of sitting in a blind, however, we drove around in Allan's Land Rover. Kevin and I rode in the back, and we saw perhaps a dozen roe deer, but none of the bucks was shootable. That afternoon we moved to an estate called Wasing, where we spent the afternoon and all the next day without seeing a good buck. Just before noon of the second day on Wasing, a young muntjac stepped into an opening. I was surprised to see it, but I shouldn't have been. These little Asian deer escaped from private estates many years earlier and have multiplied and spread across much of England. In some areas they are so plentiful that homeowners consider them a threat to their gardens and flowers.

When we returned from the woods that afternoon, Allan was waiting for us. He'd had a call from Wasing. A big roebuck had been seen in one of the fields on that estate. If we hurried, we might be

2. I'd met Kevin on a hunt in Turkey, and we'd become friends. At the SCI convention that year, he heard I was going to Greenland and suggested I set a few days aside to hunt a roe deer with him.

able to find it before dark. The buck had already left the field by the time that Kevin and I got there, so we tried walking along the edge of another field the gamekeeper thought the deer might be using. We hadn't gone very far when Kevin saw it— the roebuck was running toward the woods. It was out of sight before I had a chance to shoot.

I was scheduled to fly to Copenhagen the next afternoon, but we were back on Wasing early the next morning. I could tell Kevin was disappointed that he hadn't been able to show me a good roe deer.

"I was certain I could find you a nice roe," he said.

"It's not over until it's over," I said, hoping to cheer him up. "We still have another half-hour."

Fifteen minutes later we were back at the vehicle, ready to leave, when Kevin decided to try calling. Within seconds a female came out of the woods and started trotting toward us, then stopped. Right behind her was a roebuck.

"Take him! Take him!" Kevin urged.

He needn't have told me twice. I already had the cross hairs on the little deer's shoulder. It dropped in its tracks when I shot. It was an old buck, with impressive, heavily gnarled bases on its antlers. I think Allan and Kevin were happier than I was that I'd taken it. I'd had a super hunt during my brief layover in England, and taking that deer was merely frosting on the cake.

Diana of Denmark was that country's major hunting company when my flight from London landed in Copenhagen on 26 July 1995. Greenland had opened muskox hunting the previous year, and I'd booked a hunt at the SCI convention. Two months later, I got a call from Jan Thrysoe, the outfitter Diana uses for its hunts in Greenland. Jan worked for the Copenhagen police department, but he and his wife had been stationed in Greenland for six years. While he was there, he and his partner, a biologist in Greenland, were responsible for opening up hunting before Jan was transferred back to Denmark. Jan said he and his wife were going to the United States and would later be driving a motor home to Nova Scotia to visit a son's girlfriend. He wanted to know if he and his wife could stop by and meet me in Havelock.

I liked him as soon as I shook his hand. Jan and his wife stayed three days at our lodge. I was disappointed to hear that he wouldn't be able to personally guide me because he had to work. A few weeks later, he called from Denmark to say he'd been able to get a week off work by promising to put on a police training course the next winter. He asked if I would be interested in hunting a transplanted muskox herd that had been released in southern Greenland eight years earlier. If I did, he would guide me. I would be the first nonresident to hunt a muskox south of the Arctic Circle on the world's largest island.

Airline schedules don't mean much in the Danish territories of Iceland and Greenland, especially when a North Atlantic storm blows into the region. It was a lesson that would be brought home for me several times during my hunt for a Greenland muskox.

Jan Thrysoe and I left Copenhagen at 7:30 P.M. for a four-hour flight on Icelandic Air to Reykjavik in Iceland. We left our hotel for the airport early the next day to continue on to Greenland, only to have our 9 A.M. flight delayed twice because of bad weather in Greenland. We finally left at noon. It was a two-hour flight, and we spent another hour circling because of the fog.

When our fuel began running low, our pilot finally put us down on a former U.S. Air Force airstrip outside Narsarsuap, a village of two or three hundred people, where we stayed in the only hotel. We would have nineteen to twenty hours of daylight, the desk clerk said. The next day a Greenland Air helicopter flew us to the village of Ivittuut on Greenland's southern tip, our base for this hunt. I found it interesting that the airline used helicopters to serve smaller villages that had no landing strips. Ivittuut certainly qualified as small, even though it had a Danish naval station.

Old Eric the Red, the Norseman who named the island more than a thousand years ago, obviously had a perverse sense of humor. According to various sources, of its 840,000-square-mile landmass, only about 130,000 square miles are not covered with an ancient ice cap averaging five thousand feet deep. Only a very narrow strip about a mile wide along Greenland's southern tip outside the Arctic Circle is considered habitable. Fishing and fish processing were

Greenland's only industry when I was there, and raising sheep seemed to be the only agricultural activity possible. Farming was out of the question, at least on a profitable scale.

After we landed in Ivittuut, Ole Huttel, the head of the village, escorted us to his modern office, where we met our guide, Per. Per drove us to his home in the nearly deserted mining town of Arsuk, about two miles outside of town. The lead and zinc mine had operated since the early 1900s but had shut down three years earlier when the price of lead and zinc crashed and made mining unprofitable. Most of the homes there were abandoned and deteriorating, but Per's was well kept and freshly painted. Per put us up in rooms in the village's old hotel. No one worked there, but it had been partially kept up. A generator that ran twenty-four hours a day provided heat and lights. We appreciated the heaters when the temperature dropped to freezing at night.

According to Per and Jan, muskox had been trapped in the north of the country eight years earlier and had been released in the south. There were now about 150 of them, and I would be the first North American to hunt one. All the other muskox hunts had taken place in the north.

To reach my hunting area, we waited until the fog lifted so we could get past the icebergs safely; then we left Ivittuut in a modern fishing boat, towing a runabout. Four hours later, we went ashore and put up two tents. It was not a good campsite. When the sun was out, which was more than nineteen hours a day, swarms of flies covered us. We could only wait for evening or for a breeze to come up to give us relief from them.

After getting our camp organized, we went out in the small boat and ran along the shore, glassing for muskox as we went. When we reached a spot where a glacier ran into the sea, we went ashore and walked to a place where Per knew there were fossils. On the way we spotted a muskox bull on the other side of the river. According to Per, the young animal was stranded. It apparently had swum the river and would have to swim back to reach the area the muskox inhabited.

It was the only muskox we saw that day. At 3:30 A.M., just as the four-hour night was ending, we left our camp by boat again and drove about an hour along the shoreline. We landed and took off on foot to check a spot where Per said we might see a few muskox. The farther we went, however, the thicker the fog became. We eventually had to stop and wait three hours for it to lift. When it did, we walked another two hours until we could look down from a high, rocky ridge into a big valley. We found a herd of about fifty muskox almost immediately. According to Per, we were looking at one-third of all the muskox on this part of the island.

One of the bulls was larger than the others. We glassed it for twenty or thirty minutes before I decided to take it. It was an old male, but its horns were worn down and broken at the tips. It would not rank high in a record book, but it was in a spot where we could stalk it. Jan and Per agreed with me. We had only three

more days to hunt, and the weather forecast wasn't good. If we waited another day, we might not get to go out again. They also weren't sure where to look for the area's other muskox.

As we moved closer to the herd, a curious cow saw us and moved very close to where we were bent over, motionless. She watched us for several minutes but finally turned away and moved off. A few minutes later, we came within a hundred yards of the bull I had selected. I sat down, rested my elbows on my knees to steady my rifle, and killed the bull with two shots. Our assessment of the animal had been correct. It was an old bull, and its horns had heavy bases, but the tips were broken off and worn. Jan and Per said they thought it was the last of the bulls from the original transplant.

After taking pictures of my muskox, we spent another hour skinning it, then began carrying the hide and the meat back to the boat. It took five or six trips, but we got every edible bit of meat out, as required by law. We had thought the flies were bad before, but they were so thick while we were handling the meat that it was hard to see. We were exhausted by the time we reached camp. Mercifully, the wind came up and the flies went away.

It wasn't as windy the next morning, and there was no fog, so we were able to take the boat back to Ivittuut. Along the way we took the time to pull into two bays to see a scenic waterfall and a huge glacier. We hunted seals for an hour or two the next day, but cold rain, wind, and fog forced us back to shore. That evening Per invited us to his home for a salmon dinner with his family.

It had rained most of that day, and it was raining when we got up the next morning. As Jan had predicted, the helicopter flight that was supposed to pick us up at 11:30 A.M. was canceled because of the bad weather. There was no rain the following day, but a thick fog delayed the helicopter again, which meant Jan and I would miss the last flight out of Narsarsuap to Iceland that week. Jan, who had to be back to work at the Copenhagen police department on Monday, tried to charter a helicopter for us, but it also had to turn back. It looked as if we wouldn't get to Copenhagen for quite a while. However, when Jan learned a military plane was flying from Narsarsuap to Copenhagen the next day, we chartered a fast, modern fishing boat for the five-and-a-half-hour trip around the southern tip of the island. The open water was rough, and both Jan and I got seasick, but we felt better when we hit Shelter Bay's calmer water. We were in a hotel in Narsarsuap by 10:30 P.M., just as the sun was going down.

We weren't allowed to board the military plane the next day because I had a commercial airline ticket, and I was convinced we would be stuck there for at least two more days. But Jan learned a twin-engine chartered aircraft would be arriving to evacuate two injured fishermen to Iceland. We were able to get on this plane and arrived in Reykjavik at 2:45 P.M. There was a flight to Copenhagen at 4 P.M., and the international airport was an hour away, but we hired a taxi and made it. Jan went home, and I took a cab downtown to a hotel. After Greenland, my room was uncomfortably warm. When I opened the window, the noise of the city assaulted my ears. I didn't get much sleep before I left early in the morning for the long trip back to Moncton, but it felt great to be home instead of trying to get off that frozen island.

I had always wanted to take my grandson, Jeremy Demont, to Africa on a safari, and, now that he was nearly sixteen, we were on our way. I also took Brian West from the lodge and George Roberts, the friend from British Columbia who had done a report for Prince Azam of Pakistan. It would be the first trip to Africa for the three of them. We would spend three days sightseeing at Victoria Falls and ten days hunting. Jeremy and George did the hunting; Brian and I went along as observers.

The various problems I had been experiencing with airlines grew worse the more I traveled. This time we were in Frankfurt, trying to check in for an Air Zimbabwe flight that would take us to Zimbabwe, and the clerk at the airline counter couldn't find our reservations in her computer. We finally straightened it out and landed in Harare the next morning. We cleared Customs, got the permits we needed for our rifles, and caught another flight to Victoria Falls.

We spent the next three days at Sizinda Lodge. Brian and George shared one rondavel; Jeremy and I shared another.

The comfortable rondavels had stone and cement walls with thatched roofs, and there was running water and mosquito netting over our beds. In the dining area we could glass down to a water hole where zebra, giraffe, elephant, eland, waterbuck, warthog, and other animals came to drink. I guess everyone wants his grandchildren to enjoy the same things he does. I was thrilled to see that Jeremy was enjoying every minute of the safari.

We saw even more animals on a game drive later that day, arriving back at the lodge at dark in time to enjoy a campfire and have dinner. We spent two hours at the falls the next day and had lunch in the historic Victoria Falls Hotel, where Kevin White and I had stayed three years earlier. Later, we toured Victoria Falls National Park, where we saw a lot of elephant—as well as the damage they were doing to the park's vegetation—but very few other animals. Brian and Jeremy went whitewater rafting on the Zambezi River the next day, while George took a helicopter ride over the falls and park. When they returned, we did some shopping on the streets for wood carvings.

Our professional hunters met us in Bulawayo the next day. Ernest Dyasan would guide Jeremy, and I would travel with them; George would hunt with Kirk Mason, and Brian would travel with them. Our camp, a group of tents and a thatched dining area called Shangani, was only about an hour and a half from the airport, giving us plenty of time to go hunting that afternoon. We saw game, but Jeremy and

George didn't shoot that evening. The next day I watched Jeremy take a tsessebe with 14¼-inch horns and a very good warthog. Every grandfather will know how I felt. I enjoyed seeing him take his first African animals far more than if I had shot them myself.

We spent the next day looking for a trophy reedbuck for him but saw only a young male, which he passed up. I shot a very sick warthog that had a poacher's wire snare caught around its neck. Brian met us for lunch, while George stayed out to watch a water hole. Brian joined us in the afternoon and watched Jeremy take a baboon. Later, Brian shot a greater kudu. When we returned at sundown, we learned George had taken a warthog, a sable antelope, and a greater kudu. Our safari could not have been going any better. All three were enjoying experiences they would remember all their lives.

The next day we left that area and drove for three hours to a town called West Nicholson. Nearby was the main camp of Tshabezi Safaris, where Jeremy and George would hunt leopard and other game. Their first order of business was to shoot the bait for their cats. Jeremy shot an impala, and George shot a zebra, and the professional hunters set them out.

Leopard baiting involves more than just hanging some meat in any old tree. The tree must be easily accessible and visible to the hunter, yet there must be enough cover to allow the cat to approach it without exposing itself. The bait must be hidden from carnivorous birds and high enough that lion and hyena—if the area has them—cannot reach it, and it must be tied securely to the tree so that the leopard can't move it. As for the blind, it should be unobtrusive and positioned close enough to the bait tree to reduce the chances of missing the shot. Because the leopard usually shows up very late, the blind must face the setting sun, so that the cat will be silhouetted during the last minutes of light.

Ernest and Kirk knew all this, and they had their baits hanging well before noon. The next morning Jeremy and Brian shot two more impala on the way to check the baits. One of the baits had been hit during the night by a female leopard. Ernest hung the two impala in another location and moved the first impala to keep the female from eating all of it.

We hunted that afternoon near West Nicholson, where Jeremy and Ernest hunted along the river, looking for bushbuck. Jeremy found one and took it with one shot just before dark.

By now, George and Kirk were leaving very early each morning and traveling to a different area to hunt, and Brian was riding with us.

The third morning we found another leopard had hit one of the baits during the night, so Jeremy shot another impala to "sweeten" the bait. We spent the afternoon looking for a klipspringer for him but did not find one.

The leopard returned to the bait that night, and when we checked its tracks the next morning Ernest decided it was a good male, big enough to try to take. He had his men build a blind about sixty yards

from the tree. When we returned to camp at sundown, we learned George had taken a greater kudu and a klipspringer. In the morning we discovered a male lion had hit another bait during the night. It was a big one, judging by its tracks and the long mane hair it left on the meat. Kirk built a blind for the lion.

Brian and I stayed in camp when George and Jeremy went to their separate blinds that afternoon around 4 o'clock. Just after dark that evening, Brian and I were sitting at the campfire when Jeremy walked in with a leopard on his shoulder. It was a great moment to share. I was as proud of Jeremy as he was with his cat.

Jeremy, Brian, and I left to visit Kruger National Park in South Africa, and George stayed and hunted. It was an hour and a half to the border and another half-hour to the town of Messinger, where one of Ernest's friends met us in a van. We reached the park three hours later and drove up on a herd of Cape buffalo almost immediately. A short distance down the road, just before we reached one of the rest areas where we had rented a cabin, we saw elephant crossing the road. We got to our rest area just in time. The park closes its gates at 5:30 P.M., and anyone who isn't inside an enclosure at one of the rest stops by sundown can be fined—or eaten.

While Ernest prepared a *braai* (barbecue) for us, Jeremy, Brian, and I sat on the cabin's balcony and watched hippo in a pool about a hundred feet away. The next day we saw a leopard, perhaps fifteen lion, several nyala, a hyena, and another herd of elephant bathing and drinking in a water hole. After lunch we drove another three hours through hilly country to the town of Pietersburg. There were few straight stretches on that road, and we had to keep telling Ernest to slow down. He apparently knew the road, but he was driving too fast for our comfort.

After spending the night in Pietersburg, we drove to Rhino Ranch, south of Johannesburg, and met Sandy McDonald, our outfitter. This was our last day to hunt. Jeremy shot a springbok, Brian shot a blesbok, and I took a black wildebeest. Jeremy and Brian took photos of a white rhino on that ranch, which meant that on this safari they had seen all of the Big Five up close, as well as more than thirty other types of wildlife and a lot of birds.

We drove to Johannesburg the next day. George and Kirk were waiting for us at the airport, and at 4 P.M. we boarded a South African Airways 747 and began our seventeen-hour flight to New York, stopping for fuel at Isle lo Sal in the Cape Verde Islands off the western coast of Africa. Some of our luggage was missing when we reached Moncton, but it caught up with us the next day. We'd had a great safari, and the experience was something that Jeremy, George, and Brian (and I) will always remember.

Serge Tyshkevitch, the man in charge of my hunt in the Caucasus, and Nicolai Semenjuk, the Ukrainian who would be my interpreter during my stay in Russia, spotted me when I came off the plane from Moscow. It was 20 September, and I was in Sochi, a large town on Russia's northwestern shore of the Black Sea, to hunt the West Caucasian tur (like an ibex), a Caucasian chamois, and a mid-Asian ibex. Serge had arranged to have a helicopter waiting to fly us to our camp in the Imeretenpa River valley. As frequently happens in Russia, our helicopter flight was delayed twice and finally canceled. (We later learned President Boris Yeltsin was in town, and all flights were grounded while he was there.) I spent the night in the Soshi Radisson Hotel on the shore of the Black Sea.

Nicolai and Serge had arranged to meet me in the lobby at 10 A.M. to go to the airport, but it was pouring rain when I got up. Around 10:30 Nicolai called to say our flight had been delayed by the rain. We didn't lift off until 5 P.M. In addition to Serge and Nicolai, Serge's assistant, Antolia, and a local guide went with us.

Our camp was a very small cabin— about nine feet by twelve feet—with an attached lean-to where we ate outside. It was in a wooded, narrow valley surrounded by steep mountains, a long way from tur habitat. Our dinner that evening was a cold salad, cheese, and bread. (For breakfast they had more cheese, cold sausage, and bread with coffee.)

Nicolai stayed in camp when Serge and I left at 7:30 to go hunting the next morning. Red deer were roaring in the forest all around us, but when we went after one of them, all we saw was a quick glimpse of a stag's antlers as it ran off through the brush. We had walked a long

The author was as proud of his grandson's leopard as Jeremy was.   Zimbabwe.

The author took this Caucasian chamois above the Imeretenpa River Valley.   Its best horn was 8⅞ inches long.   Russia.

way to get there, and we would have to climb a lot higher on that steep mountain to reach the tur. We finally saw a few tur along the snow line, but there was only one good male, and it was too far off to try to shoot it. We headed back to camp at 3:30 P.M., arriving there after three hours of steady walking. On the way off the mountain we spotted a female chamois that paid no attention to us at all. Dinner that evening was a cold salad with boiled potatoes.

We hunted from that cabin for five days. We even tried staying out one night to avoid the long trek to the hunting area and back, but we saw very little game and almost no male tur. On the fourth day we did see a brown bear and her cubs and a lone chamois, the only male chamois we had seen in that area. After a very long stalk, I made a good shot. Its longest horn was 8⅞ inches long. I was happy to have it. I had booked hunts to collect four different types of chamois on this trip, and taking the Caucasian variety meant I had only three to go.

We finally left that area and walked four and a half hours back to the first cabin, where the helicopter was scheduled to pick us up the next morning. When it arrived, it flew us to another mountain and dropped us off above the tree line. Our camp there consisted of two very small tents, one for the interpreter and me, the other for the three guides. Even before we got the tents up, Serge spotted a band of tur far above us. The local guide, the interpreter, and I left the others to finish setting up the camp and began climbing.

It took us nearly three hours to reach the top, but we found the herd we had seen from below, as well as two others. One of those herds had only males. A half-hour later we had stalked within 250 yards. That was close enough, I decided. I found a rest, selected the tur that seemed to have the best horns, and shot it. Its horns were 35 inches long and would rank fifth in the SCI record book. The helicopter wasn't due to pick us up until two days later, but my chance to take a red deer had passed. They were in the forests at least a thousand feet below where we were.

On Saturday, when we were supposed to fly out, the weather turned sour, and the helicopter didn't show. We watched for it again on Sunday, when the sky had a few open patches of blue, but no helicopter came. On Monday the storm hit us with a fury—the wind blew the heavy rain almost horizontal. We spent all our time in the little tents, trying to stay dry. All our food was gone, except for the tur meat. We also were running low on fuel for our little propane stove. There was no wood anywhere nearby, so we couldn't build a fire. My tent was too small for my duffel bags, so I tried to keep them dry by stretching plastic bags over them, but the bags weren't big enough.

The rain kept up and the wind blew all that day and well into the next morning. We had no mat or anything other than the canvas tent bottom under our bags, and they were getting wet as the water accumulated around our tent and started seeping through. We tried to drain it but couldn't. It was just too windy.

The 35-inch horns of the author's western tur ranked number five in the SCI record book. Russia.

The author and his guide Volen pack out the author's Balkan chamois over a planked walkway fifteen feet above a rock-filled river in the Rhodope Mountains. Bulgaria.

Finally, late in the afternoon, the wind subsided just long enough to allow us to move to higher ground. Things didn't improve, though. It dropped to freezing that night. Nicolai had no warm clothes, so I loaned him some of mine. He was happy to get them, even though they were as damp as everything else in my duffel bags. It was snowing and blowing in the morning, and our sleeping bags somehow had snow under them. To stay warm and to try to dry out our clothes, the four of us crowded into one of the tents and fired up the little stove, consuming some of our precious propane. By now, we were eating just one meal a day—tur meat and tea. When the rain and wind gave us a brief reprieve, we went outside to find the mountains around us were totally covered with fog.

That evening the wind was so strong I expected it to rip my little tent at any minute, but it somehow managed to make it through the night. The next morning, though, a heavy gust tore out one end of my shelter. Nicolai and I worked for at least ten minutes with some light twine I had, trying to save what was left of the tent. The wind was so heavy we had to brace ourselves to keep from being blown over. My guides were having the same problems with their tent. Anatolia didn't leave their tent, however. He had a terrible toothache and a swollen jaw. In addition to his pain, he couldn't get warm. He had only a small blanket and a sheet of plastic in which he rolled himself up. That evening a major lightning storm with more rain bombarded us. To conserve our propane supply we used the little stove only to heat up our tur meat. All the coffee was gone.

One morning we woke to find the rain and wind had subsided a bit. Nothing lasts forever, not even bad weather, and it looked as if we might get out that day. I took a sponge bath and changed into damp but clean clothes. By 10 A.M., though, the clouds and fog rolled in again, making it doubtful that anyone would fly that day. At noon the four of us sat down and held a council of war. We had been out of touch with the outside world so long I was wondering if a war had broken out. With Yeltsin in town, near the border with the Republic of Georgia, where there were serious problems, anything could have happened.

We knew we couldn't stay where we were, so we decided to wait until 2 P.M. If the helicopter didn't come by then, we would walk back to the cabin in the forest, five hours away. We would have to wade a river three times, but we would have wood for a fire while we rested up. From there we could walk to a village two days away. While we were talking, we suddenly heard the *whomp, whomp, whomp* of a helicopter coming toward us. The pilot told us that all helicopters had been grounded for six days after a cyclone hit Sochi.

We were back in town at 1 P.M., in time to catch the 3 P.M. flight to Moscow. When we got there, I checked into a hotel and placed a call to The Hunting Consortium, my booking agent in Virginia. Bob Kern and his staff were relieved to know I'd gotten out. I was a week behind schedule.

I was supposed to have been hunting in Romania while we were trapped on the mountain, and I was overdue in Bulgaria. Margaret at the booking agency's office suggested that I fly to Bulgaria and hunt in Romania later. She called me back later and faxed me a new itinerary.

She said I could catch a 7 A.M. flight to Frankfurt and a noon flight out of there to Romania. I had a problem, though. Because I was a week late, my visa and rifle permit had expired, and the government offices wouldn't open until around 10 A.M. While I slept, Margaret arranged for me to be taken to someone who could take care of my rifle permit (for a very high fee) at 5 A.M. I was unable to change my visa before the 7 A.M. flight, however. There was a flight at 11 A.M., but I didn't have my visa problem straightened out by then. I had to buy another ticket and pay an exorbitant fee, but I was on the 1:30 P.M. plane to Bulgaria from Moscow. It had been quite an experience, one I hope never to go through again. I did get the tur and chamois I wanted from Russia, but I never really got to hunt a red deer.

My last request to the Russians when I left was to be sure to notify Margaret that I hadn't made the flight to Frankfurt she'd booked and that I now was flying direct to Sofia with my rifle—and no papers for it.

No one met me at the airport outside Sofia when I landed in Bulgaria on 7 October, and my Bulgarian visa had expired. It took some explaining, but the people at the immigration gate kept my passport and kindly allowed me to step outside to see if there was anyone waiting for me on the other side. No one was there. I didn't have local currency to make a phone call, so I went back inside and found someone to call the number Margaret at the Hunting Consortium had given me. We reached a man who said I should buy a visa and wait for someone to meet me outside the airport. So I had my visa renewed, cleared Customs, went out to the curb, and waited—and waited. Two hours later, I asked someone to call the number again and learned someone actually was on the way.

Thirty minutes later, my interpreter (a woman named Lily) and a driver in a new van showed up. After getting all my gear aboard, we drove three and a half hours southwest to a hunting lodge in the Rhodope Mountains near the town of Devin, close to Bulgaria's border with Greece. I had hunted Balkan chamois there in 1991 but had gone home without one. I was hoping this second trip would have a better ending.

The cook, a man named Rossen, remembered me from my earlier visit and had a fine dinner waiting for us when we arrived at 9:30 P.M. I'd had a long day. Immediately after eating, I said good night to everyone and went to my room—a suite with a sitting room and bath.

After breakfast the next morning, my guide, Volen, and driver, Yassen, and I drove to the top of the mountain, where Volen and I went off on foot to glass the openings in the forest below us. We saw a few females but no males. According to Volen, male chamois are hard to find in October because they seldom leave the forest during the day. The locals hunt them only early in the morning and late in the afternoon.

We walked off the mountain at 10 A.M., meeting Yassen at the bottom. That evening they took me to a high seat, and my guide and I sat there until around 8 P.M., waiting for a wild boar to show up. It was a comfortable, elevated blind about twenty-five feet up on timbers. It was only about seven feet square inside, but the floor was carpeted, the walls were covered with felt, and there were windows on each side. They even had an office-type swiveling chair for me to sit in.

Soon after the moon came out, about a dozen sows and young boars came out of the forest. They trotted up to the corn my hosts had set out and began chasing each other around and squabbling over it. An hour later, a large boar appeared, and I shot it. As many animals do when heart shot, the boar whirled around and made a mad dash into the forest. We found it dead about seventy-five yards from where I'd shot it. It was a good boar, with seven-inch tusks.

We were back on the mountain again early the next day but saw only the same female chamois we had seen the previous day. At 3 P.M. we drove to another area, left the vehicle at the end of a two-track road, and started climbing. It was an interesting place. A little creek ran through the bottom of a steep, narrow canyon, and someone had built a long, wooden walkway about fifteen feet above the rocks and water. At its end was a wide valley. We followed the planked walkway for about a half-mile, then climbed as high as we could get and began glassing. We immediately found several chamois, including a male, a half-mile away on the other side, but the cliffs were so steep we never would be able to reach it from our side. It was frustrating to be so close but so far away. As we left the mountain, we made plans to drive around to the other side and see if we could find the chamois again in the morning.

The driver dropped us off above the cliffs at sunup, and Volen and I took off on foot to look for the chamois we'd seen the previous afternoon. We found it, and I shot it, even though it wasn't the trophy I had wanted. It was 10 October, and I was due back in Sofia the next day and in Romania the day after that. I didn't want to go home without a chamois after two trips to the region. The best horn on my Balkan chamois was 9¼ inches long, easily making the SCI record book. However, this was the largest of all the chamois subspecies, with the longest horns—some of them nearly twelve inches long.

As it turned out, I had time to look for a better head. At lunch I learned that flights left Sofia only on Monday, Wednesday, and Friday, and no one would be able to meet me in Bucharest until Friday. I spent the next two days at the lodge, then was driven to Sofia on Thursday. The wildlife commissioner there measured and checked my trophies and also issued the export and veterinary permits I needed. I then got a room in the Park Hotel Moskva and left for Romania the next afternoon, but not without a few minor problems. My interpreter wasn't allowed to accompany me into the airport, and after I had already checked my baggage at the airline counter someone wanted to see my rifle.

The officer and I climbed down the belt and rummaged through all the baggage until we found my rifle case. After he checked its serial number against my papers, he cleared me to leave for Romania.

The weather was beautiful when I landed in Bucharest on the afternoon of 13 October. I met my interpreter, Bulbesch Adrian, and we drove five hours to Dejani, a village in the Brasov District, where I would hunt a Carpathian chamois in the Fegarus Mountains. We wasted no time getting under way. The first two hours of the drive took us through flat, fertile land with many small farms. Then we reached the mountains, where crews were working on the narrow and dusty road. Because of heavy truck traffic and construction, we didn't make good time.

Around 9 P.M. we reached the wildlife office in Foresby, where we left our car. We drove another forty-five minutes to a cabin higher on the mountain in a four-wheel-drive vehicle. I was pleasantly surprised to see the cabin was constructed of posts and beams and was nearly new. It also had electric lights, thanks to a generator. After my sleeping arrangements in Russia, I was tickled to see the large, comfortable room assigned to me.

I had arrived two weeks late, but the hunt organizers went out of their way to accommodate me. For example, when my guide wasn't available the first day, the company's hunting director and a forester took me out. We left the cabin at 7 A.M. and climbed for three hours to get to the top. We found ourselves on a large, open plateau. At our second spot to glass, we found a small herd of chamois about three-quarters of a mile away.

We were able to get within shooting range, but I decided not to take either of the two males in the bunch. It was only the first day, and I wanted one with better horns. After lunch, we worked our way along the edge of the plateau, stopping often to glass the slopes below us. We found another herd about the same time it saw us, and the chamois ran off before we could do anything. We were back at the cabin by 4:30 P.M.

My regular guide, a man named Strole Emil, arrived before daylight the next morning, and we again climbed the mountains behind the cabin. This time we saw two brown bears running across the plateau. After seeing them, I was afraid we wouldn't see any chamois in that area. I was wrong, because Emil spotted a good buck a few minutes later. It was below the edge of the plateau, and to stalk it we would need to stay behind a small ridge.

Fifteen minutes later, we were crossing the ridge when a male chamois jumped up and stood there, staring at us. Emil was saying, "Shoot! Shoot!" but I waited until I had checked its horns with my binoculars. I thought we might be able to find a better male, but Emil said it was a gold-medal trophy. There were bear in the area, which undoubtedly would affect the hunting, so I decided to take it. Just before the little animal went out of sight about two hundred yards away, I put the cross hairs on its shoulder and killed it.

After photographing the chamois, we left it where a young forester could find it and bring it down. I still hadn't taken an exceptional chamois trophy, one that would rank in the record book's top ten, but my Carpathian chamois was a good one. Its ten-inch horns would make the *SCI All-Time Record Book of Trophy Animals.*

After dinner, Emil drove me to another area. We spent the night in an elevated blind where Emil said bears were feeding. He said I also might have a chance to take a wolf. Three or four different bears were attracted to the bait that night, but the moon wasn't bright enough for shooting. The wolves bypassed the place that night. During breakfast, I was told I'd hunted in the former presidential hunting reserve, where only the presidents of Romania hunted in years past.

We left for Bucharest the morning of 17 October. I had to buy another ticket after being delayed in Russia, but I was in Vienna at 6 P.M. that same day. I now needed only an Alpine chamois, which had been introduced to the Czech Republic, to complete my quest for four chamois subspecies on this trip.

I drove with my Czech interpreter, Zuzana Kocickova, and my driver, Roman Macoszek, from Vienna to the border of the Czech Republic, where I received a visa

and a rifle permit. Three hours later, we reached Hotel Zerotin in the village of Vellce Losing. It was 11 P.M. before I got to bed. After breakfast the next morning, we drove about three and a half miles to the hunting company's office in the village of Loucna and picked up my guide, a man named Václav.

Václav drove us into the Jeseniky Mountains in his four-wheel-drive vehicle, passing on the way a large dam that was under construction. When we reached the top, we pulled off on a side road and parked our vehicle at its end. A trail led uphill, and we followed it on foot for a while, but it soon became so foggy we couldn't see and had to turn around. We tried driving up another mountain, but it was foggy there, too. We went back to the hotel for lunch without ever getting to hunt.

The fog had burned off by afternoon, and we returned to the first mountain. We were on the same trail, probably less than a half-mile from our vehicle, when we spotted two or three female chamois bounding away from us. We left the trail and hiked in the general direction they had gone. We jumped them several more times. We also pushed a male out of a little draw, but we never had a chance to get a good look at it.

Fifteen minutes later, we were crossing a small ridge when the male jumped up again, and I quickly shot it. Its horns qualified for the SCI record book, but, more important to me, I'd taken four subspecies of chamois in less than a month.

Václav and I carried my chamois to a road at the bottom of the mountain, then went back to the hotel. He skinned it that night for a life-size mount.

I still had two days before I was scheduled to leave the Czech Republic, so Zuzana drove me to a shopping area in a village ten miles away. It was an interesting old village, but I saw nothing I wanted to buy.

Poland was only thirty-six miles away, so we drove to the border to have lunch there the next day, only to learn I couldn't cross the line without a visa. I could have gotten one, but I would need a new visa to return to the Czech Republic. My rifle was at the hotel, and, because it wouldn't be shown on the new visa, I could have lots of problems when I wanted to leave for home with my rifle. We turned around and stopped at another village for lunch. The next morning I was driven back to Vienna, where I arranged for a taxidermist to prepare my trophies and ship them to my taxidermist friend, Kevin, in North Carolina. I flew to Frankfurt and home the next day. I had been gone thirty-two days. It had been quite a year. I'd hunted in eight countries in Africa and Europe and had taken fine specimens.

I would be heading for the bottom of the earth in just three months.

STARTING AT THE BOTTOM OF THE GLOBE, 1996

The Weatherby Big Game Trophy is the highest honor a hunter can receive. The Weatherby Foundation has issued only one such award each year since 1956, and it is awarded only to those who have contributed to wildlife conservation and excelled in hunting. I was deeply honored when Ed Weatherby and actor Steven Kanaly presented me with the award at a black-tie dinner in January 1996. More than four hundred people attended. I felt especially honored because the previous winners included such people as Jack O'Connor, Warren Page, Prince Abdorreza Pahlavi, Valentin de Madriaga y Oya, Francois Edmond-Blanc, James R. Mellon, Rudolf Sand, Dr. Jim Conklin, and many others well known in the hunting community.

A month after receiving the award, I was among eighty-three passengers setting sail from the southern tip of South America on a fifteen-day excursion in Antarctic waters. Before the trip was over, we would have visited the Antarctic Peninsula, the South Orkney Islands, South Georgia Island, and the Falkland Islands. To begin this expedition I flew to the southern tip of South America by way of Montreal, Miami, and Santiago, Chile. I boarded the M.S. *Explorer* on 22 February 1996 in the town of Ushuala.

I already had hunted on six of the seven continents when I realized that if I wanted to see the entire planet I would have to visit the fifth-largest, and least known, of all of them. I booked passage on an Antarctic excursion in February 1996. It was the middle of the summer in the Southern Hemisphere. We set sail with eighty-two other passengers. It took us two days to cross the Drake Passage, the water that separates Antarctica from South America. The Pacific, Atlantic, and Indian Oceans meet there, and, because of a continuous high wind that circulates clockwise around Antarctica, the Drake Passage is considered the most unstable body of water on the planet. At a certain point Antarctic waters mix with these oceans, and, within just a thousand yards, the water temperature suddenly drops 5 degrees Fahrenheit. It was there that we saw our first icebergs, something we would see more frequently as we continued south.

We were fortunate because the Drake Passage was smoother than usual, the captain said, and we had lovely weather. Nonetheless, the ship did a lot of rocking and rolling, and some of the passengers got seasick. I was spared, probably because of the medicine I was taking to avoid seasickness. Lecturers on the trip included a marine biologist who discussed life cycles of the penguins, seals, and whales we would see; a well-informed history professor who talked about the explorers, whalers, and early military personnel who had visited the Antarctic; and an ornithologist. I learned a lot about the Great White Continent on that cruise.

We spent our days on deck watching whales, seals, and icebergs. When we reached the peninsula, the ship stopped once or twice each day, and we went ashore in inflatable Zodiak boats to see the penguins and seals, or just to explore for a couple of hours before heading back to the ship. The scenery was awesome, with lots of glaciers, drifting icebergs, and beautiful passages flanked by sheer cliffs of ice. It was our ship's last voyage of the summer, and we could go only as far as 66 degrees south before we would constantly encounter icebergs and thick sea ice.

The temperature dropped to freezing only the two or three nights we spent at the southernmost points of our voyage; elsewhere it stayed above freezing during the day. We did experience Antarctica's notoriously high winds, which suddenly roar across the glaciers from the interior of the continent, then go away just as quickly. We were told that it is these winds that break up the ice and move the icebergs out to sea.

Life aboard ship was comfortable, with buffet breakfasts between 6:30 and 7:30 A.M., a buffet lunch at 1 P.M., and a sit-down dinner at 7:30 P.M. At dinner there were two choices of entrée, an appetizer, soup, salad, and dessert. Hot soup was always waiting for us when we returned from going ashore. After dinner, there were movies and videos on Antarctica in the lecture hall. When we returned to our cabins, we would find the maids had tidied up our rooms, turned down the beds, and left lists of the places, activities, and lectures scheduled for the next day. We were seeing Antarctica in style.

When we came upon a pod of humpback whales one evening, the crew put out the Zodiaks, and we followed, running up as close as forty feet from them. It was exciting.

At Deception Island we sailed through a narrow passage into the center of an old volcano that had filled with water. Early whalers had discovered the sheltered bay and used it for a base of operation. According to one of the lecturers, a sudden eruption in 1967 had buried a Chilean and British scientific base there. When we went ashore to see the local hot springs, I went swimming with about twenty others. (We are now among the few people in this world who can say they have gone swimming in Antarctica.) The water in the pool was uneven in temperature—in some places so hot we couldn't stand it and in others very cold.

The captain tried to sail down the eastern side of the peninsula in the Weddell Sea, but we ran into heavy ice and had to turn back. That ice, by the way, means the farther south a ship goes, the greater the distance it may be from the mainland. Only a very narrow strip of the northern end of the continent outside the Antarctic Circle is free of ice, and only during the short summer.

We went ashore frequently on this part of our tour and walked among thousands upon thousands of penguins and their fuzzy youngsters. (We saw seven different types on this trip, and most of them were molting.) It would be two to three weeks before they could head out to sea again. Some of the older penguins had regrown their feathers, and we watched them in the water from the ship's deck. It was amazing how fast they could swim.

On 29 February we left the peninsula and sailed to Elephant Island (named for its giant seals, not for the pachyderm). Two days later, we reached the South Orkney Islands in the Scotia Sea between Antarctica and South Africa. This region is particularly rich in history. British explorer E. H. Shackleton's boat had been crushed in the ice off the mainland at the beginning of the twentieth century, and he and his men somehow survived on the ice floes until they were able to reach Elephant Island. From there the survivors of his party made it to South Georgia Island in an open boat. Their ordeal in the world's most hostile environment lasted three years.

Nearly a hundred years later, we traveled the same route in a modern ship with sailors who knew the Antarctic waters, now charted, better than any of the early explorers. The sea was very rough, and it was hard to sleep, move about, or eat. The ship would suddenly tilt, sending everything to the floor, but our Filipino waiters apparently were used to this and managed to keep—as the English would say—a stiff upper lip. Many of the other passengers were seasick

on this leg of the trip, but again I was spared. (I took thirty seasick pills with me and had only one left when I got off the ship.) Some of the others were sick even while taking the pills.

When we reached South Georgia Island, where Shackleton was buried, we visited his gravesite and a deserted whaling station, where we saw an amazing amount of equipment and old ships that had sunk at the wharves. We wanted to visit a couple of other beaches, but the high seas kept us from going ashore. It was around this time we began to notice green on the land again. Since leaving Argentina, all we had seen was white. My ears pricked up when one of the naturalists mentioned that South Georgia Island had two herds of reindeer on it. The animals' ancestors were brought from Norway in 1911 to provide the whalers a respite from whale meat. The herds did well and now are well established on both sides of a range of mountains and glaciers.[1]

We sailed another two days across even rougher seas to East Falkland Island. A Customs official came aboard at Sea Lion Island and cleared us to enter the British Crown Colony. The weather was pleasant now (in the high fifties during the day), and we went ashore with lunches the crew packed for us. The beach was covered with sea lions, Rockhopper penguins, and various birds. Some of the passengers joined a naturalist for a three-mile hike and came back talking about

---

1. Believing I had discovered something, I mentioned this to Jack Schwabland, who wrote the text of the SCI record book, when we met a couple of years later. "I know," he said. "It's in the record book."

The author's ship (in background) stopped frequently, and, although there was no hunting, the stops enabled those on the boat to explore the shoreline. Antarctica.

The author and his party hunted glacier bears from a small inflatable boat by moving along the shoreline of Akwe Lake. Alaska.

the sights they had seen on that bleak, rocky, windswept island. We sailed the next morning to the town of Stanley, the capital of the Falklands.

Stanley was our last stop before returning to South America. On 7 March, the day we left the town of some two thousand people, we visited the local shops and a small museum filled with mementos and information about the ten-day war with Argentina in 1982. Nothing really had been settled by that conflict. Although the British won and continue to administer the Falkland Islands, the Argentines still claim the islands, calling them Islas Malvinas. This longstanding territorial dispute over the two hundred or more islands in the Falkland chain came to a head after the announcement that the islands had potential for oil exploration. For now, wool production and commercial fishing are the principal industries.

Around 11 A.M. we drove past rows of small, neat homes with flower gardens to a British Army airport, where we caught a four-hour flight to Santiago and flew on to Miami.

I was home the next day, having traveled 3,440 nautical miles. Only one other Canadian was aboard our ship; the others were from the United States, the United Kingdom, France, Germany, Sweden, Scotland, Switzerland, Australia, Bermuda, Puerto Rico, several South American countries, and Japan. In addition to seven different types of penguin, we had seen eight types of seal (including many of the largest elephant seals), whales, and many species of birds. There is no animal life in Antarctica except for the species that visit the coastal waters during the short summer. It had been a great experience on yet another unusual place on this planet of ours.

Fifty-three days after leaving Antarctica, I was flying toward the other end of the earth, on a flight from Seattle to Yakutat in Alaska, with a stop in Juneau along the way. I had booked a seven-day hunt with Ken Fanning's Alaska Guide Services for what hunters call the *glacier bear* or *blue bear*, which is blue-gray or blue-black—a rare color phase of the American black bear found only in a small area of Alaska.

Ken greeted me as I stepped off the plane, and with him were his son Kip and my guide, Ron Warren. A room was waiting for me at The Yakutat Lodge, a short walk from the airport. There I learned there were no roads into Yakutat—everything came into the little village by air or barge—and there were only fifty miles of road in the entire glacier country. I left my gear in my room, and Ron took me a short distance out of town, where I checked my rifle's zero. It was still shooting where I wanted it to, despite all the rough handling my gun case certainly must have undergone on the airlines. The next morning we flew twenty minutes in a floatplane to the hunting area at Akwe Lake. It was raining when we landed, which was not unusual in that part of the world in April.

Ken had built a small plywood cabin, using a tarp for the roof, on the lakeshore. Ron fired up a small heater as I sorted my gear and stored what I wouldn't need. It was quite comfortable. After getting squared away, we took off in a small inflatable boat that Ron had brought with us and rowed around the lake, which was a half-mile wide and a mile long. The mountains that loomed above us on three sides were steep and covered with snow from about halfway up. Ron said my chances of finding a glacier bear were around twenty percent. We were there at just the right time, when the bear were coming out of their dens, he said. The trees were just starting to sprout new leaves, so it would be a while before our visibility became more limited.

We saw ten different black bear that first day. The lower slopes were covered with thick brush, and it was surprising how quickly they could disappear. We traveled up the valley on foot the second day—a steep, long climb—and saw more bear, but all had black coats. The next day we glassed from the lake, and the following day we climbed another valley. We were seeing a lot of black bear, but none had the light-colored, glossy coat of the glacier bear.

To glass a meadow on Sunday afternoon, Ron climbed a tree and announced that he was watching something that might be a glacier bear a long way off. To get a better look at it, we returned to the lake and covered the slope with our spotting scope. Twenty minutes later, we finally located it more than a mile away and determined that it was a sow bear with a small cub. The mother had the distinctive coloration of a glacier bear! It was safe from us, though. Although I would not have shot it, females with cubs were protected by Alaskan game laws. I felt fortunate just to have seen it.

Two days later, we had seen more black bear and at least one brown bear, but the only glacier bear we could find was the sow. A plane flew in for us at 6 P.M. on Tuesday and took us back to the lodge. Ken talked me into staying longer and going out again to look for a bear. I agreed and spent the next two days on his boat, fishing for halibut about five miles from shore with five other fishermen. I caught halibut, rockfish, and a skate that resembled a stingray, and someone caught a king salmon. At 6:30 P.M. the second day I had dinner and a quick change of clothes, then flew with Ron to Harlequin Lake. We landed on wheels on a gravel bar at the edge of the water. Ken's camp was a half-mile away, and we had to carry everything to it, including our inflatable boat, outboard motor, fuel, and all our food and gear, across three fast-flowing streams while wearing waders. It took several trips.

It was the first time anyone had used the camp that season, and it was a mess. It was larger than our first camp. It had plywood walls and a plywood floor, and a plastic tarp covered its roof and both ends. The wind had torn out one end during the winter, and everything inside—including all the foam bed pads—was wet and sandy. It was much colder there, probably because the wind was blowing to us over the two large glaciers less than a mile away, which fed the lake. Everything was covered with sand that the wind had picked up along the way. It was too late (and too dark, even with a lantern) to do much with the place, so we crawled into our sleeping bags on the floor.

The wind died down the next day, bringing us pleasant weather for our first day at Harlequin Lake. We spent part of that morning cleaning up our camp and hanging the foam mats on branches to dry. That done, we headed back to the lake, inflated the boat, installed the outboard, and went hunting. About half of the two-by-five-mile lake was still covered with ice, and there were some very large chunks of ice hung up on the bottom. We saw no bear at all that day.

We hunted for four days, seeing twelve different black bear and another brown bear (but no glacier bear) before we returned to Yakutat on the afternoon of 12 May. Before flying to Seattle the next day, I went out with Kip to check his crab pots and gather the catch. I was back in Havelock the next day.

Tony Rivera, a Mexican hunting outfitter and houndsman, and Marcello Sodiro of Argentina, with whom I had hunted deer, jaguar, and tapir in Paraguay three years earlier, were waiting for me at Viru-Viru Airport a few miles outside Santa Cruz de la Sierra, Bolivia. It was 13 July 1996, and I had gone there to hunt a jaguar with them. To reach Santa Cruz from Moncton, I flew to Toronto, Miami, and La Paz. Counting all the layovers at each stop, I spent twenty-five and a half hours in the air and in airport lobbies.

When we left the airport, it was rainy and cold—about 30 degrees Fahrenheit, which surprised me. I knew this was the Southern Hemisphere's winter, but I had thought it would be a little warmer.

Fortunately, it was the last gasp of Bolivia's rainy season. It didn't rain again during my entire stay in that country.

As it turned out, I could have taken my time getting there. A few days earlier, the Bolivian government had declared the establishment of a seven-hundred-thousand-acre national park in the area where Tony and Marcello were hunting. Tony and Marcello were allowed to finish their hunt, but they would have to take me somewhere else. Unfortunately, all their equipment was at their old camp, a full day's drive. While Marcello drove there to disassemble the camp and pack things up, I waited in a hotel. Santa Cruz was an interesting, modern city of around a half-million people, and it had colorful colonial-style architecture, well-manicured gardens, spacious homes, and covered sidewalks, something I'd not seen before. Pedestrians apparently appreciate the sidewalks during the rainy season in that tropical city.

I spent most of my time resting and reading while we waited for Marcello to return. Tony kept busy by talking with members of the local hunting club, trying to track down a new place to hunt. When Marcello returned, Tony had located a spot where Bolivian hunters regularly collected jaguar. Around 10 A.M. on 13 July we left Santa Cruz in two heavily loaded vehicles, driving east toward the Brazilian border, where a small portion of the great Mato Grosso slopes over into Bolivia. Two hours later, we stopped at an open-air restaurant in a village

The hunters could glass a lot of glacier bear country from this high peak above Akwe Lake. Alaska.

A very good South American white-tailed deer from Ecuador. The largest, though, come from Venezuela. Equador.

called Yapacing for lunch. We returned to the trucks only to find that one had a flat tire. After fixing it, we spent the next three hours on a rough dirt road, looking for a suitable camping area.

We were up early in the morning, following a small pipeline past a few natural gas wells. I was struck by the irony of it all. Bolivia has great mines and huge natural gas and crude oil reserves, yet it is one of the poorest nations in South America. Our little dirt road was a long way from anywhere, yet literally hundreds of poverty-stricken indigenous people were living in mud huts along it. There were perhaps twenty dwellings in one village, and we stopped there to arrange for a local hunter who knew the area to help us. While Tony and Marcello were speaking with the man in Spanish, I looked around the place. It reminded me very much of some of the places I'd hunted in tropical Africa. In addition to the huts there were *ramada*s (thatched roofs supported by poles without walls). The people lived and cooked mostly outside. There was no running water or electricity, nor could I see any sign that they had built outhouses. They apparently answered nature's call behind their huts wherever and whenever it struck them.

At 9 A.M. we had driven about two miles past the village when the road suddenly ended at the edge of a shallow river. We pitched our tents in a spot that was completely surrounded by a thick rain forest. It was a good campsite, and we were fortunate to have good weather— it never climbed above 80 degrees

Fahrenheit during the day or below 50 degrees Fahrenheit at night. Despite being so close to the water, the mosquitoes were bad only at dawn and dusk, and (for once) my mosquito repellent helped keep them off me. There were small flies, though, and whenever the air grew still they would swarm around me. After a few days in that jungle, all of my exposed skin was covered with tiny welts from their bites.

The Yapacing River would be our only "road" through that miserable jungle. It was perhaps three hundred feet wide, and its banks and bottom were sandy. Bamboo, ferns, vines, and broad-leaved plants grew right up to its edge like impenetrable walls. In places, the limbs of the trees grew far out over the water and, in the river's narrowest places, formed a canopy. The only way to get through the jungle was to chop paths with machetes. After our first day of hunting, Tony and Marcello hired another man to help move the boat over the countless shallow sandbars we encountered.

We hunted from that camp for eight days. Although Tony's dogs tried to run several fresh tracks, they never were able to catch up to a jaguar. The jungle was so thick that even they couldn't follow a cat through it for very far. The only game I saw were small caimans, like alligators, which would glide off the banks as we approached.

I wasn't too disappointed about not taking a jaguar. I would not have been able to ship it home, anyway. I only wanted to experience the hunt.

Two days before we planned to leave, the wind came up and covered everything in our camp—including us—with thick layers of fine sand. When we returned to Santa Cruz on 22 July, the first thing I did was to take a shower and wash it off.

Tony, Marcello, and I met in the hotel's coffee shop to say good-bye. I arranged to meet Marcello and his father a month later in Ecuador to hunt a South American white-tailed deer and take a side trip to the Galapagos Islands, off the mainland. I also was interested in a project Tony was involved with in Mexico. He planned to use trophy hunters to capture jaguar in southern Mexico with tranquilizing darts and to equip the cats with radio collars so scientists at a Mexican university could study them. I told Tony I would be interested in darting a jaguar when he got the project going. It offered all the excitement of hunting jaguar with a gun, and, because jaguars were darted at point-blank range, there was an element of danger, too.

I spent that night in a hotel in Miami and was back in Moncton the next day. I'd had a tough and physically demanding hunt in one of the world's thickest jungles and never fired a shot—and I'd enjoyed every minute of it.

I suppose few North American deer hunters have given it much thought, but the white-tailed deer (along with its primary predator, the mountain lion) is one of the two most widespread large mammals in the Americas. Whitetail can be found from southern Canada all the way south to Peru.

Most scientists recognize thirty-eight subspecies on the two continents, thirty of them in North America. The whitetail at my lodge in New Brunswick are classified as northern woodland whitetails (*Odocoileus virginianus borealis*) and have the largest bodies and antlers in North America. In comparison, a big buck in South America weighs less than a hundred pounds and typically has only four points per side, including eye guards.

Generally speaking, the various subspecies grow smaller as one gets closer to the equator, and larger as one goes farther south of it. The largest of the eight South American subspecies (*O. v. cariacou*) is found in Venezuela, the southern end of the range of whitetails east of the Andes. I hunted in Ecuador, however, for a subspecies known as the Ecuador whitetail (*O. v. ustus*).

As we had arranged in July on my jaguar hunt in Bolivia, my Argentine friend Marcello Sodiro met me in Quito, Ecuador, on 20 August 1996. With him was Braden Escobar, our outfitter, and our guide, Maxwell Munoz. Marcello and I took rooms at the Santa Maria Hotel and spent the next day in Quito, while Braden and Maxwell made last-minute arrangements for horses and more supplies. We left the following day in two vehicles—Braden and I in one, Maxwell and Marcello in the other. Maxwell kept stopping to buy things without telling Braden, so it wasn't long before our two vehicles got separated. We finally got back together when Braden and I stopped for lunch. Soon after that, we left the main road and headed for the mountains. It had been raining, and the unpaved road was full of deep, slippery, muddy ruts, but we managed to reach our destination—a little ranch house where we would spend the night—without getting stuck.

There was no electricity, but we had lanterns and flashlights and were able to get our gear inside and find places for everyone to sleep. It was a lot colder than I had expected. Quito is on the equator but is at twelve thousand feet elevation. We would be hunting at fourteen thousand feet, where the temperature never climbed above 50 degrees Fahrenheit during the day.

At daylight the next morning we left the house in the rain on horseback with several local men, riding toward the snowcapped mountains that rose up above us. I was glad I had bought rubber boots and a poncho in town. Four hours later, we spotted two bucks across a wide canyon, but it was raining so hard we decided to set up a camp in the valley and try to find them later. At 3 P.M. the rain had let up, and we rode back up the mountain and found a good place to sit down with our binoculars.

"Up there, by that dead tree," Braden suddenly said. "Two bears."

Sure enough, he had spotted two spectacled bears. I set up my spotting scope and watched them for a while. They resembled our black bear, but they had shorter noses and distinctive white markings on their faces. Marcello was

looking for a bear, so he and one of the local men began a stalk that would take them within two hundred yards of the bears. Braden and I were watching the bears when Marcello shot—and missed—and the bears ran off.

The only deer we saw that afternoon was a small female. We saw two more does the next morning, but no bucks. It looked like a good place for deer, so we moved our spike camp there. It was raining so hard we couldn't go out again that afternoon, and during the night we got some wet snow, but it didn't last long. We split up in the morning, with Marcello and the two local men going one way and Braden and I another.

We were on a high ridge glassing across a canyon when we heard two shots far below us. Marcello had shot a deer for meat, a little buck that had shed its antlers.[2]

At the insistence of the local men, we took the horses and a tent and built another spike camp farther down the valley, where we spent the afternoon glassing from various spots without seeing a deer. The next morning our local guys moved us again. Braden and I weren't happy with them. We were spending all our time moving our camps and doing very little hunting. By mutual agreement, we all rode back to the ranch, got our vehicles, and drove back to Quito, arriving there soon after sundown. Braden knew where we could find whitetail along the coast.

---

2. Deer close to the equator have no set season for growing and losing their antlers. There is no set breeding season, and individual females can come into estrus any month.

We left Quito at 6 o'clock the next morning and drove to Braden's home in Guayaquil, where his father was a mango exporter. Three hours later, we reached a village called Punta Blanca and checked into a seaside resort on the Pacific that belonged to a friend of Braden's father. It was the off-season, and only the caretakers were there. Braden, Marcello, and I took turns cooking our meals.

We hunted at night, driving around, looking for deer with a jacklight—the only way we could hunt there, Braden said. Two nights later, we came around a bend in the road and surprised a small buck. I quickly stepped out of the vehicle and shot it. It was a beautiful little deer, with smallish antlers. I would later learn that SCI lumps all eight South American subspecies into a single category it calls *South American white-tailed deer.* The antlers on Ecuador's whitetail cannot compete with those in Venezuela and elsewhere, however.

Marcello was proof that hunting deer at night isn't always successful. He went out four nights in a row without seeing a buck. The day before guests were expected to arrive at the resort, we drove about twenty miles to a seaside fishing village called Salinas to get a new spring for one of the vehicles. Then we drove back to Guayaquil, where we went our separate ways.

Braden and I—along with Braden's friend, Jose Vera, who knew the islands well—flew to the Galapagos Islands in the morning, and Maxwell and Marcello went back to the mountains to hunt deer. It was Saturday, 31 August, when we landed

at an army airport on the small island of Baltra. From there we took a ferry across to Santa Cruz Island, just a quarter-mile away, and caught a bus to Puerto Ayora, the island's only town, about twenty-four miles farther.

The Galapagos chain consists of about two hundred islands, but only eight of them are of any size. Santa Cruz and San Cristóbal are the only two inhabited by humans. The islands are covered with volcanic rock, but wherever sand occurred we found sea lions and iguanas. We saw land and marine iguanas, as well as tortoises that weighed up to five hundred pounds.

Braden had brought some of his deep-sea fishing gear, so we tried to rent a boat for three days to visit the islands and do some fishing. It wasn't easy to find a decent boat. Most of the boats didn't look like anything either of us wanted to go out in, but Jose managed to hire a small one that seemed seaworthy enough. I caught a small tuna the next day and saw a sea turtle, porpoises, and a killer whale. The temperature on the islands was about 70 degrees Fahrenheit, but it was cooler on the water.

We spent the next two days touring Santa Cruz Island and Santa Fe Island, seeing tortoises, iguanas, and many different birds. Santa Fe had a few small bushes but was uninhabited. We decided to leave on 3 September. I'd seen enough. All the islands we'd visited were the same.

After a night in Quito, Braden and Maxwell's sixteen-year-old son and I left for the Amazon Valley. It was a six-hour drive, and we traveled down to lower elevations and into the jungle forest to the village of Misabualli on the Napo River, which joins the Amazon in Peru. When Braden got us rooms in the Jungle Hotel, my first thought was that there never was a place more appropriately named. The hotel's cabins had been built high on the bank overlooking the tropical river, and we had to cross the river in a canoe to reach the bank. The canoes were very long, perhaps thirty-five feet, and were designed especially for riding the rivers.

I tried to get some rest that afternoon, but it was very hot, and our rooms did not have air conditioning. I did sleep that night, and was up in time to take a tour of the river at 7 o'clock in the morning. Indigenous people were living in thatched huts all along the river.[3] The river was their only means of transportation, Maxwell's son said.

One of the places we visited was a small museum that displayed the things the local people used to gather food, including handmade spring traps and poisoned arrows. We learned that we were only about three hours by boat from the territory of primitive South American Indian tribes who still regularly killed visitors with poisoned darts from their blowguns. We also visited a wildlife refuge.

We returned to Quito that afternoon, and Braden dropped me off at a hotel. As soon as he pulled away, I realized I had left my backpack in his vehicle, and it had

my passport, glasses, and airline tickets in it. I had no telephone number for him and could find no one in the hotel who spoke English. We had arranged for him to take me to the airport at 4:30 A.M. for my 7:00 A.M. flight. If he overslept, I wouldn't be able to leave that day. He was on time, however, and my backpack was still in his vehicle. I was home thirteen hours later. It had been quite a trip.

It was 29 September when I landed in Istanbul. I was expecting to find someone from my travel company when I cleared Customs, but no one was there. The people at the police station were helpful, and, when I told them the company had already obtained a permit for my rifle, they used the airport's intercom to page the man. We then drove to a hotel downtown.

At dinner that evening I met my interpreter, a young man named Denis Engin. He and I flew on to Ankara the next morning, changed planes, and arrived in Ezerum later that day. I was in Turkey to hunt a Mideastern brown bear, a small cousin of the North American brown bear.

Two of the men I'd met when I hunted ibex and chamois in Turkey in 1993 picked us up at the Ezerum airport. One was my guide, the other was our driver—and both were named Mustafa (I never learned their last names). We would be hunting in a place called Yusufeli, they said. We had a good, flat road for the first two hours. When we

---

3. While going down the river we encountered local people in two narrow dugouts, each with a cow standing in its center. I have often wondered how they loaded or unloaded those animals.

turned onto a side road and headed for the mountains, however, it became narrower and more winding. It was already dark when we arrived at the small house where I had stayed in 1993, but I quickly changed into my hunting clothes and unpacked my rifle and ammunition. Bears are hunted over bait at night in Turkey, and we were going to check the baits. Nothing had hit them, however.

Ismail, my chamois guide on my previous trip, was at the house when we returned. It was good to see him again. Our dinner that evening—like most of the meals served while I was there—consisted of cheese, sliced sausages, bread, and tea.

Hunting from a high seat at night can be boring when nothing comes to the bait. I spent much of the next night staring at the moonlit slopes around our blind, but nothing came in. The next night I saw a bear crossing a hillside above the blind. I found the bear in my scope and sent it rolling down the mountain at my shot. It didn't stop rolling until it reached the brush across a little creek below us. Stumbling around in that thick stuff at night with a wounded bear was something none of us wanted to do, even though we were sure it was dead, so we left it, planning to return in the morning.

When we returned, we found where the bear had tumbled down the hillside. There was quite a bit of blood, but the bear was gone. Although we tried to track it, my Turkish guides weren't African trackers, and we soon lost the trail.[4] The next night I shot a wild boar to add to our bait. I was impressed with my scope's light-gathering ability. I was shooting my Ruger M77 in 7mm Remington Magnum, and it was equipped with a 40mm Swarovski 2.29X variable scope. With only the moonlight, I was able to see the animals and the cross hairs and shoot accurately.

I finally shot a bear the fourth night I was there. It was an old boar, and I shot it on the same hillside where I had lost the first bear. As with my first bear, it rolled all the way down to the creek when I shot. This time, however, it did not get up and walk away.

My guides skinned it and boiled its skull that evening. We left for Ezerum at 5 A.M., and I caught a flight to Antalya. My outfitter, Orhan Konakci, and I spent the remaining days of my hunt near the small town of Akseki, looking for a trophy wild boar. We saw only sows and piglets, though.

On 10 October I flew to Moscow and hooked up with Andre Ovcharov, a Hunting Consortium representative, and Oleg Stouper, who would travel with me as my interpreter. They helped me clear Customs and drove me downtown to the Congress Hotel. I had returned to Russia to hunt a Karaganda argali, a large wild sheep found only in the Karaganda region of eastern Kazakhstan. At breakfast the

---

4. Although we did not recover that bear, I had to pay the full trophy fee for it. In Turkey, as in many other places around the world, a hunter pays for all animals wounded and lost.

next morning I met two hunters who had just finished an ibex hunt and were on their way home. They joined us when Andre and Oleg took me on a tour of the Kremlin and Red Square. That evening we all went to a fine restaurant for dinner. It was good to have more than one person with whom to speak English again.

At 12:30 P.M. the next day, Oleg and I flew more than three hours to Kazakhstan and landed outside the town of Karaganda. (With the three-hour time change, it was 7:15 P.M.) Waiting for us in the airport's lobby was Alexander Ovcharov, who was in charge of the hunt, and a driver. From Karaganda we drove northeast to the poverty-stricken little village of Qaraghayly. Alexander had rooms waiting for us in a rather large government building of some sort. When he left us for the night, we were the only ones there.

A local hunter named Bulat and two foresters picked us up in a Russian Jeep the next morning. Bulat would be my main guide. I learned on the way to our camp that although everyone worked for the government, none had been paid for five months—the government was bankrupt, they said. An hour after leaving Qaraghayly, we reached the area where I would be hunting.

Bulat wasted no time. He was ready to go hunting as soon as we parked the vehicle. Alexander, Oleg, and I followed him to the top of a mountain and worked our way along the topmost ridge, glassing all the canyons below us as we went. There were sheep in that barren, arid range—we

saw two small rams right away, then three ewes, and a fair trophy ram that I passed up. In that afternoon's hunt we found three rams in their beds nearly a mile from us. I took a good look with my spotting scope at the largest ram and decided it was a good one. To reach it Bulat and I had to back off down to the valley, climb the mountain's backside, and come down on it from above. When we finally got there, however, we couldn't see the sheep. We hadn't spooked them, so they were somewhere below us. But where?

We had picked a rocky knob before we began our stalk to guide us to where the rams were bedded, but, once we were on that side of the mountain, we discovered the place was covered with rocky knobs. After more than an hour of sneaking around, checking everything in sight with our binoculars, Bulat grabbed my arm and pointed below us. The rams had been sleeping on a ledge below us, but they had spotted us first and were running off. I sat down quickly, got a good rest, and held slightly in front of the best ram. When I saw dirt fly up behind it, I bolted another cartridge into the chamber, led the ram even more, and killed it with my second shot. Bulat was tickled. I'd taken a trophy Karaganda argali ram by 1 P.M. on my first afternoon of hunting.

It was a beautiful sheep, with a dark-brown coat, a very dark face, and white underparts and rump patch. (Its 58¼-inch horns still rank number three in the most recent SCI record book.) After we had photographed and skinned it, we were heading off the mountain to a farmhouse

The author took this Karaganda argali ram by 1 P.M. on his first day of hunting. The last he looked, its 58¼-inch horns ranked number three in the SCI record book. Kazakhstan, 1996.

where we were invited to have lunch—with the food we had brought.

As I'd experienced in Mongolia, the family had prepared mare's milk the previous day and kept it in a churn overnight, making a crude form of cottage cheese. I didn't care for it the first time, and it didn't taste any better in Kazakhstan.

It was 14 October, and I still had a week left in my hunt, but I decided to try to get back home. While the guides were fleshing and salting my ram's cape and horns, one of the men left for Karaganda to get my airline tickets changed. I reached Moscow on 16 October and Moncton two days after that, after stops in Frankfurt and Toronto.

Before I cleared Customs in Toronto, I learned my ram's horns and cape needed to be fumigated before I could import them to Canada. While I waited for my next connection, I called Pine Ridge Taxidermy in Toronto and arranged for the company to take care of that detail and mount my ram. I don't think anyone has ever had such a successful argali hunt with fewer hours of hunting. I'd been lucky, of course, but Bulat deserved the credit. He knew the area and where to find its sheep.

My last hunt in 1996 got off to a bad start. As we were flying between Toronto and Houston, the Air Canada pilot announced we would have to make an unscheduled stop in Memphis because the plane's windshield somehow had been damaged. Getting out of Memphis usually wouldn't have been a problem, but this was the Thanksgiving holiday in the United

States, and every plane leaving there was fully booked. Six and a half hours later, another Air Canada flight to Houston stopped and picked us up. I'd missed my flight to Costa Rica and had to spend the night in Houston.

I arrived in Costa Rica on 27 November, a day late, but Mexican outfitter Tony Rivera was in the San Jose airport to meet me. When I'd hunted with Tony in Bolivia in July, we'd arranged this hunt with an outfitter named Ricardo Guardia. Although I would try to take the best buck I could find, this would not be a regular trophy hunt. Ricardo and Tony had a special permit to collect deer for a University of Mexico research project. They would send to the university tissue samples and blood from any deer I shot for a DNA study to determine the exact subspecies of whitetail found in Costa Rica.

Our hunt wouldn't get under way for another couple of days, so Tony and I visited the zoo and toured the city. Finally, at 3 P.M. on the third day, Ricardo and his friend Serge, a doctor, picked us up at our hotel, and we left San Jose in two vehicles. Our destination was the small town of Liberia, four hours away on the Guatemalan border. Things are never rushed in Latin America, so I wasn't surprised when, instead of leaving for the hunting area, we got rooms in a local motel, and Ricardo and Serge went to meet with some local hunters who were arranging things. We still hadn't gone hunting three days later.

We would be hunting in an area up the coast that could be reached only by a three-hour boat ride, but we would have to wait for the tide to come in. We slept late the next morning, had lobster for lunch at a restaurant overlooking the Pacific Ocean, and finally got away at 3 P.M. It was dark when Ricardo brought the boat ashore. We slept under the stars on the beach that night.

There apparently was no shortage of deer there. We left our camp at daylight; almost immediately we found a small buck, and I shot it. We packed it back to our camp, Tony collected the tissue and samples he needed, and we returned to San Jose in time to book a flight to Mexico City the next day. My Costa Rican deer hunt, once it got under way, didn't take long.

Tony and I spent the next night in Mexico City, then flew on to Tampico on the Gulf Coast. From there we took a taxi to a ranch owned by Tony's brother near a village called Aldama. We were to spend four days there. Along the way, Tony stopped and met some people he knew and picked up some supplies for us. The brother seldom used the ranch, and it was deserted when we got there. We stayed in the house and got our own meals while we hunted white-tailed deer on the ranch. There were deer, but they were hard to see because of the brush. We had rain and fog most of the time, and we were constantly wet.

After two days without seeing a buck, we moved to another ranch the local hunters had told Tony about. Instead of a house, our camp in this new place consisted of two tents. It was on a higher mountain, and, although it got very hot during the day, the weather was better, and there was less brush. After the first day of hunting there, I discovered ticks on my body. After that, I kept inspecting myself every chance I had. I apparently had picked them up while walking through the brush.

The only deer we saw during those four days jumped across the trail so quickly that we couldn't tell whether it was a buck or a doe. On 8 December Tony and I decided we'd had enough. We drove back to Tampico and flew back to Mexico City. When I called home from Houston the next morning, I learned that Jan's father had died, and the family was holding his funeral that day. I wouldn't be home in time to attend it.

That trip with Tony was my last in 1996. I'd gone swimming in Antarctica and had hunted in Alaska, Bolivia, Ecuador, Turkey, Kazakhstan, Costa Rica, and Mexico, taking two more races of white-tailed deer, a Mideastern brown bear, and a super Karaganda argali. It had been a full year.

JAGUAR, WALRUS, AND TULE ELK, 1997

After my wife's father died, Janice and her mother needed to get away from New Brunswick, so we flew to Mexico on 25 March 1997. Janice's friend Nancy Thomas came along. Our hotel in Cancún was the Crown Princess Club, a posh place with great food, even better weather, and a beautiful beach. I enjoyed sitting in the sun, relaxing, and visiting the town's tourist attractions, but I left all that after five days to hunt a jaguar. Janice, Nancy, and her mother stayed for nine more days.

I hired a taxi, and we drove four hours and fifteen minutes from our hotel in Cancún to another hotel in a place called Chetumal. After checking into the Holiday Inn, I left my luggage in my room and went to the lobby to wait for Tony Rivera, my guide in Bolivia and Ecuador a year earlier.

It was Tony who had told me about a young Mexican biologist's research project. To learn how many jaguar there were, how they hunted, and how far they might travel, he would capture live cats, fit them with radio transmitters, and monitor their movements. If he could get the funding, he planned to track them from four tall towers.

Tony had come up with a way for the program to pay its own way, using sportsmen who would pay for the privilege of hunting a jaguar with tranquilizing darts. The hunter not only experienced a real hunt but also got to take photos with "his" jaguar and enter its measurements in Safari Club International's record book. The jaguar would wake up no worse for the wear and walk away, wearing a collar that allowed the biologist to follow it over the next two or three years. It would be the first such scientific study of these magnificent animals. The biologist had been on every successful jaguar darting hunt and planned to write a thesis on the project for his master's degree.

I planned to hunt a jaguar for one week with Tony, then travel about three hours to another spot to hunt brocket and white-tailed deer, ocellated turkey, and white-lipped peccary with his brother, Eduardo. When Tony met me at the hotel, he was with Cuauhtemoc "Temoc" Chavez, the biologist in charge of the project. An hour or so later, J. Y. Jones and his brother Scott joined us, and we all went to dinner. J. Y., a Georgia ophthalmologist, was on a quest to take forty-two types of big-game animals in North America with the same Remington Model 700 .30-06 rifle. Jaguar were protected, though, so he would have to take his with a dart.[1]

---

1. J. Y. Jones would later describe his hunts for North America's big game—including a darted jaguar—in his book *One Man, One Rifle, One Land* (Safari Press, 2001).

Lunch in Chetumal before the author's jaguar hunt. From left: Tony Rivera; J. Y. Jones; Tony's brother; Irvin Barnhart; the author; and Gary Ingersoll. Mexico.

Soon after this photo was taken, the author's jaguar was fitted with a radio collar and given an injection. Minutes later, it walked away. Mexico.

The hunting world is not as large as it might seem. On our way out of Chetumal, we met fellow Weatherby award-winners Irvin Barnhart and Gary Ingersoll from Houston. They would be hunting with Eduardo while J. Y. and I hunted with Tony.

Tony's camp was in a thick jungle four hours from Chetumal in an area he had not hunted previously, and we reached it after dark. His men had arrived a couple of days before us and had already set up tents and had built a thatched *ramada* where we would eat. They also had been busy cutting trails through the jungle with machetes and staking out live goats to attract jaguar, just as the shikaris used to stake out cattle to attract tigers for the maharajahs in India. If one of the goats were eaten, Tony planned to try to catch the cat alive with his hounds.

We left camp each morning at 5 A.M. and checked the goats, then returned to our tents. It was warm at night, over 70 degrees Fahrenheit, but it climbed to 90–95 degrees Fahrenheit and was downright hot and humid during the day. We spent most of our time resting in hammocks and reading, except when we checked the baits each morning. After a week without a jaguar touching our goats, I returned to Chetumal to hook up with Eduardo.

In Chetumal I met the three men— Gab Michel, Huck Spalding, and Jack Schwabland—who would be hunting with me. I had wanted to meet Schwabland, author of the text in the SCI record book, for a long time. He was a walking encyclopedia on the world's game animals.

The following day the four of us, plus Eduardo and three men, left in four vehicles and drove five hours to Eduardo's tent camp, in a jungle that was as thick as the country around Tony's camp. None of us took an animal or even chased a jaguar, after walking for five straight days. On Friday we moved to another area and drove out from a motel to hunt each day.

Jack shot a brocket deer, but it was the only game any of us saw the next day. That afternoon Tony and his helper, Francisco "Pancho" Zavala Castillo, drove into camp. A jaguar had killed one of the goats, Tony said, and we had a chance of catching it. I grabbed my bags and was ready to leave with him a few minutes later.

The next morning, a Sunday, we found the jaguar's kill and put the dogs on its trail. They were out of sight in an instant, barking and howling constantly as they ran off. A few minutes later, we could hear them barking treed. The jungle was so thick that Pancho had to cut us a trail with his machete, and it took us a while to reach them. As we approached, the jaguar roared. It was nothing like the roar of a lion, but it was a thrilling sound.

The hounds had bayed a female jaguar and its two- to three-month-old cub. My first glimpse of the cat made me think of the leopards I'd taken in Africa; I could see the differences. Jaguars, even females, are larger and more muscular, especially in the shoulders. They also have larger heads. Instead of spots, they have rosettes. They really are gorgeous animals.

Tony and the biologist had given me some training with the dart gun. It was powered by a CO_2 cartridge, and the drug-filled darts were heavy, which meant its trajectory was like a rainbow. I would have to get close and put the dart into muscle, preferably the cat's thigh. If I hit the lungs or stomach, it could kill the animal, they said.

As soon as we reached the tree, Tony, Pancho, and the biologist caught the dogs to keep them from injuring the female or killing the cub on the ground. While they were doing this, I crept up on the tree and waited until Tony nodded to let me know that the dogs were tied up. When I had a clear shot, I sent a dart into the jaguar's rump. Tony carried a handgun in case the jaguar came at us before the drug took effect, but it wasn't necessary. The cat merely climbed higher in the tree; the dart seemingly had no effect. Tony said I shouldn't worry. I'd placed the dart properly, and it would take effect soon.

Sure enough, after at least three or four minutes, the jaguar became groggy and started moving its head from side to side. It lost its balance and dropped to the ground. Pancho immediately tied a bandanna over the cat's eyes to protect them. Then he measured its paws, girth, length, and the circumference of its head, plucked some hair from its belly, and drew some blood. Before attaching a radio collar around its neck and a metal tag in one of its ears, he dug some feces from its rectum. Then we made the usual "trophy" photographs, as I held the cat's head. It gave me a strange sensation to be handling such a large, meat-eating—and very much alive—cat, even if it was drugged, limp, and unconscious.

Pancho gave the cat an injection to counteract the drug and protect against infection. Then, to keep another predator from finding and killing it, we waited at a safe distance and watched. The jaguar woke up gradually, stood on wobbly legs, and walked off into the jungle with its cub. Darting it had been an interesting experience.

We drove back to Chetumal the next day and learned that Jack and Huck hadn't seen anything other than Jack's brocket deer. Huck and I flew to Cancún that evening, and Huck caught the next flight home. I spent the night in Cancún and flew to Moncton the next day. It was quite a shock to leave that hot, humid jungle and step out of an airplane to find everything covered with snow. All the time I was in southern Mexico I hadn't needed a jacket or a sweater.

I suspect if you were to walk around the halls of any hunters' convention and ask everyone you encountered to name the world's largest predatory game mammal— an animal that is four times the size of the largest polar bear or brown bear—few, if any, would think of the walrus. (The elephant seal is not considered a game animal, though it is larger. It lacks the ivory tusks that have made trophy hunters seek out the walrus.) A walrus can weigh up to two tons and can reach eleven feet or more in length. Unlike the big brown bear, which will eat grass, berries, and other vegetation, a walrus is strictly a carnivore.

Although it subsists mainly on the clams and mussels it finds on the ocean floor, there are many reports of walrus killing and eating seals. There is one species of walrus, and there are two subspecies (Atlantic and Pacific). I hunted the Atlantic walrus.

In the Inuit language, Igloolik means "place of more than one house." When Jay Walderden from Wisconsin and I arrived at the village of Igloolik on 15 July 1997, my first impression was that it would be hard to find anything else to call it. A string of typical North Country plywood and sheet-metal homes for perhaps 1,200 people had sprouted up on the featureless Foxe Basin coastline. The beach was covered with gravel and rocks, many of them stained red by algae. It was summer, so there was no snow, but offshore—for as far as we could see, which was not very far because of the fog—was floating ice.

To get to Igloolik we'd flown from Ottawa to Iqualuit on Baffin Island. There we had rented the insulated flotation survival suits that all non-Inuit walrus hunters must wear; then we had flown to Igloolik. At $200 each, the blaze-orange rental suits were insurance policies. They would keep us alive if either of us fell into the water. They also were very warm.

I had met Jay for the first time in Ottawa the previous day, and he and I had traveled to Igloolik to hunt an Atlantic walrus, something we could not have done just two years earlier. (We'd booked our hunts through Jerome Knap's Canada North Outfitting.) After landing, we were taken to the home of Brad Parker, a Northwest Territories Department of Renewable Resources biologist. In 1996 the Hunter-Trapper Association of the village of Igloolik began selling a few walrus from its quota to sportsmen, which was a good deal for both trophy hunters and Inuit. The hunters were able to participate in a walrus hunt and take home a trophy, and the village people got the meat. (U.S. citizens were not allowed to take home the trophy.) The sale of permits helped pay for things such as schools and community buildings. Parker was a strong advocate of the program and was advising the Inuit and helping them run their hunts until the program was established.

At first Parker said we'd stay at his home and go out after our walrus the next day, but that changed after his phone rang. It was one of the guides. The fog was lifting, and there was no wind. It was time to go hunting! Of all the requisites of a safe and successful walrus hunt, the lack of wind is the most important, Parker said. It can be extremely dangerous to be out in a small boat among the shifting, floating ice floes when the wind comes up. Inuit hunters have died when windblown ice buckled and heaved and suddenly crushed or capsized them.

Jay and I loaded our gear into a truck, and Parker drove us about six miles to a place he called the Point, where the Inuit hunters camped when the ice was out. We were not alone there. There were a dozen or more tents, one of which had been set up for Jay and me to use. It was 6 P.M. when we stored our gear in the tent and headed to the boats. With almost continuous daylight in July, our guides weren't concerned about leaving so late. They wanted to take advantage of the flat, quiet water. While we waited for the guides to get squared away, I looked around the Point. Mixed with the gravel were thousands of pieces of walrus and seal bones, proof that Inuit hunters had camped and gone to sea after walrus from that spot for hundreds of years.

To get to where we would hunt, I climbed into an outboard-powered aluminum craft with my guide, Japity, his son, Jeti, and two other members of their family. They said the ice floes were about thirty miles out. Jay was in another boat with his guides, Simeonie and Johnny. For safety reasons we kept in sight of each other as we traveled.

It gave me an eerie feeling to be zipping across the flat water in the little boat. When we turned off our outboard to let Jay's boat catch up, it was so quiet we could hear bearded and harp seals barking more than a mile away. There were ice floes scattered everywhere, each sculpted into its own unique shape by the wind and water. My guide said the blue ice we were seeing was from a glacier and was hundreds of years old.

Two hours after leaving camp, we reached the walrus grounds and found three or four boats with local hunters already there. I had a strange feeling that something wasn't right, and then I realized that I wasn't seeing any shadows. The sun was below the horizon, but it was still daylight. All around us were scattered groups of large, dark shapes on the stark white ice—I was seeing my first live walrus, or *aivik*, as our guides called them.

The animals were quite noisy, some barking and roaring as we got nearer. Most of them paid no attention to us, however, and we were able to drift close to them as we searched for a light-colored male with long tusks. (Light color is a sign of age.) Several of the larger walrus had dark-stained tusks. They had been eating seal meat, Japity said. When we got too close for their comfort, the walrus simply slipped silently into the water. We must have inspected two hundred or more before Jay shot a female with very long tusks, the best we had seen until then.

I wanted a male, and finally, at 2:30 A.M., Japity pointed to a good one with seven others on a floe. As we drifted toward it, I slipped my rifle out of the case I was using to protect it from the water and loaded it with 250-grain Nosler Partition bullets—my favorite load for heavy game with my Sako .338 Winchester Magnum.

Shooting an animal as large as a walrus at forty or fifty yards would be ridiculously easy if it were not for the rocking of the boat and the fact that the hunter must hit it precisely in the brain to anchor it on the ice. I put the cross hairs of my 1.56X Schmidt & Bender scope where the brain was supposed to be, waited until everyone in the boat had stopped moving, and squeezed the trigger. At the shot my walrus stiffened, then suddenly relaxed, without moving an inch. Even so, Japity stuck it with a steel harpoon tied to a long sealskin rope, just in case it revived.

We spent a half-hour trying to get its companions to leave, but there was one that would not. We eventually tied a rope on my walrus and towed it to another floe, where my guides used a block and tackle anchored with a metal stake to slide it onto the ice. I was awed by the size of the animal. It was more than ten feet long and weighed nearly two tons. Its tusks were twenty inches long.

My guides had a unique way of packing the meat back to their camp. They cut the thick hide (at least two inches thick at the neck) into three-by-three-foot squares and sliced holes all along the sides. They then laced everything up with thin strips of walrus hide to make bundles about thirty inches long and twenty inches in diameter. Steam was rising from the carcass as they cut it up. One of the first things they removed was its two-foot-long *oosik*, or penis bone, and they presented the trophy to me.

While they were removing my walrus's wrinkled skin, they were cooking pieces of the intestines and eating raw liver. They kept its stomach intact. Inside, they said, there were close to a hundred pounds of clams and mussels that they would take home and eat later.[2] I declined their invitation to join them in eating liver and guts and ate a packed lunch instead. It was 5 A.M. by the time they were done, and the sun was above the horizon. I don't know what the temperature was, but I was warm in my insulated suit.

On the trip back to camp we came upon a line of solid ice that forced us to make a wide detour in the fog. Our guides had a good sense of direction, though, and we were ashore by 8 A.M. After hunting all night, Jay and I immediately crawled into our sleeping bags and fell asleep. Brad woke us at noon and congratulated us, wanting to hear all the details of our hunt. After lunch, he introduced us to two girls from Winnipeg, who were studying whales, and a man who was filming their project. They had been at Igloolik for three weeks and planned to leave that day.

I could see no sign of the meat from our walrus in camp, and when I asked about it, Japity pointed to several mounds of rocks behind our tent. They had buried the meat in shallow holes and would return that winter to dig it up after it had properly "cured," he said. I didn't say anything, but I was thinking that I didn't want to be anywhere near the place when they opened up their cache of rotting meat.

We spent that night at Brad's home in Igloolik and returned to Ottawa the next day. I was home the day after that. We'd had perfect weather—50–55 degrees Fahrenheit—during the four days I'd been gone. It was so warm, in fact, that mosquitoes pestered us while we were on shore. I'd had an interesting experience and had enjoyed seeing the differences between our culture and that of the Inuit. My one and only walrus hunt was not nearly as

---

2. Outfitter Bert Klineburger, in his book *Big-Game Hunting Around the World*, described how he and international hunter Watson Yoshimoto ate only seal meat and the clams and shellfish from the stomachs of a walrus while hunting off St. Lawrence Island in 1962.

Atlantic walrus, taken near Igloolik. Northwest Territories, 1997.

adventurous as when the Inuit went out in sealskin boats and hunted with whalebone spears, but it had been an adventure nonetheless.

The tule elk, a subspecies found only in California, nearly disappeared after the 1849 gold rush. Fewer than thirty were left by the time an Owens Valley rancher took steps to protect them. From his private refuge, elk were captured and transplanted all over California. When I first hunted a tule elk in 1997, experts estimated there were more than four thousand in twenty-three different locations. They may never increase unless more habitat is found for them.

Among the differences between the tule elk and their cousins is that tule elk are smaller, with shorter and wider skulls and longer rows of teeth. The ends of their antlers often have crowns or cups like those of red deer. Although the subspecies is no longer threatened, a California resident could spend the rest of his life filling out applications and never draw a permit to hunt a tule elk on public land. Private landowners, however, are allowed to sell a limited number of tags.

Tule elk supposedly are easier to hunt than other elk because they prefer open, lowland areas. I did not find this to be the case.

It was a typical San Francisco day—foggy—when I landed there an hour behind schedule on 9 October 1997. I'd booked a tule elk hunt through M.U.M. (Multiple Use Management) and had arranged to meet its representative at a restaurant about 3½ hours north of the airport. I rented a car and drove north on Highway 101 until I reached the town of Willet, found the restaurant, and ran for the door in a driving rain. Jim Settle was waiting for me inside. I followed his half-ton pickup truck in my rental car for about twenty minutes to the Shamrock Ranch, where we met Frank and Julie Sanderson, the managers of the seventeen-thousand-acre ranch.

It was getting dark when Jim and I left in his truck and drove to our hunting camp, a cabin in the mountains. It was a comfortable place with a wood stove, propane lights, and a water heater. (It also had a generator, but we used the propane lights instead.) Jim cooked our breakfast, and we made our own lunch. Frank's wife brought dinner up to the cabin.

On the drive up the mountain, Jim said the Shamrock Ranch was one of the few places authorized by the California Fish and Game Department to sell private land permits for tule elk. (Until 1992, they could not grant permits to nonresidents.) The fencing on the ranch was four-strand barbed wire for cattle, which meant the elk were free to move back and forth between the ranch and the surrounding public land. They were disturbed less on the ranch, so they spent most of their time there.

It would be hard to find a better place to hunt a tule elk. The ranch was covered with mountains and hills, with broad valleys and lots of open places—perfect conditions for spotting elk with binoculars and stalking them. Hunters had already

taken four bulls on the ranch earlier in the season, Jim said.

Before we went to bed that night, Jim fired up the wood stove until it was almost too warm in the place. During the night the fire burned down, and we woke up in a very cold cabin. The temperature was about 35 degrees Fahrenheit outside when we left at 6:50 A.M. in Jim's truck. There were many roads on the ranch, and we were able to drive just about everywhere except where the roads had washed away. Jim said I should have been there the previous week, when the elk were still bugling. I was the last hunter of the season, and the older bulls now were staying in the brush—where they were hard to find—during the day.

A coyote was the only animal we saw, after driving and glassing for two hours. Then, around 9:30 A.M., while we were sitting on a ridge and using our binoculars to cover the terrain below us, Jim and I spotted a herd of about sixty elk. They were a half-mile away, feeding in an opening near the highway close to Frank's home. They all were cows, calves, and young bulls, and we left them alone and went back to glassing. Here and there across the country below us we began seeing black-tailed deer. A few of them were good bucks.

We were back on the mountain at 3 P.M. after lunch and a nap. The temperature was about 50 degrees Fahrenheit, and the rain was pouring down. When the roads became too slippery, Jim and I decided to return to the cabin, where Frank was waiting with a salad and lasagna that Julie had prepared. It was Friday now, and Frank planned to hunt with us over the weekend. I would not be the only hunter on the ranch on Saturday and Sunday. Five men were due to arrive that night to hunt blacktail, Jim said. As I went to bed that night, I remembered that this was my father's birthday. He would have been eighty-seven.

The roads were drying out as Jim and I left the cabin at 6:50 the next morning. Frank was leaving his house about the same time in his all-terrain vehicle to check out another area, and we'd made arrangements to meet at a certain place three hours later. No one had seen an elk when we got together. Two of the deer hunters we talked with said they had seen two good bulls the previous weekend and would let us know if they saw them again. We spent the rest of the day glassing and walking without seeing an elk, though we did see several big deer. Julie and her two children were waiting for us at the cabin with ham, potatoes, vegetables, and an apple crumble dessert. We'd had good weather that day, and the cabin was warmer that night.

Frank scouted another area the next morning, and Jim and I drove around, stopping to glass from every good viewpoint we could find, working our way down the mountain. By the time we reached Frank's home, we had seen four small bulls, and we learned that the herd we'd seen there the first day had moved off the ranch. Frank had seen nothing but a few deer. That evening the deer hunters reported that they hadn't seen an elk. Jim

was convinced that the big bulls he'd seen during the rut had moved out of the country, and I tended to believe him.

Frank drove off on his ATV in another direction that afternoon and saw only a black bear. He joined us that afternoon when we drove to a long canyon we hadn't hunted yet. As we approached it, we found fresh elk tracks in the mud that led over the canyon's edge, so Frank dropped into the canyon and started working his way up. Jim and I stayed high, hoping to see any elk that Frank spooked out of the brush below us. Although Frank said he saw a lot of tracks in the bottom, our little drive produced only two or three feral hogs, a black-tailed buck, and a black bear. Frank said he'd seen every color phase of black bear from cinnamon to brown to black on this ranch.

This time Julie and the kids had brought salad, chicken, baked potatoes, and vegetables for our supper. I hadn't seen an elk I wanted, but I had no complaints about the food.

Monday was Thanksgiving Day in Canada, my last day to hunt on the Shamrock Ranch. Frank had to work that day, but Jim and I drove to the top of the mountain and hunted all the way down to Frank's place before we saw our first elk. There were about thirty elk, including five or six young bulls and a very large five-by-four that I was tempted to take. I passed it up, though.

After lunch and a nap, we were back on the mountain and climbing a trail to get to another vantage point. It was warm, the trail was steep, and I suddenly realized

I was sweating in the middle of October. We could see a lot of country from our new vantage point, but we could find no elk. We did see a bobcat, a flock of wild turkeys (the first I'd seen on this trip), and more deer before we returned to the truck.

"That's why we call it 'hunting,'" Jim said. "If we got everything we wanted every time we went out, we'd call it 'shooting.'"

Frank joined us at 4 P.M., and we followed him down the mountain to check out what we were calling "the house herd," hoping that a bigger bull had joined it. The elk were still feeding along the highway, or I might have tried to take that four-by-five bull. When my hunt ended at sundown, I hadn't seen a shootable bull. Jim and Frank invited me to return during the rut in September and try again, and I said I would.

I was back in Moncton at midnight the next night. I'd had a good hunt with pleasant companions, and I wasn't bothered about returning home without an elk.

It was 9 March 1998 when Janice and I landed at Kahului on Maui Island and drove to Kalapahai Beach. At the SCI convention in Reno two months earlier, I'd booked a four-day mouflon hunt on the Big Island of Hawaii with Eugene Yap of South Point Safaris. Janice and I decided to spend a week on Maui before and after the hunt.

It felt good to be in Hawaii after our long flight from New Brunswick. The weather was beautiful, and we had a nice hotel. Janice and I did a little touring of the island in our rental car, but mostly we just relaxed and enjoyed being in pleasant surroundings. On 16 March we flew to the Big Island and met Eugene, then drove to the large property he leased on the south point of the island. As soon as we left the main road, we started gaining elevation, driving his four-by-four vehicle up a road that had been bulldozed through different stages of old lava flows. The latest eruption had occurred just twenty years earlier, Eugene said. Our camp consisted of two cabins—one for Janice and me, the other for him—about an hour from the main road. They'd been roughly built of plywood, but both had running water and a propane heater that allowed us to take hot showers. The elevation was six thousand feet, which meant we were more than a mile above the beach we'd left only a few hours earlier.

After unloading our gear, we went for a drive and saw two nice mouflon rams almost immediately. I passed them up, hoping to find a better trophy. Before we returned to the cabin that evening, we had seen feral boars, wild turkeys, and perhaps a hundred mouflon, although nearly all of them were ewes and lambs.

Eugene prepared a salad and a stir-fry dish for dinner, and the three of us sat up talking for several hours. I found him to be friendly, easy to talk with, and interesting.

The next morning Eugene and I left Janice with the truck and walked down a mountain slope, stopping often to glass for sheep. We saw a few small rams and lots of ewes and lambs. When we were within sight of the road at the bottom of the mountain, we spotted a ram with impressive horns. I wanted to go after it, but Eugene said I should wait. Its horns curled too far back behind its head, he said, and it might be a hybrid. We left it alone and climbed back to the truck.

Hawaii had no indigenous large mammal until early explorers released swine and goats on the islands. Much later, there were several attempts to introduce various game animals, including pronghorn antelope and mule deer, but none succeeded until mouflon from Europe were introduced to Hawaii between 1962 and 1968.[1] The problem is that mouflon readily breed with domestic sheep. Some of the hybrids can grow horns very unlike those of a typical mouflon. We apparently had found one of those hybrids.

We saw more sheep before we got back to Janice at 11:30 A.M., but I passed them all up. That afternoon Janice stayed at the cabin, while Eugene and I drove to another area and tried unsuccessfully to call in a turkey. Later, we drove to still another area and glassed a ridge where Eugene had seen a big ram a few days earlier. We couldn't find the animal, and, when the wind blew in a bank of fog, the temperature suddenly dropped. I hadn't brought clothing for cold weather—I simply didn't think I'd need it in Hawaii—so we went back to the cabin. After a steak and rice dinner, Eugene and I swapped hunting stories and called it a day at 9:30 P.M.

We were warm in our cabin, so I was surprised to find frost covering everything when I stepped out of my cabin just before daylight the next day. The temperature was exactly 32 degrees Fahrenheit. We saw a lot of sheep again that day, but none that I wanted to take.

We left camp on foot the next morning, my last day to hunt, and saw a lot of sheep. The larger males were staying in the timber, Eugene said.

"You should be here in September and October," he said. "You can see a thousand sheep a day when they're rutting."

After lunch, we packed our gear and left the cabins, hoping to hunt on the way down the mountain. The spots from which Eugene wanted to glass were socked in with fog, but we did see a few females and a couple of hogs. We drove around that mountain for two hours and saw a lot of sheep, including several nice rams, but I'd already taken four mouflon and didn't want any of them.

I'd been walking constantly for three days and went to bed without dinner that evening in Kona. I was just too tired to eat. Our room at the Royal Kona Resort overlooked the water, and I fell asleep hearing the waves breaking over black lava stone on the beach. Janice and I spent the next few days relaxing on Kona and Maui before returning home on 28 March. I found I'd matured as a hunter. I hadn't fired a shot on my last two trips, and it didn't bother me at all.

Although we didn't know it until we met, Oded Eliashan and I had flown from Toronto to Edmonton on the same plane on 24 April 1998, on my first leg of a journey that would take me to the North Pole. The tour organizers of this trip, Arctic Odysseys, had told us to look for each other at the airport when we landed. After an awkward introduction, we carried our bags to the shuttle that would take us to the Nisku Inn, where we would stay overnight before flying on to Resolute in Northwest Territories. Oded was from

---

1. The SCI record book does not accept an introduced mouflon entry if the tip-to-tip spread of its horns is its widest measurement. There are other restrictions, such as weight, length of tail, mane length, and color.

Jerusalem. At sixty-seven, he was seven years older than I, but we got along fine. We both had done a lot of traveling, and both of us were looking forward to this new adventure at the top of the world.

Oded and I met again in the hotel lobby the next morning, but there was no sign of the five others who had signed on to travel to the North Pole with us. We didn't meet them until we reached the Air Canada gate. We truly were an international group, representing five different countries. Besides Oded and myself, there were Tony Baron, sixty, from Ontario; James Ottos, seventy-two, from Pennsylvania; Jim Parker, forty-one, from Texas; Majad Alkhulifi, forty-eight, from Singapore; and Arnold Schultze, sixty-eight, from Germany. After stops in Yellowknife and Cambridge Bay, we finally landed in Resolute at 5:45 P.M. local time. The temperature outside the airport was 20 degrees Fahrenheit. We were just in time to meet another group of "North Polers" on their way home. They'd had good weather but were unable to land any closer than ten miles or so from 90 degrees north latitude (the true North Pole), they said.

We met our tour leader after we arrived at the Norwhale Inn, where I'd stayed in 1990 when I hunted polar bear. Ted Hockathorn was an American from Washington State, and, as are many people with his type of job, he was personable and eager to please. After dinner and an indoctrination session in which Ted talked about the region and told us what to expect, we finally were in our rooms at 10 P.M. It had been a very long day.

It was 8 degrees Fahrenheit with wind and light snowfall outside when we all met again in the morning. We were dressed in our arctic gear and went for a short walk to try it out. We were supposed to fly on to the Eureka Weather Station at 9 A.M., but the flight was rescheduled until after lunch because the weather farther north had temporarily closed the station. Arnold Schultze and I played pool, and several of us went for another walk to pass the time. The weather had improved after lunch, so around 1 P.M. Ted had us collect our gear and head for the twin Otter on the runway about four hundred yards from the hotel. Waiting at the plane were pilot Carl Ziber from Switzerland and copilot Blair Rathmussan, a Canadian.

Our flight took us over the magnetic North Pole, where we circled and landed about ten miles away on a runway next to a dilapidated building in the middle of nowhere. The skeleton of a wrecked DC-3 was nearby. It was 4:10 P.M. Three men who had skied from Resolute to the magnetic North Pole were waiting for an airplane to pick them up the next day. The sun was shining brightly, the sky marred only by a few clouds, and the temperature was perhaps 20 degrees Fahrenheit—a beautiful day in the arctic! After taking on fuel, we lifted off again at 5 P.M., heading to Eureka via the route of polar explorer Dr. Frederick A. Cook. (He claimed to be the first to the Pole in 1908, one year before Commander Robert E. Peary, generally believed to be the first in 1909.) The sun was bouncing off the sparkling snow-white pressure ridges, and the scenery was gorgeous. Just before we landed in Eureka at 7:40 P.M., I looked down and saw a small herd of muskox. Our plane had spooked them, and they were running with their long hair flowing. I have never ceased to be impressed by this little ox's ability to survive in such inhospitable terrain.

There were eight people working at the Canadian government's weather station, and their cook had a huge dinner waiting for us—salad, steak, baked potatoes, and strawberry shortcake. We were surprised to find so much food, especially this far north. The workers told us they didn't see the sun from the end of November until March. Right now, we truly were in the "land of the midnight sun," with daylight twenty-four hours a day.

The next day we were scheduled to leave for the Pole, and everyone in our group was up at 6 A.M. and ready to go. We were just in time to watch the station personnel launch a weather balloon, a balloon three feet wide by four feet high, with instruments attached to its bottom that send data about temperature, wind, humidity, and other things back to the station's computer. It was designed to climb to ten thousand feet before it self-destructed two hours later. The station releases two balloons a day, at 6:15 A.M. and 6:15 P.M. The station transmits the information its computer gathers to Eureka, and it is forwarded to Edmonton. Along with other reports, it helps determine long-range weather forecasts.

Even before the balloon's data returned, we knew we would not be going to the Pole that day. According to a radio report from a man stationed at the fuel cache about four hundred miles north of Eureka (about halfway to the pole from Eureka), the weather near the Pole was not suitable for flying, and it was expected to get worse. There was nothing we could do but wait for a break in the weather. The station was a comfortable place, with a couple of sitting rooms stocked with videos and books, and an exercise room. I sent an e-mail to Janice and worked on my journal. After supper, Ted and some of the station workers told tales about early polar expeditions. If we were going to be stuck this far north, we couldn't have found a better place. The temperature was -8 degrees Fahrenheit outside at 6 o'clock in the morning, and it dropped to -5 degrees Fahrenheit that evening.

On 29 April we awoke to find an overcast sky still over Eureka. If anything, the weather was worse than the previous day. I took one look outside and was convinced that flying to the Pole was out, and the report from the fuel cache confirmed it. In addition to the dreary sky, a high wind was blowing over the Pole. Landing there was out of the question.[2] In contrast to the comforts and companionship at Eureka, only one man

---

2. One can fly to the North Pole and land safely only during a three-week window in the spring, during the twenty-four hours of daylight. After that, the ice weakens and breaks up in places. The tour company stationed people at the cache during the "safe" period to provide pilots with weather reports.

was stationed in a tent at the cache, with a dog as his only companion.

Since we couldn't fly north, Ted announced that we would fly over to Greenland for a break in the "big city" of Qaanaaq, a village of five or six hundred. Before I left Moncton, I had sent a message to Jan Thysen, a Dane with whom I had hunted muskox in 1995 in Greenland, to let him know I would be spending a day or so in Greenland. Jan was in charge of all the airports in the region and was stationed at Thule Air Force Base, about sixty miles south of Qaanaaq. It would be nice to see him again, if he could get away. He and his wife had visited us in New Brunswick.

We landed on the ice at Qaanaaq at noon and walked a short distance to the building where we would be staying. There were only five rooms, so we were assigned two to a room. It wasn't the most modern place I've visited, but it was comfortable and clean. The temperature now was 15 degrees Fahrenheit, a lovely day compared to what we had been experiencing, and our group walked down to the post office and a coop store. According to Ted, this was one of the northernmost villages in the world.

Jan flew in from Thule by chopper while we were shopping for souvenirs at the co-op store, and we spent some time talking about our earlier hunt and our mutual acquaintances. Qaanaaq had no hotel, so he spent the night at a friend's home.

The next morning, 30 April, Jan and I were able to spend another hour together

before he had to return to Thule; then I joined the other members of our group and toured the village museum. After lunch, everyone went for a 2½-hour sled ride. When we returned, we learned the weather had improved up north, and we were cleared for our flight to the Pole.

Because of the time difference, we left Qaanaaq at 6 P.M. and reached Eureka at 4 P.M. While the plane was being refueled in Eureka, we lightened the load by leaving most of our equipment and luggage behind—as well as tour guide Ted—to make room for three extra barrels of fuel. Our next stop was the fuel cache, where we took on more fuel and met the weatherman who had been sending the reports to Eureka. The temperature was 15 degrees Fahrenheit as we lifted off and headed north again. Our pilot cautioned us to keep our fingers crossed. If there were clouds over the North Pole, we would have to turn around. Having flown in the arctic for more than two decades, he respected its weather.

We reached the Pole at 10:10 P.M. and dropped low enough to see a small tent and two men waving at us as we started to land near them. As soon as our wheels touched the ice, though, the pilot gunned the engine, and we lifted up again. There is nothing at the Pole except frozen ocean. Although the ice was about two meters deep, it was badly broken up, and it was too risky to land there. I was surprised to see open water where the ice had separated near the Pole. As we searched for another landing site, the pilot told us the men we

The author's party had to wait until the weather allowed them to fly, but they eventually landed on top of the world. North Pole.

The author's team caught the only tuna registered in the 1998 Canadian International Tuna Cup. Halifax, Nova Scotia.

had seen below were a Norwegian and a Brit who had skied to the Pole from the mainland, a distance of about nine hundred miles, pulling a sled for fifty-six days. They had left when there were only three hours of daylight.

After circling a few times—flying around the world and through every time zone in the process—the pilot finally found a safe place to put the plane down. According to our global positioning system, we were at 89.92 degrees south latitude, less than a mile from true north, the northern end of the axis of our planet. There was no wind, and it was a sunny 14 degrees Fahrenheit.

We all unpacked our cameras and took turns snapping photos of each other and the group. Someone had brought something to drink, and we clinked our cups and said toasts. The sun was about midway in the sky when we left at midnight. Our GPS showed the ice we were on had drifted two hundred yards during the two hours since landing.

My trip home was anticlimactic. We returned to Eureka, then flew south to Grise Ford and stayed at the Coop Inn. The next morning we went out on sleds behind snowmobiles and visited an old settlement, then flew across Jones Sound to Devon Island to Cape Sparbo, where Captain Cook was supposed to have spent a winter. Our next stop was Beachey Island, where we visited the gravesites of three members of John Franklin's crew, who had died in 1845 after their ship became stuck in the ice. I had pitched a tent and slept on the

same beach in 1990 while hunting a polar bear behind a dog team. We again spent the night at the Norwhale Inn in Resolute.

At the Resolute airport the next morning, we met the two young skiers we had seen camped at the Pole. There were at least fifteen reporters from various news agencies hovering around them. My next stops were Cambridge Bay, Yellowknife, and Edmonton, where I spent the night. I was back in Moncton at 10 P.M. the next evening. It had been a great adventure. I'd been to the bottom of the world in Antarctica, and now I'd been on the top. As they say in Disneyland, it's a small world after all.

In August my friends Will Webb, Sam Burgess, Ian Olvier, and I formed Team New Brunswick and competed in the 1998 Canada International Tuna Cup out of Halifax. There were only three other teams that year—two from Ontario and one from Nova Scotia—which was seven fewer than the previous year. The Department of Fisheries and Oceans was late in setting the bluefin tuna season's opening and closing dates and the number of tags they would authorize, which made it difficult for the other teams to make it that year.

The Tuna Cup ran for just four days, Thursday through Sunday. We left port at 7 A.M. each day and pulled up lines at 6 P.M. The very first day out we hooked a tuna at 11 A.M., and all four of us had a chance to sit in the chair and fight the 570-pound fish over the next hour. All of us were so tired when we brought that tuna aboard that we were hoping we wouldn't hook another fish that day. We need not have worried. Ours was the only fish caught in that tournament. Team Nova Scotia hooked a fish but lost it, and we were declared the winner. Our one fish brought New Brunswick's first team the Canada Cup for the most points and the Oland Cup for the biggest fish, as well as other prizes for the most fish caught.[3]

On 28 August, ten days after returning from Halifax, I was back at the Shamrock Ranch in northern California, hoping to take the tule elk I hadn't been able to find the previous year. Frank Sanderson met me at the gate when I drove up in a rental car at 5 P.M., and I followed him to his house and met his wife, Julie, again. Frank was optimistic about finding a good bull for me this year. The rut was just starting, he said, as we loaded my gear in his four-by-four.

It was Julie's thirtieth birthday, and Frank had planned a barbecue in her honor, so he left me at the same cabin I'd stayed in the previous year and went home. He was back at 4:30 the next morning. Frank worked during the week, so he could guide me only on Saturday and Sunday, his days off. He'd arranged to have David Ramage guide me on Monday and Tuesday, the last two days of the four-day hunt I'd booked.

Frank and I spent the first day glassing the lower country where most of the cow elk were being seen. I passed up eight bulls

that were running with the cows, a sure sign that the rut had begun. It was a good thing we didn't find a big herd bull that morning. I'd brought my .300 Winchester—and ammunition for my 7mm Remington Magnum. After a quick trip into town to buy a box of the proper ammo, we were back on the mountain at 1 P.M. It was hot— nearly 100 degrees Fahrenheit—when Frank dropped me off at the cabin. I took a nap and was ready to go out again when he returned at 6 P.M.

The only bulls we saw that evening were young. I spent the night alone in the cabin again and was up when Frank arrived at 5 A.M. This would be the day, he promised, as we drove in the dark to an area where we'd heard a bull bugle the previous evening. At first light we left the truck and walked as quietly as we could up a dry creek. We almost immediately bumped into a cow elk. Frank whispered that we needed to wait until we had better light. About ten minutes later, we crept up to a spot from which we could look down on the opening where Frank expected to find the bull. There were about thirty cow elk in a meadow, with a good bull and several smaller bulls, but we needed to get closer.

During our stalk, we spooked another cow elk, and the herd bolted toward the mountain. The six-by-six herd bull was trying to keep its herd together, while the satellite bulls were trying to steal them. They didn't stop until they reached an

---

3. Fish caught in the tournament belonged to the captains of the boats taking them. Our captain sold our tuna to a Japanese fish buyer for approximately ten dollars a pound.

The four members of the Canadian International Tuna Cup's championship team pose for a victory photo in Halifax. From left: Sam Burgess, Ian Olivier, Will Webb, and the author. Nova Scotia.

It took two trips to California, but the author finally took this fine tule elk. California.

open hillside. After taking another look at the big bull with my binoculars, I decided it was within range. One shot put it down. Frank and I field dressed the bull before Frank left to get his truck. When he returned, Julie was with him, and she took some photos before we caped, quartered, and loaded the bull into the truck. We were back at the cabin at 9 A.M. Frank worked on the cape, fleshing it, while I measured the antlers. They scored 245 SCI points, the minimum for entry in the SCI record book. I was happy with it.

When David Ramage arrived that evening, we drove around and saw several bulls, but none was as good as the one I'd taken. Frank had to work on Monday, so David and I drove around to see if we could find a coyote. We didn't see anything, and I was glad I'd taken that bull with Frank. It was 100 degrees again at noon.

We saw a black bear and several bulls that evening, but there was nothing any better than the one I'd taken.

On Monday, my last day on the ranch, we drove out from the cabin at first light.

(It was so hot I hadn't been able to sleep.) David drove me to where I'd taken my elk, and we found the same small herd of cows right away. The bull that had replaced mine was a very good one, larger than the one I'd taken. David said no one had reported seeing that animal before. We watched it for ten or fifteen minutes before heading back to the cabin to pack up. It was so hot I had trouble sleeping when I crawled into my bed at 9 P.M., and I was awake when Frank knocked on our door less than five hours later to take me back to my rental car.

At 6 A.M. the shuttle took me to the San Francisco airport, where I learned Air Canada employees were striking. I finally left on United Airlines and flew to Boston, then took Air Nova to Halifax and on to Moncton. On the way back to Havelock, I was listening to my car radio when I heard that Swiss Air Flight 111 had crashed south of Halifax at 10:15 A.M. over water, killing all 239 people aboard. I had flown over the exact spot just an hour earlier than Flight 111.

PAKISTAN, RUSSIA, AND ANTICOSTI ISLAND, 1999

After hunting in Pakistan in 1994, I'd written in my journal that I was looking forward to hunting there again. It took nearly five years, but on 29 December 1998 I was on my way. I met up with my friend Norbert Bremer from Iowa on a layover in New York, and together we boarded a Pakistani Air flight that would take us to Paris, Lahore, Karachi, and Islamabad. Norbert had booked a hunt in Pakistan, too.

When we arrived in Lahore at 6 A.M. on 31 December, the airport was fogged in, so our plane flew on to Islamabad, which was to be our final destination. We were not allowed to get off there, however. We had to clear Customs and retrieve our luggage at Karachi, some five hundred miles to the south. So we sat on that crowded airplane until 2 P.M., when we were transferred to another plane that took us to Karachi.

There was a flight leaving Karachi for Islamabad in one hour, so we hired a couple of porters to take us with our luggage to the domestic terminal to buy our tickets. They needed help from others, but we made it. We arrived in Islamabad seven hours late, at 9 P.M. New Year's Eve.

No one met us in Islamabad, so we took a shuttle to the Marriott Hotel downtown and called Rohil Nana, our outfitter.[1] Rohil drove over right away and took us to dinner. He'd made reservations for us at the Horizon Guest House, and we moved there on New Year's Day. It was there that he introduced us to Pervez Khan, who would accompany us to Gilgit, where we would hunt ibex.

Norbert Bremer, Pervez Khan, and I left the morning of 2 January for Gilgit, a small town about one hour by air north of Islamabad. When we were over Gilgit, however, the pilot aborted the landing, turned the plane around, and headed back to Islamabad. I couldn't understand what he told the passengers, but I learned he couldn't land in Gilgit that morning because of the fog (a regular occurrence, I was told). After checking into our hotel again, Pervez took us out to shoot our rifles. While we were setting up the targets, he said we would try to fly to Gilgit the next day, and if there were no flight (as happens about half of the time, he said) we would drive to where we would hunt. I wasn't looking forward to spending fourteen hours in a crowded vehicle on narrow mountain roads, but there was no other way if the planes weren't flying.

Fortunately, the planes were flying the next day, and we got to Gilgit without any problems. Asif and Ajaz, our interpreters,

---

1. Rohil Nana's health had deteriorated since I'd seen him five years earlier, and he did not leave the city to hunt with me on this trip. A few months after returning home, his sister called to say he had died.

There are Himalayan ibex on that far slope, but there was no way to reach them that day. Pakistan.

The author's Himalayan ibex hunting crew. The hills were so steep that we all needed frequent stops. Pakistan.

met us there. According to Ajaz, Norbert and I would be hunting about fifteen miles apart in a mountainous area about four hours away. The road to the place followed the Indus River and was narrow and winding. One side of it dropped almost straight down to the water.

After we arrived, government officials held a meeting in the little village near where I would hunt. A wildlife officer presented the village's leaders with $2,250 of my hunting fee. We would be the first international hunters to hunt in this area. The money would help buy improvements for the village and would give the local people an incentive to conserve the game in their area, Ajaz said. (Norbert would later report that a similar ceremony was held at a village near where he hunted.) The five of us stayed in a room at one of the houses in the village and slept on mats that night. There were no beds, chairs, or tables in their homes, and the people sat on their floors to eat.

Norbert and his guides left us the next morning and moved on to another village, and I started climbing the mountain above the village on foot. Seven hours later, we had reached a stone hut at an elevation of about 4,500 feet. It was snowing lightly, adding to the three or four inches already on the ground. Shepherds used the hut during the summer, but it was not inhabited when we got there. My guides and the local people who had come with us ate and slept in it, spending most of the next two days feeding wood into an open fire pit in the center. They set up a little tent outside for me. There was no

way to heat it, and the temperature dropped below freezing every night.

We saw only one male ibex in the eight days we hunted near that hut, and its horns were smaller than the size I wanted to take home. On 7 January we climbed another mountain, following a route taken by a herd of female ibex we'd seen earlier that day. The trail took us over a snow-covered, 13,800-foot pass and down the other side to another stone hut, where we spent the night. Just before dark, we spotted fifteen ibex on a far-off ridge. With the spotting scope, we could see that four were males, and one was very good. It was too late to try to stalk them that day, though.

We left our miserable hut before daylight and headed toward the place we had last seen the ibex. We had to climb about two thousand feet, cross a high ridge, and then lose all the elevation we had gained, and we did it in the dark. We had planned to arrive at daylight, but a heavy fog that blocked out the sun delayed us. When it cleared around 10 A.M., we tried for an hour to find the herd but did not see it. The ibex simply were not there. They had crossed a canyon where we couldn't go, my guides decided. All of us were shivering from the cold, but we had no choice but to go on. We had to find a way around a bank of cliffs and locate that herd again. My guides were convinced there were no other ibex in the area.

There were two routes. One was dangerous because we would have to move across the face of a long row of cliffs, but it was shorter, and that was the route we chose. Before we left, the guides sent one of the local men back to our hut to tell the men to return to their village. Although the canyon was only a mile wide, it was a long way around. Four hours after we started, when we were heading downhill again, we came upon a lean-to. Our guide said we still had another five hours of walking to get to our destination, and he said we should spend the night there. Through Ajaz, I told them I would like to keep going and get past the dangerous section while the weather was good.

We climbed along narrow ledges, where one slip would have sent us tumbling straight down for more than a hundred feet. As soon as we would get past a particularly nasty spot, we would come upon another. It was dark when we finally left the cliffs behind us and approached the bottom of the canyon. I had a flashlight in my backpack, but the batteries were dead, so Ajaz and I walked with our arms locked to try to keep from falling over the rocks. I cannot describe how good the water tasted when we finally found a small stream. We had taken no food or water with us. I thought briefly about soaking my sore feet but decided against it. It was cold, and we needed to keep moving.

It was 7:30 that evening when we finally reached a trail that would take us to a small village. We then had to climb another two thousand feet, but we finally reached a collection of dirty huts around 10 P.M. I was completely played out.

The next morning, as soon as it was light, I took a look at the cliffs we had descended. From where I was, it looked impossible for anything—including an ibex—to get off them. The rest of our party finally showed up around noon, but Ajaz and I spent the rest of the day resting. My guides said Norbert had taken an ibex and had gone back to Islamabad.

The following day, after another night of sleeping on the floor, we started climbing until we reached yet another stone hut. Our local guide figured the ibex had gone to the country surrounding it, but we glassed and walked around until dark without finding them.

We tried a small drive the next morning. Two of the local men walked through the canyons, hoping to jump the ibex and push them to us. But the ibex were nowhere to be seen, and I was running out of time. To return to the village where Norbert and I had separated, we had to cross a river to reach the road. The only way to get across that deep canyon was in a little 36-inch-square wooden platform hanging from a wheel on a cable high above the fast water and the rocks in that chasm. I got on it with a duffel bag on my lap, and someone pulled me across with a rope. It was an interesting experience.

My motel room in Gilgit was cold, but I had a real, honest-to-goodness bed and a shower with hot, running water. I was supposed to fly to Islamabad the next morning, 13 January, but the plane didn't arrive. Ajaz and I spent the rest of the day driving four hours to see a fort at the Hundus Valley. We decided if the plane didn't arrive in the morning, we would drive back to Islamabad. It showed up, and we were in Islamabad before noon.

This cable car across the river was the only way the author's party could leave their hunting area. Pakistan.

There are bigger brown bears on the Kamchatka, but the author was happy with this one. Russia.

I had hoped to have time to do some laundry while we were in the town, but Norbert was waiting for me. We were leaving at 1 P.M. to fly to Quetta to hunt Afghan urial, he said. I only had time to check my bags onto the flight.

In Quetta at 4 P.M. we met a man named Zab, who loaded our baggage into a vehicle and said we were going straight to the mountains, a seven- to eight-hour drive. The last four hours of the trip took us over a rough, winding, and dusty road, and we didn't reach our quarters until past midnight. We were up at daylight, though, and left at 8 A.M. to go hunting. The mountains were quite steep, and we spent all day climbing up and down. We did see three small urial and five markhor. My guides wanted me to shoot one of the markhor, but I wanted only a urial and passed it up.[2] The men thought I was crazy.

We saw our next urial two days later. It was a long way below us, and it moved off while we were making a stalk. We never saw it again. Norbert and I planned to return to Quetta the next day and rest up before flying home. Our guides wanted us to keep hunting, so I agreed to go out until noon. I should have stayed in camp, because I didn't see an animal of any kind that day.

In Quetta the townspeople had been fasting for a month, eating only before daylight and after sundown—all without drinking any water. This was the last day of their fast, and they would have three days

of holidays, when they did nothing. We missed the holidays. We flew to Karachi the next day and rested up in our motel rooms before starting the trip home.

After stops in Islamabad and Zurich, Norbert and I said good-bye in New York. I was home the next day, without having taken either of the animals I'd gone after.

I had done a lot of climbing in steep, rough, and dangerous mountains, and I'd endured extremely primitive conditions, and I was glad to be home in one piece. That trip to Pakistan was one of my toughest hunts.

Russia's Kamchatka Peninsula, the long, thin strip of land that hangs down from the eastern seacoast of Siberia, obviously has no shortage of brown bear. When I arrived on the eastern shore of Petropavloysk on 23 April 1999, I was with a group of two dozen other men who would hunt bear for ten days on the peninsula. After leaving Anchorage, we'd flown over the Bering Sea, crossing the International Date Line in the process, so it now was a day later than when we'd left, though the flight had taken only four and a half hours. Eleven of us had booked our hunts with Robert Kern's Hunting Consortium; the other fourteen had booked with various outfitters in the United States, Canada, and Europe.

Bob Kern and several local people associated with his company were waiting for our group when we cleared Customs.

---

2. My guides wanted to sell me one of the two markhor permits left from earlier hunters and kept taking me to the markhor area. I wanted to take an Afghan urial first and had only three more days to hunt. I tried to find a markhor on my last day there but ran out of time.

Outside, he had a bus that would take us to the place where we would spend the night. I watched out the window as we drove through the streets of Petropavloysk. It was a poor town, with a lot of shacks made of weathered wood. Our shabby-looking hotel appeared to be no better, but it was fine inside. At least it had hot water and comfortable enough beds. We were the hotel's only guests.

We were scheduled to fly in a helicopter the next morning to a place called Esso for supplies and from there to fly on to our various camps. According to Bob, two to three hunters would hunt from each camp. In addition to our interpreters, there would be local guides and a crew of people who would take care of each camp and do our cooking. Because of the weather in Esso, we weren't able to leave Petropavloysk until 2:30 P.M. It was too late in the day to try to fly on to our camps, so our pilots set the helicopter down at a fishing camp about seven miles outside Esso. The town had no accommodations, they said, but we might be able to stay at this camp for the night. Bob and the interpreters found us places to stay, and we used supplies that were in the helicopter. The next day we flew to Esso, where we unloaded and sorted gear and food; then we went on to our various camps.

James Brockett of Pennsylvania and I shared a trapper's cabin about two hours from Esso. Both of Jim's hips had been replaced and he'd had a heart bypass, so he was not able to get around as well as I, but he did fine. In our camp there were two guides, a camp manager and his wife (she did our cooking), a camp helper, an interpreter, a government forester, a Hunting Consortium representative, and a mechanic for the snowmobiles from which we would hunt. The cabin was small, but it had a wood stove, and our cook kept a big bucket of hot water on it. We ate in a tent that also had a wood stove for cooking. The food was all right, but it was not up to our standards.

As I had done on polar bear and muskox hunts, I would ride on a twelve-foot sled, but this time it was hooked behind my guide's snowmobile. Jim also rode on a sled behind his guide's snowmobile. For safety, we traveled together. We spotted a good bear the first morning, and Jim took it. After our guides skinned it, we moved on, looking for a bear for me. A couple of hours later, we found a small one, and I passed it up. Our guides tried very hard to get me to shoot it. If I had, they could have stayed in camp until the helicopter returned.

My guides and I went out alone the next day and saw two different bears. Both were small, but the guides chased one with the snowmobile—giving me a wild ride—until they caught up with it. They were very upset when I refused to shoot it. That night I had my interpreter explain that I was only interested in a mature male bear. I don't think they could understand how anyone could come so far to hunt a bear and not shoot one, because we did the same thing again the next morning. We ran a small bear down with the snowmobile, and again I refused to shoot it. All the bear seemed to be about the same size.

We chased bear every day for three days, and I passed up all of them. We had a

The author's crew turned out for a photo with his bear. The author passed up a lot of smaller bear before taking this one. Russia.

The author shot this buck his first morning on Anticosti Island, then passed up dozens of others without seeing a larger one. Quebec.

snowstorm one day and stayed in camp. The next day was cold and windy, and the bear were not moving. The snow was getting too soft for the snowmobile, and the creeks were opening up. With only three days left in my hunt, I shot the next mature bear we came across. It wasn't as big as I would have liked, but it made the record book. I spent the rest of my hunt reading and talking with Jim in camp while we waited for the helicopter to come get us.

On 6 May we flew to Esso and met up with the other hunters. Everyone in Bob's group had taken a bear. We spent the evening at the same hotel in Petropavloysk and went to dinner to celebrate our successful hunts.

We left Petropavloysk the next day, 7 May, and landed in Anchorage on 6 May, losing the day we'd gained coming over. There were only twenty-four passengers on that flight, and twenty-two were bear hunters. A U.S. Fish and Wildlife Service agent had to open up all our bear hides, inspect them, and take tissue samples before we could clear Customs. Before leaving for Russia, I had arranged to leave my bear hide with D&C Expeditors in Anchorage and have one of its representatives prepare the necessary paperwork and ship it on to my taxidermist in Toronto.

I spent that night in Seattle and was home before noon the next day. There were bigger bear on the Kamchatka, but I needed more time to find one.

There are few dedicated white-tailed deer hunters in the eastern half of North America who haven't heard of Anticosti Island. Some experts say there are more white-tailed deer per square mile on that island on the mouth of the St. Lawrence River between Quebec and Newfoundland than anywhere else in North America.

Anticosti didn't always have deer. When French chocolate maker Henri Menier bought the 4,500-square-mile island in 1895, he paid to have two hundred deer captured on the mainland and released on the island. (Menier also built a railroad so that he could travel around Anticosti.) Those two hundred deer obviously did well, because Anticosti was already famous for its hunting when a lumber company bought it from Menier's estate in 1925. Lumbering ended in 1972, and today there are an estimated 120,000 deer on Anticosti, or about 27 deer per square mile, according to Quebec wildlife authorities.

Anticosti's deer can also thank a man named Charles McCormick. Originally from Ottawa, McCormick moved to Anticosti in 1926 to work for the lumber company and spent the next fifty years as its game warden. The poachers he caught appeared before an irate justice of the peace—none other than McCormick himself—and then were escorted to the dock. So protective was he of the island's wildlife that some called him the "King of Anticosti."

Ten friends and I were waiting at the airport in Saint John, New Brunswick, on 22 November 1999. A charter flight from Montreal landed to pick us up, and seventy minutes later we were on a dirt runway on Anticosti Island. It was noon,

Anticosti Island may have more deer per square mile than anywhere else in eastern North America. These stayed around the hunting lodge. Quebec.

and the only things in sight were the lodge and camps of Anticosti Outfitters.

Counting our group, there were thirty hunters in camp who had booked four-day hunts for Anticosti's white-tailed deer. My group stayed two to a room in the main lodge, and I drew Sam Burgess, a businessman from Fredericton, New Brunswick. I'd known Sam for some time. He was born in Havelock and went to school there. The lodge was comfortable and well run. Its cooks served great meals and packed lunches for us to take when we went out to hunt.

We didn't have to go very far to see the deer that had brought Anticosti its fame. There were deer outside the lodge that pestered us for handouts and ate apples right out of our hands. They were smaller than our whitetail back home, although both are the northern woodland subspecies *(Odocoileus virginianus borealis)*.[3]

At any rate, finding deer away from the lodge was no problem. They were

---

3. I saw a similar phenomenon in Texas, where the deer in the Hill Country of the Edwards Plateau also are abundant—and small. Deer numbers are lower everywhere else in that state. The animals within the Hill Country weigh a hundred pounds less than those outside it. It may be like fish in a pond: As the number of fish in a pond increases, the size of the average fish decreases. A given body of water can sustain only a certain number of pounds of fish.

everywhere. One of our guides said we should have been there the previous season before an unusually heavy snowstorm hit Anticosti. Twenty thousand deer starved over the winter. If Quebec wildlife authorities are correct in their estimate of the island's deer population, that means there were "only" 100,000 left!

Our licenses allowed us to take two bucks each, and the ten of us took sixteen deer during the four days we hunted there. I shot a buck with very good antlers the first morning, then spent the rest of my time looking for a better one. I must have passed up two or three mature bucks a day, but I never found a buck bigger than the one I'd already taken.

The hunting area around the lodge was divided into zones, and one guide and two hunters were given a specific zone to hunt each day. There were eight to ten marked trails in each zone, and we still-hunted or waited along them. We saw no other hunters in our zone, except on the roads the outfitter had built. We were lucky to have mild weather with no snow. Our guides said they usually had snow on the ground in November, with daytime temperatures under 40 degrees Fahrenheit

Scientists say Anticosti Island is a "boreal forest," with white and black spruce, balsam fir, and tamarack. What I saw of it looked a lot like the country around my lodge, except that the fir dominated. In my part of New Brunswick, we have red instead of white spruce, and we have a lot more birch and maple.

Rain and fog delayed our takeoff by a day, but we were back in Saint John on 27 November. Our group hunt had been fun, and we'd seen a lot of deer. It was a nice way to end my hunting that year.

A NEW MILLENNIUM, 2000

Iran was closed to hunting after the fall of Shah Mohammed Reza Pahlavi in 1978. Then, in 1997 and 1998, news began to spread around the hunting world that hunting had reopened and that the country's unique wild sheep once again could be hunted. I knew a few of the men who had safely visited the country, and, after talking with them at the SCI convention in February, I booked a hunt there through Kaan Karakaya with Shikar Safaris of Turkey. I planned to take four types of wild sheep: the Armenian and Esfahan mouflons, and the Kerman and Shiraz sheep. George Roberts, a friend from Rossland, British Columbia, would go along with me as a non-hunting observer.

I must admit I felt a bit uneasy when our Lufthansa flight touched down in Tehran at 2 P.M. on 6 November 2000. George Roberts and I were among the first North Americans to hunt in Iran since the Shaw's regime had collapsed two decades earlier. I remembered the television news broadcasts showing angry young men storming the American Embassy and taking its personnel hostage, and I'd heard about horrible abuses of human rights under the Ayatollah Khomeini's Muslim mullahs. I also had talked with people who'd hunted there since the country reopened, and they'd experienced no problems. Khomeini was gone, replaced by more liberal rulers. Iran

once again was reaching out, trying to join the rest of the world.

A man from the hunting company met us at the airport and helped me clear Customs with my rifle. I felt better when the officials issued the paperwork I needed to take my rifle into their country. I viewed the city with great interest from our car window as we drove into Tehran. It was as if it had its feet in two worlds at once. We passed modern office and government buildings, libraries, and museums in the modern city of fourteen million people. But we also saw buildings and homes that would only be found in that part of the world. As it was everywhere else in Asia, every type of vehicle and literally thousands of people were in the streets. Women were conspicuous by their absence. The few I saw had their head covered with veils.

We left our hotel the next morning and flew an hour to the city of Tabriz in the northwestern part of the country, where our interpreter, Mohsen Nabati, met us. Nabati drove us ninety miles to a game reserve in the Zanjireh and Yam Highlands, where I would hunt an Armenian mouflon. I knew that when the Shah's brother, Prince Abdorreza Pahlavi, established the country's reserves he also helped create its first wildlife agency and strongly supported its efforts to protect Iran's wildlife, but I was surprised to see the game department's efficient quarters where we were to stay. The room George and I shared was clean, modern, and well kept.

After I sighted in my rifle, Mohsen and I drove to a nearby village, where he bought some rice for our camp. I was interested to see what we would be served and was pleasantly surprised to find fried eggs, flat bread, and coffee on the breakfast table. (All I ate for dinner in Iran was shish kebab served over rice. A special treat for our guides was to break a raw egg over the rice.) Immediately after we ate, George, two wildlife officers, a tracker, and I, along with my main guide, a man named Massen Naatti, left in two vehicles.

The reserve was arid, rocky, and mountainous, with very little vegetation. The lack of brush made it easier to find sheep with our binoculars and spotting scopes, but it also was much tougher to stalk an individual animal. We looked over a lot of sheep after we began hiking, maybe two hundred that day, but we saw nothing my guides thought had big enough horns. We drove back to the lodge at sundown and found that Kaan Karakaya had flown in from Turkey. Kaan would be my guide for the first three sheep.

Not long after we went out again the next morning, someone spotted a large flock of sheep across a wide valley. Even with a 20X spotting scope, they were so far off that we could only tell that there were rams in the flock. We managed to get within five hundred yards of them without spooking them and, with our binoculars, determined that there were ten rams in the bunch—with one very good ram.

Getting close enough to shoot that ram was a problem. The flock had seen us, and every time we tried to move closer it would drift away, always staying out of rifle range. We eventually gave up and headed toward another valley where there was a road. When Kaan sent someone to bring our vehicle around, I was relieved that I wouldn't have to walk all the way back. My feet were killing me. I don't know how far we walked over that rocky ground, but it must have been five or six miles.

We were only about fifteen to twenty miles from Iran's border with Azerbaijan when we drove up on an Iranian checkpoint on our way back to the lodge. Again, we had no trouble with the officials, even though they could tell George and I weren't Iranians. They checked our passports and my rifle permit and waved us on.

We hunted a different mountain the next day and saw several groups of pasang, a wild goat with horns like those of ibex. The only sheep we saw that morning were running away from us. After a lot of climbing, we were back at the vehicles at noon for lunch; then we drove to the place we'd hunted the previous day. George and a driver stayed with the vehicles while the rest of us climbed a peak across another valley to glass. I was sitting down to rest my feet when my guide said he had found some sheep in the spotting scope.

This herd on a hill also had a very good ram, and we held a little council of war to decide how best to stalk it. We eventually tried circling the hill to reach a spot where I could shoot across a small canyon. The sheep spotted us before I

Guides Mohsen Nabati and Kaan Karakaya and the author with his Kerman sheep. Its horns were 27⅞-inches long. Iran.

George Roberts and the author toured the Iranian National Museum, where trophies taken by the Shah and his brother, Prince Abdorreza, are on display. Iran.

could get into position. As they were running off, I fired two shots at the ram—and missed both times.

We eventually caught up with the herd on a hillside across another valley, and this time I was able to get within two hundred yards before they spooked. Again I missed. Tired and disappointed, we walked to another road where the vehicles could pick us up. I was through hunting for the day. After eating something, I did my laundry. Any hunter who tells you he has never missed an animal is not telling the truth. When you miss an animal you've worked so hard to take and it runs away, it doesn't help to know that missing is a part of hunting.

The next day we found a herd of perhaps fifty rams. My feet felt better as we climbed a ridge we had watched them cross. The herd was on the other side when we got there, but, as did all the other herds we'd seen, it moved off before we could get close enough to shoot. It was frustrating to see so many sheep and never get a good shot at one. There simply were too many eyes and not enough cover to hide our approach.

When this herd moved into a small canyon, however, we remained out of sight as we moved up from the bottom toward them. Again they spotted us before I could find a good rest, and I again missed the only shot I had. George tried to console me, but it didn't help. I cannot describe how disgusted I was with myself after missing four shots at three different rams.

We were luckier that afternoon. We were sitting just below a ridge, glassing, when we spotted a group of rams moving toward us. When they were out of sight, we crept over to where we thought they might come out. The first ram we saw was about one hundred yards away, and I was ready. All I could see was its neck, chest, and head. My shot went through its lower jaw and into its chest, dropping it on the spot.

Its horns were twenty-six inches long around the curve, not as good as I had hoped to take, but it would place in the top ten entries in the SCI record book. I was happy to have it, because I was running out of time in this area.

A full day remained before we were scheduled to move elsewhere to hunt my next sheep. George made arrangements to hunt a pasang. The next morning we drove about three hours on roads that were no better than goat and sheep trails and came to the place where we'd seen pasang earlier in the hunt. George took my rifle and went off with the guides; I sat on a high place and glassed the countryside. It seemed as barren as the moon, and I wondered how all the sheep we had been seeing—to say nothing of the people in the little villages along the road—could live there. Around noon I heard George shooting. He had taken a nice ibex and was wearing a wide grin when he returned.

The next day was a holiday in Iran, and the planes weren't flying, so we drove some 360 miles to Tehran in two vehicles. For most of the way it was a dangerous two-way road packed with speeding, tailgating vehicles and trucks.

We got hotel rooms, and George and I went on a tour of the city the next day.

Our first stop was a spot that was supposed to give us an overall view of the city, but there was so much smog we couldn't see very far. After lunch, we visited the Shah's palace. It was amazing to see the number of objects covered with precious stones. A bed, for example, was made of gold and inlaid with hundreds of diamonds, emeralds, rubies, and pearls. Later we took a tour to see the crown jewels, which were displayed in a few rooms underground. Security was extremely tight, and there was an extensive alarm system, for there were, literally, billions of dollars worth of gems on display there. After the tour, we visited a carpet shop but decided to wait until the end of the hunt to buy anything.

We flew south to the city of Yazd the next day. Our guide, cook, tracker, and driver had driven eleven hours nonstop the previous day, all the way from our camp near Tabiz, and were waiting for us at the airport. Two hours later, we were unpacking our gear in another game department lodge. This reserve was just as barren and mountainous as the place I'd hunted my Armenian mouflon. The only difference was that there were a lot more people living in the wide valleys between the mountains. We had nice weather during the day, but the temperature dropped at night, and we would wake up to find everything covered with frost.

We spotted only two or three sheep during our first hour of glassing from the vehicle the next day. When the five of us went off on foot, leaving George with the vehicles, it didn't take long for me to realize my first assessment of the terrain had been wrong. It was barren and rocky, to be sure, but it was different from the place where I'd taken my Armenian mouflon. It had many more deep canyons and steep ridges.

Around 11 A.M. we spotted a very good ram with ten ewes far below us, and we were able to approach within two hundred yards. The ram I wanted was standing in a frontal position, looking at us, and Kaan suggested that I wait until it turned broadside. The ram apparently had other ideas, because it whirled around and bolted before I could get off a shot. After the way I had been shooting, I didn't want to risk another shot at a running animal, so I didn't shoot. Instead, we watched where the sheep went and followed them.

We had a long, steep, and rocky climb, but we finally got within 240 yards of the sheep again. The sun was at their backs, shining directly into my scope, and I had to wait twenty minutes until the ram I wanted moved enough for me to see it clearly. When it turned, I killed it with my first shot.

Scientists say the Kerman sheep is a fertile hybrid of the Laristan mouflon and the Blanford urial. I could see characteristics of both these sheep in the one I'd taken. It was like a mouflon in that it had a dark coat, a white saddle patch, and no bib of hair. But its horns looked more like those of a urial. Kaan and I ran a tape around the outer curl of the horns and came up with 27⅞ inches. Kaan was excited about it. It was the best Kerman

The author shot this Armenian mouflon in a game reserve in the Zanjireh and Yam Highlands. Iran.

The author took his Esfahan mouflon near a place called Shahrekond. Iran.

There was very little cover where the author hunted Shiraz sheep, but he was able to get within two hundred yards of this ram. Iran, 2000.

ram anyone had taken since Iran had reopened, he said.

After photographing it, Kaan and I headed toward a road in the opposite direction from George and the trucks. When we reached the road, we kept walking—and walking. At 7:30 P.M., an hour after sundown, the trucks finally found us. My feet were bothering me again, and I don't think I could have walked much farther. I now had two of the four sheep I had traveled to Iran for.

The next morning we packed up and drove three hundred miles to the Negriz area, where I would hunt a Shiraz sheep. I was getting used to the dry, rocky terrain that was home to Iran's wild sheep, although I still wondered how they found enough to eat. The main difference between this part of the country and the place we'd left was that this area had far fewer game animals.[1] It also was colder. It rained off and on, and we had flurries of snow that capped the mountains above us. We again stayed in the game department's lodge.

On the third day we left long before daylight and drove several hours to a village, where a game guard was waiting for us. Although we found no rams that morning, I could tell this guy was a dedicated sheep hunter by the way he moved around the mountains. At noon we returned to the man's village to pick up another game scout. The place had a little store, housed in a small mud hut with a twenty-by-twenty-inch window from which customers ordered what they wanted. I bought soft drinks and cookies for everyone, including some children.

Later that day, after hunting two different mountains, we were coming off a hill when we came across some very fresh sheep tracks. Moving carefully, we peeked over the edge of our ridge and saw seven or eight rams. One was a good one, but it was too far away to shoot from where we were. There was very little cover, but by using the terrain to keep out of sight the local guide and I closed the distance to two hundred yards without the sheep seeing us. I had plenty of time to take a good rest and concentrate on my shot. The ram tried to run off but made only twenty yards or so before it collapsed.

After taking photos, we sent someone to go after the trucks. While we waited, I got to talking with the game guards and learned that I was the first foreigner to hunt there since the Shah had been deposed. Two of the men had horrible scars. They'd been hit in shootouts with poachers, they said. One man had been hit in the neck, and the bullet had gone through and struck the top of his shoulder. It was a miracle he had survived. Another had a scar where a bullet had gone through a muscle in his arm.

Kaan had to return to Turkey the next day, but the rest of us drove 120 miles to Shiraz, where we spent the night. The following day we drove about 250 miles to a place called Shahrekond, where I hunted an Esfahan mouflon. There were

---

1. We did see a herd of about eighty wild asses. As my guides had done in Kazakhstan when I was there in 1993, my Iranian guides called them "zebras." These were a light tan color, with white underparts.

lots of sheep there, but, as we'd found everywhere else, they were hard to approach. There was no cover, and all the rams we found were in large groups.

On the afternoon of our first day of hunting there, we stopped to look at some ancient Persian ruins my guides said were 2,500 years old. Pieces of the walls and rows of steps and columns were still standing. Decorative stones in the walls were the work of sculptors.

To get to the place we would hunt, we passed farms where people were growing corn and other vegetables and crossed a wide valley on a paved road. The truck traffic on that road was terrible, and the Iranian drivers we encountered drove like maniacs.

There was heavy frost on the ground when we left the game department lodge at daylight on my second day in that area. Instead of walking, we drove around, stopping at promising places to glass for sheep. There were lots of them. We tried to stalk a flock with fourteen good rams, but the sheep were gone when we reached the spot where we had seen them. When we saw them again, they were crossing another mountain across the valley from us.

I wasn't happy with the attitude of the local guides. They seemed to think the way to hunt sheep was to chase them down, and they complained when I tried to explain I wanted to shoot my animal in a fair-chase manner.

I took a long shot at a running ram right after lunch but missed it. I was glad

I did, because it wasn't a trophy. As we were leaving the area at dusk, a small herd of rams ran across the road and up the side of a hill. When they stopped on the ridge to look back at us, I shot and killed what I thought was the best ram in the group. I'd wanted to take a ram with horns thirty inches or longer, and the horns on this one were three inches short of that goal. It was a mature ram, though, and I was glad the hunt was over.

I wasn't scheduled to fly back to Tehran until Wednesday, so we drove into town the next day and visited the game department's offices, where I bought a two-day license. We spent the next two days looking for a better ram but never saw one before we had to leave on 27 November.

After stopping briefly in Esfahan, a clean, beautiful city, we flew back to Tehran and spent the day shopping. We left for Frankfurt at 3 o'clock the next morning, and I was home on 29 November. My only major hunt of the year had been interesting but disappointing in certain aspects. We had traveled from Iran's northern border with Azerbaijan to one hundred miles from the Persian Gulf and were never out of sight of mountains. The people were friendly, but at several roadblocks the police searched for liquor and drugs, which are regulated by the Islamic Republic of Iran's tough laws. Islamic fundamentalists still control Iran, but I wouldn't mind going back there someday to hunt for better trophies.

New Caledonia and Looking Forward, 2001

My only major trip in 2001 was a four-day hunt in New Caledonia for rusa deer, a large deer introduced to that island nation from the Dutch East Indies around 1870. My friend Norbert Bremer from Iowa was with me on this hunt.

Norbert and I spent two days in Australia, shopping and touring Sydney, before catching a 3:40 P.M. flight to New Caledonia on 31 July. When we stepped outside the air-conditioned airport terminal in Noumea three hours later, a blast of humid air hit us. I don't know what the humidity was, but I can tell you it was uncomfortably sultry.

I was glad the man who met us at the airport spoke English, because everyone was speaking French, the official language of New Caledonia, and another language that was probably Polynesian. The ranch where Norbert and I would be hunting was a 2½-hour drive from the airport, across green mountains and past a great deal of mining activity.

This French territory in the Coral Sea is smaller than New Jersey, if you count every square inch of land on every island and atoll, yet it produces more than twenty percent of the world's nickel. It also produces chrome, iron, cobalt, manganese, copper, lead, silver, and gold. We didn't see any farms, and it wasn't until I returned home that I read New Caledonia has fewer than a hundred acres of arable land. The rest of it is covered with forests and hilly woodlands. Rising above everything is a five-thousand-foot mountain called Mont Panie.

The ranch's owner, Mark, was waiting for us when we drove up to the low, open buildings where we would be staying. The design allowed breezes to circulate and made the buildings easy to replace after the winter hurricanes, I learned.

Our first day of hunting began at 5:45 the next morning with bread and coffee. Then our guide, Karl Babington, drove us in his Land Rover to the tip of a ridge, where we parked and glassed. We were surrounded by low mountains and brushy canyons, and there were rusa deer, lots of them. They were feeding in the openings, but when we put the spotting scope on them we could see they were mostly females and small stags. Before we returned to camp for breakfast at 9:30, we saw about three dozen deer.

No one rushes anything in the tropics. Norbert and I read, rested, and took a nap until 2 P.M., then went out again. We saw a lot of deer but no stags with good antlers. The next morning was a repeat of the previous one. Our guide said the rut was just starting, and the older males were still staying in the brush during the day. We saw fifty or sixty deer that day. It was amazing how they had multiplied in the 130 years since a dozen were released on the island.

The author and his friend Norbert Bremer pause for a photo; you can't see them, but there were rusa deer in the open country behind them. New Caledonia

One of the author's proudest moments: Gen. H. Norman Schwarzkopf and Al Cito present him the SCI International Hunting Award. Las Vegas.

A few of the author's trophies at his home in Havelock. The room originally housed an indoor swimming pool.

eventually find the deer and send its antlers to me, but I never heard from him. It bothered me to have lost that deer, but I'm certain it did not suffer.

The purpose of devoting the past eighteen years of my life to international trophy hunting was not to set a record for numbers of animals taken. I've never been interested in hunting animals I've already taken. Consider my Marco Polo argali. Its horns were not the trophy quality I had expected to bring home, and I could go back to try to take a better one, but I probably won't. Nor am I interested in hunting another elephant. I've taken one, and that should be enough for anyone. There are comparatively few animals I've hunted more than once.

The exception is white-tailed deer. I've hunted whitetail near my home all my life, and I expect to hunt them as long as I am able. I've hunted whitetail in various parts of the United States and Mexico and in South America. Those experiences—as well as the whitetail I feed at my lodge—have made me appreciate this beautiful, cunning, and extremely intelligent animal. Whitetail is the reason that, whenever I'm asked what I would like to hunt next, I say I'd like to concentrate on antlered game. There are forty different species and dozens of subspecies of deer on this planet, and no hunter, living or dead, has taken them all. Even before starting on such a quest, I know it is an unachievable goal. Several types of deer are endangered and cannot be hunted

legally, and many others inhabit places that do not welcome outsiders.

Looking ahead, I plan to spend a lot more time at my lodge. I enjoy working with Brian West in the winter, thinning trees and clearing brush and deadfalls. I enjoy sitting on my porch in the other seasons, watching waterfowl and wildlife along the edges of the lake I built in 1985. That lake, incidentally, started out to be just a little trout pond. When I learned I could make something much larger, we built a dam and made an eight-acre lake that we stocked with trout, smallmouth bass, and arctic char. The lake was so beautiful and attracted so much wildlife that we needed a place from which to enjoy it, so we built my 7,500-square-foot lodge in 1986. Since then, we have created more habitat for wildlife, planted more than 1.5 million trees, and built twelve miles of well-maintained roads.

Reforestation isn't my only contribution to wildlife. In 1999 I established the Alward Foundation, Inc., as a means of donating funds to conservation and wildlife, and the foundation will gain additional funding from an insurance policy when I'm gone.

I'm still active in Safari Club International's youth and conservation programs. Like most other members, I check the club's record books and awards issues every year to see what new World Hunting Awards programs and trophy categories they have launched. I've attended every SCI convention except one since 1984, and I look forward to the

The author's White Pine Lodge and lake from the air. More than a million trees have been planted in the surrounding area.

Janice and the author with their family. Their children and grandchildren come first in all things.

Actor Steven Kanaly presented the author the Weatherby Award at a black-tie dinner in Las Vegas in 1996. Weatherby Foundation president Andy Oldfield looks on.

next one. I like walking around the convention's exhibition hall and talking with outfitters, booking agents, and gunmakers to see what new hunts and equipment are being offered. I especially enjoy seeing my friends from all over the world at the conventions.

When I have time, I still reload my ammunition and shoot it at the range I helped build. Shooting is the next-best thing to hunting, and working up loads that provide the best accuracy for my rifles can be fun as well as challenging.

As you probably know after reading this book, I'm not a dedicated gun nut, as some hunters are. If something works, I tend to keep using it, instead of trying every new caliber that comes out. However, I do enjoy shooting and owning guns.

I have done most of my hunting with a Ruger M77 in 7mm Remington Magnum caliber. It has a Swarovski 2.2–9X42 variable scope, and I use 150-grain Nosler Partition bullets loaded with IMR 4350 in it. For much of my mountain hunting I used a McMillan rifle in .300 Winchester Magnum and a Schmidt & Bender 3–12X42 variable scope with EAW quick-detach mounts. I loaded it with 180-grain Nosler Partition bullets and IMR 4831. For heavier game I mostly used a Sako rifle in .338 Winchester Magnum with a 1.5–6X Schmidt & Bender scope with EAW quick-detach mounts. I usually loaded it with 250-grain Nosler Partition bullets and IMR 4831. For my only elephant I used a Browning rifle in .458 Winchester Magnum with Winchester factory 500-grain, full-

metal-case bullets. I also used a Weatherby in .222 caliber and a 4X Leupold scope for smaller animals. I loaded it with 53-grain Speer bullets and IMR 4895. I never was serious about trap, skeet, sporting clays, or bird shooting, though I've tried them all. I did use shotguns on a few dik-diks and pygmy antelopes.

So far, my children and grandchildren have not been bitten by the international hunting bug. My sons, Eric and Scott, and my grandson Jeremy do hunt deer locally. (I've given Jeremy the small hunting camp that friends and I built many years ago near my lodge.) They're all too busy. Eric is my company manager and financial manager, and Scott has his own trucking business, Alward Contracting, Inc. My daughter, Debbie, and her husband, Danny, have two daughters attending university. Danny works for Havelock Lime, one of my former companies. Jeremy and a partner started a realty company on the Internet after graduating from university a year ago. Eric has four children, ages five to eleven, and Scott has a two-year-old daughter. I love them and am proud of them all, and I'm thankful that everyone lives nearby so we can visit regularly.

I am not through hunting—not by a long shot, if you'll pardon the expression. As of this writing in early 2002, I'm planning a hunt for Afghan urial with Kaan Karakaya of Shikar Safaris in Turkmenistan later this year. I've booked hunts to Scandinavia to hunt the European (moose) and reindeer, and I plan to hunt another white-tailed deer in Mexico.

I'd also like to see more of China. I've planned four different fishing trips in 2002, including another try at the Tuna Cup in Nova Scotia to defend the Canadian championship title my teammates and I won by default last year.

Of all my nonhunting travels, I most enjoyed my trips to the North Pole and Antarctica. I don't know any other hunter who has visited all seven continents. I've been fortunate to have made friends around the world and to have seen so much of what nature has to offer on this planet. But there are new places to see, new people to meet, and new animals to hunt.

Life's too short not to enjoy it to the fullest.

APPENDIX A
CONSERVATION ORGANIZATIONS AND AWARDS

Life Member
Foundation for North American Wild Sheep
Game Conservation International
International Sheep Hunters Association
International Professional Hunters Association (Associate)
North America Hunting Club
National Rifle Association
Safari Club International

Founding Member/Sponsor
Ducks Unlimited
International Wildlife Museum
Havelock Sportsman Club
Nature Conservatory of Canada

Member
Boone and Crockett Associates
Canadian Forestry Association
Canadian Outdoor Heritage Alliance
Ducks Unlimited Canada
International Wildlife Museum Associates
New Brunswick Firearms Alliance
New Brunswick Record Book Club
New Brunswick Wildlife Foundation
Royal New Brunswick Rifle Association
Texas Trophy Hunters

Noteworthy Awards
SCI Record Book Entries (277)
Super Slam of Sheep
SCI Grand Slam Awards (all 13)
Grand Slam of North American Wild Sheep
SCI Inner Circles at the Diamond Level (all 22)
SCI Pinnacle of Achievement Award
SCI Crowning Achievement Award
SCI World Hunting Award
The Texas Slam
The Cazador Slam
The Super Exotics Slam
1988 Teddy Award
1989 SCI Major Award (Number One Africa)
1990 Teddy Award
1993 SCI Humanitarian Award
Canadian Government Certificate of Merit Award
1996 Weatherby Award
1997 SCI International Hunting Award

APPENDIX B
Arnold Alward's Animal Collection by Outfitter, Location, and Date

	Animal	Outfitter	Location	Date
	NORTH AMERICA			
1	Antelope, Pronghorn	Little Creek Ranch	Utah	9/88
	Antelope, Pronghorn	Crow Creek Outfitters	Montana	11/83
2	Bear, Alaska Brown	Sam Fejes	Alaska	11/89
3	Bear, Barren Ground Grizzly	Canada North Outfitters	NWT	5/94
4	Bear, American Black	Kelly Vrem	Alaska	1/87
	Bear, American Black	Self	New Brunswick	10/81
	Bear, American Black	Self	New Brunswick	10/84
5	Bear, Grizzly	Pacific Rim Outfitters	British Columbia	10/90
6	Bear, Polar	Canada North Outfitters	NWT	5/90
7	Bison, American Plains	Little Creek Ranch	Colorado	1/88
8	Bison, Wood	Canada North Outfitters	NWT	3/93
9	Bobcat	Little Creek Ranch	Texas	1/90
10	Caribou, Arctic Islands	Canada North Outfitters	NWT	10/89
11	Caribou, Barren Ground	Tracy Vrem	Alaska	8/87
12	Caribou, Central Canada Barren Ground	Webb & Freeland	NWT	9/89
13	Caribou, Mountain	Cassiar Stone Outfitters	British Columbia	10/89
14	Caribou, Quebec-Labrador	Ungava Adventures	Quebec	9/89
15	Caribou, Woodland	Gerry Pumphrey	Newfoundland	9/79
16	Cougar	Little Creek Ranch	Colorado	1/88
17	Deer, Columbia Black-tailed	Pacific Rim Outfitters	British Columbia	10/90
	Deer, Columbia Black-tailed	Redwood Ranch	California	10/88
18	Deer, Sitka Black-tailed	Sam Fejes	Alaska	11/89
	Deer, Sitka Black-tailed	Sam Fejes	Alaska	11/89
19	Deer, Desert Mule	Sonora Trophy Hunting	Mexico	12/90
20	Deer, Rocky Mountain Mule	Little Creek Ranch	Colorado	10/88
	Deer, Rocky Mountain Mule	Crow Creek Outfitters	Montana	11/83
21	Deer, Coues White-tailed	Sonora Trophy Hunting	Mexico	12/89
	Deer, Coues White-tailed	Sonora Trophy Hunting	Mexico	12/90
22	Deer, Central American White-tailed	Ricardo Guardio	Costa Rica	11/96
23	Deer, Northeastern White-tailed	Self	New Brunswick	11/95
	Deer, Northeastern White-tailed	Anocosti Outfitters	Quebec	11/99
	Deer, Northeastern White-tailed	Self	New Brunswick	10/78
	Deer, Northeastern White-tailed	Self	New Brunswick	10/90
	Deer, Northeastern White-tailed	Self	New Brunswick	11/87
	Deer, White-tailed (Antlered Doe)	Self	New Brunswick	11/88
24	Deer, Northwestern White-tailed	Elk River Outfitters	Alberta	11/93
	Deer, Northwestern White-tailed	Wild Rose Whitetails	Alberta	1/89
25	Deer, Texas White-tailed	Little Creek Ranch	Colorado	10/88
	Deer, Texas White-tailed	Little Creek Ranch	Texas	9/88
26	Deer, Southeastern White-tailed	B&G Game Ranch	West Virginia	12/89
27	Elk, Rocky Mountain	Little Creek Ranch	Colorado	1/88
	Elk, Rocky Mountain	AZ Outfitters	British Columbia	9/87
	Elk, Rocky Mountain	Crow Creek Outfitters	Montana	11/83
	Elk, Rocky Mountain	Little Creek Ranch	Colorado	1/88
28	Elk, Roosevelt	Pacific Rim Outfitters	British Columbia	10/90
29	Elk, Tule	MUMS	California	9/98
30	Goat, Rocky Mountain	Diamond M Outfitters	British Columbia	8/86
	Goat, Rocky Mountain	AZ Outfitters	British Columbia	9/87
31	Jaguar (Darted)	Echo Safari	Mexico	4/97
32	Javelina (Collared Peccary)	Sonora Trophy Hunting	Mexico	12/90
	Javelina (Collared Peccary)	Little Creek Ranch	Texas	1/90
33	Lynx	Big 4 Outfitters	British Columbia	2/92
34	Moose, Alaska-Yukon	Kelly Vrem	Alaska	9/87

Arnold Alward's Animal Collection by Outfitter, Location, and Date

	Animal	Outfitter	Location	Date
35	Moose, Eastern Canada	Gerry Pumphrey	Newfoundland	9/86
36	Moose, Shiras	Little Creek Ranch	Utah	9/88
37	Moose, Western Canada	Cassiar Stone Outfitters	British Columbia	10/89
38	Muskox, Barren Ground	Canada North Outfitters	NWT	4/90
39	Muskox, Greenland	Canada North Outfitters	NWT	10/89
40	Sheep, Dall	Yukon Outfitters	Yukon	8/86
	Sheep, Dall	Yukon Outfitters	Yukon	8/88
41	Sheep, Stone	Diamond "M" Outfitters	British Columbia	8/88
42	Sheep, Rocky Mountain Bighorn	Mitchell Cross Outfitters	British Columbia	10/88
43	Sheep, Desert Bighorn	Sonora Outfitters	Mexico	3/89
44	Walrus, Atlantic	Canada North Outfitters	NWT	7/97
45	Wolf, Gray	Alaska Sport and Recreation	Alaska	3/92

NORTH AMERICA "EXOTICS" (INTRODUCED)

	Animal	Outfitter	Location	Date
1	Blackbuck	Little Creek Ranch	Texas	9188
2	Addax	Little Creek Ranch	Colorado	9/88
3	Aoudad	Little Creek Ranch	Colorado	9/88
4	Deer, Barasingha Swamp	Little Creek Ranch	Texas	9/88
5	Deer, Axis	Little Creek Ranch	Texas	9/88
6	Deer, Eld	Little Creek Ranch	Texas	1/90
7	Deer, Fallow	Little Creek Ranch	Colorado	1/88
8	Deer, Red	Little Creek Ranch	Texas	1/90
9	Elk, Siberian (White)	Little Creek Ranch	Colorado	1/88
10	Dama Gazelle	Little Creek Ranch	Texas	9/88
11	Goat, Catalina	Little Creek Ranch	Colorado	1/88
12	Ibex, Asian	Little Creek Ranch	Texas	9/88
13	Ibex, Bezoar	Little Creek Ranch	Texas	9/88
14	Markhor	Little Creek Ranch	Texas	2/89
15	Sheep, Mouflon	Little Creek Ranch	Texas	1/90
16	Deer, Muntjac	Little Creek Ranch	Texas	9/88
17	Nilgai	Little Creek Ranch	Texas	9/88
18	Oryx, Scimitar-horned	Little Creek Ranch	Colorado	9/88
19	Sheep, Armenian	Little Creek Ranch	Texas	2/89
20	Sheep, Corsican	Little Creek Ranch	Colorado	1/88
21	Sheep, Hawaiian Black	Little Creek Ranch	Texas	1/90
22	Sheep, Multi-horned	Little Creek Ranch	Colorado	1/88
23	Sheep, Red	Little Creek Ranch	Texas	1/90
24	Sheep, Texas Dall	Little Creek Ranch	Texas	1/90
25	Deer, Japanese Sika	Little Creek Ranch	Texas	1/90
26	Wild Boar	Little Creek Ranch	Colorado	1/88
27	Yak	Little Creek Ranch	Colorado	1/88

SOUTH AMERICA

	Animal	Outfitter	Location	Date
1	Alligator	Adventure Safaris	Bolivia	7/96
2	Blackbuck	Maximo Riccardi	Argentina	4/92
3	Buffalo, Water	Maximo Riccardi	Argentina	5/92
4	Capybara	Maximo Riccardi	Argentina	5/92
5	Deer, Axis	Maximo Riccardi	Argentina	4/92
6	Deer, Brocket, Gray-Brown	Adventure Safaris	Paraguay	6/93
	Deer, Brocket, Gray-Brown	Maximo Riccardi	Argentina	5/92
7	Deer, Red Brocket	Adventure Safaris	Paraguay	7/93
8	Deer, Fallow	Parque Diana	Argentina	4/92
9	Deer, Red	Parque Diana	Argentina	4/92

Arnold Alward's Animal Collection by Outfitter, Location, and Date

	Animal	Outfitter	Location	Date
10	Deer, Tropical White-tailed	Braden Escobar	Ecuador	8/96
11	Ibex, Alpine	Parque Diana	Argentina	4/92
12	Sheep, Mouflon	Parque Diana	Argentina	4/92
13	Peccary, Collared	Maximo Riccardi	Argentina	5/92
	Peccary, Collared	Adventure Safaris	Paraguay	6/93
14	Peccary, White-lipped	Adventure Safaris	Paraguay	6/93
15	Cougar	Adventure Safaris	Paraguay	7/93
	Cougar	Maximo Riccardi	Argentina	4/92
16	Tapir	Adventure Safaris	Paraguay	7/93
17	Wild Boar	Maximo Riccardi	Argentina	4/92
18	Goat, Feral	Maximo Riccardi	Argentina	4/92

AFRICA

	Animal	Outfitter	Location	Date
1	Aoudad	Mukuze Falls Safari	South Africa	4/93
2	Blesbok, Common	Mukuze Falls Safari	South Africa	3/87
3	Blesbok, White	Mukuze Falls Safari	South Africa	3/87
4	Bongo	AfricSafari	Cameroon	2/91
5	Bontebok	Mukuze Falls Safari	South Africa	3/87
6	Buffalo, Cape	Mukuze Falls Safari	South Africa	3/87
	Buffalo, Cape	Tanzania Hunting Enterprises	Tanzania	8/92
7	Buffalo, Dwarf Forest	AfricSafari	Cameroon	3/91
8	Buffalo, Nile	Rocky Valley Safaris	Ethiopia	5/93
9	Buffalo, Northwestern	AfricSafari	Cameroon	3/91
10	Bushbuck, Cape	Mukuze Falls Safari	South Africa	3/87
11	Bushbuck, Chobe	Russ Broom	Zambia	6/85
12	Bushbuck, East African	Tanzania Safari & Hunting	Tanzania	8/91
13	Bushbuck, Harnessed	AfricSafari	Cameroon	3/91
14	Bushbuck, Limpopo	Mukuze Falls Safari	South Africa	7/90
	Bushbuck, Limpopo	Mukuze Falls Safari	South Africa	7/90
15	Bushbuck, Menelik	Rocky Valley Safaris	Ethiopia	4/89
16	Bushbuck, Nile	Rocky Valley Safaris	Ethiopia	5/93
17	Bushpig	Russ Broom Safari	Zimbabwe	8/92
18	Caracal	Mount Etjo Safari	Namibia	6/90
19	Cerval	Rocky Valley Safaris	Ethiopia	5/93
20	Cheetah	Mount Etjo Safari	Namibia	6/90
21	Civet, African	AfricSafari	Cameroon	3/91
22	Crocodile, Nile	Russ Broom	Zambia	6/85
23	Dik-Dik, Cordeaux	Rocky Valley Safaris	Ethiopia	4/89
24	Dik-Dik, Damara	Mount Etjo Safari	Namibia	6/90
25	Dik-Dik, Harar	Rocky Valley Safaris	Ethiopia	5/93
26	Dik-Dik, Kirk	Tanzania Safari & Hunting	Tanzania	8/91
27	Dik-Dik, Phillips	Rocky Valley Safaris	Ethiopia	5/93
28	Dik-Dik, Salt	Angelo Dacey Safari	Sudan	3/95
29	Duiker, Blue	Mukuze Falls Safari	South Africa	7/90
	Duiker, Blue	AfricSafari	Cameroon	3/91
30	Duiker, East African Bush	Rocky Valley Safaris	Ethiopia	4/89
31	Duiker, Harvey Red	Tanzania Safari & Hunting	Tanzania	8/91
32	Duiker, Ogilby	AfricSafari	Cameroon	3/91
33	Duiker, Peters	AfricSafari	Cameroon	3/91
34	Duiker, Red-flanked	AfricSafari	Cameroon	3/91
35	Duiker, Natal Red	Mukuze Falls Safari	South Africa	3/87
36	Duiker, Southern Bush	Mukuze Falls Safari	South Africa	3/87
37	Duiker, Western Bush	AfricSafari	Cameroon	3/91
38	Eland, Cape	Mount Etjo Safari	Namibia	6/90
	Eland, Cape	Mukuze Valley Safari	South Africa	3/87

Arnold Alward's Animal Collection by Outfitter, Location, and Date

	Animal	Outfitter	Location	Date
39	Eland, Central African Giant	AfricSafari	Cameroon	3/91
40	Eland, East African	Tanzania Safari & Hunting	Tanzania	8/91
41	Eland, Livingstone	Russ Broom Safari	Zimbabwe	8/92
42	Elephant, African	Rocky Valley Safaris	Ethiopia	3/89
43	Deer, Fallow	Mukuze Falls Safari	South Africa	3/87
44	Gazelle, Sahara Dorcas	Angelo Dacey Safari	Sudan	3/95
45	Gazelle, Eritrean	Angelo Dacey Safari	Sudan	3/95
	Gazelle, Eritrean	Angelo Dacey Safari	Sudan	3/95
46	Gazelle, Heuglin	Angelo Dacey Safari	Sudan	3/95
47	Gazelle, Northern Grant	Rocky Valley Safaris	Ethiopia	4/89
48	Gazelle, Red-fronted	Angelo Dacey Safari	Sudan	3/95
49	Gazelle, Roberts	Tanzania Hunting Enterprises	Tanzania	8/92
50	Gazelle, Somali Soemmerring	Rocky Valley Safaris	Ethiopia	4/89
51	Gazelle, Southern Grant	Tanzania Safari & Hunting	Tanzania	8/91
52	Gazelle, Isabelline	Rocky Valley Safaris	Ethiopia	5/93
53	Gazelle, Thomson	Tanzania Safari & Hunting	Tanzania	8/91
54	Gemsbok, Kalahari	Mukuze Falls Safari	Ethiopia	3/86
55	Gerenuk, Northern	Rocky Valley Safaris	Ethiopia	4/89
56	Gerenuk, Southern	Tanzania Safari & Hunting	Tanzania	8/91
57	Giant Forest Hog	Rocky Valley Safaris	Ethiopia	5/93
58	Giraffe	Mukuze Falls Safari	South Africa	3/87
59	Grysbok, Cape	Mukuze Falls Safari	South Africa	3/87
60	Grysbok, Sharpe	Mukuze Falls Safari	South Africa	7/90
61	Hartebeest, Cape	Mukuze Falls Safari	South Africa	3/87
62	Hartebeest, Coke	Tanzania Safari & Hunting	Tanzania	8/9
63	Hartebeest, Lichtenstein	Russ Broom	Zambia	7/85
64	Hartebeest, Western	AfricSafari	Cameroon	3/91
65	Hippopotamus	Crocodile Safaris	Zambia	7/90
	Hippopotamus	Russ Broom	Zambia	6/85
66	Hyena, Spotted	Rocky Valley Safaris	Ethiopia	4/89
67	Ibex, Nubian	Angelo Dacey Safari	Sudan	3/95
68	Impala, Black-faced	Mount Etjo Safari	Namibia	6/90
69	Impala, East African	Tanzania Hunting Enterprises	Tanzania	8/92
	Impala, East African	Tanzania Safari and Hunting	Tanzania	8/91
70	Impala, Southern	Mukuze Falls Safari	South Africa	3/87
	Impala, Southern	Russ Broom	Zambia	6/85
71	Klipspringer	Rocky Valley Safaris	Ethiopia	4/89
72	Kob, Western	AfricSafari	Cameroon	3/91
73	Kudu, Abyssinian Greater	Rocky Valley Safaris	Ethiopia	4/89
74	Kudu, East African Greater	Tanzania Hunting Enterprises	Tanzania	8/92
75	Kudu, Eastern Cape Greater	Mukuze Falls Safari	South Africa	3/87
76	Kudu, Southern Greater	Mukuze Falls Safari	South Africa	3/87
	Kudu, Southern Greater	Russ Broom	Zambia	6/85
77	Kudu, Lesser	Rocky Valley Safaris	Ethiopia	4/89
78	Lechwe, Black	Russ Broom	Zambia	7/85
79	Lechwe, Kafue Flats	Russ Broom	Zambia	6/85
80	Lechwe, Red	Mukuze Falls Safari	South Africa	3/87
81	Leopard, African	Russ Broom	Zambia	6/85
	Leopard, African	Russ Broom	Zambia	6/85
82	Lion, African	Tanzania Hunting Enterprises	Tanzania	8/92
	Lion, African	Russ Broom	Zambia	6/85
83	Nyala, Southern	Mukuze Falls Safari	South Africa	3/86
84	Nyala, Mountain	Rocky Valley Safaris	Ethiopia	4/89
85	Oribi	Russ Broom	Zambia	6/85
	Oribi	Russ Broom	Zambia	86
	Oryx, Beisa	Rocky Valley Safaris	Ethiopia	4/89

Arnold Alward's Animal Collection by Outfitter, Location, and Date

	Animal	Outfitter	Location	Date
87	Oryx, Fringe-eared	Tanzania Safari and Hunting	Tanzania	8/91
	Oryx, Fringe-eared	Tanzania Safari and Hunting	Tanzania	8/91
88	Puku	Russ Broom	Zambia	6/85
89	Reedbuck, Abyssinian Bohor	Rocky Valley Safaris	Ethiopia	4/89
90	Reedbuck, Chanler Mountain	Tanzania Safari & Hunting	Tanzania	8/91
91	Reedbuck, Common	Russ Broom	Zambia	7/85
92	Reedbuck, Eastern Bohor	Tanzania Safari & Hunting	Tanzania	8/91
93	Reedbuck, Nigerian Bohor	AfricSafari	Cameroon	3/91
94	Reedbuck, Southern Mountain	Mukuze Falls Safari	South Africa	3/87
95	Reedbuck, Sudan Bohor	Rocky Valley Safaris	Ethiopia	5/93
96	Rhinoceros, Southern White	Mukuze Falls Safari	South Africa	3/87
97	Roan, Angolan	Mount Etjo Safari	Namibia	6/90
98	Roan, East African	Tanzania Safari & Hunting	Tanzania	8/91
99	Roan, Southern	Russ Broom	Zambia	6/85
100	Roan, Western	AfricSafari	Cameroon	3/91
101	Sable	Russ Broom	Zambia	7/85
102	Sitatunga, East African	Tanzania Safari & Hunting	Tanzania	8/91
103	Sitatunga, Zambezi	Crocodile Safari	Zambia	7/90
104	Springbok, Black	Mukuze Falls Safari	South Africa	3/87
105	Springbok, South African	Mukuze Falls Safari	South Africa	3/87
106	Springbok, White	Mukuze Falls Safari	South Africa	3/87
107	Springbok, Kalahari	Mount Etjo Safari	Namibia	6/90
	Springbok, Kalahari	Mount Etjo Safari	Namibia	6/90
108	Steenbok	Mukuze Falls Safari	South Africa	3/87
109	Suni, East African	Tanzania Safari & Hunting	Tanzania	8/91
110	Suni, Livingstone	Mukuze Falls Safari	South Africa	3/87
111	Tiang	Rocky Valley Safaris	Ethiopia	5/93
112	Topi	Tanzania Safari & Hunting	Tanzania	8/91
113	Tsessebe	Russ Broom	Zambia	7/85
114	Vaal Rhebok	Mukuze Falls Safari	South Africa	3/87
115	Warthog	Russ Broom	Zambia	6/85
	Warthog	Tshabezi	Zimbabwe	8/95
116	Waterbuck, Common	Mukuze Falls Safari	South Africa	3/87
	Waterbuck, Common	Russ Broom	Zambia	6/85
117	Waterbuck, Crawshay	Luangwa Crocodile	Zambia	7/90
118	Waterbuck, Sing-Sing	AfricSafari	Cameroon	3/91
119	Waterbuck, East African Defassa	Tanzania Hunting Enterprises	Tanzania	8/92
	Waterbuck, East African Defassa	Rocky Valley Safaris	Ethiopia	3/89
120	Wildebeest, Black	Sandy McDonald	South Africa	8/95
	Wildebeest, Black	Mukuze Falls Safari	South Africa	3/87
121	Wildebeest, Blue	Mukuze Falls Safari	South Africa	3/87
122	Wildebeest, Cookson	Russ Broom	Zambia	6/85
123	Wildebeest, Nyasa	Tanzania Hunting Enterprises	Tanzania	8/92
124	Wildebeest, White-bearded	Tanzania Safari & Hunting	Tanzania	8/91
125	Zebra, Burchell	Russ Broom	Zambia	6/85
126	Zebra, Harman's Mountain	Mount Etjo Safaris	Namibia	6/90

EUROPE

	Animal	Outfitter	Location	Date
1	Bear, European Brown	Cazatur	Bulgaria	10/91
2	Bison, European (Wisent)	Cazatur	Bulgaria	10/91
3	Wild Boar	Hunting Consortium Ltd.	Bulgaria	10195
	Wild Boar	Cazatur	Spain	10/91
4	Chamois, Alpine	Hunting Consortium Ltd.	Czech Republic	10/95
5	Chamois, Balkan	Hunting Consortium Ltd.	Bulgaria	10/95

Arnold Alward's Animal Collection by Outfitter, Location, and Date

	Animal	Outfitter	Location	Date
6	Chamois, Cantabrian	Cazatur	Spain	10/92
7	Chamois, Carpathian	Hunting Consortium Ltd.	Romania	10/95
8	Chamois, Pyrenean	Cazatur	Spain	10/92
9	Deer, Chinese Water	Kenneth Whitehead	England	10/92
10	Deer, European Fallow	Cazatur	Bulgaria	10/91
11	Deer, European Red	Cazatur	Bulgaria	10/91
12	Deer, European Roe	Cazatur	Bulgaria	10/91
	Deer, European Roe	Kevin Downer	England	7/95
13	Deer, Hog	John Willet	England	10/92
14	Deer, Pere David	Kenneth Whitehead	England	10/92
15	Deer, Scottish Red	Sports in Scotland	Scotland	10/92
16	Deer, Spanish Red	Cazatur	Spain	10/91
	Deer, Spanish Red	Cazatur	Spain	10/91
17	Goat, Feral	Sports in Scotland	Scotland	10/92
18	Ibex, Beceite	Cazatur	Spain	10/91
19	Ibex, Gredos	Cazatur	Spain	10/91
20	Ibex, Ronda	Cazatur	Spain	10/92
21	Ibex, Southeastern Spanish	Cazatur	Spain	10/92
22	Mouflon, European	Cazatur	Spain	10/91
23	Muntjac, Reeves	Kenneth Whitehead	England	10/92
24	Muskox, Greenland	Diana	Greenland	7/95
25	Sheep, Soay	Kenneth Whitehead	England	10/92
26	Deer, Sika	Kenneth Whitehead	England	10/92

ASIA

	Animal	Outfitter	Location	Date
1	Saiga	Trans Soviet Outfitters	Kazakhstan	9/93
2	Sheep, Altai Argali	Safari Outfitters	Mongolia	9/90
3	Sheep, Gobi Argali	Safari Outfitters	Mongolia	9/90
4	Sheep, Karaganda Argali	Hunting Consortium Ltd.	Kazakhstan	10/96
5	Sheep, Marco Polo Argali	Trans Soviet Outfitters	Tajikistan	10/93
6	Bear, Asian Brown	Larry Rivers	Russia	10/91
7	Bear, Kamchatka Brown	Hunting Consortium Ltd.	Russia	5/99
8	Bear, Mideastem Brown	Hunting Consortium Ltd.	Turkey	10/96
9	Wild Boar	Hunting Consortium Ltd.	Turkey	10/96
	Wild Boar	Safari Tours	Turkey	10/96
10	Caribou (Reindeer)	Larry Rivers	Russia	10/91
11	Chamois, Anatolian	Safari Tours	Turkey	11/93
12	Chamois, Caucasian	Hunting Consortium Ltd.	Russia	9/95
13	Deer, Siberian Roe	Safari Outfitters	Mongolia	9/90
14	Gazelle, Hillier Goitered	Safari Outfitters	Mongolia	9/90
15	Gazelle, Jabin	Rohil Nana	Pakistan	11/94
16	Gazelle, Mongolian	Safari Outfitters	Mongolia	9/90
	Gazelle, Mongolian	Safari Outfitters	Mongolia	9/90
17	Gazelle, Persian Goitered	Trans Soviet Outfitters	Turkmenistan	9/93
18	Gazelle,Tibetan	China Wildlife Conservation	China	4/94
19	Ibex, Bezoar	Safari Tours	Turkey	11/93
	Ibex, Bezoar	Safari Tours	Turkey	11/93
20	Ibex, Mid-Asian	Trans Soviet Outfitters	Tajikistan	9/93
21	Ibex, Sind	Rohil Nana	Pakistan	11/94
	Ibex, Sind	Rohil Nana	Pakistan	11/94
22	Ibex, Siberian	Safari Outfitters	Mongolia	9/90
23	Moose, Siberian	Larry Rivers	Russia	10/91
24	Deer, Indian Muntjac	Nepal Wildlife Adventure	Nepal	4/93
25	Sheep, Armenian Mouflon	Shikar Safaris	Iran	11/00

Arnold Alward's Animal Collection by Outfitter, Location, and Date

	Animal	Outfitter	Location	Date
26	Sheep, Kerman	Shikar Safaris	Iran	11/00
27	Sheep, Shiraz	Shikar Safaris	Iran	11/00
28	Mouflon, Esfahan	Shikar Safaris	Iran	11/00
29	Sheep, Chinese Blue	China Wildlife Conservation	China	4/94
30	Sheep, Himalayan Blue	Nepal Wildlife Adventure	Nepal	4/93
31	Sheep, Siberian Snow	Larry Rivers	Russia	10/91
32	Tahr, Himalayan	Nepal Wildlife Adventure	Nepal	4/93
33	Tur, Dagestan (Eastern)	Trans Soviet Outfitters	Russia	9/93
34	Tur, Mid-Caucasian	Trans Soviet Outfitters	Russia	9/93
35	Tur, Kuban (Western)	Hunting Consortium Ltd.	Russia	9/95
36	Sheep, Blanford Urial	Rohil Nana	Pakistan	11/94
37	Sheep, Punjab Urial	Rohil Nana	Pakistan	11/94
38	Sheep, Trans-Caspian Urial	Trans Soviet Outfitters	Turkmenistan	9/93
39	Wapiti, Altai	Safari Outfitters	Mongolia	9/90
40	Wolf, Gray	Trans Soviet Outfitters	Tajikistan	10/93

SOUTH PACIFIC

	Animal	Outfitter	Location	Date
1	Deer, Axis	Nimrod Safaris	Australia	5/88
2	Blackbuck	Nimrod Safaris	Australia	5/88
3	Banteng	Nimrod Safaris	Australia	5/88
4	Buffalo, Asian Water	Nimrod Safaris	Australia	5/88
5	Chamois, Eurasian	New Zealand Wildlife Safaris	New Zealand	4/88
6	Deer, White-tailed	New Zealand Wildlife Safaris	New Zealand	4/88
7	Deer, Fallow	New Zealand Wildlife Safaris	New Zealand	4/88
8	Deer, Hog	Nimrod Safaris	Australia	4/88
9	Deer, Red	New Zealand Wildlife Safaris	New Zealand	4/88
	Deer, Red	New Zealand Wildlife Safaris	New Zealand	4/88
10	Deer, Javan Rusa	Nimrod Safaris	Australia	5/88
11	Deer, Sambar	Nimrod Safaris	Australia	5/88
12	Deer, Sika	New Zealand Wildlife Safaris	New Zealand	4/88
13	Tahr, Himalayan	New Zealand Wildlife Safaris	New Zealand	4/88
14	Wapiti	New Zealand Wildlife Safaris	New Zealand	4/8B
15	Wild Boar	Nimrod Safaris	Australia	5/88
16	Wild Goat, South Pacific	New Zealand Wildlife Safaris	New Zealand	4/88